A

B O O K

The Philip E. Lilienthal imprint
honors special books
in commemoration of a man whose work
at University of California Press from 1954 to 1979
was marked by dedication to young authors
and to high standards in the field of Asian Studies.
Friends, family, authors, and foundations have together
endowed the Lilienthal Fund, which enables UC Press
to publish under this imprint selected books
in a way that reflects the taste and judgment
of a great and beloved editor.

The publisher gratefully acknowledges the generous support of the Philip E. Lilienthal Asian Studies Endowment Fund of the University of California Press Foundation, which was established by a major gift from Sally Lilienthal.

Rifle Reports

Rifle Reports

A Story of Indonesian Independence

Mary Margaret Steedly

UNIVERSITY OF CALIFORNIA PRESS
Berkeley · Los Angeles · London

University of California Press, one of the most
distinguished university presses in the United States,
enriches lives around the world by advancing scholarship
in the humanities, social sciences, and natural sciences.
Its activities are supported by the UC Press Foundation
and by philanthropic contributions from individuals and
institutions. For more information, visit www.ucpress.
edu.

University of California Press
Berkeley and Los Angeles, California

University of California Press, Ltd.
London, England

Library of Congress Cataloging-in-Publication Data

Steedly, Mary Margaret, 1946–.
  Rifle reports : a story of Indonesian independence /
Mary Margaret Steedly.
    p. cm.
  Includes bibliographical references and index.
  ISBN 978-0-520-27486-0 (cloth : alk. paper)
  ISBN 978-0-520-27487-7 (pbk. : alk. paper)
    1. Indonesia—History—Revolution, 1945–1949—
Personal narratives, Indonesian.   2. Sumatera Utara
(Indonesia)—History.   3. Karo-Batak (Indonesian
people)—History.   I. Title.
  DS644.S73 2013
  959.803′5—dc23

                                      2012047748

Manufactured in the United States of America

21 20 19 18 17 16 15 14 13
10 9 8 7 6 5 4 3 2 1

In keeping with a commitment to support
environmentally responsible and sustainable printing
practices, UC Press has printed this book on 50-pound
Enterprise, a 30% postconsumer waste, recycled,
deinked fiber that is processed chlorine-free. It is
acid-free and meets all ANSI/NISO (Z 39.48) requirements.

This book is dedicated, with respect and admiration, to all the eager girls and daring boys of Karoland's 1945 generation, who imagined independence in myriad ways and saw how it turned out.

Contents

Illustrations

MAPS

Acknowledgments

The fieldwork on which this project is based was conducted in Indonesia over a total of fourteen months between 1993 and 1995. Most of this time was spent in North Sumatra Province, in the city of Medan and its outskirts or the highland district of Tanah Karo. Fieldwork was funded through the generous support of the Harry Frank Guggenheim Foundation, the Social Science Research Council, and the Harvard University Clark and Tozier Funds, all of which I acknowledge with gratitude.

Research was conducted under the auspices of Lembaga Ilmu Pengetahuan Indonesia (LIPI, the Indonesian Institute of Science). At LIPI, my special thanks go to Drs. Kalam Sebayang, who not only saw my proposal through the review process in record time but also introduced me to several key informants in Jakarta. My research sponsor was the late professor Masri Singarimbun, of Gajah Mada University, in Yogyakarta, Indonesia. I was accompanied in this research by research assistants Jabatin Bangun, Fariana beru Bangun, Julianus Limbeng, Sri Alem beru Sembiring, and Satria Sembiring Pandia, all of whom contributed in important ways to this project.

My deepest thanks go to the men and women who shared their memories of life during wartime with us. I will not forget the warmth of their hospitality and the richness of their recollections. This may not be exactly the story they would have told of that extraordinary time, but I hope that they and their families recognize the sincere admiration for their aspirations and the sympathy for their hardships with which I have shaped my version of it.

During my first period of research in Karoland, in the mid-1980s, I was formally adopted by a Karo family, Bapa Petrus Sitepu and Nandé Petrus beru Ginting, of Jalan Dr. Sofyan in Medan. I returned to the Sitepu household in the 1990s, enjoying the companionship of my now-grownup siblings, Petrus, Nova, Cici, and Ninin. All of them helped with this project; more important, they made my time in Medan fun. Sadly, both Petrus and Bapa Petrus have passed away since then.

An all-important early write-up year was spent at the Bunting (now Radcliffe) Institute, where the supportive, interdisciplinary environment contributed to my initial formulation of the ideas in this book. I appreciate this opportunity and thank the fellows as well as the ever-helpful staff and administrators, especially Judith Vichniac and Florence Ladd, whose vision of an intellectual refuge nurtured so many women. Toward the end of the writing process I enjoyed a different kind of respite during a sabbatical year spent in Charlottesville, Virginia. The "red house" there was a wonderful country retreat that connected me to memories of Karoland and to the comfort of family and friends.

Thanks are due Benedict Anderson, Sepideh Bajracharya, Steve Caton, Webb Keane, Michael Herzfeld, Nancy Florida, Julie Kleinman, Smita Lahiri, James Siegel, Patricia Spyer, Karen Strassler, and Tinuk and Philip Yampolsky, all of whom read parts (or all) of the manuscript and made useful suggestions and corrected errors. Philip helped especially with the material on Karo music in chapter 7 and was always quick to provide an obscure reference, a bad pun, or a grammatical correction. Ken George, as always, deserves much gratitude for his wit and generosity. Over the years his friendship has been steadfast, and I am sure I have inadvertently stolen some of my best lines from him. As fellow Indonesianists at Harvard, Byron and Mary-Jo Good have been supportive and enthusiastic over the long time it has taken to complete this book. Special thanks also go to Steve Caton, who suggested the subtitle. Numerous students have contributed in ways large and small to this project; my debts to them are so many that I must, with apologies, simply issue a blanket expression of gratitude. I am grateful for the two anonymous readers for the press, whose serious engagement with my manuscript has saved me from numerous errors and whose suggestions have made this a much better book than it would otherwise have been. Thanks also to Illiana Quimbaya, who provided a critical piece of information on very short notice. Errors and infelicities that remain are, of course, my own responsibility.

At the University of California Press, editor Stan Holwitz began the process of shepherding this book to completion; Reed Malcolm took over down the road. Thanks to Stan for his faith in this project and to Reed for taking it on, after all this time. I would also like to thank acquisitions coordinator Stacy Eisenstark and senior editor Suzanne Knott.

Julia Yezbick and Denise Waddington helped prepare the images, and Peter Gueth prepared the maps, with a last-minute assist from Troy Liston. An earlier version of chapter 7 appeared as "Modernity and the Memory Artist: The Work of Imagination in Highland Sumatra," in *Comparative Studies in Society and History* 42, no. 4 (2000): 811–46, and is reproduced here with permission of Cambridge University Press.

Finally, my most heartfelt gratitude goes to my mother, Margaret Steedly Hemingway, and my brother, John Wesley Steedly, for their patience and support, and for the special warmth of homecoming.

Technical Notes

ON LANGUAGE

Bahasa Indonesia is a modified version of Malay, the native language of the coastal populations of parts of Sumatra, Borneo, and the Malay Peninsula. Malay also served as a maritime lingua franca throughout the region, both before and during the period of Dutch colonial rule. However, it was not until the post–World War II proclamation of national independence that bahasa Indonesia gained much purchase beyond the multiethnic cities and ports of the archipelago. Only in the last decades have mass literacy, the expansion of state bureaucracy, and a greatly enlarged media footprint made the notion of Indonesian as a common national language more than an aspiration. In the 1990s, when most of these interviews were conducted, my informants were likely to be more comfortable speaking cakap (bahasa) Karo or else a hybrid combination of Karo and Indonesian.

The Karo language is one of a group of related, though more or less mutually unintelligible, languages of the Sumatran uplands classified as "Batak." Karo is lexically closer to Malay than are the other Batak languages, though these are mutually unintelligible as well. They share a basic syntactic structure and some cognate words, which do not always coincide semantically. My informants regularly moved back and forth between Karo and vernacular Indonesian. Except where it seemed especially relevant to the content or context of the story, I have not indicated such code switching in the translated text. While it might be linguistically illuminating to explore this in more detail, I felt that fully notating interviews in this way would detract from the sense—and the artistry—of my informants' accounts. Where necessary, I have inserted bracketed notations to indicate the language being used, as for example *bapa* [K., father] or *bapak* [I., father, sir]. In translated sources, both written and oral, words that are foreign to the language of the original are italicized, as in the following statement, in which the speaker switched back and forth between English and Indonesian: "*To be a good wife, to be a good*, whatever, *member of* society." Similarly, I use italics to indicate song lyrics and poetry embedded in my text.

Pronunciation of both languages is similar. Karo is said to be more melodic, with heavier stress placed on accented syllables. I have indicated in Karo, but not in Indonesian, the acute *e (é)* but otherwise in both languages follow the conventions of the "new" orthography adopted in 1972 (e.g., *maju* rather than *madjoe*). The only exception to this is for some proper names and for quotations dated prior to 1972.

ON NAMES AND TERMS OF ADDRESS

Karo society is composed of five patrilineal megaclans, or *merga*, each of which is further divided into a number of subclans (also known as *merga*). Either the clan or the subclan name may be used as a surname, though certain conventional usages are broadly adhered to. For instance, a man of *merga* Ginting Suka would never be referred to merely by his subclan designation Suka, whereas it would be quite unusual for a man of *merga* Perangin-angin Bangun to use anything more than the subclan name Bangun. Women are not regarded as properly "having" a clan name and are referred to as a "woman of" *(beru)* their natal patriclan, for example, *beru* Ginting, *beru* Bangun.

Karo generally avoid the use of personal names for reference or address, using instead either clan nicknames, kin terms, polite euphemisms, or teknonyms. After the birth of a couple's first child, they are referred to as the "father of" *(bapa)* and "mother of" *(nandé)* the child. Perhaps because of the sense of social freedom and equality of the time, my informants from the "Generation of 1945" tended to be more casual in this regard. Some adhered to the conventional forms of address and reference, but others were comfortable with the use of personal names. I follow my informants' example here and use the name by which they referred to themselves or by which others referred to them.

Kinship terms are given in the standard anthropological abbreviations, as follows:

B = brother

D = daughter

F = father

H = husband

M = mother

S = son

W = wife

Z = sister

In combination, terms should be read sequentially, for example, MB = mother's brother (K., *mama*). It should be noted that Karo use these terms to indicate a specific kinsperson or to designate a person belonging to a general kin category.

The Outskirts of the Nation

Each year on August 17 the highland town of Kabanjahé, like every other district seat in Indonesia, celebrates the proclamation of national independence. Banners, billboards, and strings of electric lights decorate the broad main streets. *Perjuangan* (struggle) and *Merdeka!* (independence), the keywords of nationalist mobilization, appear everywhere, from cigarette advertisements to T-shirts. Freshly painted gateways at the entrances of side streets and public buildings mark off national time in red-stenciled numerals: on the left side, 17-8-45, the date of the independence proclamation, and on the right, 17-8 of the present year (figure 1). Schoolchildren begin practicing their parade routines weeks in advance.

Kabanjahé is the capital of Tanah Karo (I., Karoland), an administrative district in North Sumatra Province. It is ordinarily the kind of place that travelers pass through on their way to somewhere else. All the main roads that cross the Karo plateau meet in Kabanjahé, spinning off the market square in pinwheel formation. Long-distance transportation is funneled through the terminal on the edge of town, but all the local buses pick up passengers at designated spots around this central square. Villagers returning from the market or from a visit with city-dwelling grandchildren, or on their way to a wedding or funeral, cluster on the street corners or loiter in the coffee shops, waiting for their bus and exchanging news. This is where you can pick up the latest gossip about deaths, marriages, scandals, and school admissions. Students

FIGURE 1. Ceremonial gateway, North Sumatra, 1995. Photo by the author.

going home for the weekend and young people heading to rural harvest festivals shed their cultivated urbanisms—Jakarta slang, languid gestures—as they mix with these inquisitive commuters.

Tanah Karo is a prosperous farming district, and Kabanjahé is the site of its largest retail market. On Mondays—the traditional market day—the town is still flooded with shoppers, but now the market is open every day, and Mondays have lost much of their special excitement. The market itself is an open-air maze of stalls packed with the everyday necessities and cheap treats of rural life. The entire complex forms a square enclosure bounded by a wall of street-side shops, each side pierced by a gateway of grim, black-thatched towers. Cabbages, pineapples, leeks, and bananas spill out from these gates and onto the adjacent streets and sidewalks, where they share space with plastic-ware, cheap clothing, and locally made products, such as brooms, rice winnowers, knives and machetes, rattan baskets, cylinders of palm sugar, brass pesticide-spray tanks, bird cages, and bamboo spoons.[1]

The town of Kabanjahé got its start shortly after the turn of the century as a Dutch colonial subdistrict station and mission post. Government offices, courts, medical facilities, schools, and churches were soon followed by auto repair shops, restaurants, retail stores, and even a movie theater, but aside from an annual livestock fair and horse race there was little in the town to interest Europeans. The cool highland climate was an invigorating change from the equatorial swelter of the lowland plantation zone, but Dutch visitors preferred to stay in the nearby resort town of Berastagi. "These Dutch people didn't like Kabanjahé," one woman told me. "They liked Berastagi better. So that's where they built their houses, Dutch houses, with the tile roofs." Berastagi offered dramatic vistas of wide skies and smoking volcanoes, photos of which adorned many a European traveler's album. There is no view in Kabanjahé except of cornfields.

Not many signs of colonial days remain in Kabanjahé, for much of the town was burned to the ground in 1947 by retreating nationalist fighters. Rebuilt after the war, its public buildings owe more to the no-frills internationalist architecture of the 1950s and the plain, unadorned style favored by the Karo Protestant Church than to either the white-columned grandiosity of urban colonial architecture or the cozy charm of Berastagi's shuttered bungalows and flower gardens. Like the market gates, newer government buildings are supplemented with the conventional ornaments of Karo architecture: high-pitched, multigabled roof-lines, sometimes shaggily thatched; brightly colored gable insets woven with traditional designs; auspicious images of the lizardlike spirit-messenger *beraspati* zigzagging along the walls; and on guard from each roof peak the black, arching profile of the wild ox.

Although it has small but established communities of Chinese and Javanese residents and its civil servants may come from all over the province, Kabanjahé is a self-consciously Karo town. This identity has been actively fostered both by the district government and by the Karo Protestant Church, which has long been the self-styled defender not just of Karo manners and morals but of language and culture as well. The church's headquarters are here, and its influential presence has stamped the entire town with an industrious Calvinist respectability. The comfortable present-day fit between Protestant ethic and Karo custom was, so to speak, tailored in Kabanjahé.[2]

Most of the time the town bears its place in the nation lightly. Many of the stores and cafés that line the streets have Indonesian names, but Karo, rather than Indonesian, is the language of the streets, the shops, the churches, and even the government offices. Radio shops have about equal numbers of Karo and Indonesian music recordings on display, as well as some Western selections, but Karo pop is mostly what you hear on the streets.

A stranger who has traveled elsewhere in North Sumatra will notice a special politesse in Kabanjahé, which is a result of the Karo assumption that even strangers may turn out to be relatives. Westerners here are not the oddities that they seem in villages farther off the beaten path, but neither are they a significant source of income. Bus conductors and pedestrians will try to shoo out-of-place tourists back to Berastagi or direct them to the "traditional" village of Lingga, assuming they've lost their way, but a word or two in Karo invites responses of courtesy and delight and messages to be delivered to distant kinfolk living somewhere "over in the West." In short, Kabanjahé doesn't just fit into family networks; it runs on them: you go to your auntie's market booth to buy sugar or oranges, and you take your uncle's bus back to the village; you meet a sister-in-law on her way to a ceremony and learn the news of long-unseen relatives; you carry a letter for a homesick niece or a prescription for an ailing grandmother. These are the everyday expectations of a persistently local sort of place, one that, without diminishing its enthusiasm for education, technology, and other modern opportunities, looks more to the surrounding highland villages than to the cities of the lowlands for its cultural standards.

But on August 17 Kabanjahé's standard is the nation. At the soccer stadium on the edge of town, schoolkids, scout troops, civil servants, soldiers, elderly veterans, and casual spectators assemble for the morning's official flag ceremony. Just as it happens throughout Indonesia—as it has happened every year since 1945—precisely at 9:00 A.M. the *bupati* (district head of government) reads the familiar words, in their familiar, rhythmic intonation: *Pro-kla-ma-si. Ka-mi bangsa In-do-né-sia . . .*

> Proclamation. We the Indonesian people hereby declare Indonesia's independence. Matters concerning the transfer of power and other matters will be executed in an orderly manner and in the shortest possible time.
> Jakarta, dated 17–8-05[3]
> In the name of the Indonesian people,
> Soekarno — Hatta

The flag raising follows immediately. A white-uniformed drill team composed of student representatives of all the district's high schools marches to the reviewing stand, where an "heirloom duplicate" flag is presented to one of its members. She (for on every such occasion that I have witnessed the flag's recipient has been female) then delivers the "Grand Old Red-and-White" (Sang Saka Merah-Putih) to the team of four, who perform the actual raising of the flag. Once the sergeant-at-arms has formally reported the ceremony's successful completion, the national anthem, "Indonesia Raya," is sung in heartfelt unison by the crowd. This entire ceremony is synchronized across the nation: you can see on national television the same ceremony (though done with considerably more panache) led by the president in Jakarta and imagine it being performed in exactly the same way, and at exactly the same moment, throughout Indonesia.

The main event of the day in Kabanjahé is the parade. By the time the flag ceremony is over the town is already filling with spectators. They stand or sit on the street curbs along the parade route. Young men clamber up on overhanging gateways or sturdy signs to get a better view. By midday it seems that the entire population of the highlands must be assembled around the market square and down the long main street to the reviewing stand set up in front of the *bupati*'s residence. City parades feature floats, but here there are just uniformed civil servants and groups of marching children from each of Kabanjahé Sub-district's forty-six elementary and middle schools. Drum bands and majorettes are costumed in extravagant, gaudy fancies, and some of the children are dressed in ethnic costumes—not just Karo, but Javanese, Balinese, Toba, Simalungun, Malay, Acehnese. Others appear as typical *perjuangan* figures: boy-guerrillas camouflaged in passion fruit vines and waving bamboo spears with red-painted tips; ragged evacuees carrying huge baskets on their heads; occasionally a girl dressed as a nurse in white, with a neat cap and black bag. The rest of the children march in formation, wearing their everyday school uniforms.

It's a long way from the soccer field to the center of town, and the marchers have to circle the whole town before the parade ends at the reviewing stand. The smaller kids are usually exhausted by the time they arrive. As each group passes the stand, the drum band performs one song and a quick marching drill, and the head drum majorettes execute a stylish back-dipping curtsey to the "inspector of the ceremony" (a role taken in turns by various high civilian and military officials), who snaps back a crisp military salute in response.

One Indonesian friend, who was living in Jakarta, sniffed when I said I was interested in these small-town celebrations. "They're just behind the times out there," she said, "poor imitations of Jakarta." Another friend, whom I had invited to one of these all-day affairs, grumbled that this was just another instance of the "militarization" of everyday life. "What do you mean?" I asked.

"Empty ritual."

But it's not empty ritual or cheap imitation for the enthusiastic crowds who line the streets, listening to group after group play the patriotic Karo song "Erkata Bedil" (Rifle Reports) on melodeons and snare drums. One woman I saw grabbed her restless son by the shirt collar and, pointing to a group of children dressed as evacuees, told him sharply, "Pay attention! This is what we went through for independence!"

. . .

The Indonesian struggle for national independence was the first successful war of liberation in post–World War II Asia. It became a model and inspiration for anticolonial and national struggles worldwide. As a result of its historical precedence and predominantly bourgeois-nationalist (rather than Marxist-internationalist) orientation, as well as its success in welding a nation from diverse and dispersed populations—some thirteen thousand islands, with several hundred linguistically and culturally differentiated groups—in a relatively short time *and* in the absence of some precolonial entity on which to base its territorial claims, Indonesia became a model and inspiration for theories of nationalism and state formation as well, from Clifford Geertz's work on new states in the 1960s (Geertz 1973a,b,c) to Benedict Anderson's "imagined communities" in the 1980s (Anderson 1991). Since that time there has been a proliferation of local histories, memoirs, and biographies written by and about veterans and political leaders of the struggle. Nevertheless, academic studies of Indonesia's War for Independence have continued to attend mostly to a small segment of the total national spectrum, focusing geographically on Java, politically on urban elites, and experientially on men.[4] Without denying the centrality, both before and after the fact, of Java-based elite men in the project of postcolonial state formation, this book shifts attention to one of the neglected parts of that spectrum: rural women and men in the Karo highlands of northern Sumatra. Karo villagers took up the cause of Indonesian independence with an enthusiasm perhaps unexpected in formerly stateless hill people who had been, in James Scott's (2009) phrase, adept at the "art of not being governed." That their enthusiasm found expression in ways often at odds with the state-building projects of the political center is rather less surprising.

The "imagining" of a national community, as Webb Keane has pointed out, "entail[s] a process of imagining its components as well. Thus, to the extent that a 'center' defines itself and its authority by

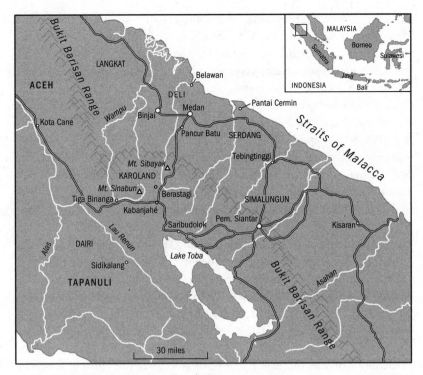

MAP 1. North Sumatra, with inset of Indonesia.

defining the 'margins,' we should be attentive to the assumptions that underlie our own concepts of 'the local,' and their possible complicity with the 'center's' claims to legitimacy" (1997:37). Likewise, we should also remain alert to "push-backs" from the margins—attempts, successful or not, to reimagine or even to relocate the nation's center.

For more than a century, Karoland and its people have been included in colonial and postcolonial state-building projects mostly as an afterthought. Forcibly incorporated into the Dutch East Indies empire in the early years of the twentieth century, the Karo highlands remained a disregarded backwater through forty years of colonial rule, significant mostly because of its proximity to the profitable plantation zone of Sumatra's East Coast Residency, for which it served as a convenient leisure destination. During the independence struggle, the republic's Java-based political leaders rarely noticed events in Karoland, except when they failed to meet the expectations of the central government or the military chain of command. Since independence, even though Karo claim to have the highest percentage of college graduates of any ethnic group in Indonesia, they have been routinely stereotyped as either rural bumpkins or urban thugs. Yet Karo histories, both before and during the independence struggle, are filled with the kind of "hidden pretenders to thrones, back-country claims to occult powers, and sheer provincialism" that Keane (1997:37) sees as proof that "people have a fair capacity for strong alternative views, perhaps even self-deception, about their own importance and agency in the world." It is this sense of ambivalent national belonging, in which Karo are simultaneously incorporated and marginalized, marked as transgressively "local" by their very enthusiasm for the cause of independence, that I highlight by referring to the "outskirts" of the national community.

For most Indonesians, the armed struggle against the Dutch took place "at some distance" (Siegel 1997a:192). Rural populations were relatively sheltered from the fighting, and local participation was sporadic and preferential. Thus, writing of East Java, William Frederick notes that nationalist youths "identified themselves with a supra-village world" and were in turn "seen by the village communities they entered as outsiders" (Frederick 1997:221).[5] In some parts of the archipelago, word of the struggle for independence came only in the garbled form of rumors of "Astrimis" (from D., extremist; Tsing 1993:79); in other areas news of war did not arrive until well after the fighting was over (W. Keane, pers. comm.). But in the Karo highlands and throughout the former Dutch residency of Sumatra's East Coast, much of the fighting took place in the countryside rather than in cities and towns. Karo villagers were in the thick of the action from the first clash with Allied peacekeeping troops in December 1945, through two Dutch military campaigns and a near-total evacuation of the district's population, to the mass demonstrations in 1950 that finally brought the province into the republican fold. "Everyone was in motion," recalled Kumpul beru Muham, a schoolteacher and ardent nationalist, "and everyone wanted to step forward. There wasn't anyone who regretted independence. I think everyone supported it." But the beginning of independence was also marked by outbreaks of extreme social violence. In a climate of fear and uncertainty, in which the spirit of liberation was strong but a sense of common purpose was mostly lacking, Karo followed a variety of paths, to futures variously imagined as "independence."

Rifle Reports is an ethnographic history of that extraordinary time, as it was recalled by some of the people who have lived to tell of it. It can be read as an anthropological study of the gendering of wartime experience, of the mutual enfolding of home and nation in one corner of Indonesia's "imagined community," and of the actions and aspirations of Karo women and men in the struggle for freedom from Dutch colonial rule. It is, in short, one of the many stories of Indonesian independence that could be told from the outskirts of the nation. How, I ask, might stories such as these complicate or even unravel conventional understandings of what nations are and how they come into being?

But this is also an inquiry into the work of storytelling both as memory practice and as ethnographic genre: how stories of personal experience are told and received; how past events are recalled and reworked in storied form; how narrative plausibility is constructed or dismantled; how the art of narration constitutes its subject(s)—in short, how stories inhabit social space and sociality abides in stories. Such an inquiry demands close attention not only to the content and context of Karo narratives but also to their contours. Matters of form and style, poetics and politics, genre and "audiencing practice," memory and forgetting, are as crucial to my analysis as are questions of historical accuracy and authentication. Throughout, I tack back and forth between the poetic and the evidentiary, attentive to a number of shifting temporalities: the events of the struggle, the time of the story's telling, the representation of time *in* the story, the rolling present of recollection and of writing, as well as the variously conjoined points in between.

Memory, as Maurice Halbwachs (1992) says, is an effect of community. It is constructed in dialogue, activated by interrogation, and framed by the conventions of narrative plausibility. Personal memory may be constricted by official limits on public discourse, by the formal shape of public commemoration and rituals of remembrance, by the lack of an interested or knowledgeable audience. In the face of what seemed a national campaign to forget all of the experience of the independence struggle except for a few plausibly heroic (and notably Javanese) events—the battle of Surabaya, the burning of the city of Bandung, the "general assault" on Dutch-held Yogyakarta—and a few officially recognized national heroes (mostly male and, again, mostly Javanese), male veterans frequently gathered for a nostalgic exchange of war stories; indeed, their word for these get-togethers was, literally, *nostalgia*. In these *nostalgia* sessions, as Luisa Passerini (1987:19) notes of Italian workers' accounts of life under fascism, "personal memory combines with the collective memory, and individual mythology turns into a tradition" that is shared by the storytelling group as a whole. Karo women, with the partial exception of those few who were active in associations of veterans and veterans' wives, spoke of their experience to a different, mostly unwilling, audience: their children and grandchildren, whose knowledge of the independence struggle mostly derived from school textbooks, TV movies, and comic books. Yet they, too, persevered in their storytelling. With the fiftieth anniversary of independence approaching and most remaining eyewitnesses to the war in their sixties or older, I thought it was important to document those remembered experiences—especially the stories of women, whose part in the struggle remained almost entirely unrecognized.

Between 1993 and 1995 I interviewed more than a hundred people, three-quarters of them women, about their experiences during the independence struggle. They included former soldiers, militia officers, and government officials, as well as teachers, church elders, choir directors, midwives, nurses, entertainers, businesswomen, spirit mediums, and housewives, but the majority were small-scale farmers and traders. Some were people I had known for more than a decade; with others I had only the most transient of contacts. All but a few were ethnically self-identified as Karo. Many were living in or around Medan, the sprawling capital of North Sumatra Province, with their children or grandchildren; some had moved to Jakarta; but most remained in the towns and villages of the Karo highlands. Most were from the so-called Generation of 1945, who came of age during the independence struggle, and so their accounts were no doubt colored by memories of youth, just as their experiences of the period were tinted by the enthusiasms and hopes of that adventurous life-phase. I collected local histories, self-published memoirs, photos from family albums, mimeographed testimonies and historical accounts, old recordings of songs, patriotic comic books, and much more. I read faded typescripts and listened to family stories, hoary jokes, and second- and thirdhand yarns swapped in casual conversations in coffee shops and on bus trips. I haunted record shops and used-book stalls, attended Independence Day celebrations in the Karo highlands, explored archives in the Netherlands and in Jakarta, and was fortunate to receive from friends and colleagues copies of documents I never would have discovered on my own. Not all of these materials are cited here, but all, in one way or another, contributed to the shaping of this book.

"IT ALWAYS RAINS ON INDEPENDENCE DAY"

In 1993, the first year I attended the Kabanjahé festivities, it rained all day. The marchers were wet and cold, but though some of the younger children ·

looked miserable the parade went on as planned. Standing on the convenient raised portico of a women's health clinic, which offered a good view of the route if no protection from the rain, I met two elderly women wearing jaunty yellow velvet caps, sarongs, and military-style jackets. I never learned their names, but it was our brief encounter that brought this project into focus for me. Huddled under an umbrella, they posed for my camera and explained that they were veterans of the independence struggle. They showed me their medals. "What did you do?" I asked.

"Whatever they told us to do. Mainly we buried the dead." Later I learned that their home village was not far from Raja Merahé, the site of the final and most disastrous battle in the Karo highlands. On July 31, 1949, a Dutch convoy was attacked by two Karo battalions and an Acehnese assault brigade. There were forty-five casualties on the Indonesian side, including most of the Acehnese, who, armed only with swords, had attempted to take on Dutch tanks. Witnesses said that many of the wounded soldiers, who were unable to escape, were run over by the tanks. Two weeks later the final cessation of hostilities went into effect; at the time of the battle a diplomatic agreement had already been reached between the Dutch and Indonesian governments.

"It always rains here on Independence Day," my neighbor on the parade route explained the following year, as the rain dripped from our umbrellas. Karo take this as a kind of soggy tribute, whereby the suffering of the struggle is commemorated in the form of precipitation—though they also recognize that it is, after all, the beginning of the rainy season.

On August 17, 1995, the golden anniversary of Indonesian independence, there was no rain. There had been an extraordinary deluge the night before, however, and the chilly highland air made that evening's official reception and torchlight parade into acts of endurance for spectators and participants alike. The rain began as the procession was preparing to depart. Representatives of various local social and religious organizations, young soldiers, and high school students stood patiently at parade rest in the downpour with their flickering torches. The recently appointed *bupati*, Col. D.D. Sinulingga, was smartly uniformed in military dress whites, and, as he started out to salute the marchers, his adjutant dashed up with an umbrella. Colonel Sinulingga shooed him away and, umbrellaless, stood at salute in the rain as the entire procession passed by.[6] After circling the town, the torchlight parade ended just down the road from the *bupati*'s residence, in a moment of silent prayer at the Taman Makam Pahlawan, the National Heroes' Memorial Park.

FIGURE 2. The National Heroes' Memorial Park, Kabanjahé. Funeral of Selamat Ginting, 1994. Photo by the author.

SPEAKING FOR THE DEAD

"A town can only be called a town if it has a heroes' cemetery," Indonesian historian Taufik Abdullah comments. There may be "hundreds of heroes' cemeteries . . . scattered around the country" (Abdullah 2009:2), but Kabanjahé's is the only district-level military cemetery in Indonesia with the official status of Taman Makam Pahlawan, "heroes'

FIGURE 3. Nurses Muli beru Sebayang *(standing, right)* and Tiolina boru Pasaribu *(standing, left)* with friends, near the village of Pernantin, May 1, 1949. Photo from personal collection of Bapa Ruth Ginting *(far left)*.

memorial park," having been formally dedicated as such before a government directive restricted this designation to national cemeteries at the provincial level or above.[7] It might seem like a terminological quibble, but the fact that the Karo district has a heroes' memorial park rather than a "garden of happiness" *(taman bahagia)* is a matter of considerable local pride.

Looking through the gateway, you see a flat, grassy expanse broken only by long lines of white markers. Some of these are crosses, others are dome-shaped Muslim *nisan*, but most are simple white stones, for at the time of the independence struggle few Karo had accepted either Christianity or Islam. As of 1996, there were 735 people buried there.[8] Many of them had died in military service during the struggle; all were recipients of the Guerrilla Star or had been awarded Class A veterans' status.

Only one of them was a woman. Her name was Muli beru Sebayang; she is standing in the right foreground of figure 3. She was in the medical corps of a Karo militia brigade and died during the last days of the war, but not in battle. One of her fellow nurses told me that she had come down with dysentery and died before she could be taken to a field hospital. A male companion of hers recounted a different story: she began menstruating heavily and bled to death.

I don't know which of these accounts (if either) comes close to the truth. The dysentery story may be a polite euphemism, because Karo don't like to speak of reproductive processes or sexual functions. But it is also possible that the menstruation story is a transcoded fantasy of what can go wrong with women's bodies in times of war. There may have been another story altogether that her colleagues, friends, and family did not know or perhaps did not wish to share. The photograph, which seems a compelling form of historical evidence, is, like the gravestones, the material trace of an absent voice. It reminds you of how much you don't know.

Speaking for the dead is, in any case, the task of monuments and poets. In 1963, the Karo composer Djaga Depari gave voice to the dead freedom fighters in a song titled "Sora Mido-ido" (Voice of Appeal). Depari composed his music on the violin, which he thought could capture most effectively the melancholy vocal quaver characteristic of Karo singing. Although he was sometimes criticized for his "Indianized" melodies, Depari more or less single-handedly set the standard for Karo popular music in the 1950s and 1960s. "Sora Mido-ido" is one of his best, and best-loved, songs, and it has become a Karo classic. It begins:

> *Terbegi sora bulung-bulung erdeso*
> *ibabo makam pahlawan si lino*

Hear the soughing of leaves/o'er the deserted Heroes' Memorial Park, and, in its repeated long o's, sound as well as sense evokes the chill loneliness of the burial ground:

> *Bagina sora serko medodo*
> *cawir-ceré sorana mido-ido.*

> A grievous wail
> Clear and bright, the voice of appeal.

Depari was himself a veteran of the independence struggle and an employee of the district Office of Information, but his words invoke the authority of neither his own experience nor his government position. Instead, they draw their moral force from local memory, natural history, and the consecrated ground of national commemoration. Just as the hardships of the struggle are said to be mourned in the August 17 rains, the freedom fighters' lament is given voice in the "grievous wail" of leaves in the wind.

> Dark billows shading our charred villages,
> orphans' and widows' tears dropping down,
> a shriek that cuts to the soul—these
> were the consequences of chasing after freedom.
> Listen! you who guide the sails,
> avoid greed and triviality,
> our breath and blood were the price of this freedom,
> don't squander our nation's sacred gift.
> The waters were red with the blood of our warriors,
> the marshes yellow with our tears,
> the skies dark with the smoke of burned villages,
> we were chasing after freedom.
> Give your hand to our lame companion,
> sing a lullaby to the orphan child,
> let there be peace and compassion for those of one stable,
> this is the freedom fighters' lament.[9]

The song hinges on the moral obligation to repay a debt. Its title, "Sora Mido-ido," makes this point elegantly. The root word *ido* means "a credit or claim held against another, the return owed for a loan or labor." *Mido*, its adjectival form, carries the additional meaning of "angrily reproving." Depari's reduplicative usage *mido-ido* not only suggests a repeated and emphatic appeal but also underlines the *ido* within the reproach—the claim registered against an unredeemed debt.

The moral nature of this debt is further stressed by the phrase *kahul bangsanta*, an ambiguous phrase I have translated as "our nation's sacred gift." The Karo word *kahul* derives from the Arabic/Malay *kaul*, meaning "vow," but pertains especially to a religious observance pledged in return for the fulfillment of a wish or prayer. In Karo, however, it refers specifically to a living animal offered to the tutelary spirits of the land or forest on behalf of a community or individual. The animal so pledged—usually a white chicken or goat—must be without defect or deformity; it is not killed but released into the spirits' care. This pure, living gift is not intended as a scapegoat or sacrifice but rather (like Jesus, according to one Karo hymn) as the token and conduit of a continuing spiritual guardianship. Speaking from the nation's consecrated ground of remembrance, and in the name of the state's own acknowledged heroes, the poet addresses his words to the country's leaders: *you who guide the sails, / avoid greed and triviality, / . . . don't squander our nation's sacred gift.*

Local pride and popular memory converge more on the song's patriotic images than on its dark interrogation of freedom's human cost. Burned villages, heroic warriors, and grieving women are the subject matter of billboards and painted gateways, war monuments, and patriotic dramas throughout the Karo area. In this struggle, villages *were* burned, warriors *were* heroic, and women *did* grieve. It requires no great insight to say that the burnings, heroism, and grief were not always as simple and straightforward as these patriotic icons like to suggest or that there is more to the story of independence than this. Nevertheless, we may do well to remember that these images are based in Karo experience of the independence struggle and that Karo today understand them as key signifiers of their own collective part in the nation's birth. These scenes of repetition and remembrance—*lieux de mémoire*, Pierre Nora (1989) calls them, sites of memory—inscribe the nation's history in the lives of its citizens, and their memories give it life.

THE NATION AND THE PEOPLE

Equally ambiguous in the phrase *kahul bangsanta* is its second term, which, following its most common current usage, I have translated as "our nation." J.H. Neumann's Karo-Dutch dictionary (1951) identifies *bangsa* as a Malay word, meaning "people (D., *volk*), descent group, family or kind." It can refer to a species or a shared quality (*bangsa kuc-ing*, the cat species or someone who has catlike qualities), a ruling lineage (*bangsa taneh*, the "people of the land" or village founders), or the inhabitants of a territory (*bangsa Indonesia*, the Indonesian people). The *-nta* ending is the possessive form of the first person plural inclusive *our*. It is not entirely clear how expansively inclusive the *our* is in this case, whether it refers to the audience for the Karo-language song ("our people") or the broader imagined community of "our [Indonesian] nation."

Nationalist state ideologies are inclined to identify "the state with the nation and the nation with the people" (Chatterjee 1993:155)—and, I might add, the people with the population. Such identifications not only obscure the complex and ambiguous currents at work within the national community but also serve to legitimize the state's exercise of force on its own citizens. This is certainly the case in Indonesia, where military command under both the Sukarno and Suharto regimes was justified by the moral myth of struggle, and state violence was largely directed against groups perceived as insufficiently committed to the nation's birth.[10] One way to begin to undo this association, says

Chatterjee, is by making visible "the many risky moments in this narrative of anticolonial nationalism, the alternative sequences that were suppressed, the marks of resistance that were sought to be erased" (Chatterjee 1993:156). This is not so much a matter of seeking counter-hegemonic resistances and oppositions to state power or even to state rhetoric. Nor is it a matter of uncovering the "true history" behind the mask of ideology or of recovering the silenced subaltern voice. As Chatterjee warns, we should not underestimate "nationalism's capacity to appropriate, with varying degrees of risk and varying degrees of success," stories of marginality and dissent. That is why I began by introducing the reader descriptively to the Karo area through an account of Independence Day celebrations. By taking such public sites of memory as a parade, a popular song, and a national cemetery as narrative points of departure, I aim to deflect readerly expectations of access to a historical memory unmediated by ideology or to unambiguous autobiographical "voices," and at the same time acknowledge Karo pride in their part in the nation's founding.

While criticizing the tendency of nationalisms to depend on an illusory inevitability, we too often allow a similar inevitability to invade our analyses of nationalism. We forget how unlikely such projects may have appeared at their inception, what options might have been available (or not), and what the stakes for inclusion may have been for those on the outskirts of the nation. Throughout this book I highlight the contingency of the nation form, the nature of the state, and the difficulty of aligning local and national worlds of belonging. I approach the social dramas of Indonesian nationhood through the stories, experiences, and memories of some of the women and men of Karoland's 1945 generation, tracing the variously tangled and perhaps incompletely understood ways that they, and others like them, contributed to the founding of the Indonesian nation. Their stories make up a mutable field of meanings and actions, changing over time and according to circumstance, inflected by generation, class, status, and political affiliation as well as by personal histories, family memories, state ideologies, and local knowledge. The routes they follow are divergent, difficult, sometimes wavering, and rarely obvious, but they are clearly marked with the signs of gender. Gender is written into the scripts of nationhood, in voices that speak of patriotism as well as violence, sacrifice as well as opportunity, "tiredness" as much as bravery; in the intimate, familiar language of home as well as the aspirational rhetoric of the transcendent nation-state. "Rifle Reports," the popular song that inspired the title of this book, makes this point in romantic terms as it evokes the gendered division of space and labor in nationalist ideology: young men were called to report for battle at the front lines, while women stayed at home, tending the fields, cooking the rice.

Chapter 1, "The Golden Bridge," serves as a "reader's guide" to the book as a whole. In it I provide some general background on Karoland and its people, describe my research project and the puzzle of Karo nationalism, and offer some reflections on methodology, the interview process and its limitations, and the seductions of ethnographic intimacy. Questions of gender, narrative, violence, and memory, which are at the heart of my analysis, are also addressed.

The chapters that follow are arranged in roughly chronological order, though with an anthropologist's regard for organizing motifs, recurrent themes and social frameworks, and a storyteller's fondness for digressions and flashbacks. Beginning with the proclamation of national independence in 1945, I trace the events of the struggle in Karoland as far as the Renville peace accord of 1948, which brought a temporary halt to the fighting. This turbulent period was a time of both hope and terror, as Karo struggled to comprehend what "independence" might mean and what kinds of sacrifice they might be called upon to make for it.

The arc of my historical narrative thus stops short of the war's end. Indonesia was to experience two more years of sporadic guerrilla conflict and outbreaks of internal violence before the formal cease-fire and recognition of Indonesian state sovereignty in 1949, and another eight months after that before the Republic of Indonesia took its final political form. The stories that could be told of this time would have less to do with the idea of "independence," which is my theme here, than with the intensification and rationalization of state (and military) authority, a condition that continued, in heavy-handed and sometimes brutal fashion, up to and beyond the time of these interviews in 1993–95.

. . .

In bringing together these stories of independence from the outskirts of the nation, I hope to extend recognition to the men and women of Karoland's "Generation of 1945" who, in variously tangled and incompletely understood ways, contributed to the founding of the Republic of Indonesia. *Rifle Reports* was written in acknowledgment of their efforts and aspirations and is dedicated to them all.

The nation's past is also inscribed in its untold stories: the wartime liaisons that my companions and I were warned not to ask about; the unexplained hints of family secrets; the unspoken accounts of betrayal and failure and, perhaps, cowardice; occluded memories of sexual violence and obsession, cruelty and terror; and the continuing routines of everyday life. There were the stories that went against the grain of conventional narrative enframement, so that we didn't know what to make of them—indications of dementia, or an alternative poiesis?—and those that left traces of disturbance in their wake, hints of other stories that could have been told, but weren't. There were the stories marked by the silent stones of the Heroes' Memorial Park or by the unmarked graves of victims whose lives tragically ended in the forests, rivers, and ravines of the highlands.

There were also some whose speech was otherwise silenced, like a former nurse whom I will not name here. After the war's end, she joined an organization associated with the Communist Party, and like many others, she was arrested during the mass violence of 1965–66. I was surprised when people told me that she was back, living in her home village. After considerable effort to track her down, I found her there, and, with my companions, met her one evening on the porch of her family's home. A small crowd gathered; I was worried that such an unauthorized conversation might cause trouble, but that was not the case. Age and hardship had worn away her memory of past events, or perhaps she simply had no interest in recalling them for us. She didn't remember much about the struggle, she said, but told us excitedly about her recent trip to a Bible camp near Lake Toba. I believe this was the first time she had been allowed to go on a trip outside the immediate area of her village in years. Her account of long-ago events was broken and largely incoherent, and I did not press further.

I mention this woman here not to diminish the passions, both national and personal, that inspired the actions of the many other young men and women of Karoland's 1945 generation. Most of this book is devoted to their efforts and commitments. Rather, my intention is to acknowledge the absences shot through this story of Indonesian independence and to gesture toward the uncontainable excess—never enough, never enough—of storytelling. The registers of nationalism, for good or ill, should have room enough for madness as well as sense, for grief as well as triumph.

CHAPTER I

The Golden Bridge

Independence—*politieke onafhankelijkheid, political
independence*—is no more and no less than a golden bridge,
and after we have crossed that bridge we will perfect our
society.

—Sukarno

The image of independence as a golden bridge to the future can be
found several times in Sukarno's political writings. It first appeared in
his 1933 speech "Mentjapai Indonesia Merdeka" (Achieving an Independent Indonesia), quoted in the epigraph above, but nowhere was it
more significant than in his famous "Birth of the Pancasila" speech, of
June 1, 1945.[1] Speaking to a committee of Japanese officials, Javanese
aristocrats, and elite nationalist politicians who had been convened to
explore the possibility of Indonesian national independence, he argued
that political independence must precede rather than follow from the
resolution of such "petty issues" as the nature and organization of state
authority, the intellectual and physical readiness of the population for
self-rule, and the general level of social welfare throughout the archipelago. These were matters that could be properly dealt with only after
political independence had been achieved. "If every one of the seventy
million Indonesian people [*orang Indonesia*] has to be independent in
their hearts before we can achieve *political independence* [English in
original], I say again, we will not get an independent Indonesia before
the Day of Judgment! . . . It doesn't matter if the people [*rakyat*] can
read or not, it doesn't matter if the economy is strong or not, it doesn't
matter if the people are ignorant or clever, as long as the requirements
for an independent state [*negara*] according to international law are in
place, that is, there is a people [*rakyat*], there is a land [*bumi*], and there
is a government [*pemerintahan*]—they are already independent." What

was crucial, he insisted, was that the Indonesian people cross that golden bridge together, not divided by class, religious, ethnic, regional, or ideological differences, and without expectations for what would be on its other side. Instead, he called for passion. "Whenever a nation [*bangsa*] is able to defend its country [*negeri*] with its own blood, with its own flesh, at that moment that nation is ready for independence. If all we Indonesians [*bangsa Indonesia kita*] are ready and willing to die, to defend our Indonesian homeland [*tanah air Indonesia kita*] even if with sharpened bamboo spears, at that moment the Indonesian nation [*bangsa Indonesia*] is ready and willing, ripe for independence." This immediately begs the question: If "the people" were not yet "independent in their hearts," then what would impel them to defend the nation with their lives?

That Indonesia was an already-existing nation, a spiritual entity, was for Sukarno self-evident. He based this claim on its "God-given" territorial integrity (which "even a child can see" on the map) and on the historical precedent of the precolonial kingdoms of Srivijaya and Majapahit, whose reach exceeded the insular limits of Sumatra and Java, respectively. Perhaps more important for him was the common "weltanschauung" of the archipelagic population. In his June 1 speech he sketched what he saw as the fundamental concepts that made up this worldview: nationalism, humanitarianism, consensus-based democracy, social welfare, and religious faith, a set of five principles (Panca Sila) that he ultimately boiled down to one "purely Indonesian" idea: *gotong royong*, mutual assistance. Yet this vision of a territorially, historically, and culturally united Indonesia, so apparent to a political leader in the nation's Javanese center, might have been less clear on its outskirts, among those whose place in the national community was neither so obvious nor so privileged: peasants and rural villagers, ethnic outsiders, Christians, outer islanders, urban laborers, women, tribal minorities, native aristocrats, and European-educated and -oriented elites.

In June 1945, as the Pacific War was winding down, it seemed that Japanese occupying forces might honor the promise to grant independence to Indonesia, and Sukarno's speech needs to be read in the context of that hope. The Japanese surrender, when it came, was surprising in its suddenness. Indonesian nationalist leaders were left uncertain and unprepared as to how to proceed. In the end, they were forced to act. On August 17, under pressure from armed youth impatient with their elders' caution, Sukarno read the brief text of the independence proclamation to a small gathering at his home in Jakarta. As word of the proclamation trickled out of Jakarta, nationalists began to mobilize support, form militia units, and raise funds to oppose Dutch efforts to retake their former colony.

"With us," explained Eben Hezer Sinuraya, a former company commander in the Napindo Thunderbolt (Halilintar) Regiment, the largest of the Karo popular militias,

> as soon as the gong of independence sounded, it was "forward march" right away! We didn't know what had to be done, but we stepped right up. . . . We stepped forward, even if we didn't know anything, we stepped forward. Later, from the inside, then we could fill it in. Otherwise, what is "Independence"? What *is* independence? At the time probably 80 percent of the Indonesian people didn't understand what independence meant, in political terms, they didn't understand. How could they understand independence? They didn't even know how to write! . . . But as soon as there was the proclamation, they joined right in. Whether it was because they were afraid or whatever, well, that's possible too, but it wasn't 100 percent because they were afraid. They really wanted to take part.

Despite its resonances with Sukarno's "golden bridge" speech, this is not the confident assertion of a self-evident national spirit. A thoughtful man, Eben Hezer seemed perplexed by the response he described. Karo highlanders, who were touched lightly by the Dutch presence, would appear to have had little reason to oppose the reinstatement of colonial rule and little material with which to imagine the grand sweep of an archipelagic national community. It may well be that Karo villagers "really wanted to take part," as Eben Hezer said—but what did they think they were taking part in?

Anthony Reid has recently characterized Indonesian nationalism as "anti-imperial" and argued that it was through the "alchemy of revolution" that an ascribed colonial identity (I., *inlander*, "native") was transformed into a "passionately felt new community." The anti-imperial struggles of Southeast Asian decolonization—in the Philippines, Vietnam, Burma, Indonesia—"sacralized the new identities which had been charted on the map by the old empires." Especially among the "state-averse" societies of the Southeast Asian uplands and elsewhere on the outskirts of state power, the colonial government was seen as an "essentially alien but necessary construct, which opened doors to a broader modernity than would otherwise be possible" (Reid 2009:26). The Indonesian state took up the mantles of modernity and necessity and attached them to a collective sense of national belonging.

Reid's assessment is a good descriptive summary of events and outcomes during the Indonesian independence struggle, but it is less satisfying as an explanation of anti-imperial nationalisms in places like Karoland. Nationalist commitment was, for one thing, not evenly spread across the archipelago or even across the many ethnolinguistic communities of northern Sumatra. Why then did Karo respond with such enthusiasm to the call for national independence, when other groups, most notably Javanese plantation laborers, who were unquestionably the most exploited population in the region, did not? How did they come to align themselves with the political movements of an urban intelligentsia almost entirely drawn from other ethnic communities? What significance could colonial borders have had for people who had never traveled beyond the limits of their own district and whose relations with neighboring groups had as often been characterized by enmity as by cooperation? What kind of passionately felt community could they have imagined? What could independence have meant to them? What, in other words, was this strange alchemy of revolution?

This is what political scientists refer to as a "puzzle": a seemingly paradoxical situation or event that may serve to illuminate aspects of more general phenomena—in this case, the nature of decolonization, peasant political consciousness, mass violence, and the nationalisms of post–World War II Asia. There is no shortage of possible answers to this puzzle. Resistance "from below" is a well-worn topic in a range of disciplines and places, both historical and contemporary. Slave revolts and peasant uprisings, riots and crowds, millenarian and cargo cults, religious movements, royalist pretenders, supernatural signs and rumors, and prophecies of the "world turned upside down" have all been widely examined, generating an equally wide range of explanations: psychological, political-economic, cultural, sociological. In some cases, they are said to be the outcome of external pressures—global economic forces, national or international politics, the intensification of state power—in the absence of intermediary mechanisms capable of alleviating such damages. Others find the explanation in the psychic disruptions of colonialism, the anxieties of modernity, the collapse of state authority, the contradictions of capitalist exploitation, or any of a range of other forces.[2]

In his classic essay on anticolonial violence, Frantz Fanon celebrated spontaneous popular violence as a "cleansing force" in the struggle against colonial oppression (1963:94), arguing that although the "rank and file of a nationalist party is urban," only the colonized peasantry

revolution

constitutes a revolutionary force, "for they have nothing to lose and everything to gain" (1963:60–61). Violence "frees the native from his inferiority complex and from his despair and inaction" and enables the "liquidation of regionalism and of tribalism" that prevent the colonized from entering the modern world (1963:94). Fanon regarded local values and customs as an atavistic burden, but for other analysts these are precisely the moving force of rebellion, whether in the form of the "moral economy" of subsistence agriculture (Scott 1976); the figure of the "social bandit," a Robin Hood–like folk hero who serves as a spokesman and template for demands of economic and social justice (Hobsbawm 1959); or the fundamentally religious worldview that underlies the "rebel consciousness" of subaltern actors (Guha 1983).

In *Peasant Wars of the Twentieth Century*, Eric Wolf emphasized the role of "tactically mobile" middling peasantries as vanguard agents of popular revolt. Paradoxically, he noted, it is "this culturally conservative stratum which is the most instrumental in dynamiting the peasant social order," because they are also "the most vulnerable to economic changes wrought by commercialism, while [their] social relations remain encased within the traditional design." This is the group most exposed to ideas emergent in the cities, primarily through the experiences of their children who are sent away to school, join the urban workforce, or extend their commercial activities into urban markets. "The middle peasant," Wolf concludes, "is caught in a situation in which one part of the family retains a footing in agriculture, while the other undergoes 'the training of the cities'" (Wolf 1969:291–92).

Issues of mediation and mediating groups are also central to Miroslav Hroch's (1985) analysis of the "social preconditions of national revival" in nineteenth-century Europe. For Hroch, it was the small-town intelligentsia of teachers, journalists, civil servants, students, and clerics, readers of newspapers, and members of political clubs who served as the primary disseminators of nationalist ideas from the city to the countryside. Moving beyond the assumptions of ethnic primordialism, he hypothesized that nationalist mobilization was most likely in regions characterized by dense networks of communication and mobility and by moderate levels of social change. The presence of schools and the development or intensification of commercial agriculture and petty commodity production all supported the kind of discursive context that contributed to the spread of nationalist ideas.

More recently, insurgency studies have turned from the liberatory to the brutal aspects of irregular warfare. Some have focused on the traumatic experience of victims, whether to assess the extent of violence, to advocate for reparations or repair, or at the least to recognize their suffering (Daniel 1996; Das 1990, 2007; Fassin and Rechtman 2009). Others look for an inner logic of mass pathology or cultural affinity (Hinton 2005), regard ethnic conflict as one of the "darker sides" of territorial nationalism in a globalizing world (Appadurai 2006), or focus on the manipulations of elite or state actors who directly provoke violent outbreaks (Aditjondro 2001; Aretxaga 2003; Taussig 1989, 2005). A common conclusion is that violence comes to be regarded as a legitimate response through the demonization or "dehumanization" of outsiders, as typified by the notion of ethnic "cleansing." As Appadurai (2006:6) puts it, when social uncertainty intersects with such Manichaean notions of "us" and "them," violence itself can "create a macabre form of certainty."[3] *violence as certainty*

One might argue that there are too many explanations here rather than too few, so that it is possible to select from the menu of options and find an explanatory fit in virtually any given case. Yet all are partial. Each can tell us something about Karo participation in the nationalist struggle for independence, but none precisely fits the situation—or, alternatively, fits equally well in cases where participation was not so widespread and enthusiastic. Neither the Fanonian "wretched of the earth" nor a "tactically mobile" middle peasantry, inspired neither by religious beliefs nor by notions of social banditry, Karo were close enough to the lowland urban centers to feel their influence but sufficiently disadvantaged by mission paternalism and colonial neglect to remain minor actors in a political field dominated by other players.

Where a political scientist might aim to solve the puzzle of popular nationalism in Karoland, I want to retain a sense of puzzlement, to use it *anthropol.* as a guide in tracking both the unaccounted-for events of the independence struggle and the memories and stories that have been produced *okay w/* around them. This means regarding stories as more than just sites for *uncertainty* information retrieval or strategic positioning. It means attending to their *uncertainty* form as well as content, to the shape that memory takes in narrative, the *can be* layers of interpretation through which it is pressed, the way it circles and *s.t.* circulates, how it escapes, is recaptured, and escapes again—or doesn't. *product.*

This chapter sets the stage for that exploration by introducing Karoland and its people, sketching their historical engagement with the colonial state of the Netherlands East Indies, and acknowledging a few of the key sources that drew me to this project. I then describe the methodological issues and concerns of my research project and discuss problems regarding memory and narrative, as they affect the exposition and presentation of materials here. But first, I want to consider some of the social and performative aspects of this fieldwork in memory's war zone, focusing on what I have called the "audiencing practice" of the ethnographer (Steedly 1993).

AUDIENCING PRACTICE AND ETHNOGRAPHIC SEDUCTION

Much has been written in recent years about both the doing and the writing of ethnography—its reenactment of colonial power relations, its duplicities, its fictive nature, and so forth—and not enough about its audiencing practices—its ways of listening and reading. A useful step in the latter direction is Antonius Robben's (1996) essay on the risk of "ethnographic seduction, transference, and resistance" in interviews with the victims as well as the perpetrators of violence. The ethnographic interview, Robben argues, is constructed in a "dialogical alliance" between interrogator and respondent, and he carefully examines the affective flows and blockages that constitute that vexed but necessary alliance. In his view, the ethnographic sensibility predisposes the interviewer to buy into the narrative produced by her interlocutors, to soft-pedal or avoid issues of culpability or of suffering, to shrink from confronting distortions, dissimulation, or duplicity on the part of informants. Out of a notion of good manners or bad faith or a sincere desire not to cause pain, the ethnographer may accept, tolerate, or fail to recognize the strategies of concealment and disguise through which interviewees evade uncomfortable or embarrassing revelations. Informants, for their part, attempt to "captivate" the ethnographer through displays of courtesy, generosity, openness, humor, pathos, and rhetorical flair in order to draw the ethnographer into their particular version of past events. They may resist sharing certain kinds of experience, out of a sense of public shame or a concern not to show themselves in a bad light or because of the personal value that these heavily affect-laden accounts may have for them.

Robben's conclusion is that we need to recognize the seductive forms of transference and countertransference in ethnographic interviews in order to overcome them and so to penetrate the "manifest discourse" of the interview to discover "deeper truths." Mine is different. While I recognize the ethical importance that endeavoring to uncover the facts about acts of violence can have in certain circumstances, my purpose here is not to eliminate or even to "cope with" the biases of seduction or countertransference. Rather, I use them to examine the broader field of operations in which the narrative experience of (any) storyteller and (any) audience is shaped. After all, ethnographic sympathy is not the only thing standing in the way of truth. The ethnographic encounter is not the starting point of narrative seduction, just another step along the way.

Because of my long and affectionate association with Karoland and its people, I was peculiarly prone to such seductions. The nostalgic double time of the interview, in which youth was recalled from the perspective of age, further softened the tenor of our interactions. I was, I'll admit, seduced by narrative. I was enchanted by the enthusiasm, wit, and dramatic flair of my informants' stories, no less than by the shared intimacies and pleasures of local knowledge: of language and its nuances, of familiar place-names recalling earlier visits, of the workings of kinship and the shape of sociality, of the savor of shared meals. I was grateful that my informants were willing to take the time to meet with me and charmed by the cordiality of their welcome.

From my first extended period of fieldwork in North Sumatra a decade earlier, I had some facility (now rusty) in the Karo language. This was crucial for establishing credibility and making contacts with older Karo informants. Most Karo today speak Indonesian, and some long-time urban dwellers are fully fluent in both languages, but older people are as a rule more comfortable speaking Karo, and they took it as a sign of respect if our conversations at least began in that language. During my earlier fieldwork I had lived for nearly three years in a predominantly Karo neighborhood in the city of Medan and had traveled extensively through the highlands. I had also been formally adopted by a Karo family of the Sitepu subclan. This gave me a set of ready-made kinship relations and a structure of clan and village connections on which new relationships, transient or more long-lasting, could be pinned.

What may have been more important was that I was a familiar fig-ure (at least by reputation or by well-worn, often embarrassing, anec-dote) in the north Karo villages where my adopted family hailed from and where I had visited regularly. In the villages of my matrilateral kin, Kuta Mbaru and Mardinding, I was introduced as "Petrus's older sis-ter" or "the girl Rasimah [my Karo mother] adopted"; in my father's village, Berastepu, I was "one of the Sitepus from the Rumah Mbelin side," referring to the village ward identified with his lineage. Traders at the Berastagi market remembered me as "Nalem's friend," because I had often visited her parents' fruit stand there; elsewhere I was known as "the keeper's companion," after my former research assistant Juara Ginting, whose skills as a soccer goalkeeper had made him something of a local celebrity. These old friends were no longer around—Nalem was now married and living in Jakarta, and Juara was studying anthropology in the Netherlands—but their fellowship of a decade before continued to define my identity in Karo communities. Before, I passed myself off with the familiar status of college student, which many of my informants' children or grandchildren shared, but now I came with the title of "professor" and a position at an American university with a name familiar even in highland Sumatra. Fortunately, Karo are not much impressed by such things. I was granted a few more amenities while traveling because of them, however, and had fewer opportunities for unorthodox encounters. Karo seldom use unadorned personal names except for children, relying instead on teknonyms (terms of address derived from the name of one's eldest child or grandchild, such as Nandé Batin, Jabatin's mother), generic clan nicknames (e.g., Iting for an elderly woman of the Ginting clan, Tigan for a Tarigan grandmother), or kin terms (anakku, "my child"; bibi, "auntie," father's sister), but our informants frequently addressed me simply as "Meri," an approach that both situated me as child to their elder and shocked by its simultaneous expression of affection and foreignness.

Although I occasionally conducted interviews alone, more often I was joined by one or two research assistants.[4] They were all students or recent graduates of the University of North Sumatra, in their twenties, and single, now resident in Medan but with roots in rural Karoland. One was an anthropologist; the others were all in the Department of Ethnomusicology. Jabatin Bangun, from the north Karo village of Batu Karang, accompanied me on most of the interviews, until the demands of finishing his thesis got to be too much. His classmate Fariana beru Bangun was also a frequent companion. Her parents, both from south Karo and veterans of the struggle, were among those we interviewed, and they provided several photos from their family album. In the last few months of research Julianus Limbeng, Satria Sembiring Pandia, and Sri Alem beru Sembiring joined us. The other regular member of our crew was the youngest of my adopted sisters, Linzi Magdalena beru Sitepu, better known as Ninin, who drove us all around the highlands, including places that I would never have imagined a car could reach. In Karo villages it is rare to see a woman driving a car, and so I was (to my relief) regularly upstaged as a curiosity by Ninin, who got used to the chorus of kids shouting, "Mami maba motor!" (which can be roughly translated as "lady driver"), whenever we arrived in a new village.[5] Sometimes Karo friends and relations came along with us, and frequently we had an audience of curious neighborhood children or family members of our informants.

My Karo companions and assistants met our informants on the grounds of everyday kinship and common acquaintance. This guaranteed that our conversations were guided by the conventions and restrictions of Karo social etiquette, somewhat mitigated by the tolerance that Karo elders show for the cultural missteps of urban youth. Interview settings ranged from late-night gatherings in the bare front rooms of village houses, with kids peering in the windows, to elegant city living rooms over cups of sweet tea. There was one beautiful afternoon in a gazebo overlooking a highland lake, with a group of village women enthusiastically singing Japanese songs they remembered from their school days. Occasionally the conversation got edgy, as silences and stone-walling marked certain topics off-limits. Some meetings were as informal as dropping in on an auntie or chatting with family members while watching TV. We placed no pressure on informants to participate, although in a few cases sons did push their reticent mothers to take part. On two occasions overzealous village officials called together all the local veterans for awkward formal gatherings in which little more than bland commonplaces could be exchanged.

Most people were eager to tell their stories. The interviews were relatively open-ended, although they were, to be sure, influenced by the concerns that we as interviewers brought to the conversation. I was interested in women's experiences and in local understandings of nationhood and modernity, two topics that had impressed me in earlier conversations about the independence struggle in Karoland. My ethnomusicologist assistants wanted to know about songs and musical performances. We began, as Karo conversations must, by working out proper terms of address, provisionally calibrating personal relationships to the specific demands of kinship. We also asked for such personal data as education, marital status (then and now), and village of origin; other than that, we tried to allow informants to shape the narratives themselves. Not infrequently, they told *us* what to ask. In one of our first interviews, two of my Karo aunts explained how we should be questioning them:

> NANDÉ MADASA BERU GINTING: How you ask the questions, that's what's most important, so we'll understand. Say: "At that time back then, how was it?" so we'll understand.

NANDÉ RIKSON BERU TARIGAN: "What about this time? This time, what happened to you?" Say it that way, please, so it's clear.

ND. M.: Right, otherwise we won't remember.

ND. R.: "Tell us what happened to you in the war, what happened in the evacuation," that's how you should say it, like that, please. So we'll know what to say. For example: "At the beginning of independence, what happened to you?" You already asked us that. So now, "How was it during the war? When the enemy came, what happened then?" Like that.

Rather than following this advice, we simply asked people what happened to them during the struggle, including what they thought was important or interesting, starting from the beginning and going on until the end. We tried not to interrupt with questions and, unless they asked for guidance, we allowed them to determine for themselves the appropriate points of beginning and ending. These were usually, but not always, the 1945 Proclamation of Independence and either the evacuees' return to their homes (mostly in 1948 or '49) or the mass demonstrations of 1950 that brought the province into the newly recognized Republic of Indonesia. They frequently added as a prologue an account of the Japanese occupation of 1942–45.

"Oral sources," Alessandro Portelli (1991:46) says, "are *oral* sources." This is worth noting for two reasons. First, the transcribed interview is not the same thing as the conversation it claims to reproduce. A radically thinned record, it loses the sensuous immediacy of sight and smell as well as sound—the background noise and interruptions, the nuances of intonation, tempo, vocal inflection, rhythm, volume, and gesture. For me, these conversations are intimately connected with the smell of a smoky wood fire, the earthy taste of a sardine stew or fragrant rose tea, or the indescribable, spicy-sour flavor of Karo seasonings. More than that, they echo with the sound of everyday speech, its jumble and humor, so hard to convey in written form—all the more so as the texts here are second-order transcriptions, reworked from Karo or Indonesian, or more often a mix of the two, into English. For this reason, it is important to engage with them ethnographically— to dwell on context as well as text, to circle around the written, translated words of the transcript, and to fill in the gaps of implicit social meaning, local knowledge, and cultural poiesis—or, at the very least, to recognize the absence of these.

Second, "oral historical sources are *narrative* sources" (Portelli 1991:48). As such, they require some attention to formal characteristics, literary genre, and storytelling technique. As Portelli notes, conversational narratives seem less fixed by genre than written ones. In the former, "historical, poetical, and legendary narratives often become inextricably mixed up. The result is narratives in which the boundary between what takes place outside the narrator and what happens inside, between what concerns the individual and what concerns the group, may become more elusive than in established written genres, so that personal 'truth' may coincide with shared 'imagination'" (Portelli 1991:49). This is not to suggest that oral sources are any more, or less, truthful than written ones but, rather, that they must be approached *truth* with an agile attention to style, genre, and performativity, all of which are both more pressing and more difficult when one is working in a relatively unfamiliar linguistic terrain.

In times of war, as Kalyvas (2006) points out, reliable information from the countryside is "costly" and hard to come by. This was true throughout Indonesia during the independence struggle, but nowhere more so than in Sumatra.[6] Communication lines between the republican center in Java and the outer islands of the archipelago had been largely disrupted or destroyed during the Japanese occupation. The nationalist blockade and embargo on travel in the province meant that little traffic (or news) from the hinterlands reached the urban centers of the lowlands prior to the first Dutch military campaign of 1947. In Karoland, rumor flourished at every level. Disinformation campaigns and "psywar" tactics spread false reports; cultural misunderstandings and prejudice on all sides led to expectations of violence as well as to actual violent acts.

Primary and secondary sources, both oral and written, continue to bear the "stamp of rumor" (Pandey 2002:188). Few individuals on either side have been eager to admit that war crimes or atrocities were committed. Few victims of violent acts remained to tell of them; nor, I imagine, would survivors have been willing to do so. Personal heroics and sacrifices become the foci of both memory and narrative; other, less dramatic occurrences fade from retrospective view. Stories are borrowed, reworked, embroidered, retrofitted to the measure of a celebratory nationalism. Eyewitness accounts have over time become formulaic, and it is never clear when these retellings are based on personal experience or imagination. Recollections of violence may have been exaggerated by the climate of rumors, disinformation, fears, and fantasies that Karo attributed to Dutch psywar tactics, or they may have been overlaid with powerful, and literally unspeakable, memories of more recent terrible events, most notably the massacres of alleged communists and fellow travelers that took place in Karoland in 1965–66. In the aftermath of these and the rise to power of General Suharto's authoritarian, military-dominated New Order regime, certain radical or leftist individuals and organizations have been almost entirely erased from both written and oral accounts of the struggle. However much the enthusiasm of the masses, the travails of evacuees, and the antics of volunteer youth militias may capture popular imagination and ethnographic interest, the accepted point of view of the independence struggle remains that of the Indonesian National Army.

Under these circumstances, it is tempting to want to fill in or correct the historical record—to recover suppressed voices, unearth the credible testimony of eyewitnesses, measure the truth or falsehood of each statement, offer the dead at least the minimal respect of a numerical count, however speculative it may be.[7] This effort seems particularly urgent in the case of nationalist and protonationalist movements, in which elite and urban biases may be intensified by state efforts to celebrate or sanitize the conflict in the form of its own "national primeval myth" (Abdullah 2009:2). To attempt such things, one would have to approach these stories forensically, as if they were crime scenes to be sifted for evidence, or—at the very least—to figure out what crimes might have been committed, who the perpetrators were, and who the victims. I don't mean to dismiss this desire or the aspirations for social justice and historical accuracy that motivate it. I have, where possible, cross-checked events, dates, and places with written sources as well as with other interviews. I have noted where stories agree or conflict, where they intersect, overlap, or diverge. I have tried to recognize where the constraints of genre shape the content of stories and where my own imagination has rewritten a scenario in dramatic form. I have also left some mysteries unresolved. Throughout, the presence of the not-entirely-reliable ethnographic author-narrator in the text should serve to remind readers (including the ethnographer herself) that these are *stories*, not "voices" speaking "truth to power."

One of ethnography's greatest seductions is its "granularity," its tendency to exceed the demands of theory by reveling in the plenitude of surface detail.[8] This descriptive excess generates a range of pleasures. For the ethnographer in the field, it suggests her initiation into a body of arcane knowledge and a particular (different) way of being in the world; it evokes sensuous memories of taste, smell, sound, sight, touch. For the knowledgeable specialist or native reader, there is the pleasure of finding familiar names and terms inscribed in an academic text, where they sit, unassimilable but delicious, like raisins in dough. For the reader unfamiliar with the locale or period, it conjures a terrain that is concretely different; it gestures toward an unknown, but plausible, world and hints how much more of that world there is, beyond the limits of the text.

Over time, as we became more proficient in the period's history, we were seduced by its special terms (*kyoring* for military drills, *béréng* for anti-aircraft guns), key figures (Selamat Ginting, Djamin Ginting, Rakutta Berahmana, Payung Bangun), standard acronyms (Pesindo, Napindo, TKR, TRI, BHL), and recurrent images. We learned that the eating of *béwan*, a coarse hedgerow weed, shorthanded an entire catalogue of privations during the evacuation of the highlands, that class positions could be charted in cloth, that "ignorance" could signify either heroism or vulnerability, that a "double twist" was a hairdo as well as a British-made machine gun. We learned the dates that encode famous battles, such as May 7 (the battle of Berteh, in 1949), and visited places unrecorded on maps, such as Batu Roring, a wooded hilltop near the village of Mardinding, where village girls brought food and supplies to a guerrilla camp during the second military campaign, and Tiga Cinder, a contraband "standing market" at the river ford that marked passage between Dutch-occupied Karoland and territory claimed by the Republic of Indonesia—"standing" (rather than seated) so that buyers and sellers could make a quick getaway if police, on either side of the river, Dutch or republican, showed up. We realized the importance of bridges and rivers in the topographic imaginary of the struggle, because so many stories were built around them: the Bengali Bridge, which marked the forward watch post for the Karo troops at the Medan front; the "bamboo bridge" over the Dog River (K., Lau Biang), where a squad of Indonesian soldiers were ambushed by the Dutch; the Snake River (M., Sei Ular) ford, where fleeing refugees were fired upon by Dutch fighter planes; the bridge near Kandibata, which was blown up by nationalist troops after the refugees from Kabanjahé crossed over, fleeing the Dutch advance; the bridges at Tiga Pancur and Lau Lateng, which were destroyed "in one night" by the inhabitants of the village of Gamber;[9] Tepas, where one woman arrived too late, after the bridge had been destroyed, and so spent an entire night carrying her two children, her injured husband, and their rice supply, across the ravine;[10] the *rambingen* bridge, a terrifying single rattan cable stretched across the deep Lau Renun gorge, where one man fell to his death and many evacuees refused to cross out of fear;[11] the rivers that held the bodies of suspected "collaborators," "spies," and other victims of internecine violence.

The accumulation of details contributes to the plausibility of ethnographic accounts and personal testimonies. <u>Details like these ground memory and its stories in a concrete structure of feeling, an intimate cultural discourse of struggle and violence, danger and anticipation, patriotism and fear</u>—the interwoven strands that made up Karoland's golden bridge to the future. This is not a matter of evidence that adds up forensically, that explains or concludes; rather, it is about the pleasure evoked by recollection of a particular place and time. That pleasure, fraught as it is with complicities and complications, duplicities and perhaps a certain disingenuousness, is a thread that runs through this book, weaving together the traces, textures, and tones of a moment when the Indonesian nation might have been imagined "together," for the first time.

THE SETTING

Kabupaten Karo, an administrative district of the province of North Sumatra, is located in the interior highlands at the upper end of the Bukit Barisan mountain range, which runs like a spine down the length of the island of Sumatra. It lies between the sprawling metropolitan area of the provincial capital, Medan, to the east and Lake Toba, the world's largest volcanic lake, to the south; its northwestern edge borders the province of Aceh. The district roughly coincides with the wide plateau from which its name derives, stretching southward from the two active volcanoes, Mounts Sibayak and Sinabun, that anchor its skyline as well as its imagination. Volcanic soil and high-altitude climate suit the district for agriculture, its proximity to the urban centers of the lowlands fit it for commerce, and so Taneh Karo (K., Karoland) has become one of Indonesia's prime areas for growing vegetables, fruits, and flowers for urban markets both national and international.

Wide as the vast, lonely sea. That is how songs and narratives have conventionally described the cool, open spaces and broad vistas of the Karo plateau, in implicit contrast to the crowded, sweltering lowlands. Between these extremities lie the forested hills of the *dusun* (piedmont zone; lit., "hamlet" or "orchard," indicating an outlying settlement area), which makes the rise to the plateau in short, steep stair-steps: in less than seventy kilometers you reach an elevation of thirteen hundred meters as you pass onto the plateau at Mount Sibayak's lower slope. A series of deep-cut river courses slash the smooth planes of the plateau, shaping patterns of settlement, travel, and alliance across the highlands,

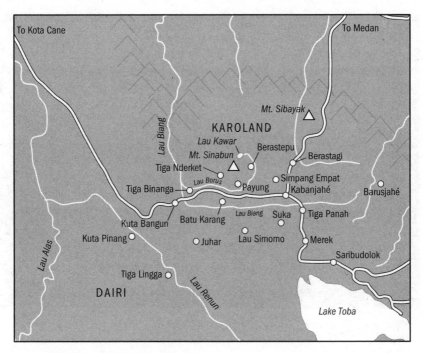

MAP 2. Taneh Karo, North Sumatra.

as well as between upland and lowland communities (Bronson 1977). At its encircling edges, the plateau crumples into the stony ridges and folds of the mountain's steep, rugged base.

Even before the introduction of commercial agriculture in the early twentieth century, the plateau's rich soil and relatively abundant water enabled the construction of large settlements, some with as many as several thousand inhabitants divided into a number of semiautonomous *kesain* (K., village wards or neighborhoods). The villages of the Karo highlands were composed of massive log dwellings, each housing eight or more related families. You can still see a few of these old houses today, preserved for tourists or falling into ruins; in colonial-era photographs, their steep gabled roofs, covered in black thatch and topped with protective images of *bénténg*, wild oxen, seem to replicate the jagged mountain skyline. These multifamily dwellings constituted minimal social units. Each was headed by a member of the founding lineage of the village or *kesain* and contained his household and those of representatives of his key kin groups: *senina*, clanmates; *kalimbubu*, maternal or wife's kin; and *anakberu*, affines via sisters' marriages.[12]

FIGURE 4, Northern Karo plateau, with Mount Sinabun in the background. Photo by the author.

I have written in some detail elsewhere about how mission language programs, in conjunction with European notions of primordial identity, colonial realpolitik, nativist movements in other parts of the archipelago, and the practical constraints of print-capitalism, combined to generate a sense of what we would now describe as an ethnic identity in early twentieth-century Karoland (Steedly 1996; cf. W. Keane 1997). Suffice it to say here that such a standardized, territorially delimited notion of abstract cultural belonging does not appear to have predated European involvement in the affairs of Sumatra's east coast. Early accounts may have followed local terminology when they divided the population into Muslim "Malays" of the coast and pagan "Battas" (or Bataks, as became the common usage) in the interior, but it is not clear that these terms indicated much more than the mutable categories of religious or political affiliation.

The ethnolinguistic subdivision of the category "Batak" was initiated by the work of H. N. van der Tuuk, a linguist employed by the Dutch Bible Society. He recommended that the generic term *batak*, which had become a pejorative equivalent of "heathen" and "pork eater," be replaced by specific toponyms such as Toba and Pakpak (of which he

FIGURE 5. Batu Karang, one of the largest villages in the Karo highlands, c. 1925. Anonymous. Photo reproduced with permission of the Koninglijk Instituut voor de Tropen.

considered Karo a dialect subcategory). Subsequent cultural elaboration produced ethnic typifications based usually on the territorial extent of particular mission "fields" and their spheres of social influence (Joustra 1901; Kipp 1990; Beekman 1988:130–62; van der Tuuk 1971; Voorhoeve 1955; Steedly 1996).

Karo society as a whole was composed of five megaclans, or *merga*. Little more than patrilineally transmitted proper names, these were unranked, dispersed, noncorporate groups that stretched across the Karo plateau and through the *dusun* regions of upper Deli, Serdang, and Langkat in East Sumatra and into the adjoining Tapanuli Residency to the southwest, where they overlapped or coincided with the clan designations of other highland groups. Clan names mainly served to mark the extent of recognized siblingship and thus to negatively define the bounds of marital exogamy.

Merga were made up of formally associated aggregates of named subclans, also called *merga*. There were no commonly known accounts, either historical or mythical, of *merga* origins and no assumption that all clan or even subclan members were descended from a common apical ancestor (Singarimbun 1975:70–71). Lineages, which were usually assumed to share descent from a common, though frequently unknown, ancestor, might be considered quasi-corporate entities. The founding lineage of a village, or *kesain*, was collectively regarded as the ultimate owner of the land (K., *bangsa taneh*, "people of the land," or *si mada taneh*, "founders" or "those who made the land"). The village or *kesain* head, as lineage representative, was responsible for the distribution of agricultural land in the form of heritable use-rights. Lineages were frequently designated by place-name, as, for instance, Sitepu Rumah Mbelin, which designates a man of the Sitepu subclan of *merga* Karo-Karo, from the founding lineage of *kesain* Rumah Mbelin in the village of Berastepu.

These patrilineal descent groups—clans, subclans, and lineages—were woven into a multilayered and frequently contradictory network by marital connections among families. Marriages revised or remade hierarchically complementary relations between ritually superior *kalimbubu* (wife givers) and their subordinate *anakberu* (wife receivers); these spun out both generationally and laterally to encompass the in-laws of in-laws in hypothetically infinite extension.[13] Marriage between cross-cousins (K., *impal*, MBD-FZS), which enabled the continuation of maternal as well as paternal descent lines in the following generation, served as a conventional ideal, though not a prescribed practice. With a few formalized exceptions, the principle of clan exogamy was strictly adhered to, but unconventional alliances were sufficiently commonplace that status hierarchies among individuals and groups were situationally adjustable, even reversible, rather than fixed.

Forms of address placed every individual in a particular asymmetrical relationship with his or her interlocutor. Notions of the "sameness," or interchangeability, of all clan members meant that, at least in terms of social etiquette, relatedness was not measured in degrees. Strangers could become kin through marriage, adoption, or fictive equivalence— as when one subclan was designated to be the "same as" another for reasons of calculating kinship. These strategies of incorporation permitted the extension of kinship to newcomers, acquaintances from other Batak groups, or even to distant foreigners.

This emphasis on ⌐fluid, expansive relations⌐ of asymmetrical affinity complemented a descent-based political system that was acephalous and relatively egalitarian. Highland communities were fissiparous, characterized by internal rivalries among lineage mates and feuds with neighboring communities and hedged with a multitude of built-in checks and balances that made any consolidation of power difficult, "proof," as Assistant Resident Van Rhijn remarked acidly in his 1936 memorandum of transfer, "of the aversion to authority which the Karo possess in such high degree" (1936:37). Beyond the level of the village or even the *kesain*, there were little more than occasional, transient political linkages, governance being largely embedded in individual kin relations and the juridical regulation of these rather than in formal institutional structures. *aversion to authority*

FEELING COLONIZED

European settlement in East Sumatra began in 1863, when a Dutch consortium established the first tobacco plantation on "empty" land leased from the Malay sultan of Deli. By 1890, the East Sumatran *cultuurgebied* (D., plantation zone) had become one of the most important revenue sources in the Netherlands East Indies, with about 150 agricultural enterprises producing tobacco, rubber, palm oil, and other valuable commercial crops. The spread of plantation agriculture engendered numerous conflicts in the region. In 1870, Karo lowland chiefs and their allies responded to what they saw as the planters' unauthorized appropriation of village land by attacking and burning the offending enterprises. This "Batak War" was quickly put down by the Dutch, and an "autonomous" native government (D., *inlandsche zelfbestuur*) was established for the residency, headed by the Malay sultans of Deli, Serdang, Langkat, and Asahan. Although Karo grievances were acknowledged and compensated by the Dutch, sporadic attacks on European plantations continued.[14] Fearing that these could form the basis for an alliance with the Muslim Acehnese, with whom the Dutch colonizers engaged in an intense struggle for dominance in the region, colonial officials and planters came up with a plan to "make the Bataks our friends" by converting them to Christianity. Sponsored by the Deli Planters' Association, in 1890 the Nederlandsch Zendelinggenootschap (NZG, the Dutch Missionary Society) established the first mission post in the small Karo village of Bulu Hawar, in the *dusun* region of upper Deli, about halfway between the lowland city of Medan and the highland plateau.[15]

Both the colonial government and the NZG missionaries had a stake in establishing a zone of shared interests with the independent people of the highlands, who, they felt, might form a "bulwark" against the spread of Islam. In 1901, the NZG accepted the invitation of two headmen in the village of Kabanjahé to open a mission post there. Construction of the missionary's house had not yet begun when the village was attacked by an alliance of Karo leaders hostile to both the European presence and to the ambitions of the Kabanjahé headmen. Colonial troops were predictably called in to protect the mission and to pacify the unruly chiefs. Following a short and effective Dutch military campaign, Karoland was incorporated in 1904 as a district of the Residency of Sumatra's East Coast. A centralized governmental structure, ostensibly based on local custom, or *adat*, was established and a hereditary bureaucratic elite invented to run it. Turning to an obscure tale of honorific titles bestowed by the sultan of Aceh, the Dutch resuscitated the nearly forgotten institution of the Raja Berempat (Four Kings) of Karoland—and added a fifth for good measure to cover an outlying stretch of territory on the edge of the plateau. Accorded the title of *sibayak* (the Karo equivalent of the Malay honorific *orang kaya*, "rich man"), these rulers served under the supervision of the Dutch district *controleur*. Below them was arrayed an equally artificial hierarchy of hereditary officeholders: *raja urung* (the chief of a cluster of genealogically related villages), *pengulu kuta* (village headman), and *pengulu kesain* (village ward chief).

At the time the treaty of annexation was signed, Assistant Resident Westenberg (1904) verbally pledged the signatory chiefs that village lands would never be alienated to foreigners. The promise was kept, though perhaps only because of a lack of investment opportunities there. With little incentive for exploitation, Dutch administrators adopted a laissez faire attitude. They built a road linking the Karo plateau to the markets and military garrisons of the lowland population centers, but otherwise left matters of social welfare to the underfinanced and overextended NZG mission and economic development to the highlanders themselves.

Improved transportation, new markets, and the introduction of new crops enabled a dramatic shift from subsistence dry-rice farming to the small-scale production of fruits and vegetables for lowland and overseas export in the course of a few decades. By the 1920s, a state-funded school system had been set up at the primary and intermediate levels, and several private middle schools had been established by progressive local rulers.

Karo highlanders entered the colonial era competitively handicapped by a relative lack of educational and economic opportunities, but by 1940 they had developed and exploited a profitable niche in the East Coast Residency's sociopolitical ecology and were on their way to catching up with the modernizing ventures of the other groups in the region.

However minor Dutch interventions may have been in the Karo area, their effects were not trivial. Colonial conquest and administrative reorganization had forced some headmen from office, extended the authority of others, created territorial boundaries and formal courts of law, and established a hierarchy of governance where none had existed. All-weather roads linking Karoland to the urban centers of the lowlands made travel easier and created new occupations—truck driver, mechanic, broker, café owner, clerk, shopkeeper—and new routes to wealth and influence. Literacy and a concomitant "progressive" (i.e., Westernized) outlook marked a generational as well as an incipient class divide. Land values soared as a result of the rapid expansion of commercial agriculture, especially in regions near the main roads and markets and in villages where government-subsidized irrigation projects had been put in place or where highly profitable tree crops had been introduced. Even locally these economic benefits were not evenly distributed. In some villages a few families came to hold most of the irrigated land while others lost control of their fields permanently. In other places anxieties about the sudden disparities of wealth found intertwined expression in fears of crop theft and accusations of sorcery. These new points of conflict and resentment settled into the already existing fault lines of Karo society, generating unlikely alliances with urban political activists and sporadic outbreaks of mob violence during the late colonial period and the Japanese occupation. They continued to shape political allegiances and antipathies through the independence struggle and to trouble social relations for decades afterward.[16]

Dutch colonial rule in East Sumatra came to an abrupt end in March 1942, when, after putting up only a token defense, the overmatched Dutch military forces surrendered to invading Japanese troops. Villagers in Karoland recalled the unexpected appearance of Japanese soldiers on red bicycles, the sudden arrest of European missionaries and administrators, and the crisp discipline and casual brutality of the new occupying force. The Japanese were at first welcomed as liberators, but attitudes soon changed to resentment and fear. "That was when we learned how it felt to be colonized," said Nandé Tobat beru Sembiring, a former army nurse we interviewed at her modest home in Jakarta:

NANDÉ TOBAT: From the behavior of the Japanese. That was the worst, the Japanese time. It was really hard. Just imagine, there was no cloth! Say we had harvested ten cans of grain from our fields, they'd only let you keep three of them. Bring us seven cans, they'd say. So we didn't eat rice anymore, we'd have to beg them for it. They'd give us whatever they felt like, and then only the old broken grains. And this was *our* rice, mind you! Well then, don't you start to feel the pain of colonization? There wasn't even any cloth, or even any more salt. When the Dutch were here you didn't really feel it, you just didn't have anything. You couldn't get ahead. Everything just stayed the same. When we really felt it was in the Japanese time.

Didn't feel it

Karo men recalled the humiliation of having to bow to Japanese soldiers on the street and the shame of being publicly slapped for failing to do so. They spoke of hiding from press gangs seeking laborers for road-building projects or the notorious Tanjung Tiram saltworks. Even more disturbing was the Japanese treatment of Karo women. During the first months of the occupation, Japanese soldiers would turn up unexpectedly looking for food or girls, both of which they would simply appropriate as they liked.

MADASA BERU BERAHMANA: After Japan came, the market closed because everyone was afraid of the Japanese. They controlled the entire city of Kabanjahé. Everyone was afraid. We'd also heard that they were really— they were hunting for women. So at that time we were still girls, I was seventeen or eighteen at the time, so we all migrated out of Kabanjahé. I went to Perbesi-Tiga Binanga, where I had relatives, to avoid being approached by Japanese soldiers. They would ride out on horseback in the evenings looking in the houses for where there were young girls. So because of that we girls went to the villages, to avoid that.

Karo described the three years of Japanese occupation as worse than nearly four decades under the Dutch. "They took the good food, we got the yams," the schoolteacher Kumpul beru Muham complained. "The pigs—they cooked rice for the pigs, but what we got was mixed with [feed] corn. You had to cook it all day, and it was still too hard to chew," said Nandé Timur beru Ginting. There was no cloth in the markets, so villagers were reduced to wearing gunny sacks, barkcloth, or even thatch. Bapa Mul Sembiring, of Gurukinayan, recalled wearing pants made out of locally processed rubber, which melted in the lowland heat. "We had nothing because of Japan, nothing."

During the first year of the occupation, local resources such as rubber and rice were shipped to Japan to support the war effort, but the breakdown in Japanese commercial shipping in mid-1943 meant that raw materials could no longer be exported from Sumatra and manufactured imports such as cloth became scarce in local markets. A new policy of provincial self-sufficiency reduced the already limited supply of essential goods. Rice and cloth were stockpiled for distribution to government employees, Japanese civil and military personnel, and city dwellers who would otherwise face extreme hardship.

Japanese military policy also changed in 1943, as preparations stepped up for an anticipated Allied invasion of northern Sumatra. A coast watch was instituted, and demand for corvée labor to build roads, fortifications, and airfields intensified. Indonesians were given a role, albeit limited, in the defensive preparations. In May, a recruitment drive was begun for Heiho "auxiliary" soldiers, intended mainly to serve as manual laborers alongside Japanese troops in Malaya, Burma, Vietnam, and India. The program had no educational requirements, the pay was low, and the training was rudimentary, but it offered the first real military instruction for Sumatran youths. In November, a second program was instituted, which offered military training for the "volunteer" officer corps (Gyugun) of a planned defensive home guard. The Gyugun program was more ambitious and selective than the Heiho; cadets underwent a rigorous six-month program to teach them leadership skills, riflery, drill training, and military theory, as well as Japanese values and discipline. "I was still a young kid at the time, you understand," recalled Mena Pinem, "and yeah, I saw all my friends too in Gyugun uniforms, all dressed up, [I thought] why them and not me? Something like that. I wanted to wear one of those long Japanese swords."

Responsibility for local recruitment for these programs was given to BOMPA, the newly created Agency to Assist in the Defense of Asia (I., Badan Oentoek Membantu Pertahanan Asia). Led by local political figures, BOMPA was a propaganda organ intended to build support for the war effort. Some considered its participants to be "sellers of young men's heads" (Surbakti 1978:94), collaborators and pawns of the Japanese. Others took a different view. "Look here," Mbeligai Bangun, of Batu Karang, said, "if it weren't for Japanese training, not one of our soldiers would be soldiers. That was how Japan helped us, they were really cruel but they were the ones who trained the soldiers." The BOMPA recruitment drives provided one of the few venues in which nationalist sentiments, in however guarded a form, could be publicly articulated. "We put on plays for [the Heiho recruits]—stories in the Karo language once a month," said Nandé Santoso beru Sebayang, a schoolteacher in Kabanjahé who was an active participant in the BOMPA rallies. "The Japanese watched, but they didn't understand. . . .

Suppose we did a story, 'The Sun Also Rises.' Because the Japanese love the rising sun. So by this so-called rising sun, we'd mean the light of independence. You had to be clever."

In September 1944 the Japanese government, having experienced a series of drastic military setbacks, offered a vague promise of political independence for Indonesia at some time in the future. Propaganda and recruitment efforts were stepped up. Nationalist themes could be expressed more openly than Nandé Santoso's veiled references to the rising sun of independence. The Indonesian red-and-white flag and the national anthem, "Indonesia Raya," banned in the early days of the occupation, were now publicly permitted.

On August 17, 1945, two days after the Japanese surrender to Allied forces, Sukarno proclaimed the independence of the Republic of Indonesia. As British troops from Lord Mountbatten's South-East Asia Command arrived to oversee the Japanese surrender and the release of prisoners of war, Indonesians began to mobilize in support of the nationalist cause. Continuing the efforts of the BOMPA propaganda campaign, rallies were held in villages and towns throughout the province to raise money and recruit volunteers to defend the republic. In the euphoric atmosphere of independence, a range of military and paramilitary organizations formed, some affiliated with political parties and others little more than street gangs. Many were only weakly subject to centralized command structures; some were little more than the private armies of aspiring political leaders. As a result, ideological conflicts, interethnic animosities, personal grudges, family feuds, and resource competition quickly escalated into clashes between rival units.

Beginning in 1946, fighting between nationalist militia groups and British occupying forces broke out around the provincial capital of Medan, intensifying as British peacekeeping forces were replaced by returning Dutch troops. In July 1947 the Dutch launched the first "police action" (D., *politionele actie*) in the form of an all-out assault on nationalist encampments around the city. Fleeing the fighting, lowland refugees flooded into the highlands. In the months that followed, Karo highlanders themselves became refugees. Virtually the entire noncombatant population left their homes at the urging of nationalist leaders committed to a scorched-earth policy, as Dutch troops moved across the Karo district. Villages were burned and crops destroyed. Thousands of people—mostly women, children, and older men—were forced to seek refuge in the republic's shrinking territory. Several hundred thousand people lived for as much as a year in desperate conditions in forest huts and jerry-built camps. In 1948 a treaty was signed, and the refugees were sent home to rebuild their villages and to provide a base of support for guerrilla units, which continued the conflict through a second military campaign. In December 1949 Indonesian national sovereignty was internationally recognized.

The independence struggle was a time of social instability, fear, and unpredictable violence. It was also a defining moment of social transition, marking, as Karo see it today, a self-willed and decisive collective break into modernity. Many of the people set in motion by the forces of independence—refugees and guerrillas, students, workers, soldiers, villagers who had lost their goods, their homes, and sometimes their families in the struggle—stayed on the move after the war's end. Farmers migrated downstream to the coastal lowlands, establishing squatters' claims to the fallow fields of the former tobacco plantations on the outskirts of Medan. Soldiers were sent to distant parts of the archipelago to put down local rebellions, in the process developing a sense of entitled national belonging. Even people who stayed behind were in motion. Bus lines crisscrossed the highlands, linking lowland migrants to their homes in Taneh Karo, connecting traders to local and international markets, or bringing highland travelers to Padang Bulan, Medan's outpost of Karo settlement. Today direct bus routes take passengers from the corners of the Karo district on a "straight shot" to Jakarta. However insignificant the villages and farms of Taneh Karo may appear when viewed from the metropole, this is not one of Indonesia's "out-of-the-way places" (Tsing 1993).

SOURCES AND ABSENCES

My first stay in Karoland was for a period of almost three years, 1983 through 1985. I was conducting dissertation research on Karo spirit mediumship, but it sometimes seemed that my informants were more interested in telling stories about the independence struggle than in answering my questions about mediumistic initiations and spirit encounters. Stories about spirits relayed their sense of marginality or "stuckness," of being out of place in the modern world, a condition they described in a poetic metaphor as "hanging without a rope," unable to move either forward or backward. Talking about the independence struggle, in contrast, was a way not only of placing themselves firmly within the nation but also of mapping the modern. Like Sukarno's golden bridge to the future, their stories of the struggle had an anticipatory quality, of looking forward to a brighter coming day, even when that once-future prospect was now long past.

Three sources I encountered in the 1980s encouraged me to think more about Karo accounts of the independence struggle. Their sometimes harmonious, sometimes discordant resonances led me to consider stories of the struggle from the intersecting perspectives of gender and class, nationhood and modernity. The first of these sources was the man I called "Pak Tua" in my previous book (Steedly 1993). An itinerant gambler, raconteur, and sometime healer, he told amazing stories of his own escapades and exploits, some of which appear in that book. Pak Tua had been a company commander in the radical Wild Tiger Brigade (I., Barisan Harimau Liar, commonly abbreviated as BHL), the peasant militia group that has been blamed for the most unrestrained violence of the wartime period in northern Sumatra. Pak Tua's stories were neither nationalistic nor even, in any obvious sense, patriotic, but instead bespoke a grassroots, class-based solidarity. He offered a sympathetic, often funny account of the young volunteers, who more or less fumbled their way toward independence without much idea of where they were headed. In his stories of the struggle, Pak Tua portrayed himself as a trickster who became an officer without anyone realizing that he couldn't read or write. When the fighting was over, though, he found himself increasingly at odds with the modern world and out of step with the disciplinary agendas of the state. "Nowadays it's difficult," he said. "You can't go on any longer in the proper way, but you have to go on anyway. That's the situation now."[17] Unlike many of the other untrained and unskilled Wild Tiger volunteers, Pak Tua exploited his position of marginality with a great deal of gusto, and some profit. The last I heard, he was involved in the prostitution business, making beauty charms for the girls and invulnerability spells for their protectors, and had become a ubiquitous informant for thesis-writing anthropology students at the local universities.

A very different but equally compelling source was the recording of a song by a Karo woman named Sinek beru Karo, made in the late 1950s and still available in bootleg cassette form in the '80s. Sinek's performance gave an autobiographical twist to the traditional improvised genre of blessing song known as *katoneng-katoneng*, which she used to recount her experiences during the 1947 evacuation. Tracing the trajectory of personal experience in simple and striking images, her performance directed attention to the gendered poetics of remembrance and at the same time raised the possibility of localizing the nation in narration.

What made Sinek's song seem so unusual to me was not the sentimental patriotism it displayed but the way it transported the ordinary
routines and extraordinary experiences of women into the space of public discourse. Karo women have generally been granted little voice in
social deliberations or in the collective self-representations of oratory
and storytelling. Neither did they have much to say that could be fitted
into the conventional frames of formal public speech, except in formulaic lamentations for the dead and the displaced discourse of spirit
mediumship. Evacuation stories were different: women (but rarely men)
told them repeatedly and enthusiastically. In these accounts, narrative
set-pieces of flat pathos and bare-bones intensity were strung along
recited lists of place-names, mnemonic chains by which women's experiences could be held as well as shared. The subject matter of women's
stories was endurance, not heroics; they depicted ordinary, daily acts
transformed by the startling circumstances of warfare. Sinek turned the
everyday objects and events of women's lives into the stuff of art, in a
nationalist vein.

> There in the thick forest, where the ravines were deep,
> that's where we stayed
> until it was dark, brother,
> and it began to rain, too.
> We needed a shelter,
> there wasn't even a field-hut.
> We needed to cook our rice,
> we didn't dare to light a fire.
> Not to mention we hadn't brought a cooking pot,
> we hadn't even brought rice for cooking.
> And to add to that, brother,
> the planes kept shelling from above.
> We didn't dare to light a fire.[18]

My third source was the excellent two-volume history *Perang
Kemerdekaan di Karo Area* (The War for Independence in the Karo
Area) and *Perang Kemerdekaan di Tanah Karo, Karo Jahe dan Dairi
Area* (The War for Independence in Karoland, Lower Karo and the
Dairi Area), written by retired army lieutenant colonel and amateur
historian A. R. Surbakti (1978, 1979). Like most Indonesian accounts
of the independence struggle, Surbakti's history was written in good
nationalist style and went to considerable lengths to avoid controversy.
Most national histories view the struggle from the perspective of its
leaders in Java and assess the value of local action by how closely it
conformed to the standards and commands of the center. For Surbakti,

who was an officer in the Karo Halilintar (Thunderbolt) militia, the center is northern Sumatra, and the perspective is Karo. His local partisanship exceeds the limits of patriotism; it generates a text that, by "provincializing" Java, both hews to and undermines the official national line.[19] The peasant rebels of Pak Tua's comic stories found themselves out of place in the modern nation for which they had fought; Sinek's song situated independence in the spaces of women's domestic routines and wartime wanderings; Surbakti depicted the war as the last of a long line of Karo struggles against Dutch colonialism, as if "Indonesia" had been the objective of local history all along.

It is hard to imagine war stories in which the enemy plays so small a part. Aside from the missionaries, who were recollected sympathetically by a few people, the only Dutch person recalled by name was a notoriously brutal officer by the name of Van der Plank, who was said to have summarily executed Karo men in several highland villages in the last days before the 1949 cease-fire (Surbakti 1979:303–5). Stories of the Japanese occupation are filled with individual soldiers, occasionally friendly, other times cruel, some of them identified by name. But the Dutch rarely rise above the shadowy generic category of "the enemy." Dutch convoys are the target of nationalist militia attacks, and Dutch planes drop bombs from above, but only rarely are there any visible— much less named—Dutch characters in Karo stories.

The reason for this is partly demographic: there were not that many Dutch soldiers involved in the fighting in Karoland. The Royal Dutch Legion of the Indies, the KNIL, was largely composed of native recruits, mostly from Ambon in eastern Indonesia but including some Sumatrans as well.[20] They seem to have carried the main burden of fighting in Karoland. After the first two weeks of the 1947 "police action," Dutch troops ventured out of the occupied towns of the highlands mostly for "mopping up" operations or to escort supply convoys. During the second military campaign of 1948–49, much of the fighting was handled by the "Blauwpijpers," the military guard of the Negara Sumatera Timur (NST, the State of East Sumatra), the Dutch-backed "puppet" government of the province set up in 1948. Villagers told me how surprised they were to meet what they took for "black," Malay-speaking Dutchmen and how intriguing they found the notion that there were others, more or less like themselves, at the other end of the archipelago. They occasionally also admitted that some local boys had gotten themselves on the wrong side of the struggle and turned up in the Blauwpijpers. They told poignant and sympathetic stories of the turncoat NST

supporter Nerus Ginting Suka, who had veered from anticolonial agita-
tor to royalist collaborator over the course of his long political career.
They obsessively recalled the rumors of mysterious *kaki tangan musuh*
(collaborators, lit. "feet and hands of the enemy"). They remembered
fights between politically or personally antagonistic militia units,
confrontations between militia leaders, and the interminable efforts of
the army to "rationalize" (i.e., incorporate) the semiautonomous volunteer militias. It was the un-otherness of these indigenous opponents and
ambivalent supporters of the republic that made them both interesting
and comprehensible. The Dutch may have provided the occasion for
the independence struggle, but it was in these ambiguously Indonesian
figures that the identity of the national community-in-the-making was
working itself out.

GENDER IN A TIME OF STRUGGLE

"I can save you some trouble," said one young village headman when I
explained that I wanted to talk to women about their part in the war.
"Before the war, women cooked. During the war, they cooked. Now—
they're still cooking. What kind of struggle is that?" He might have
added that Karo women carried the main burden of family leadership
while young men were away at the front, that they suffered the most
from the material privation imposed by the war, or that they were
responsible for the economic support and material sustenance of
nationalist forces. Women grew the crops that not only fed the soldiers
but also financed a part of the struggle. They spied on the enemy;
carried messages, food, and weapons to the troops; tended the sick and
wounded; buried the dead; entertained the soldiers; hid the guerrillas;
worked in government offices, field hospitals, and jungle camps; gave
speeches; and, yes, cooked the food. But fighting was for men, and the
rest was just business as usual.

Noting the general lack of critical recognition for women's contemporary writings about World War I, Margaret Higonnet (1994:160)
suggests that this may be because "many of these forgotten texts are
about *women*"—and thus not recognizably war stories at all. The identification of warfare as appropriately male action and the battlefield as
a properly masculine domain has made possible the exclusion of women
from the field of war literature. Women writers have responded to their
literary "exile" (as Higonnet terms it) by creating stories that "fold
war back inside a domestic frame." Such stories invite a rethinking of

[handwritten margin note: don't we also have to take this narrative seriously?]

wartime's gendered fronts: surveying the dimensions of wartime domesticity as well as exploring the shape that war takes within domestic space; examining the effects of the conceptual separation between home front and front lines, and of the ways in which that separation is maintained, in women's as well as men's stories of wartime experience.

In Karoland this spatial separation is reflected in a proliferation of love songs. One of these is "Erkata Bedil," a popular Karo song that, translated as "Rifle Reports," provides the title of this book. The song was brought to my attention by Bapa Ruth Ginting, one of my Karo grandfathers, who sometimes accompanied us on interviews. In its first verse, participation in the struggle is figured in gendered terms:

> *Erkata bedil i kota Médan, ari o turang*
> *Ngataken kami maju ngelawan ari o turang*
> *Tading i jenda si turang besan ari o turang*
> *Rajin ku juma si muat nakan ari o turang.*

> Rifle reports in Medan city, O sister dear,[21]
> Telling us to report for battle, O sister dear.
> You'll stay behind, sweetheart, O sister dear,
> Tending the fields, cooking our rice, O sister dear.

I liked the punning assonance of the song's first lines, in which sound *(erkata)* is echoed by saying *(ngataken)*, a figure I have mimicked in translation with the duplicative use of *report* to signify both the sound of gunfire and the commanded presence of volunteers at the battlefront. I liked how this blurred the distinction between cause and effect, event and narration, and how it unsettled agency by dwelling on the power of words, sounds, and inanimate objects to make things happen. Bapa Ruth was not interested in such poetic nuances. He wanted me to appreciate the song's straightforward limning of the division of nationalist labor—men fight, women do the cooking. His was not the dismissive attitude that inspired the headman's question, "What kind of struggle is that?" On the contrary, Bapa Ruth thought that too much attention had been paid to the front-line martial engagements represented in the song's first couplet and not enough to the support activities delineated in the second. Staying at home and cooking the rice was an act of social preservation, moral consequence, and patriotic valor of greater importance than the destructive changes wrought by masculine violence. Attention to what he called the "suffering and sacrifices" *(penderitaan dan pengorbanan)* of Karo women—his version of what I more neutrally described as *peranan dan pengalaman wanita,* "women's roles and experiences"—could, he thought, restore the equilibrium of value or even produce a counterhistory that shifts the moral balance toward a sacrificial model of citizenship and sociality grounded in maternal, domestic values.

What Bapa Ruth did *not* say was that the song's sharp separation of gendered space and action covers only one phase of the independence struggle and only a portion of the population. In mid-May 1946, Karo militia volunteers were first sent to the front lines encircling the city of Medan. At the same time, the moderate nationalists who had recently gained control of the Karo district government began a massive indoctrination campaign to enlist grassroots support for the cause of independence. "Erkata Bedil" was this campaign's informal theme song. Its implicit point of view may have been that of the departing soldiers, but the song's primary audience was the young unmarried village women whose labor could be mobilized at home, "tending the fields, cooking our rice." By fostering a kind of libidinal investment in the work of war, it *produced* the kind of experience that it appears in retrospect to have been a reflection of. The home-front mobilization of female labor that the song describes ended in July 1947, when the fighting shifted into the highlands. After that, home front and front lines were hopelessly entangled, and the clear patterns of gendered activity the song details caved in.

"Erkata Bedil" joins the theme of male leave-taking that is a staple of Karo poetry to the sweet sentimentality of Malay and Indonesian popular music. *O gentle sweetheart,* the duet refrain goes, *how shall we bind our promise? Our vow, our vow, together forever, O sweetheart.* In the second verse, the girl addresses her departing lover, asking him to remain faithful while he is away.

Adina lawes kéna ku médan perang ari o turang
petetap ukur ola melantar ari o turang
adi ué nina pagi pengindo ari o turang
sampang nge pagi si malem ukur ari o turang

If you go off to the field of battle, O brother dear,
Fix your resolve, don't you waver, O brother dear.
If fate permits, O brother dear,
there'll be a time of heart's ease coming, O brother dear.

This fusion of romantic desire and national service haunts the memory of the generation of '45, especially its artists. Bapa Ruth, like some other male veterans with a literary bent, wrote serialized love stories in his spare time. These nostalgically filtered the independence struggle through a young man's (mostly unhappy) experiences of romantic attachment. His tribute to the "suffering and sacrifices" of women takes a similar emotional tack. Intended to place women in the spotlight as nationalist subjects, it does so from the mythologizing viewpoint of masculine imagination: women's primary significance lies in their unreflective, dutiful support for men of action.

One of the most striking features of many of the interviews we conducted, especially with women who actively participated in nationalist organizations, was their insistence that, despite the extreme hardships they experienced, the years of the independence struggle were the best of their lives. This had nothing to do with the poignant love songs that defined the spirit of the times for men like Bapa Ruth. It had to do instead with an enlarged sense of personal self-worth and a potential that was not limited to childbearing and -rearing. Women's memories of the social equality of the struggle, as romanticized in their own way as the memory of love during wartime, cast a special glamour over this period in their lives.

Like many visionary nationalists, Sukarno spoke of women, especially peasant women, as equal members of the nation. "Without women our revolution cannot possibly succeed," he wrote, quoting Lenin approvingly (Sukarno [1947] 1984:241). The independence struggle was a time of dramatic new opportunities for Karo women. New possibilities were opened up by the egalitarian rhetoric of nationalism and by the practical demands of military mobilization. Women's right to basic education was recognized. They were encouraged to attend public rallies and to speak in them. They were given the same basic military training as men, though not the opportunity to use it. They took on new responsibilities and imagined a future of extraordinary promise. Some women were able to create new and egalitarian sorts of domestic arrangements, outside the control and surveillance of parents and kin. They were allowed to interact freely with men in ways that would previously have been unacceptable. They saw themselves as equal actors in the struggle for national independence. They took on social roles that, however restricted they might appear by contemporary standards, were far broader than the limited possibilities traditionally accorded to them.

Just before the opening of the 1947 military campaign, Sukarno published an extended essay titled *Sarinah*, which was, he explained, the name of his childhood nurse. (Indonesia's first department store is also named after her.) The book, a "token of gratitude" to her for teaching him to "love the little people" like herself, is subtitled *kewajiban wanita dalam perjuangan Republic Indonesia* (The Responsibility of Women in the Struggle of the Republic of Indonesia). It was intended for use as a course of study for women to promote their consciousness of equality with men. But for all its sentimental invocations of the simple peasant woman Sarinah, the book was directed at a different audience: the educated urban elite. Studded with Dutch, French, and English phrases, with discussions of primitive matriarchy, modes of production, and the role of women in the French revolution, with quotes from Bachofen, Rosa Luxemburg, Gandhi, Marx, Lenin, and the Bhagavad Ghita, *Sarinah* traced the evolution of women in society "from the cave to the city." The unspoken implications of class difference lying beneath the homogeneous narrative of gender here cast a troubling shadow over promises that, once the independence of the nation was fully achieved, the state's guarantees of social justice and social welfare would ensure the full independence of women. Predictably, these guarantees—such as they are, today—are most effectively invoked by those who come to them from positions of relative privilege.

Conventional histories of Indonesia's independence struggle are almost entirely silent on the subject of women. This is due in part to their continuing emphasis on top-down institutional arrangements, party politics, statecraft, and military strategies. It is also partly an effect of idealized notions of brotherhood and male bonding that, as Christine Dobbin (1980) has pointed out, underpin the historical imagination of Indonesia's war for national independence. Personal accounts of battlefield heroics, elegiac depictions of soldiers as the nation's "fallen flowers," and a stream of patriotic films, plays, and songs in which female characters serve as surrogate mothers, devoted wives, or love interests for male protagonists have fostered a view of the independence struggle as an arena for displays of masculine prowess. Identifications of women with domesticity and, more broadly, with the people as a whole, create a two-sided image of woman in war, in which she may figure as the maternal ideal of nationhood or as the suffering victim of wartime aggression but only rarely as an active participant in the struggle for independence.[22]

Incorporating women's experiences in an analysis of social processes does not simply reverse the discriminations of male-dominated historiography and nationalist hagiography while reproducing their basic assumptions; it radically expands and transforms the analytic field. By placing women's wartime experience at the heart of my story, I intend to decenter the military strategizing and sporadic moments of combat that have dominated Indonesian histories of the independence struggle and to highlight instead the daily activities, the routine as well as the extraordinary, of an entire population, male and female, in a period of intense political mobilization, random violence, and extreme social dislocation.

Gender is woven into wartime remembrance in love songs and in patriotic speeches, in the constructed separations of social space and the commonplace tropes of nationalist rhetoric. It is inscribed in family memories, local legends, and authorized biographies; in origin myths, folktales, textbooks, Bible stories, and proverbs; in the etiquette of kinship, the orderings of traditional authority, and the enacting of conventional roles. It exists in the socially inflected desires and hopes that were spun into forms fresh or banal in newspapers and dime novels; in the platitudes of coffee-shop chat and the affecting commonplaces of lovers' discourse. Following the storylines of gender in a time of war leads not to truth unhegemonized but only further into the thickets of social memory, power, and aspiration in which we all live.

the goal is not truth

PARTIAL RECALL

"Now I'm going to tell you something I'll bet you've never heard before," said Bapa Ruth Ginting, our sometime travel guide. "The rice they gave us at the front, it was red! It was wrapped in teak leaves, you see, each portion, and the leaves stained the rice. They turned it red. That's what I remember about the food at the front." Bapa Ruth's claim to originality notwithstanding, just about every Karo man who served in the popular militias mentioned the red rice of the Medan front to us. It was a sensuous hook that seemed to capture the essence of life at the front: a mix of violence and anticipation that could cast a defamiliarizing glare on something as ordinary as a packaged meal of rice. No doubt their rice wasn't always red, though the former soldiers, in a rush of nostalgic remembrance, recalled it that way.

Medan's streetside vendors and food shops commonly served (and still do) individual meals wrapped in banana leaves, but because of the number of servings that had to be prepared every day for the soldiers at the front, alternative wrappers had to be found. When the teak trees that lined the Medan-Berastagi highway were cut down to blockade the road, their large leaves were put to use in the *dapur umum* (public kitchen; the open-air cooking stations where the soldiers' meals were prepared). The kitchens were overseen by staff officers or, more often, by their wives. Karo girls from nearby villages sometimes helped out, but most of the work was done by Javanese estate laborers. They cooked the rice, topped it with boiled cassava leaves or stews made with vegetables trucked down from the highlands, and folded each individual portion in a leaf wrapper. Militia leaders notified the kitchen staff of their unit's position and current strength (which varied considerably from day to day), and the correct number of ready-made meals would be delivered to them.

The unexpected redness of the soldiers' rice contains, but does not draw attention to, this entire backstage apparatus of food collection, preparation, and distribution, which linked uplands and lowlands, home front and front lines, the labor of women and the battles of men. It also hints at, but does not display, other less attractive aspects of military mobilization, such as the exploitation of plantation laborers, crop levies on farmers, appropriations and downright theft of property from civilians, political infighting, and competition—sometimes violent—between armed units over strategic resources (van Langenburg 1976; Stoler 1988). These are subsumed by the nostalgic pleasures of sensuous recollection, the minor strangenesses of wartime experience. *strangeness of wartime*

Despite the passage of nearly half a century, Karo stories of life during the independence struggle seemed remarkably precise and vivid. By invoking concrete details and named places, they located memories in a familiar space. Seemingly trivial matters provided a material ground for narration. Not surprisingly, food was a common theme. "No salt," they said. "We had to eat *béwan*," people told me over and over. "You know what *béwan* is, don't you?" Then they would describe this hardy weed—how it looks, how it has to be cooked, what it tastes like. However concrete or compelling these memorable images may be, they are always the outcome of selective narration and partial recall.

Aside from the obvious concerns raised by a historical study's dependence on the memories of events nearly fifty years past and by the special difficulties of working with sometimes elderly informants, we faced three specific problems in conducting interviews. The first of these, which has been particularly significant in those rural areas with histories of political violence, is fear. Having seen during the war and afterward the potentially fatal effect of a casual remark or an unreflective commitment, some villagers were unwilling to risk making a recorded statement on any topic, however innocuous it seemed. In some cases my government clearance and the approval of the village headman were sufficient guarantee of informants' safety; in other cases, these were precisely what informants were afraid of.

2. A second, more common problem was the tendency of others (mostly, but not always, the male relatives of female informants) present during interview sessions either to monopolize the conversation or to channel the narration into what they deemed an appropriate or interesting form. This included appropriative commentary and explanation from the sidelines; downright interruptions when informants ventured into areas the sideline observers thought were uninteresting or inappropriate; lectures (to me) on the proper way to conduct interviews ("she doesn't really understand this, so you have to ask lots of specific questions"); lectures (to informants) on how to tell a story properly; and unsolicited expositions on the aims and methods of social science—which, in New Order Indonesia, seemed to be oriented toward the collection of material details that could be strapped onto a set of prefabricated conclusions. Remarkably, informants were rarely deterred by these interventions. Nor, once they had begun, did they seem particularly distracted by our occasional interruptions.

The third problem, and perhaps the most pervasive, was the impact of government screening on both the shape of historical memory and informants' interpretation of our aims. In the mid-1980s, new applications for veteran status (and thus military pensions) began to be reviewed, under revised and broadened eligibility guidelines that for the first time recognized women veterans. At the same time the status of all veterans was reevaluated for pension approval. Applicants underwent a complex review process (referred to in Indonesian as *skrining*) during which they were required to fill out complicated forms, interrogated about forty-year-old details of their military record, and asked for corroboration of their claimed (and in some cases already acknowledged) service. Substantial bribes were often necessary to ensure the processing of applications. Some well-connected individuals with only tenuous claims to veteran status were approved; others with what seemed more legitimate claims were rejected. An applicant's memory lapse could have serious repercussions, and it is thus not surprising that many informants—despite our insistence that these interviews were unrelated to *skrining*—worried about making mistakes, particularly regarding dates. Others thought we might be able to help them apply for pensions. While many informants were concerned about the adequacy or authority of their own narratives, we were also frequently warned about the *veteran palsu*, "fake veterans" who appropriated others' stories or who in one way or another didn't measure up to the standard of a "real" veteran. In these circumstances, experiential authenticity became a valuable commodity; memory, as a result, was highly contested ground.

"I was from the Japanese army," Nasip Perangin-angin began his account of military service. "All of us former Japanese soldiers here, and I in particular, went into the TKR. Tentara Keamanan Rakyat [People's Security Army] it was called at that time. Then the TKR changed to TRI, Tentara Republic Indonesia [Army of the Republic of Indonesia]. Then from TRI to TNI [Tentara Nasional Indonesia, Indonesian National Army]. TNI Company 2, Battalion 3, Regiment I, that's under the leadership of Djamin Ginting. The battalion commander was Nelang Sembiring." A somewhat more elaborate account of military service, in the classic Karo form of a traveler's tale in which temporal sequence is plotted by movement from place to place, came from Bapa Tabonal Ginting. Like Nasip Perangin-angin, he too began his well-rehearsed narrative with a record of institutional reorganizations and affiliations.

BAPA TABONAL GINTING: At the beginning, you see, first there was the proc-lamation of August 17, 1945. That was the beginning of our independence. So because of that, there was the BPI here, the Barisan Pemuda Indonesia [Indonesian Youth Brigade], then there was Pesindo [Pemuda Sosialis Indo-nesia, Socialist Youth of Indonesia]. After that the Allies came to Berastagi, so all the young men in the village of Pernantin, eighty-nine in all, went there. When we arrived [the Allied troops] had already gone back [to Medan], so we went home again. After we got back here, instructions came again: "All of you go to Bandar Baru," so we all went there. When we got there, the head of our group wouldn't let us go straight to the front, so we all went home again. After that we went to Pancur Batu, that was during the First Aggression [first Dutch military campaign], that's when our friend Marulla was killed, and Gading Ginting was crippled.[23] From there we retreated to Sibolangit and from there on to Kabanjahé. It was in '47, the Dutch came in from Siantar and then to Saribu Dolok. So from there we retreated to Lau Simomo. We defended Lau Simomo. Captain Pala Bangun's battalion defended it. After that, we went to Kuta Bangun. . . .

This is a good, if elliptical, illustration of what I call the "pension testi-monial." With its circuits of abrupt arrival and sudden departure, extreme narrative compression, and insistent repetitive beat of facticity, it is a story whose main virtue is its verifiability. Bapa Tabonal provides relevant details of his military career, names commanding officers, offers selected sites for further interrogation—and eliminates whatever might cloud or complicate the simple signs of military service. The names of places can be synchronized with well-documented incidents: the battle of Berastagi (November 25, 1945); the creation of a defensive post at Bandar Baru (late April 1946); the move to the Pancur Batu front (the end of May 1946); the Sibolangit-Kabanjahé retreat following the collapse of the Medan front (late July 1947); and the shifting Lau Simomo–Kuta Bangun front during the defense of the highlands (August–December 1947), which identifies his militia affiliation as the Napindo Halilintar Regiment. The names of comrades dead or injured in battle add to its proofs.

Any conversation is marked by evasions and constraints. In Indonesia, these are often warnings of an approach to dangerous political terrain. After General Suharto came to power in 1966, following what was officially described as a communist-backed coup attempt, all forms of antigovernment activity or sentiment were rigorously and sometimes violently suppressed. Harmony and acquiescence were glorified and enforced as key social values. Ethnographic research on topics bearing on religious, ethnic, race, or class differences or on political dissent was unlikely to receive government approval. For this reason, I usually described my project, in official as well as informal contexts, as a study of Karo women's "roles and experiences" during the independence struggle. Focusing on women defined my research as suitably nonpolitical in Indonesian terms, since the political arena was considered a fundamentally masculine space (though, ironically, it had the opposite effect on grant applications in the United States, where, in the 1990s, "gender" could be regarded as a political rather than an academic area of interest). In addition to facilitating government clearance, this provided a certain protection for informants by designating a "safe" realm of discourse, but it also set limits on what we would be told.

What we tried to create in our interviews was an informal conversational setting comfortably open to view. This was in part to avoid any association with the private interrogations of the *skrining* interview and also to avoid arousing local suspicion about what might have been said in private conversations. In the context of public discourse, secrets could remain appropriately unspoken, suspicions unvoiced, and events that might embarrass or endanger informants undisclosed. Certain things I don't understand and could not ask; others I learned but cannot repeat. I do not know what people did not choose to tell me in front of their neighbors or family. Party politics, which played a significant role in youth mobilization and indoctrination, was mostly forgotten or omitted. No doubt certain other aspects of the struggle—acts of violence or collaboration or cowardice, as well as more benign social improprieties—were downplayed, given a positive spin, or left out altogether. Individual heroics were occasionally played up or in some cases may have been invented outright. I have no access to the truth of narrated events and no wish to break the implicit trust of what was willingly shared with us.

Except in a few cases, I have used my informants' real names. I do so despite the ethnographic convention of using pseudonyms to protect the confidentiality of sources and the privacy of confidants. But if this book is to have any value for the families of the women and men who shared their stories with us, it is as a record of their personal contributions to the cause of national independence, of which they spoke with considerable pride, and as a record of their visions of the stakes in that struggle. The reader should recognize, however, that the use of real names required all parties, ourselves included, to exercise a necessary discretion (or even dissimulation) in our interviews and that it is my responsibility to continue this discretion in the act of writing.[24]

[handwritten margin note: Are they reading this book?]

As important as what could and could not be said in our conversations is the issue of whom we did and did not speak to. Obviously, these are survivors' tales: survivors not just of the war itself but of the intervening decades and in particular of the political violence that brought General Suharto to power in 1965. Karo politics until that time had been left-oriented, and the massacres there, though undocumented, were devastating. Many who were associated with left-wing political organizations either during or after the independence struggle were killed or imprisoned; those who were "implicated" (the Indonesian term, *terlibat*, needs no explanatory predication) and lived to tell were not much inclined to talk about the past.

Most of our informants were identified through personal contacts in veterans' circles. The northern plateau, which is the part of the Karo district I know best and where my adoptive Karo family hails from, is where the greatest number of interviews were conducted. The north Karo population was strongly divided between supporters of two popular militia organizations, the Halilintar Regiment and the Barisan Harimau Liar. A third armed force, the Indonesian National Army (TNI), drew its Karo recruits largely from the eastern side of the plateau. I know this area less well and so conducted fewer interviews with veterans and affiliates of the army than with those of the militia units. The majority of our informants were associated with the Halilintar Regiment. This was in part because of that organization's numerical and political predominance in the Karo district but also because my initial contacts were with former Halilintar leaders, who then introduced me to others, and so on. The BHL was smaller and more radical, both in its politics and its actions; correctly or not, it has been blamed for much of the internecine violence of the period. Like the Halilintar Regiment, the BHL was affiliated with the Indonesian Nationalist Party, but since 1965 it came to be associated by many with the Communist Party—mainly, I believe, because of its reputation for ferocity rather than any ideological affinity. Not surprisingly, many (though by no means all) of the ex-BHL members I met were reluctant to speak of their experiences and actions.

TALKING ABOUT REVOLUTION

Certain words we learned *not* to use. Foremost among these was *repolusi*—or, sometimes, *polusi* (K./E., revolution). Following the standard usage of Sukarno and other "Old Order" intellectuals, English-language accounts routinely describe what most Indonesians now call the War for Independence (Perang Kemerdekaan) or, more commonly, the independence struggle *(perjuangan kemerdekaan)* as the "Indonesian revolution." At first we did the same. We soon realized that the word *repolusi* meant something different to our informants. In the village of Payung, my assistant Jabatin Bangun opened an interview with a group of women veterans by asking them to tell us "what happened here during the time of the revolution." Their replies puzzled us at the time.

NANDÉ SENANTIASA BERU BANGUN: Here in this village?

J.B.: Right.

ND. S.: What do you think? Whoever we hated, just drag them off.

J.B.: I mean, what did you do?

ND. S.: We didn't get mixed up in the revolution. Not us.

J.B.: Yeah, but didn't you do anything like gather up food, and stuff like that at the time?

ND. S.: Not during the revolution. The revolution, you know, that was all about people hating each other. We didn't know anything about that, we were just girls. We didn't have any business with that. We didn't know about this incident or that one. We heard, well, that one, he's gone. That one disappeared. Well, we heard. We heard, but we didn't get mixed up in it.

J.B.: That's not what I meant. I meant, what were you doing while that was going on, if you were in, say, the public kitchen, or training . . . ?

ND. S.: Oh, we were in the public kitchen.

NANDÉ USMAN BERU PANDIA: Right, when it was a little safe here.

Repolusi was not another word for *perjuangan*, the armed struggle against the Dutch enemy. In a literal sense it referenced the violent events of the so-called Social Revolution of 1946, a period of roughly three

weeks when political power was forcibly transferred from the traditional
rulers who had governed under the Dutch and Japanese to the new
Republican National Committees, a transition that had been effected
with considerable brutality in East Sumatra. But in Karoland it signaled
something broader and more terrifying: the outbreaks of popular violence that occurred sporadically across the highlands between 1945 and
1949. If *struggle* referenced the organized armed resistance to a foreign
enemy in defense of sovereign national territory, then *revolution* referred
to a broad range of uncoordinated actions at the same time as, but only
loosely connected to, that struggle, much of it targeting fellow Indonesians. Popular violence was, at one time or another, directed against local
officials who had cooperated with the Japanese or the Dutch; village
moneylenders, entrepreneurs, and wealthy landowners; lowland refugees
and political prisoners, including those who were ethnically Karo; supporters of left- or right-wing political organizations or members of rival
fighting units; and those who signaled, intentionally or not, some perceived affinity with the Dutch. But in a broader sense, *repolusi* stood not
for a specific moment or event but for a condition of pervasive fear and
indiscriminate violence, in which *anyone* could become a victim.

Stories of *repolusi* emerged hesitantly in our interviews, almost as an
afterthought. This was surely due to the awkwardness of their fit within
the conventional storyline of national success and, more important, due to
their relentless reconfiguration, especially during the New Order period, as
part of a long series of left-wing betrayals of the nation. Had we not mis-
used the term *revolution*, we might never have heard about incidents like
these. Once we learned to distinguish between *perjuangan* and *polusi*, we
were mostly able to avoid such awkward moments as the Payung interview
quoted at the beginning of this section ("We didn't do anything in the
revolution, we were just girls"). In following their usage in this book, my
intention is not to take a stand on whether the struggle was or was not
sufficiently "revolutionary"; nor is it to accept either the New Order
regime's depoliticized view of the War for Independence or the army's self-
glorifying representation of itself as the sole guardian and protector of
national sovereignty. Rather, I do so in order to highlight the thread of
internal violence that ran through the euphoria and commitment of independence.[25]

Out of tact and political caution, we did not often bring up the events
of repolusi ourselves; however, we were attentive to moments when our
informants introduced the subject and would encourage them to tell us
more. For this reason and because of the vivid, indeterminate nature of

these memories of violence, it is difficult to assess the significance and extent of popular violence in Karoland. In the chapters that follow, I regard repolusi as a constant possibility, one that could "step forward" at any time. This book is not a history of violence, but it is one that anticipates the aftermath of violence at every moment.

TELLING DETAIL

Personal acts of remembrance and forgetting are inevitably shaped by the claims and insistences of official history. They are marked by the constraining demands of the present, the mediations of interlocution, and the occasions and conditions that came between the story's then and the telling's now. Memories are framed by habits of mind and lineaments of genre—the form of a song, a story, a poem, a book, a phrase, an anecdote. They are inflected by the rhythms of poetry and music and everyday speech, hitched to the potency of a vivid image. They are also shaped by the storyteller's wit and skill, which can sometimes spin a story on a telling detail.

> NANDÉ MENDA BERU TARIGAN: One day something happened that was amazing. Or, maybe somebody else wouldn't think it was amazing, but I did. The Dutch attacked [the village of] Suka. We women ran away across the rice fields. I was carrying my clothes in my arms and my blanket like this [folded on her head], because I couldn't stand the cold. I only had this one red blanket. So this red blanket really annoyed my companions. Anyway, I didn't want to let go of this blanket. So because the one behind me was scared to see my blanket, we were walking on the dike, you know, so she came up, she shoved me. She said, "You're the one these Dutch are looking for! We're in danger on account of you, not to mention that blanket of yours!" she said.

Nandé Menda was the wife of Lt. Col. Djamin Ginting, the highest ranking Karo army officer during the struggle. He died in 1974 while serving as Indonesia's ambassador to Canada—having been, as Indonesians say of out-of-favor army generals, di-duta-besar-kan, "ambassadorized," following Suharto's rise to power. In 1994, when we met, Nandé Menda was living in an impressive house in downtown Jakarta, within walking distance of the upscale Plaza Indonesia shopping center. We spoke in her living room, where we were joined by her friend Roncah beru Barus. Both women were prominent members of Jakarta's Karo Christian community. They had known one another for more than fifty years. Roncah lived all the way across town and didn't have a car or a phone, but the two of them met or talked every day. Nandé

Menda's memories were as well-polished as the room; each story was a little comic gem. Roncah, who must have heard them many times before, was still an appreciative audience.

Nandé Menda came from the piedmont market town of Sibolangit, near the first Dutch mission post in East Sumatra. Her marriage was a love match; no one had approved except for Roncah, who like Nandé Menda was a schoolteacher in Kabanjahé at the time. "She was the only one who would go with me when I went to tell my parents about the marriage, just her," Nandé Menda said. "My husband, until the day he died, remembered that one good deed." Her other fellow teachers had objected to the groom, a former trainee in the Gyugun officer corps, because of his association with the much-resented Japanese. *His* family objected to the bride because they considered her an overeducated lowlander.

The couple was living in Kabanjahé in 1947 at the time of the Dutch invasion. Nandé Menda was sent to the relative safety of her in-laws' home in the village of Suka, on the eastern side of the Karo plateau. To a young schoolteacher used to the plantation zone's cosmopolitan lifestyle and tropical climate, Suka must have seemed dirty, backward, cold, and unwelcoming. When she first arrived there, she made the mistake of airing her sheets in the sun. The villagers thought they were a signal to Dutch bombers and made her take them in. Later, during the evacuation of the village, they figured the Dutch planes flying surveillance must be looking for her because she was the commander's wife. That red blanket folded and carried on her head, vivid as a bull's-eye from the air, was the last straw.

> She shook my arm and my blanket fell . . . into the water! Wah! What could I do, I couldn't stand to be parted from my blanket, I had to go in after my blanket. So I followed after them from behind, they got across the fields, and the Dutch [soldiers] and I were still down in the fields. I was walking, I was holding on to my blanket, but fortunately they didn't pay any attention to me because I was just following behind on my own. Because they thought, oh, it's just another woman evacuee, whatever.

Wrapped up in Nandé Menda's warm blanket and white sheets are ideas of comfort, home, modernity, cleanliness, and propriety—all the hallmarks of the bourgeois, Dutch-inflected domesticity that was a main objective of elite women's education at the time. The garish manufactured blanket carried on her head might have been a parodic stand-in for the earthy red-brown handwoven cloths known as *uis gara* (lit., "red cloth") that Karo women wore wrapped into flat, pillowlike turbans *(tudung)*.[26] It is this implicit contrast between red blanket and *uis gara*—tokens of modernity and tradition, of urban and rural lifestyles— that her story plays upon.

But there is more than this to be unfolded from Nandé Menda's red blanket. Karo tend publicly to downplay disparities of wealth, but they also measure the minutest calibrations of prestige in the quality and cut of clothing. One of the things they seem to have resented most about the Japanese occupation was the lack of available cloth, all of which had been stockpiled for the war effort. Only those with the proper connections could get any cloth at all. Riano Perangin-angin, for instance, explained his decision to join the Heiho military auxiliary corps in textile terms. "It wasn't because we wanted to go," he said. "We didn't have any clothes, you see, during the Japanese time there weren't any clothes. All our clothes were patched, we even used bark to make clothing. They took all the cotton out of mattresses, pillows." Two years after Japan's surrender, sheets and blankets were still more than an extravagance and a conspicuous display of social superiority: they could be seen as the perquisites of a collaborator.

While I may be able to lay out for the reader some of the resonances of the content of Nandé Menda's story, more difficult to convey is its droll style. This being one of my first entries into the domestic world of Jakarta's rich and famous, what I remember best about the occasion was the contrast between the grand formality of the setting and the apparent ingenuousness of her account. This skill at moving between down-home and cosmopolitan styles was something I later learned to expect from the most successful members of Karoland's generation of '45, but at the time it came as a surprise to me. There was an unexpected note of light self-mockery in her storytelling: without looking quite foolish, Nandé Menda managed to tweak her own rather imperious manner and to tell a story that was genuinely entertaining. In it, motives and action are simple and straightforward, and the only violence committed is against a beloved blanket. Read it again: this is a story for children.

SIGNS OF VIOLENCE

About four months after Nandé Menda's flight across the rice paddies there was another encounter between Dutch troops and Karo women. This one was disturbing enough to be mentioned in a report of the North Sumatran governing commission (Recomba) dated November 26, 1947, which cites an earlier report by Kabanjahé's civilian administrator,

A. J. Ph. Gonggrijp—"the contents of which, incontrovertibly true, give in a few words a quite thoroughly shocking picture of the tragic results of the campaign of lies of which this population is the victim." Gonggrijp's appended report repeats a story he had heard from the battalion commander stationed in the south Karo village of Mérék, not far from Suka:

> On foot patrol through the territory our soldiers suddenly encountered a dozen Karo-Batak women, who the moment they were seen, flung themselves without thought into a deep ravine located nearby. Considerable time spent searching for any movement on the edge of the ravine yielded no single result, so that it may well be assumed that these women indeed smashed themselves to bits in the deep and silent abyss. (Indonesia Rapportage 1945–50)

This unfortunate incident, said Gonggrijp, demonstrated the local population's "fear and loathing" of the Dutch, a situation he attributed to "atrocity propaganda." This is a fairly standard blame-the-victim military stance, in which responsibility for violence is denied both in a general sense (accusations of violence against the Dutch are a "campaign of lies") and in the case at hand (false propaganda, not the presence of the patrol, is the cause of the women's apparent deaths). To me, what is more interesting is the report's placement of violence within a field of narration. It says that stories, in the form of "lies" and "propaganda" about violence, are what makes violence happen. Event and representation here reverse their usual order. The propaganda campaign, of which these Karo women were already "tragic victims" before they became actual victims of their accidental run-in with Dutch soldiers, functions in the report to contain a moment of horror and to clarify a seemingly incomprehensible situation.

As Gyanendra Pandey (1992:27) notes, histories of violence tend to dwell on context. In such accounts, context—in this instance the narrative background of "atrocity propaganda"—appears to make sense of violence by circling it, filling in the space around it, considering what preceded, instigated, or precipitated it, exposing the state of mind or cultural values that contributed to it. Contextualizing violence is a way of neutralizing it, making it seem like a familiar, knowable, and thus manageable condition. "Its contours and character are simply assumed," Pandey writes, "its forms need no investigation."

Rather than explaining the occurrence of violence, Karo stories trace its signs and effects. They dwell upon its aftermath rather than its causes and observe it indirectly through the reactions of others. Here is another

story of Nandé Menda's, this one recounting the 1948 Dutch bombing
of the town of Kota Cane in republican territory:

NANDÉ MENDA BERU TARIGAN: It was early in the morning, I was still asleep.
Suddenly there were shots in Kota Cane—*dor rar rar rar rar*—my husband and
the officers who were with him all ran out of the house. At that time I didn't
know I had any strength at all, I was sick at the time. But apparently the
strength came. I ran, under—the house was high, I went underneath. The house
had a ladder down to the river, behind the ladder is where I sat with my baby—
fifty-two times I counted the shots from the airplanes, two of them in turns. . . .
It seems my servant didn't leave me, she was holding on to one of the house
columns, crying there. Her brother—there was one other there—ran from one
post to the other, ran nonstop for about an hour. Even so, there was something
amusing, I looked at the river—apparently there was someone in the river. If
the plane fired, he dived, he thought he'd be protected by the water—if the
plane stopped firing, he came out. That was what I watched in my fright.

Less detached but equally observant is the following account of the
same event, which was told to me by Nandé Petrus, my adoptive Karo
mother. She was about nine years old at the time of the bombing:

NANDÉ PETRUS BERU GINTING: About nine o'clock in the morning, we were
still in the house, the planes came. I don't know how many there were,
people said there were five. I don't know because we immediately—as soon
as we heard the sound of the plane, there was a deep ditch near the house we
were staying in. As soon as we heard the plane we ran to the ditch, that's
where we took shelter. For a long time we heard the sound of bombs. We
thought the bombs were nearby. We heard the sound of bombs. Nonstop. So
my friend's mother, she was crying. My baby, my baby, one of her children
was left behind in the house. A little boy. We weren't big yet and he was
younger than us. We were staying in the same house. My baby, my baby, she
said. . . . So, to make it short, now it was safe again. Safe. We hadn't eaten
yet, breakfast wasn't even cooked yet. Safe again. So then, there wasn't any
sound of airplanes. So, it's safe now, we said. Let's go out. We came out, we
went straight to the house. There was this sawmill, right there by the sawmill
was where we bathed, that's where we saw this water buffalo, meat scattered
all around, dead. There was a person there too. There we couldn't tell which
was human flesh and which was water buffalo flesh. Because there was
this—I still remember the one who took care of the water buffalo, his name
was Parli. I still remember. There was just the one water buffalo left, and he
was the herder. He wasn't senile, just sort of slow. So when the airplanes
came, he apparently kept on herding the water buffalo. Along the road. So
when the plane dropped a bomb the water buffalo was hit, and he was hit
too. So it was—that's why the flesh was all together, like I said. It was horrible, you know. "Look at that, Mother," I said to your granny Karo. "Eyah!
don't look at it," she said, she was scared too. "Don't look," she said. So
when we got to our house—it was nothing but ashes. Word was that our

house was the first one that was hit. It was good luck that none of us stayed in the house. Good luck. So the house was turned to ashes, then we saw that our friend's baby was dead. Hit by the bomb. . . . He wasn't in the house, but nearby. He'd gone out of the house, but nearby, he didn't hide, just a kid, you know. He was running around. He was dead, hit by the bomb.

Nandé Petrus told the story of the water buffalo over and over, in increasingly gruesome detail: meat draped on trees, human and buffalo all mixed together, you couldn't tell which was which, some people wanted to cook it, it shouldn't go to waste, they said, but *she* wouldn't eat any. "Eeuw!" her kids shrieked, running from the room or turning up the TV whenever she started in.

. . .

Rifle Reports is a story of Indonesian independence as it appeared from the outskirts of the nation. Neither a record of victimization nor a celebration of resistance, it is not a story about violence, but it is one in which violence can emerge at any moment. To speak of it as a *story* is not to pass judgment on the truth or falsity of the various accounts of which it is composed but rather to emphasize its constructedness, the fashioning of narrative connectivity, or what Clifford Geertz (1973d) has referred to as the fictional—"made"—nature of ethnographic writing. To speak of it as *a* story is not to assert its unity or to deny the multitude of sometimes discordant elements, contesting versions, and disparate visions of which it is composed, nor is it to claim some imaginary fullness or repletion, as if it were possible to "fill in" the story of independence in some thorough way. Surely other stories can be told of these events; I hope they will.

In telling this story I have tried to attend deeply to the words and the experiences of my Karo informants, but, except in the Bakhtinian sense that any text is a patchwork of other people's words and ideas, some of them referenced or quoted and others so thoroughly absorbed that they may not even be recognized by their appropriator, this is not the kind of collaborative, multiply authored project that James Clifford (1988:51) has recommended as an "alternate textual strategy." Nor is it intended to produce a more complete account of Indonesia's independence struggle by including the voices of those hitherto left out of official or academic consideration, for narrative proliferation does not lead toward, but rather away from, fullness. My aim is to clear a space for broader and more complex visions of agency, citizenship, and social violence, of subjectivity and state formation.

From the transcribed texts of recorded interviews I have selected, brought together, juggled, and recombined stories, phrases, commentaries, bits of conversation, jokes, scenes, and songs. Sometimes these narrative fragments enhance and build on one another; other times they are contradictory, rattling. Some of these bits and pieces I chose to make a point, but more often it was the other way around: the point emerged from puzzling over a story or remark I found compelling, typical, moving, odd, surprising, or just plain baffling. Around them I have arrayed a range of other fragments: my own comments and reflections, pieces of published histories, newspaper accounts, fiction and poetry, items fished from colonial archives, literary criticism, anthropological commonplaces, the theoretical touchstones of academic legitimacy.

Mostly absent from my account is the everyday noise that accompanied all our conversations: traffic on the street, voices from the kitchen, pans clanging, children crying or laughing, sideline commentaries, hawkers' calls and neighbors' greetings, the television in the background, the hiss of the tape recorder. Rudolf Mrázek has recently written movingly about the tension between voice and noise in his own interviews with elderly Indonesians. "Most of the memories and (I guess) dreaming that I have recorded in Indonesia . . . happened in places where the noise of traffic deafened much of what was said, remembered, or dreamed. I have witnessed and was part of it as the voices struggled to be heard in that modern space" (2010:73). Sometimes, on the other hand, noises evoked a space that was less than modern, as was the case with some old recordings of song performances that I found in a radio shop. In these, the barking of dogs and the crowing of roosters were captured along with the murmur of audiences' voices and the crackle, pop, and hiss of old tape and antiquated recording equipment. In either case, the residue of "outside" sound is a reminder of the complicated multiple temporalities in which these preserved voices were situated.

In putting this material together I have been faced with certain problems of exposition—among them how to convey to a nonspecialist audience a dense and highly localized account of events that, even in the generalized form of a national history, are largely unfamiliar to most Western readers; how to suggest, in English translation, the nuances of both Karo and Indonesian language and discursive styles while acknowledging the impossibility of such translation; how to lay out an unfamiliar social framework so that personal narratives are not reduced to an illustrative function but become themselves the point of explication; how to impede the too-rapid leap to understanding or easy identification on the part of the reader (or, indeed, the author); how to balance the comprehensible and the mysterious in my account; and most important, how to respect my Karo narrators' own purposes and understandings without *dealing* privileging their accounts as truths neither subject to ideology nor *with* inflected by interests. I have opted for a narrative style built upon apparent digressions, an accumulation of discursive layers, careful attention to detail and texture, shifting temporalities, and self-conscious interventions. My intention is to produce an account that moves toward difficulty rather than simplification, one that compels as well as enacts the strategies of patient and engaged reading, aiming not to get to the bottom of things but rather to sink experience ever deeper into the dense narrativity of everyday life.

I want to avoid two traps of ethnographic writing, the generic and the (auto-)biographical: to resist, in other words, the urge to "redeem the fragments" of local pasts by locating them in a "world of meaningful interconnections" (Comaroff and Comaroff 1992:16–17) that exists largely on the printed page. As Lila Abu-Lughod (1993:7–13) has argued, ethnographic generalization can make the described community appear more coherent, unified, and undifferentiated—in a word, more "other"—than might actually be the case. One way to disengage this exoticizing tendency is to focus closely, as Abu-Lughod has done, on the lives of a few individuals, entering into the general frameworks of sociality and ethnographic representation through their particular experiences and viewpoints. By putting the individual at the center of the ethnographic narrative, however, this approach risks replacing otherness with identification, substituting the hypothetical unity of the speaking subject, history's eyewitness, for the imposed coherence of meaningful context, and so taking the "voice" (the informant's, the ethnographer's) as the site of both truth and authenticity. So it is with stories rather than their tellers that my text mostly engages: stories that multiply and echo and differ; stories that won't stay put, that change from one telling to the next, or that are oddly frozen, caught on a memorable image or a polished phrase; stories that force their audiences, and even their readers, to engage in practices of creation, skepticism, enjoyment, recognition, masquerade, mystification. This is a narrative space of multiple beginnings and misleading middles, thick with encounters and calamities, trials and errors, secret risks and bad-faith pledges, with no end in sight: moments caught up on the run and passed along—in family memories, mythic reconfigurations, social frameworks, poetic inventions, genealogical inscriptions, durable jokes, memorable commonplaces, and snatches of song.

What accumulates in all these tellings and retellings is _incompleteness:_ a sense of multiplying absences, gaps, inconsistencies. The details do not add up. Consider, for example, the narratives of violence I have presented above. They do not complement or contradict one another, do not add anything to one another, in an informational sense. They are not counterposed to bring out the uniqueness of the individual voice, to present the eyewitness as a privileged source of truth. They do not make suffering comprehensible, explicable, or even bearable. Quite the contrary, their affective resonances _reduce_ the comprehensibility of violence, render it inexplicable both in motivation and outcomes, reveal the unbearability of its effects, blur the clarity of its details, and refuse the easy explanations of context. Like the noncanonical fragmentary sources—poems, songs, myths, workers' diaries, local traditions, family genealogies—that Gyandendra Pandey (1992:50) suggests are of "central importance in challenging the state's construction of history," these stories, taken together, can demonstrate that "what the official sources give us is also but a fragment of history."

CHAPTER 2

Buried Guns

FAREWELL MY HERO, read the banner over the house. MAJ. SELAMAT
GINTING (RET.), COMMANDER, SEKTOR III NAPINDO HALIL-
INTAR. WE WILL CONTINUE YOUR ASPIRATIONS TO FILL UP INDEPEN-
DENCE.

It was nearly dark by the time we arrived in Kuta Bangun, a midsized
village in the central region of the Karo plateau. Even without the banner we couldn't have missed the place. It was bustling with the kind of
activity that signaled a ceremony, and the shoulder of the road was
lined with city cars: low-slung Toyota sedans and Daihatsu Charades,
SUVs and Land Rovers with government license plates. The funeral
announcement had appeared in the Medan papers the day before, April
23, 1994. It being a Saturday, the news quickly spread through the
kitchen crews at Karo weddings all over the city. By the time the funeral
party arrived from Jakarta the airport was packed with Selamat
Ginting's friends and former comrades-in-arms.

Selamat Ginting was a charismatic and often-controversial figure on
the national as well as the local stage. His life had been marked by ups
and downs. The youngest son and heir to the office of *raja urung* (subdistrict head) of Kuta Bangun, he turned from a prospective career in
the colonial civil service to anticolonial activism. He was one of the
founders of POESERA, a Karo produce-marketing cooperative that
served as cover for an underground nationalist organization during the
Japanese occupation. During the independence struggle he headed the

71

largest of the Karo popular militias, the Napindo Halilintar (Thunder-bolt) Regiment—later known by the territorial designation "Sektor III," an area that covered part of the Karo highlands and the adjacent Dairi district. He resigned his military commission in 1949 and went into business, but politics was his real calling. In the early 1950s he spent two years in military prison, having hidden a large cache of guns and ammunition rather than turning them in to the army at the war's end. Soon after his release he was elected to the national legislature, where he served for two terms. A passionate Karo partisan and dedicated Sukarnoist, he became an outspoken critic—one of the very few—of the New Order regime.

The memorial service in Jakarta had been attended by a long list of public figures, including a son and daughter of former president Sukarno, Guntur and Sukmawati. Another of Sukarno's daughters, Megawati Sukarnoputri, who was at that time the chairman of the tepidly oppositional Indonesian Democratic Party (Partai Demokrasi Indonesia, PDI), sent a condolence wreath of lavender orchids.[1] When the funeral party arrived in Medan, another brief service was held in a vacant lot near the rifle range outside the city limits. It was sweltering, people said, and hundreds of mourners showed up. The service lasted only about an hour, because the family had to leave for Kuta Bangun, where the Karo bereavement ceremony (K., *kerja céda até*) was to be held. Burial with military honors would follow, in the National Heroes' Memorial Park in Kabanjahé.

It was the season for landslides, and so, mindful of the weather, we decided to delay our departure for Kuta Bangun until the next morning. Then the car wouldn't start, so we had to wait until church services were over and the auto repair shops opened. We didn't leave Medan until noon and arrived well after the ceremony had begun.

I'd never spent much time in what Karo call the *gunung-gunung* (hilly) region of the central highlands and so was expecting something like the dense, chilly villages that you find perched on Mount Sinabun's cloudy slopes or in the dry, flat expanses of the Kabanjahé corn belt. But here the warmer climate, wide green wet-rice fields, and rolling hills were pleasantly surprising signs of lower elevation. The houses were mostly plain, single-story dwellings, strung along the roadside; many were built of concrete, but a few, including the house where the funeral ceremony was being held, were of unpainted boards.

Inside, we paid our respects and settled into a corner. The women's choir from the local church arrived and led a short program of hymn singing and prayer. It was announced that the funeral service the next day would be conducted following the liturgy of the Karo Protestant Church rather than *secara adat*, according to custom, with the explanation that Selamat Ginting's final wish had been for a Christian burial. Some people found the story of his last-minute deathbed conversion too good to be true, for his commitment to the old ways of ancestor veneration was well known. ("My parents and grandparents have taken care of me in this life," he told me. "Why should I turn away from them in the afterlife?") But, as one of the preachers there said, it was the "hardness" of his position that made this reversal seem all the more miraculous. It was a sign of God's grace, he said, a divine message to the Karo people.

I had just met Selamat Ginting and his wife, Piah Malem beru Manik, that March, shortly after my arrival in Jakarta for research clearance at the beginning of my project. Kalam Sebayang, my case officer at the Indonesian Institute of Science, was one of Selamat Ginting's many "nephews," and he arranged for and accompanied me on a visit to their home on Satria Street in Jakarta. It was not a particularly affluent neighborhood, and the house, though large, was unremarkable; it showed the casual disregard for fashion typical of Karo homes, country or city. Rollaway furniture allowed the front room to be used for occasional guests like us or emptied quickly to accommodate large gatherings or political meetings. The only decorations were cabinets of wartime memorabilia and a wall full of certificates and portraits, arrayed (typically, as I would learn) around a large picture of Sukarno in his prime. Among the photos on the wall were several of Piah Manik in uniform, wearing trousers and carrying a pistol. In one she was with a group of other women (figure 6), and in the other she was on horseback. These reminded me of one of the first things I'd heard about her—that she was nicknamed Beru Rengga Kuning, after the cross-dressing heroine of a popular Karo folktale, an appellation that balanced her husband's equally legendary nom de guerre, Kilap Sumagan, the "great thunderbolt."[2]

From the beginning they both spoke to me in the Karo language, as if a Karo-speaking foreigner were the most ordinary sort of visitor; they seemed neither amused nor impressed by my facility in that language. I slipped immediately into the discourse of kinship, addressing him as "Bayak" (grandfather) and her as "Karo," which is a kind of pet name for a grandmother of Karo-Karo clan; they called me "Meri," without honorifics or formality, as grandparents or friends might. This being a

FIGURE 6. Piah Malem beru Manik (in dark uniform) with companions. Pergendangen, Taneh Karo, 1949. Photo from collection of Selamat Ginting and Piah Malem beru Manik, hung on the memorabilia wall of their home, Jakarta, 1994.

first meeting, I decided not to record the conversation. We talked for four hours that night, mostly about politics and current events—or rather Bayak talked and the rest of us listened. The doctors had put him on a diet of "grass," he said, which left him feeling a little weak; he invited me to come again in a few months, when his health had improved. "We'll stay up all night and talk," he offered cheerfully. "I can tell you everything you need to know about women in the struggle." Their fiftieth wedding anniversary would be in August of that year; he was planning a grand celebration in his home village of Kuta Bangun, and he invited me to attend that too.

My next meeting with Piah Manik was at the funeral two months later. "Bapak is gone," she told me sadly. "Now your book will never get finished."

"Bapak" was how she usually referred to her husband in our conversations. It is the formal Indonesian term of address or reference for an adult man, literally meaning "father" but roughly equivalent to the English "mister." Other times she spoke of him as "Pak Ginting," Mr. Ginting. A standard Karo etiquette of referentiality would have similarly avoided personal names, but done so by stressing relations of kinship to others: "your grandfather," "So-and-So's father." I thought at the time that this was simply an Indonesianism that had crept into her vocabulary as a result of long residence in Jakarta. It may have been that, but I now think it was more: a way of formalizing and "deprovincializing" her account by marking her husband's identity in national, Indonesian terms. Whether she intended it this way or not, her unconventional mode of reference encouraged me to think of Selamat Ginting as sui generis, which in many ways he was.

The day of the funeral had the kind of dazzling clarity that is occasioned by the experience of loss. Women in flat, heavy turbans and the dark colors of mourning clustered in the open yard (figure 7). Here and there fringed palms, set off by the brilliant early-morning sunshine, broke the encircling vista of low, field-checkered hillsides. Canopies had been erected on three sides of the yard; the fourth side was made up by the open veranda of the house. Lined with mats, the canopied spaces were marked for the seating of members of the three general categories of kin—*senina*, clanmates; ritually superior *kalimbubu;* and *anakberu,* who are charged with performing the work of the ceremony. On the side facing the house were areas for "dear friends" and "wartime companions." These spaces filled up as the day went on; by lunchtime there was hardly a place to sit. The open coffin, which had remained in the house through the night, was brought out onto the porch for a final public viewing.

Like any Karo ceremony, this one was filled with speeches, dancing, and eating. A five-piece orchestra *(gendang)* had played most of the night and off and on throughout the day. In addition to the requisite orations by family members, on this occasion there were also tributes from Selamat Ginting's political associates, the head of the district veterans association, and representatives of the three main military units that had operated in the Karo area—Selamat Ginting's Halilintar/ Sektor III command, Regiment IV of the Indonesian National Army, and Brigade "A," the militia organization also known as the Wild Tiger Brigade. Everyone admired Megawati's wreath, prominently displayed to the side of the porch: the Sukarno name was still magical in veterans' circles. Three high school students read a poem titled "For My Selamat Ginting" in the breathy declamatory style popular in Indonesia:

> My father, my Selamat Ginting, my retired officer,
> Liberty or death you proclaim.
> You stand straight and firm 'mid the flames of struggle,
> Days without eating, nights without sleeping,

The spirit of struggle never extinguished.
Forest after forest you crossed with your soldiers,
Mountain after mountain you climbed with full conviction,
River after river you forded.
Not a handful of earth did you cede to the colonizer.
O Selamat Ginting,
Hero who will ne'er come again,
Who determined the history of the nation's struggle,
Who increased the stature of the state,
You are the hero of independence.
Unforgettable hero,
Your name is inscribed in gold ink in the history of the nation.[3]

The poem may have been unadulterated Indonesian hyperbole, but what followed it was a classically sweet moment of Karo understatement. As the orchestra began to play "Perkantong Samping"—to me the loveliest and most poignant of Karo ballads of the independence struggle—Selamat Ginting's wartime companions were invited to dance in his honor. Dressed in their best clothes, the old veterans formed a single semicircular line facing the open coffin. With graceful bows and nuanced gestures, they danced their respects to the bereaved family, who received them in solemn dignity.

"Perkantong Samping" means "side pockets," and it refers to the unfashionable cut of the uniforms worn by the militia volunteers of Sektor III.[4] The song was composed by Lt. Naksi Sinulingga as a riposte to snubs by the notoriously style-conscious girls of Juhar, a large and prosperous village of the southern highlands:

Hey, Side Pockets!
    That look don't sell, you say.
    'Cause you think, little sister,
    it's clothes that make the man.

Your attitude's so dated,
    that's why you talk this way.
    You just don't realize
    a man can change his clothes.

The real target of this song was not the snobbish Juhar girls. It was, instead, the regular troops of the army's Regiment IV, who looked good in their government-issue uniforms but (as the Sektor III volunteers would say) weren't much for fighting:

Take a look at the *kayang-kayang* fruit
    so beautiful to see.

When it's ripe it's not fit to eat.
Unripe it's not worth cooking.

There were more verses, describing in this same vein other beautiful but useless creatures (the iridescent dung fly being one particularly memorable example). Now, though, it was just a lovely old melody that seemed to quiver in the luminous highland air. What came to mind as I ran through the lyrics to myself was not lingering resentments and occasional clashes between volunteers and regular troops but rather an image of shy young soldiers and pretty village girls of fifty years ago, like the ones who inhabit those slightly out-of-focus black-and-white snapshots in family albums.

Against the melodic background I heard Piah Manik's voice addressing her dead husband. This was, as far as I know, her only public speech of the entire ceremony. Speaking slowly and pausing between sentences, she began by mentioning his plans for their golden wedding anniversary, which would have been held *soon, you said. . . . It'll be fun, you said that too. . . . I, I'm not very good at talking. . . . You were the one who did all the talking. . . . But never again. . . . So then, don't*—and suddenly she shifted into the stately cadence of sung lamentation:

—leave me, beloved
await him
our wartime companions
Ginting clan, beloved
this loved one
this beloved
receive—

Fragments of her lament wound around the music as she greeted the dancers, embracing a few of the men who wept openly. Her deep, calm singing was in the old Karo style, its soothing beauty enhanced by the soft rounded vowels that bespeak a southern highland home.

beloved beloved
answer us one more time, beloved

. . .

Back in Jakarta two months later, I stopped by the house on Satria Street to pay my respects. Thinking of my unrecorded conversation with her husband, I suggested to Piah Manik that she too had a story to tell; maybe someday when she felt like it we could record that story. A cluster of younger family members gathered to offer encouragement

FIGURE 7. Kin group dancing at Selamat Ginting's funeral. Kuta Bangun, April 25, 1994. Photo by the author.

and advice. Their interest soon dissipated and they drifted off, leaving only Granny Iting—Selamat Ginting's sister—as our audience. The two women rehearsed various familiar anecdotes, searching, as it turned out, for the proper starting point. Then they told me to turn on the tape recorder, and Piah Manik began, precisely, with the story of how she planted Japanese guns in the rice field known as Juma Pali.

Did her husband have to die for this story to come out?

"First," she said, "this was still Japanese time. We were in Kuta Bangun. We'd been married nearly five months. So, that's when Bapak took a truckload of Japanese weaponry. There were rifles. Bren guns.[5] Bombs. Pistols. He hid them in Lau Lisang, the river—"

"Juma Pali, it's called," Iting interjected from across the room.

"—at Kuta Bangun. This is how it was. He hid them first, along the side of the road. Then he called his friends from Kabanjahé. Bapa Berah, Bapa Cita Ngena, Zain Hamid. Pasang Sinuhaji was their driver. So: 'Where can we put them? Let's put some of them where we can get to them after independence,' they said. Then they all spent the night at our house in Kuta Bangun. They brought some, the little ones—pistols and bombs—to the house. There were maybe forty pistols. I'd seen a pistol before, Bapak had one he'd gotten from a Japanese soldier. So they told me, 'Here, hide these pistols.' They gave me the responsibility. That's when I planted the pistols in Juma Pali."

Once past the long and dramatic story of the guns of Juma Pali (about which more later), Piah Manik's recollections took the form of a chronicle of residences: her friend Nandé Santoso's house in Kabanjahé, the bungalow of Vice-Governor Dr. Amir in Berastagi, the abandoned plantation house at Batang Kuis, the forest camps and field huts of military campaigns, the one-room rented house on Besi Street, the house she had built on Sutomo Street while her husband was in jail. "I was always getting dropped off somewhere, you know," she explained later. "Even when we moved back to Medan, it wasn't like army officers' families. I was usually put up in someone's house, that's why I'm so confused. We just stayed with anyone who had room." Finally the list of places where she'd been dropped off became too long for recollection. Did Tanah Lapang come before or after Kuta Nangka? Where did she go after Juhar? Did she stay in Tiga Binanga after the cease-fire or move directly to Medan? "Stop the tape!" she demanded. "We'll do this another time, I don't remember what comes first anymore. If Bapak was here, he'd know. I'll remember it later."

FAMILY STORIES

Every family, as Maurice Halbwachs (1992:63) notes, "has its own peculiar memory," which is formed in the convergence of collective frameworks with the particular conditions and circumstances of its members' lives. "Foremost in this memory," he writes, "are relations of kinship." These give to the memory of the family its double character, in which abstract social principles are embodied in the unique physiognomy of individual family members, and conventional roles and responsibilities are made to seem both natural and binding by the affections generated within the family circle. Because family memory is preserved not only in the personal recollections of its members but also in such transferable forms as names, stories, genealogies, souvenirs, and styles of action, it traverses generations and crosses the consciousness of individuals.

Everyday objects and activities anchor the memory of the family in chronotopically indeterminate scenes of domestic routine; in contrast, places of residence—a house near the market, a grandmother's village, a field hut with a leaky roof—specify precisely the sites and sequences of remembrance. Halbwachs (1980:156) remarks that most groups "engrave their form in some way upon the soil and retrieve their collective remembrances within the spatial framework thus defined." The marks of a group's presence can outlast its actual span of habitation, being passed down in signs and stories that become "genealogies of places, legends about territories" (de Certeau 1984:122). These overwrite and entangle earlier traces of habitation and in turn are subject to the overwritings and entanglements of others. Places like the house on Besi Street or the Juma Pali rice field serve as signposts in the terrain of remembrance, even after those places—or the groups that inhabited them—have themselves disappeared.

The memory of the family is not the sum of recollections of all its individual members, but neither is it a homogeneous set of shared traditions, ideas, and images of the past. The collective frameworks governing social life provide the common referential schemes that make memory possible, but they also ensure that personal remembrance will reproduce the conditions and limits of social being. Gender is perhaps the most obvious, but by no means the only, instance of this. Of all social institutions the family is perhaps the most profoundly and universally shaped by notions of gender difference and transected by gender divisions. These guide the ordering, perpetuation, and reproduction of family space; they designate the kinds of experiences available to family members and inflect the values and orientations through which events are turned into stories. The relative mobility of men and women, the kinds of domestic practices or social virtues expected of them, the opportunities for speech and action open to them, the limits on knowing imposed on them according to their sex: family memory does not overcome these conditions; it invests in them.

Though Piah Manik told the story of the buried guns of Juma Pali as if it were her husband's history that she, as its guardian, was now duty-bound to recount, the tale was transmuted in the telling into another kind of story altogether. It became the bookending incident, twice-told, in our construction of a narrative of her life leading up to and during the struggle for independence. It was a story told with other interlocutors—Granny Iting was one—and composed of fragments of other people's stories, family memories, legends of places. In telling, or retelling, that story, I too have ranged through an array of sources: primarily the recollections of other family members and friends, but also colonial accounts, local histories, maps, genealogies, my own recollections of places and times. And while I have mainly tried, through my recounting (or recasting) of it, to illuminate some of the gendered dimensions of a narrated life, I have also attempted to remain true to its affective core, as a work of both mourning and pride.

. . .

About a month later, we began again. This time we met in Medan at her brother's house. I wanted to fill in her family background as well as her wartime experience, so, picking up the theme of houses, I asked where she and her family had lived in Medan during the Japanese occupation. "In Japanese times? I wasn't, we hadn't gotten married yet. I was still a girl. My father's house was on Laksana Street. Well, actually, our first house was on Japaris Street." From that point we tracked and backtracked the sequence of her temporary residences, including the difficult period when her husband was in prison and she supported them by taking in boarders and selling snacks, up to his election to the Indonesian national assembly in 1955: "He was elected, then he went to Jakarta and I stayed here on Cut Nyak Din Street. We were apart most of the time. While I was on Cut Nyak Din Street both of the children were born. So then after Cut Nyak Din we stayed in a hotel in Jakarta. . . . He was elected twice, two sessions."

My final questions reprised the story of the buried guns. I wanted to pin down the dates of these events. Were the guns buried before or after the Japanese surrender? I asked. We measured the time by the height of rice plants. They'd been about ten centimeters high, she said; that would mean it was within a month of sowing, when the tender plants were still in danger of being damaged by field mice. In Kuta Bangun the *merdang merdem* celebration that marked the end of the planting period was usually held in August, so it would probably have been no later than the end of August or early September.

Even plotting time in this way, against a local ritual cycle and according to the natural growth of rice, seems to miss the point here.[6] What her account follows is not a chronicle of events but rather what de Certeau calls a "spatial syntax" of temporary habitation. Time spans— five months, seven months, a year—are used more or less interchangeably as marks of transition rather than measures of temporal duration. It may be argued, with de Certeau (1984:115) that all narratives are in fact "travel stories," but Piah Manik's stories emphasize the pauses in a life in motion and the effort to domesticate all these sites of transient dwelling. This I found to be a common narrative strategy in Karo women's stories of wartime travels. It suggests why their stories should so frequently be interspersed with detailed descriptions of everyday labor and why memory in these accounts tends to coalesce around the most ordinary of household objects—a cooking pot, a red blanket, or a Good Morning–brand hand towel.

[margin annotation: memory coalescing around objects]

THE KINGDOM OF KUTA PINANG

> PIAH MANIK: See, my grandfather, my father, and my husband, they were all different, but they were all movement men. My grandfather [MF] was close to the Dutch, he was the village head in Lau Tawar. Whenever they went from Sidikalang to Sembetek they'd stop over in Lau Tawar. So they gave him a medal. Then my father—well, *his* father had been the raja in Kuta Pinang. His father—actually it was his uncle, his father's youngest brother— because he was incompetent they removed him from office. They took the kingdom. . . . It went to court, but my father never won.

"Did you have the chance to go to school, Karo?" I asked. She had, she said, but only intermittently. Fondness and filial obligation had kept her from getting much of an education. Her father moved to Medan to further his political plans around 1940, when she was ten years old. Before then, she had spent most of her time with her granny Pinem—her mother's mother—in Lau Tawar, about ten kilometers from her father's home village of Kuta Pinang. In the words of her husband's biography, she was so "spoiled" by her grandparents in Lau Tawar that they neglected (I., *lupa*, lit., "forgot") to send her to school (Bangun and Chairudin 1994:62). After they moved to the city, she had no time for school.

Kuta Pinang was one of the so-called Karo villages on the western side of the Renun River (Lau Renun), which formed the territorial boundary between the colonial residencies of East Sumatra and Tapanuli. Villages here were much smaller than those on the Karo plateau; in 1909 the German geographer Wilhelm Volz estimated that Kuta Pinang had about two hundred inhabitants, which put it on the large side for the region. The total population of her grandfather's "kingdom" *(kinirajän)* was probably not more than five hundred all told, or about the size of a village ward *(kesain)* on the Karo plateau. So when Piah Manik speaks of her father's "lost kingdom," you have to realize that it was a small one at best.

Although the inhabitants of this crumpled landscape of stony ridges and steep grassy hills had close social and cultural ties to the Karo communities on the other side of the river, they had been, for reasons of colonial convenience, incorporated in 1906 into Tapanuli's Dairi district. A kind of cut-and-paste afterthought in the Sumatran rounding off of empire, the Dairi district covered administratively inaccessible portions of what were perceived as three distinct ethnolinguistic homelands—Karo, Toba, and Pakpak. Traversed diagonally by three mountain ridges, Dairi was a sparsely populated region with little arable land and few resources beyond such forest products as camphor, benzoin, rattan, and varieties of wild rubber. These had formed the basis for long-standing debt relations with buyers from the west coast ports of Sinkel and Barus. A major trade route from southern Aceh to the lowland sultanates on the east coast passed through the region as well.

In July 1904 Kuta Pinang served as an overnight bivouac for Dutch troops under the command of Overste G. C. E. van Daalen on his return march from campaigns of conquest in southern Aceh. His adjutant, Lt. J. C. J. Kempees, described it as "quite a large kampong [I., village], of outstanding prosperity." The Dutch soldiers spent a pleasant day there, "wandering at ease and weaponless" among "peaceful, and even friendly" villagers. "Along the kampong flowed a great river with glass-clear deep water, in which there were large swimming holes. A pity, that to experience this pleasure one had to descend along a steep footpath 200 meters, and afterwards climb back up again" (Kempees 1905: 206–7). Dr. H. M. Neeb, the expedition's medical officer and photographer, kept his camera at hand and "snapped away cheerfully at a moment's notice." One of his photos is the portrait of a young woman alone on a grassy hillside (figure 8). The tranquility of this image is in stark contrast to the casual brutality recorded in Neeb's famous photographs of the Van Daalen expedition's massacres in Alasland, which had taken place a few weeks earlier.[7]

When Louis van Vuuren, the district's first *civiel gezaghebber* (civil administrator), arrived in the region in 1906, he found the Karo villages of Lau Renun, tucked in their steep valleys and surrounded by groves of coconut and areca palms, to be "cheerier" than the unbroken forest of southern Dairi. The terrain, crosscut with wild ravines and deep gorges, was "magnificent," he wrote, though difficult of passage. Van Vuuren's mandate, as described in his *Eerste maatregelen in pas geannexeerd gebied* (First Measures in Newly Annexed Territory), was to prepare the area for governmental incorporation. With that aim in mind he enthusiastically inventoried crops, speculated on the possibilities of introducing coffee, benzoin, and rubber cultivation, considered laying

FIGURE 8. Young Karo woman in Kuta Pinang, 1904. Photo by H. M. Neeb, in
Kempees 1905.

in wet-rice fields, and recommended transportation routes. He located villages and mapped the main paths through the region. But his primary task was to construct the administrative and juridical territories through which colonial *rust en orde* could be established and maintained. To accomplish this, he recorded genealogies.

The Tapanuli territory had originated as a subsidiary district within the residency of Sumatra's West Coast, and government there took the form of direct rule. Unlike in the indirectly ruled East Coast Residency, where "autonomous" native states maintained what the Dutch liked to think of as traditional patterns of authority, in Tapanuli only the lowest level of the administrative hierarchy was granted even the illusion of self-rule and customary precedent. It was nevertheless crucial, Van Vuuren (1910:19) argued, to "rule the land with and through the chiefs who according to folk-concepts have the greatest right to authority." To do so, "one must quickly determine who those chiefs are."

This was no simple matter. Some local rulers refused to report to the colonial representatives; others sent a "family member" (D., *familie-lid*, in this context almost certainly a representative of the chiefly lineage's *anakberu*, whose formal role it is to serve as spokesman of his superior kinsmen) in their place. Administrative choice often fell on the most vociferous claimant to chiefship or on the one who had been quickest to take advantage of this new power source. Given the limited facility of Dutch officials in the local languages, much of the negotiation of power was carried out through translators, who thus wielded a great deal of influence over the decision-making process.[8] In such a situation, Van Vuuren (1910:45) explained, difficulties could be forestalled and "rightful claimants to succession" identified, by careful attention to the genealogical records of local chiefs, for "through studying the constructed family trees [D., *stamboomen*], much that was once dark and incomprehensible becomes bright and clear."

The plan seems to have worked to Van Vuuren's satisfaction in the Toba and Pakpak areas, but it was less successful in the Karo villages, where clearly bounded juridical territories and unambiguous hierarchies of rule were not to be found. This was not surprising, as missionary-ethnographer Meint Joustra (1910:25) wryly remarked, for here, as in Karoland proper, "very little value is attached to keeping up with clan genealogy, very much in contrast to what one finds in Toba-land." Van Vuuren's *stamboomen* traced the neatly branching lines of patrilineal descent, but they missed the dense, multivalent networks of charisma and obligation formed through ties of marriage. While it is true that lineage identity and rights to property and position were inherited through patrilines, social action was also embedded in the asymmetrical mutuality of the *kalimbubu-anakberu* relationship. Marriages, both recent and long past, formed in perpetuity relations of symbolic debt and credit, which both crosscut and exceeded the territorial bounds of lineage authority. At every level of public decision making, these relations were engaged through practices of deferral and mediation. Chains of lateral cross-clan linkages could be activated to make claims for help or blessing, to counter or dispute the actions of others, to rally political support, or simply to order the everyday interactions of social life.

"In spite of all my efforts I have been unsuccessful in creating a *landschap* [subdistrict] here," Van Vuuren complained. "In fact, I have not even been able to follow the descent of the chiefs, so that no genealogies have been constructed for this part" (van Vuuren 1910:55). Instead, he created five juridical subsections *(negeri)*, each conforming roughly to the area of dispersal of a particular local lineage segment, with the chief *(pengulu)*—or chiefs, in cases of multiple claimants—of its originary village serving as subsection head. One of these, the Manik *negeri*, roughly coincided with the kingdom of Kuta Pinang.

Piah Manik's grandfather, Tenah Manik, was the *pengulu* of Kuta Pinang at the time of the Dutch conquest. He died shortly thereafter and was replaced by his youngest brother, the "incompetent uncle" of her account. When the latter was removed from office, the kingdom of Kuta Pinang was absorbed into an adjacent subsection. Her father, Raja Mula Manik, tried repeatedly and unsuccessfully to reclaim the headmanship of Kuta Pinang and continued to use the title of *pengulu* even after he had moved on to grander political arenas. He brought several lawsuits to the colonial court but without success. Finally he tried a different route to power, establishing underground connections with Japanese agents and moving to the provincial capital of Medan.

> PIAH MANIK: So he thought: "What can I do to get this kingdom back?" That's why he was looking for a way to get the Japanese in. So you see, my father, my grandfather, and my husband, they're all different. All of them were political, but in different ways.

. . .

Reading colonial accounts of bureaucratic rationalization and resistance, I am struck by how much seemed to depend on talk. Not just the kind of talk recorded in the reports of planning committees and boundary commissions, the optimistic assessments of tax bases and natural resources, or the official memoranda composed with an eye to career advancement, but the local talk that took the form of family histories, lawsuits, adat perorations, sagas of migration, and tales of village founding and fissioning. Telling the right story in the right place could, for those ambitious Karo men who encountered the soldiers and bureaucrats of Holland's overseas empire, generate an authority that was, by and large, narratively exercised as well. The right talk was especially important once the other traditional routes to power and prestige—hospitality, gambling, and warfare—were curtailed or prohibited by colonial regulation.

What kind of talk mattered here? It depended, of course, on the audi- *audience* ence. What was effective in conversation with a Dutch assistant resident or in a colonial courtroom might not hold up to the scrutiny of one's kinsmen or local rivals, and vice versa. But in general, and especially under the pressure of similar tendencies in colonial discourse, the most successful talk seems to have been that which reflected masculine prowess, individual agency, justification or explanation by antecedence, and the (patri)lineal transmission of names, rights, and properties.

Speaking with authority meant more than simply having something authoritative to say; it also meant having the authority to speak. In Karo terms this mostly meant having someone else to speak for. An etiquette of multilayered deferral mediated the expression of personal desires and grounded social authority in oratorical displacement. In the customary arenas of kinship negotiations, ceremonial discourse, and the adjudication of legal claims, the mediating spokesmanship of the *anakberu* softened and deflected personal desires by detaching speech *speech +* from agency; the officiating presence of the *kalimbubu* legitimated those *agency* desires by public acknowledgment and blessing; the concurrence of clan and lineage mates (*senina*) rearticulated individual interests as common goals.

Authoritative speech was virtually by definition male. Women had little access to public speech except in song: in the highly personal mode of funeral lament, the relatively depersonalized genres of blessing songs (*katoneng-katoneng*), and the formulaic rhyming duels of courtship (*ndung-ndungen*).[9] Women's exclusion from public discourse both reflected and reinforced the ambiguity of their position in the patrilineal kinship order. Temporary members of their natal household before marriage and dependent outsiders in their husband's family after it, women were largely left without a constituency to represent. As permanent jural minors, women could not speak for themselves in public deliberations or in formal oratory; what was perhaps more important was that, since women only rarely had someone else to speak for, they had very little occasion to speak authoritatively at all.

Power to command could also be asserted by force of arms or by force of personality—what Karo referred to as *dolat*, the quality of sovereignty or personal charisma. What legitimated and extended these individualized forms of power building was the leader's capacity to create alliances or to represent effectively the interests of others in disputes and negotiations. In a pattern common throughout the uplands of island Southeast Asia, aspiring Karo leaders might also claim to speak for powerful outsiders, especially those with whom they had personally established reciprocal trade or tributary relations.[10] Local authority was frequently shored up by the receipt of gifts from outside as well. Karo histories are replete with stories of powerful outsiders, such as the sultan of Deli, the lord of Aceh, and the king of the mountain spirits, who bestow honorary titles, regalia, and wealth on those they favor.

It is this kind of cosmopolitan orientation to power that Piah Manik implied by referring to her male relatives as "movement men" (I., *orang pergerakan*). Like the English *movement*, the Indonesian term derives from a root *(gerak)* meaning "gesture" or "shift in position or posture." The term *pergerakan* ordinarily denotes political involvement of a specific kind: that is, participation in activities shaped by the intellectual agendas of modern Indonesian nationalist organizations. Here, however, *movement men* refers in a more general way to individuals who looked outside their communities of kin for new sources of power and spokesmanship, in order to strengthen their own standing at home. This more spacious definition, which can accommodate acts of hospitality to Dutch travelers or a conspiracy with Japanese agents as easily as armed support of a Java-based nationalist political party, suggests a continuity of masculine agency across the spectrum of strategic political allegiances.

From this viewpoint it is not much of an imaginative stretch to envision Raja Mula Manik turning to the Japanese in order to get his kingdom back. Since Japan's 1905 military victory over Russia, Indonesian nationalists had from time to time looked wishfully for Japanese support in their struggle against Dutch rule.[11] The granting of "European" legal status to Japanese residents of the Indies in 1899 and the establishment of a Japanese consulate in Batavia a decade later had stimulated commercial relations between the two countries. In the cities and towns of the archipelago, Japanese shops ("Toko Djapan") and itinerant traders created a market for housewares and other cheap goods of Japanese manufacture. By the end of the Great Depression, when Japan's share in Indies imports reached a peak level of 32.5 percent, the presence of Japanese commercial travelers was notable even in the Sumatran hinterlands (Sato 1994:4).

By 1940 Japan was looking at the Dutch East Indies not just as a market for manufactured goods but also as a source of the raw materials needed for industrial and military expansion. Oil was the most significant of these, but essential items for acquisition in the Indies also included such Sumatran raw materials as salt, rubber, tobacco, coffee, and forest products (Sato 1994:5; Broek 1942:126–29). It was around this time that Raja Mula Manik, with his options for appeal under the colonial legal system exhausted, struck up a friendship with the Japanese man whom Piah Manik referred to as her adopted father and whose name she remembered as "Samoto." Shortly thereafter, Raja Mula Manik moved to Medan with his family, where he set himself up as a dealer in native rubber. Using this commercial cover, he established contact with the city's Japanese consul, Hayasaki.

This kind of opportunistic reaching out to power cannot be conceived of as "choosing sides," in any ideological sense. But the connection, which resulted in a fairly durable political alliance, did bring the *pengulu* of Kuta Pinang into the orbit of the urban community of political activists, nationalist educators, and radical journalists—and under the surveillance of the East Sumatran Political Intelligence Service (Politieke Inlichtingendienst, PID). On December 8, 1941, he was among a group of men arrested under the provisions of the War Powers Act and sent to an internment camp in West Java.[12]

A FAITHFUL COMPANION

What would it mean for a girl to grow up in the company of all these movement men? What kind of stories would she have to tell? One of the chapter titles in her husband's biography (Bangun and Chairudin 1994) describes Piah Manik as a "faithful companion" *(pendamping setia)*. The phrase could also serve to define her own narrative presentation of self, for she diligently places herself in the shadow of powerful others— first her father, then her husband. Autobiographical expectations would seek the subject of narration in the narrating self, but how do you recognize the subject in the story of a faithful companion?

Patricia Meyer Spacks has described the protagonists of prominent Western women's autobiographies as "selves in hiding." In the written

lives of such influential and controversial public figures as Emma Gold-
man, Eleanor Roosevelt, and Golda Meir, Spacks (1980:132) finds a
common tendency to "hide from self-assertion" and to "stress uncertainties of the personal, denying rather than glorifying ambition,
evading rather than enlarging private selves." Something like that self-
effacing style is also apparent in Piah Manik's narrative of her life. In
the following passage the urban world of politics is refracted through
the description of domestic work.

> PIAH MANIK: Our first house was on Japaris Street. My father apparently
> was connected with the Japanese. This was still Dutch times. It seems he had
> a connection with the Japanese, my father did. Well, so no one would know,
> he acted as a latex dealer. This latex, it wasn't regular rubber latex, it was
> *jelutung*, wild rubber.[13] You get it in the forest. Then process it at home.
> Cook the sap, put it in . . . in a big wok. It's like cooking palm sugar. Put it
> in, take it out, then beat it to get out the bark and all. Until it's clean. Once
> it's clean, hang it out to dry, then sell it. But this was just so, father just did
> it so, so if he was connected to the Japanese, no one would be suspicious.

Note that it is not her own labor that Piah Manik describes here but
rather a kind of agentless practice associated with—though not performed by—her father, who acted as a dealer in the product of this process. Throughout her account, similar vignettes of work anchor the rush
of events in familiar patterns of repetitive action but at the same time
submerge the self in the routine of everyday tasks and domestic duties.

narrating the experience of others

Another recurrent form of narrative self-effacement is the anecdotal
substitution of the experience of others for her own. In our second interview, from which this account of her early life is taken, I had hoped to
draw out the connection between two powerful men who had figured so
prominently in her life: her father, Raja Mula Manik, and her husband,
Selamat Ginting. This was a purpose on which our interests converged.
She presented her life story as a now-necessary supplement to a historical
record rendered suddenly incomplete by her husband's death. Her life
story had become an opportunity to speak not just about herself but also
for someone else. In other words, it provided an occasion for her to speak
with authority. Piah Manik claimed a place of public respect by locating
herself in the shadow of prominent men as a "faithful companion" and a
dutiful daughter and by speaking on their behalf. It is thus not surprising
that her narrative often veered way from her own experience to follow
the actions of her absent husband or father. Here, for example, the story
of how a Good Morning–brand towel saved her father's life fills the
vacant space of the autobiographical subject.

PIAH MANIK: So a few months later, the Japanese were getting closer, and our house was under surveillance. My mother had just had a baby. So when the baby was about two months old, Japan was getting closer, closer. They arrested my father. The Dutch did.

So then we went back to Kuta Pinang, me, my mother, and Koran, the baby, who was still little. After we went back to Kuta Pinang, my father was put into a detention camp for Japanese.

They took him to Cimahi [West Java], he was imprisoned there by the Dutch, in their camp at Cimahi. But at the same time they were taking him to Cimahi, in the middle of the way, the Japanese attacked. They were going to bomb the ship. But because my father and his Japanese friend had arranged a code—What's your code? father asked him. He said, take a towel, a little white towel, Good Morning brand, wash it, and lay it out to dry. So the men up above [in the plane] will see something white down below and they won't bomb the ship. So father got to Cimahi, and that's when the Dutch were defeated and Japan came in.

Luisa Passerini (1987:19) notes the importance of stories like this in constructing "memories of self." By seizing on "key features involving fathers and generations," a narrator can affirm personal recollections as part of "a tradition shared by a family, a circle of friends or a political group." Such stories are also a way to fasten the enclosed spaces of domestic life onto an invisible scaffolding of public events. Diverting her narrative trajectory to include the tale of her father's close call, Piah Manik covers the battle of the Java Sea and the end of Dutch rule in the Indies in the span of a white hand towel. This kind of towel is still a common item in Indonesian markets. Thin, cheap, marked in red with Japanese characters and the English slogan "Good Morning," it is the most mundane sort of mnemonic link between then and now, between ordinary domestic activities—bathing, doing laundry—and the grand events of national history.

The Japanese invasion of East Sumatra began on March 12, 1942; two weeks later, after only token opposition, the Dutch military force in Sumatra surrendered unconditionally. By May a new central military administration (J., *gunseikanbu*) for Sumatra, had been set up under the command of the Twenty-fifth Japanese Army Division. Government positions formerly held by Dutch officials were restaffed by Japanese and, at the lower levels, Indonesian employees. In Medan, the former Japanese consul Hayasaki was appointed mayor. He quickly drew together an informal advisory council composed of local intellectuals and nationalists across a rather wide political spectrum. Along with several prominent local lawyers and journalists this group included the consul's prewar contact Raja Mula Manik, who had just returned from Dutch internment in Java. For a civilian, Hayasaki seems to have had a good deal of influence in the inner circles of the East Sumatran *shu-chokan* (residency administration), and his native advisers—"the first to which the Japanese appeared willing to listen," according to Reid (1979a:93)—were thus in a pivotal position in the new regime.

> PIAH MANIK: So my father came home, they brought him here to Medan. They took him home to the village, after that they gave him a job. He was the assistant to the *gunseibu* [regional military administration] here, in Japanese times.

One of the key activities in which members of Hayasaki's advisory group took part was the recruitment of Indonesian volunteer workers and military trainees. In May 1943 a program was set up to produce auxiliary troops (Heiho) for the Japanese army. Heiho volunteers were given some basic military training, but they were mostly expected to perform menial duties or manual labor. Few who were sent overseas returned. In the Karo area, Heiho recruiting was directed by Nerus Ginting Suka, a former radical journalist and political internee, who headed the BOMPA propaganda program.

> PIAH MANIK: But no matter what [my father's] job was, rice was still hard to come by. So he and my uncle [K., *mama*, MB]—what was that uncle's name?—Nerus Ginting. They were, you know, together in the Japanese time. All the village boys who wanted to go into the Heiho, they came through our house.
>
> Well, we were staying on Jalan Laksana here in Medan. Sometimes there were twenty in one day, or thirty in one day. But however many there were, they all ate at our house first, they ate here one time. They'd arrive, then they'd all eat, then the next morning they were turned over to Uncle Nerus, my father would explain it all, then they'd be put in the army barracks.

The horizon of Piah Manik's world does not extend far beyond her family's new home on Laksana Street. A parade of "movement men"—her father, "Uncle Nerus," the village boys who had signed up as Heiho volunteers—pass through the house, mainly, it seems, at mealtimes.

> PIAH MANIK: It was like this: six *gantangs* of rice, say, that's enough for ten people, there are twenty more to feed. So, add yams. This is how to cook the yams so they get soft. Once the rice water comes to a boil, put in the yams. Put in the yams, cover the pot, mix it with the rice so it tastes good. We served goat intestines, curried, called it curried goat. That's how it was for several, or more, I guess for a year or more.

The emphasis on food here is not coincidental. By the end of the Japanese occupation most of the East Sumatran population was living in near-starvation conditions, but the cities faced food shortages almost from the beginning. This was partly the result of the increased demand put on local resources by the occupying forces and partly because of damage done to roads and railways at the time of the invasion. Produce grown for market often could not be transported or distributed. As Japanese levies on farm crops increased, peasants turned more to subsistence production, thus adding to the distress of urban populations. Price controls, labor conscription, forced sales to government agencies, and the use of fallow estate land for rice and vegetable production did little to alleviate the situation. Rumors that rice was being stockpiled for the war effort or hoarded by well-connected officials created bitter resentment toward "cooperators" like Piah Manik's father. Her account of kitchen politics can thus be read as a disclaimer of privilege in the form of a recipe.

Karo political activists associated with an array of quasi-underground associations frequently gathered at the house on Laksana Street. Among them were the organizers of POESERA, the Karo marketing cooperative: Tama Ginting, a leader of the Karo branch of the PNI-Baru, one of the first anticolonial political organizations in Karoland, who had been arrested along with Raja Mula Manik in 1941; Rakutta Sembiring Berahmana, who had been active in the Japanese propaganda organization BOMPA and would become the first *bupati* of republican Karoland; and Raja Mula Manik's nephew and future son-in-law (*kéla*, ZS, DH), Selamat Ginting, who was in his early twenties at the time.[14]

PIAH MANIK: So once we were done and all the Heihos had gone, and things were back to normal, then Pak Ginting, Tama Ginting, Rakut' Sembiring [Berahmana], there were about six of them, then they would come in. They were involved in politics, underground politics. Back then, Pak Ginting was my father's secretary, in the Japanese time. So that's where he learned about politics and all, about how it would be after independence.

He was the secretary, and if you were a secretary, well, you'd know just what the situation was with the Japanese and all that, he'd know it all. So that's when those six fellows were staying there in one room on Jalan Laksana.

At the time when there was no rice, they didn't have any spare clothes either. They soaked their clothes in the bathroom. Two changes of clothing each, one to wear and one to wash. Every one of them was lazy. They didn't want to wash, they were all lazybones. Because they were all, you know, aristocrats [I./K., *keturunen raja-raja*]. So my mother said, "Come on, my girl, just stamp on these clothes, put in some soap and if you're not up to washing them, just tramp on them a bit, then rinse them, when they're clean hang out your brothers' clothes," she said. So I washed all their clothes. Hung them out, but nobody ironed them. As soon as they were dry, they put them on.

The contrast between the diverse political activities and contacts of these young movement men and Piah Manik's domestic routine is striking. While the difference in the scope of action—their autonomy, mobility, ambition; her containment and subordination—is immediately obvious, what I find more interesting is the way her restricted perspective reframes their activities in the terms of her own. There is no recognition of ideological differences among the assorted political actors who enter the household. Collaborators, antifascists, royalists, socialists, populists, and traditionalists: all this mix of eclectic and sometimes contradictory affiliations blurs into the generic category of "politics." This is, to be sure, politics from the viewpoint of a teenage girl, but it provides a useful corrective to more institutionally focused accounts of anticolonial resistance in East Sumatra. Like the earlier Karo movement men who struck up deals with powerful outsiders to enhance their standing at home, ambitious young nationalists like Selamat Ginting and his friends were looking for a power base rather than for political guidance. Ideological consistency—except perhaps in a broadly anticolonial sense—took a back seat to strategies of personal influence building.

Folding the movement back into domestic space turns cooking, shopping, and doing the laundry into political acts. This domestication of political space shifts attention away from the conflicting interests, ideologies, and institutions that have dominated conventional readings of movement politics in East Sumatra and instead figures the movement as a series of activities or tasks to be accomplished, without regard to personal interests, ambitions, or ideologies. The other side of this approach—namely, the politicizing of domestic space—sustains a similar effacement of the personal. It does this by demarcating a kind of "public interior" without room for introspection, few private thoughts or feelings, and no reflections or desires. There are no scenes here that do not bear on the movement and Piah Manik's relation to it, including the circumstances of her marriage. Offstage, there may be space for a private self, but it is not part of this story.

MARRYING COUSINS

PIAH MANIK: Like I told you before, there wasn't any rice, so I had to go fetch rice, or yams, from Pancur Batu [a town on the outskirts of Medan].

I'd take the train. I was just twelve years old then. [Pak Ginting] was studying with my father back then. Sometimes he'd go buy vegetables at the
Central Market, I'd fetch the yams. Mother would always say, "The one
she's with, he's going to be her husband." . . . He wasn't married yet. His
mother was my father's sister, so he and I were cross-cousins. That's why my
mother said, you know, that he was my husband.

Karo myths, legends, and local histories frequently turn on chance
encounters between cross-cousins (*impal*, MBD, FZS). A young woman
meets a wandering stranger; to her surprise he turns out to be the son of
her father's sister, who had married into a distant community and been
forgotten by her family. This opportune meeting leads to a wedding,
which reunites—one generation down—the brother and sister separated
by a necessarily exogamous marriage.[15]

Sisters are not literally forgotten by their brothers upon marriage,
but it must seem that way to girls who are expected to leave their homes
and join a husband's family. In the practical arrangements of everyday
life as well as the formal obligations of Karo custom, a woman's
connection to her natal household can be tenuous if not reinforced or
reinstated by a pattern of recurrent cross-cousin marriages. So it is not
surprising that women frequently cultivate close and companionable
relationships with their brothers' daughters and that they are often
eager to arrange marriages with them for their sons. Such a marriage is
supposed to create an alliance of interests and affections between the
women of a household and to reinforce the ties between families of
birth and of marriage.

A "proper" *impal* marriage, that is, one between an actual mother's
brother's daughter and a father's sister's son, is usually a matter not of
individual preferences but of family commitments, and it is carefully
regulated to emphasize duty rather than choice. A young man should
not pass over a close cousin for a more distant relation or choose a
younger cousin over her elder sister. Courtship is neither expected nor
allowed. Instead, the young man's mother approaches her niece's family; if they agree to consider the match she will ask the girl herself. No
matter what the actual circumstances of the marital arrangement might
be, the appearance of personal disinterestedness should be maintained—
as if the marriage were intended only to promote the collective welfare
of the families involved (Singarimbun 1975:153–60).

Whether or not such a marriage has actually been proposed for them,
children frequently have to endure the teasing of their elders about
their *impals*—infant "husbands" or preadolescent "wives," the more

incongruous the better—with whom they are supposed to have close but somewhat reserved relationships. This often leads not to romance but to antipathy. I have seen little boys react with fury, or with embarrassment and pride, to such jokes about their baby cousins, to the amusement of their tormentors in either case. Young people consider *impal* marriages unromantic. They generally prefer to make their own arrangements, and parents sometimes have to exert a good deal of emotional pressure on unwilling cross-cousins in order to make the match. Faced with such parental arm twisting, young men may simply stay away from home, but this is not an option for many girls, who until marriage are more restricted in their mobility and more tightly bound to their natal family.

Piah Manik was about thirteen years old when she was approached about marrying her *impal*. The match's main supporter was her aunt (*bibi*, FZ, HM), Selamat Ginting's mother. Joking predictions notwithstanding, neither Piah Manik nor her own mother seems to have been impressed by this "lazy" cousin's potential as a husband. Selamat Ginting himself thought his aunt and her daughter would be unlikely to agree to such a marriage, because "he didn't have a steady job other than running the [POESERA] cooperative and making speeches for free. He didn't take care of himself, he didn't get his hair cut, he didn't have any clothes except for the ones that were stuck to his body" (Bangun and Chairudin 1994:61). Moreover, his own romantic interests were directed elsewhere at the time.

Even if a girl is in favor of the marriage she is likely to decline politely at first. An overeager acceptance can lead to suspicions about a girl's moral character: Why is she in such a hurry to wed? This makes it difficult to actually refuse a proposal, for even a fairly strong expression of disinclination may be interpreted as a sign of modesty. Turning down an *impal's* marriage offer is a matter of delicacy and tact, for a firm rejection risks offending close family members. The usual strategy is thus to ask for time to consider the proposal.

> PIAH MANIK: So after a couple of years like that, they came to ask for me, to marry Pak Ginting. I wasn't even grown up yet. At the time I'd gone back to the village, to Lau Tawar. So they asked me. "Ask my parents," I said. If they agree, then I'll ask to put it off for a year, I thought. "In a year I'll marry him," I said. What I meant was—because he needed to get married right away, so if I said to wait, then he'd go ahead and marry someone else, I thought. So I wouldn't be the one for him. I made that my excuse. To wait one more year. That's the way, if we're right for one another, a year won't matter. But they waited for a year, so then there wasn't any excuse. I had to do it.

FIGURE 9. Selamat Ginting and Piah Malem beru Karo-Karo Manik, c. 1955 (Bangun and Chairudin 1994: front cover).

The marriage might not have come off at all if Selamat Ginting hadn't approached his older sister about his marriage plans. In the middle of July 1944 he confided to her that he was engaged to a girl from Juhar. His sister passed the news along to their mother, who quickly put an alternate plan into effect.

A meeting was set up with the appropriate family members to discuss the marriage. To Selamat Ginting's surprise, however, the bride under consideration turned out to be his young cousin Piah Manik, not his sweetheart from Juhar. But with all sides in agreement as to the appropriateness of the match, he "accepted defeat graciously" and agreed to marry his *impal*. The wedding took place on August 23, 1944. "There was no honeymoon," Selamat Ginting's biographers note dryly (Bangun and Chairudin 1994:61). "The work of leading the POESERA cooperative and giving speeches everywhere went on as usual."

For the first few days after a marriage the bride is not allowed to leave the groom's parents' house; this period of seclusion ends with the *ngulihi tudung* (returning the headcloth) ceremony, in which the new couple makes a formal visit to the family of the bride. Selamat Ginting's biography describes this occasion as tense and unhappy, but, warmed by the passage of nearly fifty years of marriage, the telling becomes a kind of sweet joke on the reluctant young couple.

> So the date was set. As it turned out, the groom had a meeting in Tiga Binanga. The departure was postponed. Likewise, because the groom's hair was still shaggy, his wife gave him some money for a haircut. Then the bride sulked because she didn't want to walk with him. The wife gave two choices: her husband could walk in front, and she would walk behind, or she would walk in front and her husband some distance behind her. In short, the two of them got into an argument, because the groom forgot to get a haircut. Hearing the fight between her son and daughter-in-law, Selamat Ginting's mother threatened to hang herself if they kept on fighting. Finally the couple quieted down and then the three of them walked together. (Bangun and Chairudin 1994:61–62)

KUTA BANGUN

> PIAH MANIK: After we were married, we stayed in Kuta Bangun. We stayed in Kuta Bangun, there you had to farm. So we went to the fields, I didn't know how to manage wet-rice fields, so we made our field in what they called Juma Pali, toward the mountain along the road to Kuta Buluh. That's where we planted the guns, I told you. There I knew what to do. I knew how to farm on dry fields. Then about seven months after we got married, Japan surrendered.

"Why did you move to Kuta Bangun, Karo?" my assistant Jabatin Bangun asked. "If Bayak was a secretary in Medan, why didn't you just stay there?" Any marriage-minded Karo girl would have known the answer to this: newlyweds are expected to live with the groom's parents, usually until the birth of their first child. So although Selamat Ginting went on with his work in Medan and Berastagi, his new bride stayed with her mother-in-law in Kuta Bangun.

> PIAH MANIK: It was, you know, because we got married. We were married, so we had to go home to Kuta Bangun. So then, after we'd gone back to Kuta Bangun, the Japanese were defeated. Right, then once they surrendered, my father moved to Kuta Buluh too.
>
> It wasn't safe anymore. But Bayak kept on trading tobacco. While he continued his politics. He was in the tobacco business. He took all our tobacco from Kuta Bangun to sell. He used it all up for the movement. His sister's tobacco, all our family in Kuta Bangun, just like that. He took my tobacco, he took it, he used it up for the movement, not a cent came back to us, no. "Where's my tobacco money?" my sister-in-law said. "Just wait

awhile," he said, "wait awhile." Well, you know, he gave it all to his friends. Back then not one of his friends was working, all the movement people were unemployed.

. . .

In *Sources of the Self,* a sweeping intellectual history of modern identity, Charles Taylor suggests that the self is narratively constituted through an "orientation toward the good." In telling her life story as in living her life, a narrator/actor will order and comprehend events in relation to certain key notions of moral value; these offer a framework for action as well as for the interpretation of acts. Ideas of moral value, notions of selfhood, forms of narrative expression, and visions of community—that is, "conceptions of what it is to be a human agent among human agents"—together form a conceptual "package" that is always historically and culturally specific (Taylor 1989:105). If lives are experienced in narration, then the forms of both narrative and life depend on the particular "packaging" of the good in which they partake.

Industry is the key value around which Piah Manik's story is organized. Tasks are to be completed, problems are to be resolved, jobs are to be done in a particular way. The self familiar to readers of Western autobiographies is one that chooses, decides, strategizes, plans, hopes, and even defers, but Piah Manik's narrated self is one who works. In her account her own diligence is dramatically highlighted by the attitudes of her husband and his movement friends, who are too lazy even to wash their own clothes and who use up her sister-in-law's profits from her tobacco because they won't get jobs.

Industry is a measure of value most often applied by women, but not all women are equally industrious, or competent, in the execution of their tasks. Piah Manik admitted that according to the standards of the village cooperative work group (K., *aron*) in Kuta Bangun, she might not have measured up either.

PIAH MANIK: There were nine of us in the *aron. Gotong royong* [I., mutual assistance] it's called, *gotong royong.* I just went with them that one season. "Come on," they said. It was just a coincidence, because I, you see, I couldn't work hard like villagers do. If we've never held a hoe like that, we'll work, you know, but if we get tired we stop. But with them, you've got to be strong. That's why, when I got home my mother-in-law said not to do it anymore because I was sore all over. So after that, "*Ih,* I can't keep up with you," I said. "If we're all done this time and finished, that's enough. Never again," I said.

But strength is less important than persistence here. Despite her inexperience, Piah Manik completed the season's work she had committed herself to, and because she persevered in this difficult task, she was in a position to take care of her husband's secret cache of guns, as you will learn in a moment. "It was just a coincidence," she explained, removing intent from the calculation of her labor's historical value. "I couldn't have known ahead of time that there would be anything to take to Juma Pali."

Diligence, industry, and responsibility are not, of course, considered strictly female virtues, but women do seem to stand in some moral relation to them. In the following passage, Piah Manik has her mother-in-law speak up for duty:

PIAH MANIK: After they'd bombed Sidikalang [in 1948], after the Dutch came in, Pak Ginting was, you know, he just gave up. Where can we go now? he thought.

I was with the medical corps in Tulasen. "You're wanted in Pancur Panggoh," they said. I went with the soldiers to Pancur Panggoh. That's when Pak Ginting—apparently he'd come from behind—he picked up my mother-in-law in the fields along with his sister. My mother-in-law said to him, because Pak Ginting was crying, my mother-in-law lamented over him too. She said, "I know you're afraid. But afraid or not, the task can't be left unfinished, my son. Finish your task. What has been taken up with effort, can't be left unfinished," she said. They wept there.

There was a chicken, my mother-in-law had one chicken left. "Kill this chicken," she said to his sister, "so your brother can eat before he goes," said my mother-in-law, to the sister and her husband.

So the chicken was killed, and when the rice was done he ate. He ate, and then once he'd eaten—he'd already ordered us to go to Perongil, to head for Aceh—after he ate, we had packed everything up. The soldiers were already marching, they were heading for Aceh. Then he said, "Let's go back. We can't go to Aceh, we're going to Taneh Karo. We'll arrange everything later in the mountains, that's where we'll make our battle plan," he said.

Piah Manik is describing here the opening of the second military campaign of the independence struggle. In December 1948 Dutch troops broke an official cease-fire agreement and began an attack on nationalist strongholds all along the Van Mook Line, which divided republican from Dutch-held territory. Selamat Ginting's troops, headquartered at Sidikalang in central Dairi, responded to the assault by advancing into Dutch-occupied territory on the Karo plateau, where they set up guerrilla bases on the forested mountainsides. After the repeated failures and privation of the first campaign, the shift to guerrilla warfare in the second soon began to show some success.

PIAH MANIK: So then, then we went back, not to Aceh, the soldiers were all lined up, they turned around, changed course, they'd been going downhill, now they advanced, going back uphill.

The troops' entry into Taneh Karo is pictured here as a sudden, spontaneous reversal—a literal turnaround—in marching orders, inspired by a mother's advice, but it had in fact been planned well in advance of the Dutch attack. It was part of the overall reorganization of local militia forces under army auspices, in conjunction with a tactical shift from conventional to guerrilla warfare.[16] This was, indeed, the plan that established the Sektor III territorial command.

Like the narrative of the Good Morning hand towel, this episode joins the narrator not just to the public history of the nation but also to a "family tradition" that links generations in the shared experience of a frequently retold story. It does so by imagining the moment not in terms of military rationalization or chains of command or strategic troop deployments but as a densely meaningful scene of maternal compassion and filial duty. The occasion of a son's or a daughter's leave-taking is one frequently and stereotypically encountered in Karo life and artistic representation. The mother's grief is expressed in the form of a sung lamentation offering words of advice and blessing to the departing child (*ngandung*, "weeping"), and a ritual meal (*mbesur-besuri*, "to satiate") is prepared by the family's immediate *anakberu* (here, the sister and her husband) to fortify the traveler's spirit.

Pivoting the soldiers' return around a tableau of maternal lament conveys "in gripping abbreviation"—as Halbwachs (1992:60) describes a similarly condensed scene from domestic life—"the idea of a family" in the Karo sense of the term. The profound local salience of this moment is, however, immediately unsettled by the presence of the nation, which is implied by the incongruous insertion of the Indonesian word *tugas* (task, duty) into the Karo text of the mother's lament. "Tapi mbiar pé, *tugas* la banci la dungi, 'nakku" (But afraid or not, the "task" can't be left unfinished, my son). The semantic field of *tugas* covers both the pragmatic and the exalted senses of the English *duty* but leans toward the former: a piece of work, usually of limited duration, given by a higher authority—as, for example, a student's homework assignment, a soldier's guard duty, a daughter's household responsibilities. It is the implication of a higher authority behind the task that makes possible its "weightier" connotation of moral responsibility, especially in the context of the nation.[17] The closest Karo equivalent is *dahin*, "work," and in fact in a second rendition of her mother-in-law's words Piah Manik uses the latter term: "Tapi adi enggo si ndahi *dahin* é, la banci la dungi" (But if we have this work to do, it cannot be left unfinished).

JAPANESE GUNS

An experienced event may be circumscribed in both duration and value, Walter Benjamin (1969a:202) writes, but "a remembered event is infinite, because it is only a key to everything that happened before it and after it." Benjamin is writing about Proust's *À la recherche du temps perdu* and how a single remembered experience can unlock an endless associative labyrinth of recollection, but an event in memory can also be infinite in its capacity to encompass a whole life's meaning. The burial of the Japanese guns at Juma Pali—the story with which Piah Manik opened her history—is that kind of event.

These guns were independent East Sumatra's "first capital in the form of weapons" (Surbakti 1978:34). Most published accounts explain that Selamat Ginting had acquired the guns by singlehandedly hijacking a munitions truck traveling across the Karo plateau and then hiding its load of weapons on a remote highland roadside.[18] This "unexpected stroke of good luck" (as he himself described the incident) may actually have been staged. According to POESERA organizer Tama Ginting, the "capture" of the guns was actually the outcome of secret negotiations set up by Raja Mula Manik between his son-in-law Selamat Ginting and Japanese officers sympathetic to the nationalist cause. As Tama Ginting recalled the scene, shortly after the Japanese surrender two soldiers showed up at POESERA's Medan headquarters and offered to surrender some weapons to the group's leaders.

> You can't imagine how delighted we were, and we agreed to accept them. Then we discussed where the weapons would be surrendered, and for the sake of secrecy it was agreed that they would take the weapons toward Kotacane, to kilometer 131 on the Medan-Kotacane Highway, a few kilometers from Tiga Binanga. . . . Selamat Ginting, Tama Ginting and Keras Surbakti departed from Medan to receive the weapons at the appointed place. In Berastagi we picked up Pasang Sinuhaji, and we all departed for Balandua in his 1933 Opel automobile. Precisely at the time that had been agreed upon, the weapons were brought by the two Japanese soldiers and placed in a hidden spot. (T. Ginting, quoted in Surbakti 1978:32–33)

Later—as driver Pasang Sinuhaji continues the story—"for reasons of safety and security, Selamat Ginting and his wife secretly moved the guns to Kuta Bangun and hid them in the Juma Pali field. . . . we all swore that whoever revealed the presence of these guns would be killed" (quoted in Surbakti 1978:33).

In late September 1945 Selamat Ginting, who had been drawing attention to himself by sporting a Japanese pistol around town, turned some of these guns over to Abdul Xarim M. S., a prominent journalist and influential member of the Hayasaki inner circle. Xarim in turn used them to bluster the jittery Medan politicians into making public Sukarno and Hatta's proclamation of Indonesian independence, an event that had taken place nearly six weeks earlier in Jakarta. The guns finally ended up with Xarim's son Nip, an antifascist activist who used them to create his own special military unit devoted to procuring weapons for the republican army. When the East Sumatran division of the TKR (the People's Security Army, as the nation's military force was then known) was formed two weeks later, about half of its limited supply of armaments came, via Nip Xarim, from Selamat Ginting's cache of weapons.[19]

Selamat Ginting didn't turn all of the guns over to Xarim and his son, though. Most of the small arms were hidden behind the bathroom of the restaurant-boardinghouse that served as an informal meeting place for Medan's young nationalists. These weapons made their public debut on October 9, the day before British troops began disembarking on the Sumatran coast, at a "giant parade" on the city's esplanade. More than a hundred thousand people—nearly half the city's population—were said to have been present to celebrate the declaration of national independence. Selamat Ginting and his friends, with the Japanese grenades "draped luxuriantly" about their shoulders, acted as security guards (Manihuruk 1979:106).

As this muscular display of bravado may suggest, there was more panache than politics to the activism of nationalist youth in those heady days. For an aspiring leader like Selamat Ginting, guns and charisma were sufficient resources to build what was effectively a personal army of friends and followers: ex-students, streetwise urban delinquents, village boys looking for action, demobilized cadets, and laborers left stranded by the Japanese surrender. By mid-December, when he turned his attention to the situation in the Karo highlands, he had already become one of Medan's most powerful militia commanders.[20]

Piah Manik's part in these events has received little attention in published histories of the independence struggle, which mostly highlight the heroic exploits, backstage squabbles, and passionate speeches of the movement's male protagonists. Her own version of the story was neither heroic nor passionate, but its simple record of unassuming bravery was compelling, particularly when you remember that she would have been about fifteen years old at the time of these events. She told me the story at the beginning of our first recorded interview and again at the end of our second, in response to my attempts to fix a date to these occurrences. It seemed to have taken on the fixity of a habitual narrative, for both tellings were remarkably similar. The text I present below is a composite of the two. I have divided it into eight "scenes" but have chosen not to otherwise interrupt the narrative flow. The story's plot—its narrative structure and chronology, the choice and order of scenes and the dialogues within them, the cast of characters, their motivation and function—follows her first telling, with the exception of the epilogic final scene ("The guns were gone"), which comes from the second. This segment and some other passages from her more detailed second version have been grafted onto the narrative framework provided by the first. The story begins with Selamat Ginting's arrival in Kuta Bangun with his friends and a car full of guns.

JUMA PALI

Scene 1: The Task

We were still out in the fields, when he came from Berastagi with his friends, all of them in a car. I was in the fields. When I got home there they all were. So didn't I have to cook rice and all, if six of them showed up in the village?

Our cooking pot, we used firewood and all, we cooked, then once it was done he explained things. After we ate it was night because he was only there one night with Bapa Berah [Rakutta Berahmana] and all of them.

He said, "Here're the guns, pistols and all, take them to the field in the morning. I'll come join you later, we won't go together," he said.

What kind of plan can I make? I thought. So then, "All right," I said.

Scene 2: The Plan

Around that time in our village we had an *aron*, a village work group. There were nine of us. We had this field, it was called Juma Pali. This Juma Pali. "Let's go to my field tomorrow," I said to them. "All right," they said.

How can I get these friends to carry the pistols to the field so I can bury them there? Because I couldn't let the Japanese find out. If they found out, our whole family would be . . . shot. Not just us, they'd wipe out the whole family.

So I got some *kedep* (rice bran), nine bags full. I shoved the pistols down into the bran, five or six in each bag. Then I said to my friends in the *aron*, "This is what we're taking to the field."

"What's this?" they asked.

"*Kedep.*"

"What's it for?"

"I'm taking it to the field to sprinkle around the rice plants (K., *pagé*), so the mice won't eat them." When the rice plants are still small, they'll die if the mice dig around them. Usually, you see, if there are mice, these mice, you see, your rice, they burrow around it, they can kill all your rice plants. Because if it's still in the first month, the seed is still there. The hulls (K., *kulitna*). The seeds have sprouted but the hulls haven't rotted. [The mice] hunt for the seeds. There aren't any seeds left but it looks like usual.

"So I can spread it around, spread it around, this bran, they'll look for the rice seeds until dawn, the mice won't eat my rice anymore," I said. I made an excuse. I made an excuse because if I didn't they'd see them. They'd see the pistols they were carrying, because I gave three or four to each of them, and there were nine of us. Nine of us in the *aron*.

Well, they believed me. Not one of them knew they were carrying guns. Because I put in a shirt first like that, with rice bran under it, and then I put rice bran on top like that too. I did all of them like that and I carried one, too.

Scene 3: The Aron Is Sent Home

Because our field was two hectares wide, it took a lot of bran. Two hectares had been planted. We didn't get a chance to harvest it even, we'd been evacuated before then.

So we brought them all to the field, early in the morning. When we got to the field, we put all the bags of bran in a field hut. We put them all there, we didn't . . . "Wait until I come," Pak Ginting had said.

Well, we all went to work. We all went to work, then it was midday. You know, usually when you go to the field you stay there till late afternoon. You bring your food along, because it's too far to go home to eat.

So around two o'clock I said, "There's no need to go on. Why don't you all just go home now?" Usually we didn't quit until four.

Bapak came to the field, he said, "Send them all home, so we can bury these, these weapons," he said.

"All right," I said. "Go on home, all of you. Bayak is here, there's—I guess he's got something he wants to do here, go on home now," I said.

"All right," they said. "But why are you sending us home?"

"Well, this field of ours is a long way from the village." Juma Pali was pretty far away. So they went home.

Scene 4: The Story of Jali

Ah, my sister-in-law's field was across the river. I went along [with them] as far as that. There was a ravine in our field and her field was on the other side. I went with them over there.

After I'd gone—there was this Jawi [Malay, i.e., "Muslim," here an Acehnese itinerant farm laborer] who worked for us. "Go get a mat so I can stretch out," [Pak Ginting] said to this fellow Jali, this Acehnese fellow that worked for us. What he meant by asking for a mat, apparently that was so I would come back to our field right away, but I didn't understand. "Tell your mother [meaning Piah Manik] to bring a mat over here," he said.

"I need a mat, mother," said [Jali].

So because this Acehnese fellow was so nice, "Let me take the mat," he said. We were still chatting over there. "Here," I said.

Bapak had already got all the guns out of the sacks of bran, he'd taken them all out, he'd cleaned them up. So this laborer of ours came up to the field hut, thinking, "I'll lay out the mat, maybe Bapak wants to take a nap." He took Bapak by surprise!

"You! Go fetch your mother over there, quick!" he said, meaning to call me.

"Bapak is calling you," he [Jali] said.

"All right," I said, "I'm coming." So after a while my friends in the *aron* went on home.

As soon as I got there, he was yelling at me. "I called for a mat, why didn't you bring it? Now I'm going to [have to] kill you both, you and the Acehnese fellow both! I'll shoot you right now," he said, Pak Ginting said.

I was shocked! "Why?" I said.

"He's seen these weapons. If anyone finds out about this, the Japanese will kill us all, not just us two. They'll kill the whole family, all of us and all our relatives without any hope of pardon. You know how these Japanese are now," he said, "*paskis* [fascists]."

"Hold on a minute," I said.

"Rather than have our whole family dead later on, better to kill the two of you now," he said.

So I said to Jali, "Oh, Jali, what did you see in the field hut?" I said.

"I didn't see anything, mother," he said.

"What was your Bapak holding in his hand in the hut?"

"I didn't see anything."

"You mean you didn't see anything at all?" No. "Really and truly?" Really and truly.

"Well, Bapak was sitting there, holding whatever, whatever, didn't you see it?" No.

"Well then, go get some water, hurry up!" I ordered him to go get some drinking water. I sent him off. Then I said to Bapak, "He didn't see anything at all in there. You got mad at him first. 'What did you see in the hut?' I said. 'I didn't see anything,' he said. So he doesn't know anything, he's never even seen a pistol: 'What is this thing?' He wouldn't have recognized it." He'd never seen one, you know, that's how it is with peasants, he was just a vagabond looking for work in Kuta Bangun. We hired him to help in our fields.

Scene 5: Burying the Guns

Well then, "If he really didn't see them," he said, "go ahead dig the hole," he said. He'd never even held a hoe from the time he was a kid.

"So how are we going to bury those guns? Show me so I can bury them," I said.

So he said, "Did you bring some cloth from the house, a bucket, thatch"—you know what thatch is, don't you?

So then—he didn't want to do it. Because he'd never even held a hoe, so I was the one who had to dig the hole, so big, like that. Put thatch first in the bottom, put the thatch in a bit thick. So then, take a bucket. Put the bucket on top of it like that. They're already wrapped in cloth, cloth, all kinds of sarongs, well, that are sort of, um, worn out, wrap them up so they won't get wet in the rain. So then cover it with more thatch. Then cover it with zinc roofing, used roofing, then close it up with earth. Then I planted sugar cane on top of it. Sugar cane, you know, you cut off the tip like that, no one would be surprised to see it around the edge of the, you know, the hut. So then we went home. I dug the hole, then put the thatch in first, then wrapped up the pistols and grenades, put them in the bucket, then I closed it up and buried it. Then I planted sugar cane on top. If you plant sugar cane, you cut off the tip and plant that. So no one would know. Just the two of us knew about it.

So then, "Don't let anyone find out," he said all the time. "No, I, well, I won't talk. Where would I talk about it? The only place I ever go is to the fields."

Scene 6: Time Passes . . .

So then the *pagé* was all done, breaking up all the clods, like that, it was chopped up fine and clean. After that I went to Kuta Buluh a lot, because Kuta Bangun and Kuta Buluh are close. I went there a lot to see my mother, then I'd go back to Kuta Bangun, like that. He [Bapak] was with his friends all the time, with Bapa Berah. They'd already taken the tobacco, all of it, the tobacco money. I don't know what it was used for, but he didn't return it. They made the, it's called POESERA, it was an association. This POESERA sold the tobacco, they sold potatoes, the point is, all kinds of produce. He was selling produce from Berastagi to Medan.

Anyway, the rice was budding, the rice was already budding. So then, I, I was going to Dairi a lot, it was, this Dairi, or Lau Tawar, you'd say, that's where my mother was from. So no one would know, no one could know about it. Then, about, mmh, five months later we were independent.

Scene 7: Guns for Independence

We were already independent, but Bapak said, "Apparently independence has already been announced in Jakarta," he said, "but here in Medan it hasn't been announced yet."

So then, the governor—maybe it was Governor Hasan, I can't remember what they said his name was—Bapak said, "Why hasn't our independence been announced yet, sir?" he said.

"Proclaim independence, you say! When we don't have a single gun! How in the world are we going to oppose anybody if we don't have any guns?" he said.

So then, "If you'll lend me a car, I can get some guns. I'll be back tomorrow," said Pak Ginting. So Pasang Sinuhaji, he found a driver, they gave him a car.

That's how they all found out we'd hidden the guns in Juma Pali. Those are the ones that went to Medan, those are the guns that were used at the very beginning of independence. Those were the guns. So that's why Juma Pali, to this day Juma Pali is famous around here, famous, you know, because that's where all those guns were.

Scene 8: Epilogue: The Guns Were Gone

So I wasn't in Kuta Bangun when all of them got the guns from the field. All those guns. So then, [Pak Ginting] ordered a fellow to come get me. "Tell her to come home," he said.

So this lowland fellow said right away—we hadn't met before— "Yeah, it seems you planted guns in your field," said this lowlander.

"Guns? What kind of guns?" I said. "I don't have any."

"*Ih*, no, you say, but Bayak has already fetched them."

"Bayak has fetched them? Where did he get them?"

"Bayak left here three days ago, he took some people to Juma Pali, they all had pistols when they left there," he said.

"No, I don't know, there aren't any," I said again. Because I'd just arrived, Bayak had fetched them, he said. So the ones that they hid in Lau Lisang were all carbines. So if he's already fetched them, fine, I said.

I went to the field, it was true, it was open, they hadn't even filled in the hole again, all the old thatch was scattered around. So they brought them all here [to Medan], because Governor Hasan said—he was the governor at the time—because "We don't have any guns, announce independence, announce it," he said. "We don't have any guns so how are we supposed to announce it?" he said. "Well, let's go get some," [Pak Ginting] said, "I'll fetch them from Kuta Bangun, there are guns," he said. So that's why he gave part of them to Pak Hasan and kept another part. Those were, you know, the first guns.

NATIONAL SERVICE

In the biographies and autobiographies of Indonesian military men, such as A. H. Nasution's *Memenuhi panggilan tugas* (To Fulfill the Call of Duty, 1982) and Ramadhan's *A. E. Kawilarang: Untuk Sang Merah Putih* (For the Grand Red-and-White, 1988), service is a means to the higher good of the nation. Soldiers' stories such as these find their fullest expression of service and self-discipline in terms of military command. Hence the habitual tendency of military autobiographies to narrate national history along a trajectory of personal achievements or promotions in rank. While Piah Manik's narrated life shares this emphasis on duty and diligence, it does not do so in relation to a "higher good" embodied in the nation or anywhere else. Duty, instead, is a moral good in its own right. Her life appears as a sequence of assigned tasks—tasks that, once encountered, should not be left undone. The scaffolding of command and authorization through which those tasks are ordered is, as in the story of her mother-in-law's lament, left obscure.

Piah Manik's story of her life may seem rather "flat" to readers looking for adventure, suspense, and heroic self-dramatization. This is partly the result of viewing a life in retrospect. Looking back over a lifetime brings a span of history under the scrutiny of the present and thus into the realm of teleology. This dilemma, common to any form of personal narrative, is, as Gusdorf (1980:42) remarks, "insurmountable: no trick of presentation, even when assisted by genius, can prevent the narrator from always knowing the outcome of the story." But the apparent flatness of her narrative is also the effect of a presentation of self as enacted through duty, rather than constituted by experience or knowledge.

Piah Manik's story is more concerned with family ties than with personal development. Her ability to complete her assigned tasks seems for this reason to have an "always already" quality to it. She is in the movement alongside her husband because she was already in it with her father. She plants rice in the field of Juma Pali because she had already learned from her granny in Lau Tawar how to work dry fields. She can run a public kitchen for her husband's soldiers during the siege of Medan because she cooked for the Heiho volunteers at her father's house during the Japanese occupation.

The story upends our narrative expectations in other ways as well. Some of its most dramatic moments—the bombing of Sidikalang, for example, as well as the retrieval of the Juma Pali guns—occur during her absence. The event that might arguably be seen as the most important of her life—her wedding—is not even described; I have gone to her husband's biography to find an account of it. The only intimation of marital intimacy is an enactment of its absence: her husband's feigned call for her to bring a mat and join him in the privacy of the field hut because he "apparently has something he wants to do." Aside from her mother-in-law, the women who might have been expected to share her life most closely—her mother and grandmother, sisters and sisters-in-law, the officers' wives, nurses, and activists who took part in the struggle with her—are hardly mentioned. Nor does she speak of her

growing sense of purpose or comprehension of the meaning that independence holds.

I don't mean to argue that Piah Manik did not maintain close personal relationships, or feel a solidarity, with the women who shared her
family life and wartime experience. Nor do I want to suggest that she did
not come to understand independence or that her practical competence
did not increase with time and experience. The narrative representation
of a life should not be mistaken for the life itself. What I am suggesting
is that whatever moral progress or personal development may have
taken place during the lifetime recounted here occurs, narratively speaking, offstage. Just as the rhetorical device of a "public interior" of domestic activity leaves no space in her story for personal concerns, feelings,
and desires, so too the fiction of disinterested diligence offers little occasion for the display of moral introspection, nationalist fervor, or
collective solidarity. Unlike those military presentations of self in service,
in which career advancement is intertwined with national destiny or
national history is punctuated by heroic exploits, this is not a narrative
of progress. And unlike the autobiographies of Western women, which
downplay public accomplishments by focusing on what Jane Marcus
(1988) refers to as the "invincible mediocrity" of domestic life, it is not
a revelation of the intimacies of the "private self."[21]

In many ways the story of the guns of Juma Pali differs from the rest
of Piah Manik's life narrative. For one thing, its organization (in both
recorded versions) is more complex; it features subplots, minor characters, perspectival shifts, changes of scene, and extended passages of dialogue. There is a dramatic shift in her narrative's spatial syntax, especially
in scenes 6 ("Time Passes . . .") and 7 ("Guns for Independence"), in
which the history of the republic is braided into a chronicle of village life.
The rice fields are prepared, Piah Manik visits her mother, POESERA
is organized, her husband and his friends use up the tobacco money,
Governor Hasan insists on the need to defend independence, and Selamat
Ginting offers to get him some guns. This is not a literal sequence of
events but rather a cluster of occurrences—at different times, in different
places—linked by the secret presence of the guns in the Juma Pali field
and the still unacknowledged reality of independence.

As this suggests, the central subject that holds the story together is not
the narrator, or even another character, but rather the cache of Japanese
guns. Nevertheless, subjectivity is more fully developed here than
elsewhere in Piah Manik's account of her life. I mean this not simply
in terms of an emphasis on her own agency, although it is true that the

narrative provides her with occasions for planning (scene 2, "The Plan"), quick thinking (scene 4, "The Story of Jali"), and creative problem-solving (scene 3, "The *Aron* Is Sent Home") as well as her characteristic diligence (scene 1, "The Task," and scene 5, "Burying the Guns"). Throughout the story motives are explored, varying levels of knowledge recognized, and actions explained. Here alone in her account of the independence struggle is there a glimpse, however partial, of the scaffolding of national political authority that stood behind local actors like her husband. Scenes 5 and 8 offer entertaining glimpses of masculine ineptitude ("He'd never even held a hoe"; "they hadn't even filled in the hole . . . the old thatch was scattered around"), and in the opening of scene 4 there is a refreshing moment of (implied) resistance to her husband's demands, followed by what seems like an extraordinary overreaction on his part.

However the story is told, the buried guns of Juma Pali seem to take on a life of their own. In the eyes of Medan's insurgent youth the guns were the new regalia that marked them as "movement men"; in the swashbuckling accounts of nationalist historians, they were the key that unlocked the door of independence in East Sumatra; in the views of skeptical British peacekeeping troops, conservative politicians, and down-and-dirty covert operatives, they were the trigger to anarchy. For Piah Manik their significance is different. In her account they are not instruments of personal advancement, national liberation, or senseless violence but simply objects around which industrious domestic acts could be performed. Her part in securing those guns retroactively confirms and prospectively guarantees her place in the movement. The guns could make things happen, but she kept them safe, for a time. In doing so she made her own life narratable. More than that, she made it remarkable.

CHAPTER 3

Imagining Independence

Word of Indonesia's independence reached the Karo highlands even before it was officially announced in Medan. According to Sektor III historian A.R. Surbakti, the news was carried by Selamat Ginting and his friends when they came to collect the buried guns of Juma Pali. In an exuberant rush of movement and emotion, Surbakti's (1978:34) account draws the reader into the action as their 1938 Ford coupé convertible speeds back toward the city, loaded now with the disinterred Japanese guns: "Their spirits seethed with joy, as if no power on earth could oppose them." When a policeman stops the car in Kabanjahé, they warn him fiercely, "No inspection, unless you want to be sent straight to hell!" The policeman steps aside. All along the road to Medan, Selamat Ginting calls out that Indonesia is free and that every house should fly the red-and-white flag.

As I picture this scene, the car full of young men and guns charges along the steep and twisting road leading down from the highlands with the noisy, reckless bravado of today's daredevil motorcyclists and fare-hungry bus drivers. Farmers stand in puzzled surprise as cries of *Merdeka! Merdeka!* drift across the fields where they are working. Idle men in roadside cafés are startled from their chess and coffee as the convertible roars past and then vanishes around another curve. What landscape of aspiration, I wondered, could accommodate such disparate figures as the soon-to-be militia leader in a borrowed convertible full of guns and the peasant woman startled by his shouts of *"Merdeka!"*?

What common hopes could they have shared with Indonesia's erudite Java-based "Proklamators," Sukarno and Hatta? What incidents and experiences, what interventions, projects, and principles, could have brought them all together in the struggle for independence?

Imagination is a seductive though not particularly reliable guide to the events of the past, and mine is probably too cinematic in its envisioning of life during wartime. This is the lesson I learned from (mis)representing to myself another scene of highland travel: the fall of Kabanjahé, when Piah Manik and several others were evacuated to Kuta Bangun ahead of the Dutch troops' advance. Every time we drove west from Kabanjahé I found myself imagining, against the familiar daytime landscape of cornfields and orange groves, *their* desperate flight, which I pictured in noirish stylings of grainy angularity: the sweep of a black sedan's headlamps as it cut around the sharp turns, racing through the night with the town in flames behind it and Dutch bombers overhead. I later realized that it was midday when Kabanjahé was burned. Piah Manik and her friends were well away by then anyway, and they weren't in a car at all, having cut across the fields from Kabanjahé on foot.

Whether grounded in fact or fancy, scenes like these are crucial to the mythopoeia of nationhood, in part because of the enthusiasm they display. In Surbakti's history, for example, dry reports of institutional arrangements and official pronouncements of the incipient nation-state ("In the above-mentioned meeting on Jalan Amplas, Mr. T. M. Hasan was invited to offer a response regarding the report of the proclamation of the independence of the Indonesian people in Jakarta, and the situation in Java related to the above-mentioned proclamation") are regularly upstaged by eruptions of popular nationalism in an effervescent mix of youths, guns, marches, and slogans. "This giant parade, in the spirit of . . . Independence or Death, bore banners and slogans expressing the desire and longing of the Indonesian people for independence," Surbakti writes of the mass demonstration that followed Governor Hasan's announcement of independence.[1] "From that moment, the cry Merdeka! . . . Merdeka! echoed everywhere. And with it the Red-and-White badge began to be worn by young men and women. Wherever we went," he concludes, switching to the inclusive intimacy of the eyewitnessing subject, "we would observe the Red-and-White badge plastered on chests, and, when meeting a friend, would offer and receive greetings with the cry . . . Merdeka!" (Surbakti 1978:36).

In the photograph of this rally most frequently reproduced in nationalist histories, the movement's sedate and disciplined leaders (usually

FIGURE 10. Pro-independence rally on the Medan esplanade, October 6, 1945 (Biro Sejarah PRIMA 1976).

identified by name) stand out against a blurred and barely visible background of unrecognizable marchers, onlookers, and grenade-carrying bodyguards (figure 10). Surbakti's account reverses this emphasis. Here the crowd appears as the locus of a visceral and relatively unguided popular nationalism, and its leaders go unmentioned. Like slogans painted on banners, or red-and-white badges plastered on nationalist chests, the parade is a legible sign revealing the "soul and spirit" of the common people. Wrapped in "a sense of pride, because Indonesia was independent, and it had become their responsibility to establish and to defend this independence," the enthusiastic young men and women of Medan begin to hail one another into the community of the nation (Surbakti 1978:36).

. . .

Karo use two terms more or less interchangeably to name the period from the 1945 independence proclamation to the time of the Dutch invasion of the highlands in 1947: *mulana merdeka*, they say, "the beginning of independence," and Zaman Merdeka, "Independence Time." What they identify by these terms is not so much the moment when Indonesia announced its freedom from colonial rule as when they started to use the word *merdeka*.[2] Few had any idea what this foreign term meant. Still, whenever they passed one of the numerous guard posts set up across the highlands to watch for intruders, spies, or collaborators, they were expected to show the proper patriotic spirit by shouting *MERDEKA!* Some, who were shy about speaking a foreign language, would only whisper: *"MERDEKA."* Others came up with nonsense words like *merdekat* and *merdekak.*

This "ignorance" (as they describe it) strikes Karo nowadays—especially those who were there at the time—as extremely funny, but the story I heard most often about the *Merdeka!* salute had a tragic edge. It was told of a number of places, but the village of Berastepu, which is located on the northern side of the Karo plateau, may have a better claim to it than most. At least my informants there said they knew Pa Tongkat, the unlucky old man in the story, and his grandson, who still lived there. Lots of wild things went on in Berastepu during the independence struggle, so this might well have happened there too.

Berastepu was a particularly contentious place in the early years of the struggle. In December 1945, conflicts in this village between two major militia groups—Selamat Ginting's Halilintar "Thunderbolt" Regiment and the Barisan Harimau Liar, the Wild Tiger Brigade—precipitated the breakup of the unified military command for the district. As a result, Berastepu, like many of the villages of northern Karoland, had separate guard posts and offices for each of the feuding militias. This meant that villagers were doubly subjected to interrogations and inspections. By the time Dutch troops arrived in 1947, old Pa Tongkat was so used to shouting *Merdeka!* every time he saw a uniform that he greeted these new soldiers the same way, upon which they shot him.[3]

This is not what Benedict Anderson had in mind when he remarked that it is nationalism's strange power to persuade individuals "willingly to die for such limited imaginings" as a bounded territory or the fellowship of unknown others. The nation, he writes, "is imagined as a *community,* because, regardless of the actual inequality and exploitation that may prevail in each, the nation is always conceived as a deep, horizontal comradeship" (Anderson 1991:7). Events like Selamat Ginting's ride or the giant parade on Medan's esplanade are compelling not just because of their enthusiastic show of public support for the cause of national independence but also because they can be used to display the unity of the people-as-imagined-community, at its very moment of realization. In such scenes, the masses are not simply called upon to witness and acknowledge their leaders' vision of a national future; they are present also to confirm that the nation was there, waiting in the wings, all along.

How this mutual comradeship comes to be recognized in the first place (flags, badges, and nationalist salutes notwithstanding) is rather more problematic than such after-the-fact imaginings suggest. Like Dante's journey through the dark woods of the *Inferno*, nationalism seems always to find itself beginning "midway through." Theories of nationalism frequently share this inclination and so do not often consider how or why—beyond such evidently inadequate explanatory mechanisms as primordial sentiment or ideological manipulation—a total national community might have imagined itself into being in the first place. Most often it is assumed that an educated (and mostly male) elite has already done the initial work of imagining for the community as a whole. The transformation of peasants or workers or, for that matter, women into "citizens"—of France, or Hungary, or Indonesia— can then slide by, under cover of the always-already mode, as the workings of false consciousness or popular consent or shared imagining. But what seems in retrospect to have been the originary self-interpellation of an "obvious" national community may have been at its inception nothing of the sort.

Zaman Merdeka was a period of mobilization and indoctrination, in which a popular commitment to independence, strong enough to move virtually the entire Karo population to sacrifice wealth, homes, and family, was forged. This commitment was motivated by a myriad of small shocks and circumstances, variously encountered; by aspirations for the future; by the excitement of songs, slogans, and a vivid rallying cry; and by the sense of injustice and diffuse but excruciating resentment. It was formed in the disciplinary routines of military mobilization, the euphoria of collective participation, and the violence of revolution. What kind of shared identity might Karo nationalists have envisioned for themselves? For the most part, they had little sense either of "Indonesia" as a real or imagined entity or even of "Karo" as an exclusive, perduring ethnic appellation. Independence was the opposite of "feeling colonized." It was "delicious"; it was the chance to get ahead and the opportunity to reopen old wounds, to redress old wrongs.

Mobilization, aspiration, and revolution: these are three ways of imagining independence. Memory marks them as distinct from one another, although the thing they scan and the time they recall are the same. Their stories have different beginnings, middles, and ends, different moods and motives. They poise their narrators quite differently in the national community-in-the-making; they reckon differently with the nation's future. In storylines taken from folklore and government interviews, built on the delicious promises of nationalist propagandists or the labile discourse of rumor and fear, shaped by nearly fifty years of heavy-handed state rhetoric, and illuminated by the nostalgia of bygone youth, Karo women and men traced their various approaches to the nation. Taken together, these do not constitute a fuller, more coherent script of national self-fashioning but rather an aporetic account, growing ever denser with absences and amnesias. What follows in this chapter is thus an essay into uncertainty, in which independence, that chimeric object of national desires, is at once unreliable guide and impossible object.

FORMATIONS

For most of the Japanese occupation, Sumatra, which was deemed less "socially advanced" than Java and hence less prepared for eventual independence, had been kept isolated from the nationalist currents on Java (Reid 1979a:105–6). Japan's worsening military and economic situation necessitated an increase in the level of grassroots involvement in the war effort, but there was little administrative coordination of activities or organizations above the residency level. Transportation difficulties meant that even after the Japanese surrender communication between the islands was tenuous. The actual control that could be exercised by the republican government from Jakarta, or even from a provincial capital like Medan, was extremely limited. Java-based political organizations might have provided the inspiration and the tacit authorization for gatherings of like-minded youth in the provinces, but this should not suggest that these local branches were necessarily under the control of, or even known to, their nominal parent associations (Kahin 2003:178).

Following the independence proclamation, nationalist leaders in Java moved quickly to establish a central legislative committee, the Komité Nasional Indonesia-Pusat (KNI-P). Decisions of this national governing body were to be implemented through a system of provincial- and district-level KNI organizations (Anderson 1972:116–17). This institutional framework was fragile and disconnected at best, and its Sumatran leadership cautious and indecisive.[4] And there were, or would soon be, other contenders for power in East Sumatra: British peacekeeping forces sent to oversee the Japanese surrender; the Netherlands Indies Civil Administration (NICA), created under Allied military auspices and made up largely of Dutch citizens released from Japanese internment; the residual authority of the Malay aristocracy; the defeated but still-armed Japanese soldiers; the newly legalized political parties; the official army of the republic; and the irregular militias that were formed during the first months of independence.

Accounts of youth mobilization in Medan at the beginning of independence present an almost impenetrable thicket of names and acronyms—Black Crows, National Control, Vanguard Brigade, National Vanguard, Mark of the Chain, Mark of the Adze, BKPI, PPPHG, PPL, BPI, PRI, TKR, TKR-"B," Napindo, Knights of Pesindo, Parkindo, Hisbullah, Sabilillah, Fifth Force, PADI, Poh An Tui, Black Bear, Black Brigade, Red Brigade, Sacred Brigade, not to mention groups identified by their home turf: Serdang Street, Gurami Street, Sepat Street, Pulo Berayan, Tembung, Kongsi Dua, and Padang Bulan, among many others. Nationalist militias formed like crystals around whatever structural seeds were available: underground political cells, local hangouts, labor associations, neighborhood gangs. These groups formed and reformed, replaced leaders and changed affiliations, attempted to claim constituencies, and, spurred on by the energetic disinformation campaign conducted by a small Allied counterinsurgency unit, fought with one another. Soon they began to consolidate into loose associations, taking on (and discarding) names and institutional legitimacy, if not much political direction, from nationalist organizations headquartered in Java.

The first formally organized youth association was the Committee for Unemployment Assistance for Heiho and Gyugun (PPPHG), established on August 25, 1945, by a group of former officers from the Gyugun officer corps led by Lt. Achmad Tahir (Biro Sejarah PRIMA 1976:72–73). The committee's immediate purpose was to provide food, shelter, and transportation for demobilized recruits left stranded in Medan at the end of the war, but it also maintained contact with former Heiho and Gyugun trainees throughout the residency. Tahir's group expanded its initiative a month later, forming the Sumatran chapter of the Barisan Pemuda Indonesia (BPI, the Indonesian Youth Brigade), a general coordinating body for youth mobilization (Reid 1979a:63, 80). It was at the BPI's September 30 inaugural meeting that Governor Hasan publicly confirmed the news of Indonesia's independence. Shortly thereafter, the BPI, drawing on its own ranks of Japanese-trained officers, created the command structure for a Sumatran division of the republican army (then known as the TKR, Tentara Keamanan Rakyat), with Tahir as its commander and Djamin Ginting, a former Gyugun first lieutenant, as TKR head for the Karo district.[5]

Riano Perangin-angin was in the Gyugun training program in mid-August 1945, when, without explanation, the training center was suddenly closed. The trainees' weapons were collected, and they were ordered to return to their homes. A few months later, he learned what had happened from his uncle (K., *mama*, MB, WF), Masa Sinulingga, in the west Karo village of Kuta Buluh.

> RIANO PERANGIN-ANGIN: Here's the story. The story goes like this. I don't remember the date, but it was either in October or November. My uncle called me to Kuta Buluh. "What is it, *mama?*" I said. "It seems we're independent," he said. "What's independent, *'ma?*" I said. "By rights you should understand this *merdeka*," he said, "because you've been to Taman Siswa [a private nationalist middle school, in Medan]." "So if we're independent, what are we going to do, *mama?*" I said. "We become the masters," he said. "We're the government. Not the Dutch anymore." "What about Japan, *'ma?*" I said. "Well, the Japanese have been defeated." "Oh," I said. "So the Netherlands are here defending what they call Hindia Belanda, meaning the Republic of Indonesia," he said. "Soon all the *sibayaks* will be replaced, the *raja urungs* will be replaced, the *pengulus* will be replaced," he said. "The arrangements haven't been made yet." So finally at the end of our conversation, "Let's form our brigade. Its name is BPI, Barisan Pemuda Indonesia," he said. "If that's what you say, all right," I said. . . . There was still a *sibayak* here then, Sibayak Kuta Buluh. So they called the *sibayak* and his staff—I don't know if he was just sort of passive, not knowing the situation yet, although he was an instrument of the Japanese—or the *pengulu*, or whoever. Well, automatically because there was no firewood, they [burned] the porch of a house. You know, on the old-style houses, the place where the weaving was done, that's the porch, it was made of bamboo. That's what they burned, for the meeting. For illumination.[6]

A second major youth association that was formed around this time, the National Vanguard (Nasional Pelopor, later known as Napindo), was based in movement politics rather than Japanese military experience. It consisted of several independent militia groups associated with the Indonesian Nationalist Party (PNI). The name was chosen as a nod to Sukarno's Barisan Pelopor (Vanguard Brigade), a Japanese-sponsored urban youth association in Java, which was one of the few nationalist organizations whose membership cut across class lines (Reid 1979a:174).[7] Some of the Napindo units had, either through negotiations with sympathetic Japanese officers or by out-and-out brigandry, managed to acquire their own weapons. The BPI may have held center stage at the "giant" rally of October 6, but Napindo groups held most of the guns.

British troops began landing in Sumatra on October 10. Their primary objective was to oversee the Japanese surrender and the release of war prisoners, but they were additionally charged with assisting in the transition to peacetime rule. To this end they used NICA as a liaison organization with the European and "nonnative" (i.e., Chinese and Indian) population and at the same time endeavored to maintain working relationships with the Malay sultans as well as the KNI as the de facto republican government.

The situation in Medan was complicated by heavy-handed Dutch efforts to regain control of the city. These led nationalists to suspect that the British were actually paving the way for a Dutch return to power.[8] On October 13 the rumor spread through Medan that a policeman on Bali Street had assaulted a child wearing a red-and-white nationalist badge. Groups of youths armed with machetes and knives rushed to the scene ("as if shocked by a high voltage electric current," the PRIMA historians say [Biro Sejarah PRIMA 1976:179]). Fighting spread through the city. By the time order was restored, at least ten people had been killed and perhaps a hundred more wounded.[9] Two days later, in a similar incident in the city of Pematang Siantar nearly twenty people died, including four Dutch soldiers who were killed when the hotel where they were billeted was burned by nationalist youths (Reid 1979a:160).

These events brought the independence struggle home to Sumatran youths who had been following the news of fighting in Jakarta and Bandung. Soon militia organizations were flooded with volunteers and requests for military training (Biro Sejarah PRIMA 1976:178–87). To handle the demand, the TKR began to call up ex-Heiho and Gyugun trainees, many of whom had returned to their home villages after the Japanese surrender. With this cadre, they established eight training centers in Medan, offering two-week lightning courses for new recruits. Similar training programs were subsequently set up in the secondary cities and larger towns of the residency.

For the young men who joined the army or one of the party-affiliated militia groups at the beginning of independence, mobilization was a continuation of their experiences during the Japanese occupation: recruitment campaigns, military training, air raid drills, and propaganda courses. They entered into the discipline and violence of army life incrementally, through a series of stagings, fronts, and "clashes." Organizations, hierarchies of command, strategies, tactics, contests of will, and acts of insubordination are, in their accounts, the elements of a coherent narrative in which personal growth ("how I learned to be a soldier") is mapped onto national destiny ("how we won the war").

This "mapping" is literal as well as figurative, for these characteristically military progress narratives take the form of travelers' tales, in which temporal sequence is plotted by movement from place to place.

> BAPA BETY SEMBIRING: I was trained for a year at Polonia [airfield] by the Japanese. Guarding the field. After Polonia, after we'd finished a year, we were moved around. Some went to Birueun [in Aceh], some here to Binjei, Padang Cermin. . . . So after Japan was defeated I was active in the struggle. All of us former Japanese soldiers went home, we were given clothes but not taken all the way home. When we got to Medan, Central [Market] was the only bus station back then. The *preman* [from D., *vrij man*, day laborers and petty criminals] there, the *pemuda* [I., nationalist youth], they said we're already independent, they said, we're independent, they were all wearing red and white. We Japanese soldiers didn't know, just that Japan said we'd been defeated in the war. So we divided up the Japanese clothes with them, with the youths. We were under the leadership of Ahmad Tahir, who's a general now. In the Japanese army we'd been under the command of Tengku Nurdin from Perbaungan. . . . Then there was an order from Djamin Ginting for all the former Japanese soldiers to return to Taneh Karo. We formed an army there. We organized a battalion. I was made an instructor.

By the time the first wave of recruits had been trained, the TKR Fourth Division had an estimated infantry strength of seven units, each with between two hundred and a thousand members, but virtually no weapons. The lack of arms may have been one reason the army-dominated BPI had been looking for allies among the stronger youth militia groups.[10] In late October the BPI merged with the Badan Kebaktian Pemuda Indonesia (BKPI, Indonesian Youth Service Corps), a politically moderate nationalist group that had a reputation for violence and was associated with the conservative but well-armed Pasukan V (Fifth Force). This new, broader association took the name PRI (Pemuda Republik Indonesia) to reflect solidarity with the like-named youth association of Java and West Sumatra. Inspired by news of the fighting in Java and "aspiring to share the sense of unity and direction which the movement in Java appeared to possess," youth groups from across the political spectrum declared themselves PRI affiliates (Reid 1979a:162–65).[11]

This solidarity was short-lived. Soon after Vice President Hatta signed the November 3 Decree legalizing political parties, the PRI officially aligned itself with the Socialist Party, changing its name to Pesindo. Required to remain independent of party politics, the TKR formally withdrew from the association. For a time Pesindo remained more or less by default the general umbrella association of militia groups throughout the residency, even though some of its strongest units, including Selamat Ginting's Halilintar Regiment, remained affiliated with Sukarno's Nationalist Party.

In the Karo district, youth mobilization had at first gone smoothly. Within days of the official announcement of independence, BPI/Pesindo chapters had been formed in Berastagi and in Kabanjahé. Building on POESERA's grassroots network of underground cells, Pesindo branches were quickly established throughout the highlands.

> RIANO PERANGIN-ANGIN: First PRI was formed, Pemuda Republik Indone-sia. After that it changed to Pesindo. . . . I don't know the exact date, I don't know exactly when. From Pesindo they all scattered. Meaning that from Pesindo there were some who went into TKR, that was what they called the army then. . . . They changed it [from TKR] to TRI, but the people were the same. Actually this Pesindo was an *"onderbouw"*—you're a college student, you should know what *onderbouw* means—an *onderbouw* of the Socialist Party. But in Taneh Karo it wasn't influenced by the political meaning. We didn't bow to the Socialist Party. Most of the Pesindo people were nationalists or could be said to be members of the PNI. Specifically in Taneh Karo. I don't know about Java, right, that was the home base of the Socialist Party. This was how it was in Taneh Karo.

Unlike Medan, where the Malay-dominated native administration had been immediately pushed aside by less reactionary political leaders, the Karo district KNI remained for a time in the hands of the same elite functionaries who had held office under the Japanese as well as the Dutch. The *sibayak* of Sarinembah Subdistrict, Ngerajai Meliala, continued to head the district government. Maintaining this administrative status quo was intended to ease the transition to a representative form of government. "For the Rajas," Surbakti (1978:98) writes, "this was a great test. They had to be able to adjust themselves as autocracy gave way to democracy, and they had to adjust their style of governance from autocratic to democratic."

Tensions between Pesindo and the district's conservative rulers were exacerbated by divisive party politics, longstanding personal and family grudges, intervillage conflicts, class resentments, and generational differences in style and education, but they were also ameliorated by the countervailing forces of kinship. Rakutta Berahmana was a nephew by marriage of the *sibayak* of Sarinembah as well as his sometime protégé. Selamat Ginting, who became the commander of the Pesindo militia in the Karo district, was heir to the position of *raja urung* of Kuta Bangun; he too had been for a time a clerical trainee in the Sarinembah subdistrict office. In fact many of Pesindo's leaders came from what Karo rather grandly refer to as the "royal circles" *(kalangan raja)* of village society in the highlands. Thus, despite the extravagant antifeudal rhetoric of some of Pesindo's more radical factions, the district KNI maintained a wary cooperation with the youth organization in its efforts to recruit volunteers, raise funds, and collect arms.

Nationalist solidarity still seemed to be holding firm in early November, when a company of the Sixth Battalion South Wales Borderers was moved to Berastagi to inventory and confiscate Japanese weapons. Relations between the British troops and local youths were cordial at first, but a series of minor incidents, such as soldiers frightening the town's inhabitants by firing guns in the streets and publicly "bothering" Karo girls, soon turned local sentiments to resentment and anger. Tensions escalated after two British soldiers were injured by blowpipe darts in a roadside ambush (Biro Sejarah PRIMA 1976:247). The next day, an officer billeted at the Merdeka Hotel "disrespectfully" took down the red-and-white Indonesian flag flying in the hotel yard and replaced it with the Union Jack.

Pesindo protests over the flag incident were ignored. When youth representative Malpal Barus warned the British commander that they might no longer be able to guarantee his troops' safety, he got the response, probably true but less than tactful, "We don't need to have our safety guaranteed by children" (Surbakti 1978:54–55). As nearby Pesindo branches began moving reinforcements into Berastagi, the British stepped up their search for weapons. Disregarding instructions from the central Pesindo command in Medan, youth forces, armed mostly with grenades and homemade gasoline bombs, attacked them. After about four hours of running battle, the British, who evidently had no wish to engage militarily, began to withdraw toward Medan. Along the highway the retreating troops encountered roadblocks and snipers armed with blowguns. According to one popular story, a hive of bees was strategically dropped onto the road just beyond the Sibolangit market as the convoy passed by (Biro Sejarah PRIMA 1976:247–48).

This incident marked the end of British attempts to patrol beyond the Medan city limits. Within days the Allied command announced that its troops in East Sumatra would be confined to an area with a radius of four and a half kilometers surrounding Medan and its harbor, Belawan. Within the boundaries of what they termed the "Medan Area," the British would be fully responsible for keeping the peace; outside these limits, the responsibility was left to the Japanese, who were increasingly reluctant to interfere in nationalist matters (Surbakti 1978:71–72). As the historians of the PRIMA group explain, "The term 'Medan Area' became popular after the British army set up signs around the city of Medan with the words: *'Fixed boundaries of protected Medan Area'*. . . . From that phrase was born in youth circles the term 'Medan Area,' which was not pronounced as in English, but had experienced a process of transformation according to Indonesian pronunciation 'area' (ah'-ré-ah), to refer to the region of Medan and its environs" (Biro Sejarah PRIMA 1976:775).

Once they had established this protected enclave, the British found themselves encircled by armed youths, who converged on the perimeter of the city, setting up camps just outside the self-imposed bounds of British authority. Groups of varying degrees of legitimacy blockaded the roads, turning back or appropriating shipments of rice, vegetables, and fruits and demanding tolls from travelers. With little experience, limited supplies of arms and ammunition, and no effective coordination among units, the youth forces were, as one former TKR officer put it, "an easy target" for Allied assaults: "The Medan Area was not defended according to the conditions of the field, the weather and the enemy; instead, emotion was given priority over logic" (Arifin Pulungan 1979:68).

ROMANCE OF THE STRUGGLE

There can be no doubt about the actual fluidity and risk of nationalist mobilization in this initial phase of the struggle. Describing the growth of military and paramilitary organizations in the first months of the struggle, the PRIMA historians write, "Both in Medan and in other areas, troops were not formed by the top leadership directly from above, but were born from the initiative of the people themselves, spearheaded by youth figures who dared to step forward and were able to act quickly and adroitly. Only the guidelines were taken from political parties or mass youth organizations, or from the army headquarters" (Biro Sejarah PRIMA 1976:273).[12] Even within the relatively firm hierarchical structure of the TKR, individual units acted independently. Volunteers moved freely from one unit to another. Troop strength "simply consisted of the number of youths there at a particular time." Youth leaders claimed the rank that suited them and held their followers more by force of personality than by military discipline.[13] "All a commander needed back then was personality," said Mulih Kwala Sebayang, who had been a sharpshooter in the Halilintar Regiment.

MULIH KWALA SEBAYANG: Ability, courage, that's all. It wasn't entirely a matter of intellect. Not all intelligence was useful. Courage was what it took. Whoever was daring, put them in front. Whoever wasn't daring, to the rear. The intellectuals, they were all staff. Back then we thought that anyone who didn't dare to fight couldn't be an officer. Only someone who dared to fight could become an officer. We didn't know that staff officers are high in rank. We absolutely didn't know. Whoever would fight, he was the leader. . . . Later we learned that military rank didn't work that way. Only those who've got an education can hold a high rank, even if they've never fired a single bullet.

It is difficult to discover, either in published accounts or in local memory, anything that contradicts this picture. As Stoler (1988:228) points out, "real confusions of motivation and affiliation" among the nationalist players were registered by observers on all sides of the struggle. But we can also detect in these statements the unmistakable inflections of what Ranajit Guha (1988) calls a "prose of counter-insurgency," which carries the assumptions of the colonial archive—or, in this case, the postcolonial state—into the second- and third-degree separations of memory and of history writing. Several interlocking and characteristically counterinsurgent themes recur: spontaneity, criminality, charismatic leadership, and primordialism. The mobilization of urban youth is often represented through nature imagery: groups formed "spontaneously, just like the pools of water in low places after the ebbing of a great flood that has washed away the fields on the banks of a river" or "popped up like mushrooms in the rainy season" (Biro Sejarah PRIMA 1976:202, 208). Although a few Dutch and Indonesian sources endeavor to "distinguish urban thuggery from revolutionary zeal," the line between legitimate and criminal activity is frequently blurred: "all accounts agree" that the period was marked by extreme violence and social disorder (Stoler 1988:232). Emphasis is commonly placed on the recruitment of *preman*—a term locally used to refer to casual or noncontract laborers but by implication also to urban loiterers, petty gangsters, and others on Medan's underworld fringe—to the nationalist cause. "In addition to young men without regular work, elements that are usually labeled 'bandits' and 'hoodlums' [I., *bajingan*] and so forth, could also be gathered into this movement" (Manihuruk 1979:103). As a result, "the security situation shifted in the direction of an unchecked rampage of criminality. Felons, bands of burglars, robbers and pickpockets were on a rampage" (Biro Sejarah PRIMA 1976:206). After a fight outside the Oranje Bioscoop, "the youth received a new sobriquet as 'extremists' and 'terrorists'" from the British (Manihuruk 1979:118). Medan was in the hands of "fighting gangs of all sorts, sometimes comprising youths of the same ethnic group or from the same part of the city, but defined by loyalty to one forceful figure who showed his decisiveness at a critical moment. The symbol of authority was always the pistol" (Reid 1979a:162). Youth leaders built their followings by tapping "communal loyalties" and thereby forged "strongly ethnocentric factions" (van Langenberg 1985:128): Matheus Sihombing, an illiterate Toba Batak youth from Tapanuli, commanded a group "mostly composed of youths from Tapanuli living in Medan, predominantly former Medan toughs." Youths from Karoland "mostly joined with Selamat Ginting," while Javanese youths supported the (Javanese) former mechanic Bedjo (Manihuruk 1979:103, 110).

Terms like *fighting gangs, communal loyalties,* and *urban thuggery* do not capture the complexity of this situation any more than the British labels *extremists* and *terrorists* do. Neither the charisma of leaders nor the primordial sentiments of followers fully account for the form and content of youth mobilization. For one thing, education and political contacts were as important as charisma in the selection and rise of youth leaders. Mobilization followed preexisting social networks. In some cases gatherings of young militants did take on an ethnic, regional, or religious coloring, but in others the common link might be Japanese training, class background, occupation, neighborhood, or school ties. Lack of communication among militia units meant that one group would usually be unaware of the organizational efforts, contacts, or activities of others or become aware of them only in situations of conflict or complaint. As a result, themes of disorder, outlawry, and lack of discipline are consistently overplayed in firsthand accounts as well as in the secondary literature of the struggle.

Alongside and often interwoven with the law-and-order motifs of criminality and spontaneity another discursive strand can be identified. To borrow a phrase from the PRIMA historians, it might be termed the "romance of the struggle" (I., *romantiknya perjuangan*). Referring to the lability and indiscipline of the army's new recruits, they write:

> We can sometimes gladly accept those courses as natural, but sometimes they make the hearts of those who know of them annoyed because of their inappropriateness. Nevertheless, all of this is nothing more than the romance of the struggle, because in fact this development is revolutionary and leads to an objective goal. The revolutionary situation at the time actually caused the spirits of our youth to become restless and unwilling to accept restraint, so

that as a result discipline became slack, but on the other hand growth was explosively rapid like the explosion of a jet that breaks the sound barrier so that here and there abnormal shocks and incidents occurred. (Biro Sejarah PRIMA 1976:187–88)

"Mold your spirits to become a young Diponegoro, a young Teukoe Oemar, a young Toeankoe Imam Bondjol, a young Singa Mangaraja," exhorted an article titled "Sikap angkatan muda" (Attitude of the Young Generation) (Purba 1946) in the Kabanjahé-based nationalist journal *Radikal*, citing for its largely Karo readership the "established trinity" (Reid 1979b) of Javanese, Acehnese, and Minangkabau heroes of anti-colonial resistance—and adding for good measure the Toba Batak leader Singamangaraja XII, who had been killed in battle against the Dutch in 1907. Models for youth emulation also included Japanese samurai, Muslim warriors, American cowboys, and the populist highwaymen of folktales and dime novels. Muhamad Radjab (1949:294), a Java-based journalist who traveled through East Sumatra in 1947, described at first-hand, and with more than a little metropolitan condescension, the style of East Sumatra's "freedom fighters": "Their long hair was swinging down to their shoulders, sometimes they were unshaven, two revolvers in their belt, the barrels cocked upward, wearing high boots that stamped around the restaurant." At first impressed by their outlaw bravado, Radjab soon learned that "these bold men" were no more than coffee shop braggarts and "heroes of the rearguard," who had never even been to the front. Furthermore, their style was out of date: "Just like in Malioboro [Street, in Yogyakarta] a year ago."[14]

Photographs—most of them, of course, posed—come closest to a direct expression of youth style. I came across a photograph of five boys and a kitten, taken in the village of Batu Karang in 1949, in a family album (figure 11). The caption read, "They were under NEFIS [Nether-lands Forces Intelligence Service] surveillance because they were considered 'the most dangerous.'"

The romantic nostalgia that attaches itself to images like this is almost inescapable. In accounts of their experiences during the first year of the struggle, men frequently portrayed themselves as dangerous, innocent boys like these. Their stories were of daring but half-baked plans, foolish mistakes, acts of thoughtless insubordination, ignorance of the rules of military order or the nature of warfare. Despite the pervasive violence they depicted, there was a kind of tenderness in the telling.

Most historical accounts continue to characterize the first phase of youth mobilization as spontaneous, disorderly, and often criminal.

FIGURE 11. Youth style, 1940s: *(left to right)* P.S. Ginting, Kilo Berahmana, Terteh Ginting, Guru Bayak Sinulingga, and an unidentified companion. Collection of M. Bangun and Nandé Lidia br. Barus.

Others, less sympathetic to the disciplinary routines of the state, have sought to uncover forms of subaltern action, independent of elite aspirations and state authority (Anderson 1972; Cribb 1991; Lucas 1991; Smail 1964; Stoler 1988). These frequently discern in the lineaments of youth mobilization such "traditional" forms of rural resistance as millenarian movements, magical practices, ascetic withdrawal, and social banditry.[15] Some identify the figure of the urban gangster-revolutionary as an indigenous form of "heroic social deviant" (van Langenburg 1985:122) known as the *jago*, or "fighting cock" (Onghokham 2003).

In a now-classic statement on the *jago* figure, John Smail argues that these urban gangsters, loiterers, and penny-ante hoodlums represent a "variation on a much more ancient rural type": "The jago, it must be understood, is no more a simple rural criminal than the classical European bandit. The jago band is an accepted, though deviant social institution; it has its justificatory myths and a collective mystique and is headed by a leader marked by strong charisma, though it is only parochial in scope. The individual jago characteristically carried an amulet *(jimat)* which usually confers invulnerability on him. He is often an adept at *pencak* [a form of martial art]" (Smail 1964:88).

In the Betawi (Malay) dialect spoken in the native quarters of colonial Batavia, the term *jago* referred specifically to a gang boss or village strongman. Part of an informal network of casual laborers, petty gangsters, robbers, and toughs that connected the city's rural outlands to its port, markets, and transportation centers, the *jagos* of Batavia were primarily labor brokers, controlling the supply of workers in specified occupations or areas of the city. Like Medan's semiorganized *preman* gangs, *jago* bands at times "enjoyed an almost symbiotic relationship with the forces of law and order" (Cribb 1991:15), but their activities also shaded into racketeering, robbery, and violence for hire. Links to the nationalist movement gave the antiauthoritarian *jago* or *preman* a new respectability, and the governmental vacuum following the Japanese surrender "gave him opportunity. The revolution gave power to many such figures. . . . [Some] were even confirmed by the Republic as regional officials or military officers" (Reid 1974:56–57). The swaggering, long-haired coffee shop braggarts described by Muhamad Radjab in the passage quoted above epitomize this outlaw style, which has become a familiar icon of heroic national bravado, particularly popular among today's aspiring young *preman* and *jagos*.

Whether or not these features—personalistic ties and charismatic leadership, cultlike solidarity, mythical charters or oaths, provincial

FIGURE 12. Youth style, 1990s: *Jago* à la Rambo. Independence Day painting outside a martial arts club, Medan, 1995. Photo by the author.

worldview, magical beliefs, and stylized arts of self-defense—characterized actual rural bandits in Java or elsewhere in the archipelago, the *jago* "type" that they identify was a familiar one in folktales and pulp fiction and remains a legendary-literary staple today. In a dizzying mimetic circuit, youth volunteers and revolutionary wannabes modeled themselves after fictional *jagos* and after those who so fashioned themselves. These stock figures have been picked up and elaborated in nostalgic reminiscences, where they are thematically linked to the common idioms of ignorance and romance. From there they have been appropriated to fill the "indigenous" slot in the tertiary literature of the struggle or rebuilt in popular imagination to the specifications of Hollywood and Hong Kong film studios. Swathed in guns and amulets, the *jago* has come to signify not just the irrational violence and passion of early nationalist mobilization but also its autochthonous roots and continuity with premodern modes of opposition to established authority.

The romance of the struggle emphasizes antistructural and carnivalesque components of nationalist mobilization: personal action rather than obedience to regulations, courage rather than intellect, violence rather than discipline, passion rather than reason, lumpen rather than elite actors, the grotesque rather than the mundane. It can support heroic self-aggrandizement or figure exceptional risk. Its flamboyant characters give the nation's narrative a dramatic focus; its humor and pathos lend plausibility, and sometimes provide light relief, to a story that is otherwise too pious to be believable or too familiar to be entertaining.

Flat, generic images like the *jago* stand in for complicated, ambiguous, and densely populated social situations. They rescript memory's contingencies according to the standard scenarios of insurgency—national melodrama, personal tragedy, heroic epic, romantic farce. They serve as figures of antiauthoritarian resistance both to the Dutch and to the disciplinary aspirations of the republic and its army, signifying the passionate spirit that was needed to jump-start the struggle but had to be subdued in the process of building a modern nation-state. As the authorized history of the North Sumatran military command puts it, "Without guidance or equipment from above they were transformed into a fighting force able to oppose the British Army trained in World War II. In fact these troops that were labeled extremists and bandits by the Dutch were in the end transformed into the Indonesian National Army, faithful defenders of the Nation of the Republic of Indonesia, the Pancasila and the Constitution of '45" (Team Asistensi Pangdam II/BB 1977:95).

SOLIDARITY

Peasant mobilization, Ranajit Guha (1983:167) points out, is based in "two closely related patterns of corporate behaviour, namely emulation and solidarity." Imitative or contagious rebellion spreads through a population by means of face-to-face relationships, a sense of collective responsibility, shared faith or values, kinship or the fabrication of an idiom of brotherhood, common experience, territorial identification, deference to traditional patterns of authority, or—"depending on the level of the consciousness of the people involved"—class position (Guha 1983:40). Partha Chatterjee (1993:163) sums up this list of solidarity's diverse (and contradictory) forms in the "notion of community." Drawing a contrast to the individualistic alliances of interests and preferences that constitute bourgeois politics, Chatterjee argues that peasant solidarities "do not grow because individuals feel they can come together with others on the basis of their common individual interests: on the contrary, individuals are enjoined to act within a collectivity because, it is believed, bonds of solidarity that tie them together already exist."

Approaches such as these regard peasants—or, more broadly, subalterns—from a "fundamentally romantic" (Ortner 1995:179) viewpoint: as a generic subjective category, with a distinctive, shared consciousness or mentality. But as Ortner points out, subalterns do not simply constitute an undifferentiated mass: "They have their *own* politics—not just between chiefs and commoners or landlords and peasants but within all the local categories of friction and tension: men and women, parents and children, seniors and juniors; inheritance conflicts among brothers; struggles of succession and wars of conquest between chiefs; struggles for primacy between religious sects; and on and on" (177). Peasant communities, in the Karo highlands as elsewhere, are shot through with competing solidarities, antipathies, opinions, interests, attitudes, and affiliations: heterogeneity is neither an elite privilege nor a distinctly bourgeois burden. Attending to these internal differences allows a recognition of "the ambivalences and ambiguities of resistance itself" (190) and permits a richer understanding not only of the "why" of peasant resistance but also of the "how"—those factors that impel, shape, or impede collective political action against forces of oppression.

Internal differences shape subaltern political action in another way as well. As Stathis Kalyvas (2003) argues, conflict situations typically involve the interaction of cleavages at various levels of political organization. Local actors call upon the support and resources of powerful outsiders for purposes of their own. Organizations of larger scale can draw strength and relevance, as well as supporters, from grassroots alliances. Neither "private" (i.e., local) interests nor "political" (extralocal) positions alone can account for such mobilizations and countermobilizations; rather, it is necessary to understand political agency in times of conflict as a "joint production" of central and peripheral intentions and interests. Political alignments may be influenced by ideological affinities or social ties, conditioned by preexisting rivalries or prior affiliations, or they may simply be matters of chance.

By the opening of the independence struggle, class divisions and inequalities were becoming significant features of Karo social life. Fairly clear class positions were staked out ideologically (if not in practice) by the army as well as by the various party-based militias. One can say with some confidence that in the Karo district Pesindo represented the small Western-oriented, town-based intelligentsia; that the Halilintar Regiment stood for the classic alliance of middle peasants and petty bourgeoisie; that the BHL was identified with the interests of poor peasants and the urban subproletariat; and that the TKR was aligned with the *pamong praja*, or bureaucratic elite.[16] But mobilization can be tracked more predictably along lines of territory or kinship than of class. Regardless of their ideological orientations, leaders drew support most effectively from those areas where they had the closest and most extensive personal relations. TKR commander Djamin Ginting was from the Suka subdistrict on the south side of the plateau, an area that became an army stronghold. BHL forces were centered in Payung Bangun's home village of Batu Karang and in other villages on the northern plateau around the foot of Mount Sinabun. The Thunderbolt Regiment's main strength was in the central *gunung-gunung* region around Kuta Bangun, Tiga Binanga, and Perbesi, where Selamat Ginting and many of his staff officers hailed from. It was also a significant presence in some feud-divided and -subdivided areas. Selandi and Gamber were BHL strongholds, but the adjacent, rival village of Payung mainly supported the Thunderbolt Regiment. Tiga Nderket and Berastepu were both in BHL territory, and both divided their support between BHL and the Thunderbolt Regiment. Even Batu Karang had a strong Thunderbolt contingent.

In some cases this distribution reflected the existence of internal rivalries, longstanding disputes, perceived social injustices, or inequalities of resource distribution. In Tiga Nderket the presence of two militias seems to have had to do with local resentment of a newly wealthy chiefly lineage, resulting in part from land-pawning practices, and in Berastepu a longstanding local rivalry was exacerbated by the disparities of wealth that resulted from the introduction of orange groves in the 1930s. But just as frequently the presence of rival militias in Karo communities had to do with more pragmatic matters such as cross-cutting kinship affiliations or with families playing the odds by placing a son—or daughter—in each of the main armed forces.

In the early phase of mobilization, rank depended on the number of soldiers under one's command. As a result, village youths endeavored to draw their friends and relatives into locally constituted militia troops held together by personal allegiances: the larger the unit, the higher the commander's initial rank. Education, family status, and wealth were, even more than prior military experience, the interrelated correlates of command. Predictably, volunteers who could activate the widest range of kin relations were in the best position to form their own units. Sempa Sitepu, from the village of Ergaji, was a TKR company commander:

SEMPA SITEPU: This was in September '45. We got together, met up with Djamin Ginting, "What's this I hear about independence?" [we said]. "Let's form a troop." We got together all the boys from around here, from Suka, Ergaji, Kuta Kepar, and around there. . . . We formed a troop. Getting together in Suka. It was about two kilometers from Ergaji, about two kilometers from Tiga Panah. That's where the *sibayak* was, he was a [distant] relative of ours. So we all got together there, about 120 of us, that's one company. Some were ex-KNIL. That had surrendered. Then we got together the village boys that looked healthy. No examination, no medical tests, nothing. Just, whoever wants to go, that's all. . . . At first it was all family connections. But after the troops were formed, we could see. Then it was apparent who were the natural leaders. That's when it changed, in the field.

When my Karo grandfather Galang "Big" Sitepu joined the Halilintar Regiment in his home village of Berastepu he brought a group of eleven men with him. For that, he was given the rank of platoon commander, "right from the village." I asked why so many others from Berastepu had joined the BHL. "It's the family system," he explained.

BIG SITEPU: There I saw sympathies were mostly on account of kinship. For instance, Payung Bangun, his *anakberu* were in Berastepu. Take my cousin, I had a cousin in Berastepu who was a bus driver. [Payung Bangun] was his *kalimbubu*. Called him. It's the family system. But not me. Me and Selamat Ginting, we weren't even acquainted. I never even knew his history. . . . [Halilintar Chief of Staff] Ulung Sitepu I didn't even know. I was from Berastepu, he was from Sukanalu way over yonder, how could I have known him? Back then, to get from Sukanalu to Berastepu—or, let's just say to Kabanjahé, not even to Sukanalu, maybe you wouldn't even get there once in three years, not once in five years, probably. How could we have known each other? I just went to village school. He'd already been to [school in] Palembang [an industrial center and port in South Sumatra] or wherever. How could I have known him? So I didn't have a system of acquaintance. I knew a lot of the Wild Tigers, including my cousin.

With its entangled solidarities and inherited animosities, the family system complicated as much as it clarified internal lines of allegiance and resistance in Karoland. The army's repeated "rationalization" projects were directed at replacing the personalistic, horizontal basis of military loyalties with a unified, vertical command structure. This goal was only partly reached, and even then with a good deal of effort, mainly because the TRI structure in Karoland had also been built upon a localized social foundation and reinforced by personalized relations between commanding officers and their subordinates. By the end of the struggle, discipline and hierarchy had been successfully instantiated as the *ideals*, if not always the outcomes, of military organization.

ASPIRATION

Imagining independence depends first on recognizing the condition of unfreedom.[17] Generating that awareness was the task of nationalist propagandists in Karoland. Soon after the proclamation announcement, political rallies—Karo called them *saranen*, "instructions"—began to be held throughout the highlands to mobilize support for the new republic, recruit volunteers for the various popular militia groups, and prepare villagers for the anticipated return of the Dutch. *Encik* (M., female teacher) Kumpul beru Muham was one of the small coterie of educated Karo women who were active in the political rallies of Independence Time.[18] "To begin with," she said, "people didn't know the difference between being colonized and being independent. So those of us who happened to know, we had to go from one village to another to explain it." Kabanjahé schoolteacher Madasa beru Berahmana recalled the *saranen* message this way:

> MADASA BERU BERAHMANA: Then in fact I joined in, every evening we went to what were called back then *saranen*. In other words, giving information, explanations, what independence meant, to the villages. And one thing I really remember, "Later when we're independent," we told or explained to the villagers, "don't be afraid any longer, we will never be miserable like what we experienced with the Japanese soldiers. So everything will be," we said, "all the income from our nation we'll use ourselves, by the people themselves, we won't be colonized any more." That's how all the explanations went.

In sensuous imagination, *merdeka* was articulated through invocations of pleasure, ease, and fulfillment and by promises of a future without limits, in which no opportunity would be lacking. Hardships were reconfigured as willing sacrifices and acts of generosity, shaped by a "love of homeland" and an ethos of communal sharing.

Nowhere in Indonesia were nationalist leaders more committed to total popular participation in the independence struggle than in Taneh Karo. The reason for this was not so much their belief in participatory democracy and universal suffrage as it was their adherence to the principles and practices of kinship. *Nandé bapa kerina la erndobah la erpilih*, Karo orators say, "all the mothers and fathers, indistinguishable, equally beloved," meaning that all members of the general class of relations identified as "fathers" or "mothers" (e.g., MZ, FBW, MFBD, or FB, etc.) are—hypothetically—identical and interchangeable. However contentious and competitive Karo social life may in fact be, its rhetorical ideals are the harmonious accord and collective agency reflected, for example, in the conventional phrase *sada pengodak sada pengolé*, "one in step and one in speech." On the basis of this inclusive, one-for-all—and-all-for-one social ethos, Karo leaders determined that everyone—men and women, children as well as adults—should play an active, conscious part in the struggle for independence.

Indonesian-language newspapers were started in Kabanjahé by the local branch of the Nationalist Party (Radikal) and the district administration (Kebangoenan, "Awakening"). These were not so much providers of news as venues for the publication of political speeches, patriotic and informative essays, profiles of national leaders, inspirational poetry, information about the new republican government, and advertisements by local businesses and prominent local figures.[19] The district Office of Information sponsored exhibitions of patriotic art and formed a propaganda theater group. Songs were composed in Karo and other vernacular languages with patriotic themes, in traditional as well as popular genres. There were recruitment drives by the army as well as various militia organizations, such as Pesindo and Napindo. Village guard units were formed and a network of command and observation posts set up across the highlands. A special military training program for women, the Srikandi Corps, was created by the army. At the subdistrict and village levels, obligatory military drills were organized for women as well as men, work groups were set up, and first-aid training classes held. Scout troops were organized for children too young for military recruitment, where they too learned to march and played war games like capture the flag. Public kitchens fed the militia recruits, with provisions and labor donated by villages on a rotating basis.

Primary and middle schools that had closed during the Japanese occupation reopened, offering instruction in Indonesian and Karo. Adult literacy classes were also set up and enthusiastically supported. Nandé Sri Arihta beru Bangun exaggerated, but not by much, when she declared, "The day after independence was announced, they said that everyone had to go to school." Her husband, Yahya Barus, continued her thought:

YAHYA BARUS (BAPA SRI ARIHTA): Everyone had to go [to school]. Especially PBH [I., Pemberantasan Buta Huruf, "Elimination of Illiteracy," i.e., an adult literacy program]. A lot of effort went into that. Because if someone started to understand letters, well, they could read. So their comprehension would be wider if they could read for themselves, right? They could read newspapers. That's why all the effort went into the literacy campaign. So people could read.

The schoolteacher 'Cik Muham was the daughter of the *raja urung* of Tiga Nderket. She taught in a private primary school in Batu Karang, a large village about five kilometers by road (half that as the crow flies) from her family's home village.

> ENCIK KUMPUL BERU MUHAM: In the morning I taught at the [village] school. In the afternoon I taught the women and girls. Military drills, literacy, and everything, cleanliness, health. At night there were rallies. . . . If I had time, I'd sew. I was a seamstress back in Batu Karang. So nonstop from morning to evening, nonstop. I taught in the morning till 1:00. Come home from school and sew until four or five o'clock if there wasn't a marching drill. Every night there was a program. Rallies, propaganda, or entertainment, there was always a program. . . . We didn't even think about clothes, you know. Who had a nice dress? Well, there weren't any, none at all. Don't think we had nice face powder, or pretty clothes, or pretty shoes. At best, [rubber] sandals. Life was hard.

The *saranen* campaign aimed to instill in the Karo population a "spirit and consciousness of sacrifice," with the result that, as Surbakti (1978:44) hyperbolically puts it, "every one of the people wished actively to struggle to defend the nation's independence." Rallies were held in villages throughout the highlands, sponsored by the Office of Information as well as by a wide range of political parties and nationalist organizations. Rakutta Berahmana, who headed the information section of the BPI from October 1945 until April 1946, was an "unforgettable public speaker" at the rallies. "In the special vernacular style, by including old folks' sayings, Rakutta had a great share in planting the spirit of struggle and consciousness of responsibility in the hearts of the people. In addition to being able to speak for hours, he could also orate while dancing. Because of that, every meeting that included his name as a speaker was sure to be flooded with people" (Surbakti 1978:44).

More often, featured speakers were local headmen, youth militia leaders, or members of the district Office of Information. Sometimes militia recruiters or representatives of the political parties and youth organizations came from Kabanjahé or Medan. "Do you remember the beginning of independence, Tigan?" I asked one of my Karo grandmothers, Nandé Rikson beru Tarigan of Gamber Village:

> ND. RIKSON: Like the very beginning? We'll be independent soon, they said at this meeting, as I remember. They had a lot of meetings at night at the beginning of independence, every night there was a meeting. No one was too lazy to attend. There's a meeting, they'd say, and everyone would gather. In

every village. . . . So, let's be committed to independence, stand firm if need be, the enemy is sure to come. The enemy is already in Jakarta, or wherever, we didn't know, we just knew about our area. But whatever happens, there's sure to be war here. So all of you get ready, all the parents, our *laskars* [I., militia fighters, guerrillas]—back then they called the soldiers *laskars*—you're to give them food. Are all of you parents ready to do that? We're ready, [they said].

Many women spoke of going to Kabanjahé—some for the first time—to attend the monthly rallies that were held there. "All of us from the villages were invited," said 'Cik Muham. "We didn't take cars like now, sometimes there was a truck, or whatever. Take an oxcart, so you'd get to Kabanjahé together with people from all the villages in Taneh Karo to celebrate the 17th, which was the occasion of proclamation day." The women's organization PERWARI (I., Persatuan Wanita Republik Indonesia, "Women's Association of the Republic of Indonesia") also organized public meetings for women in large villages and market centers.

'CIK MUHAM: We'd call a public meeting, so the playing field in Batu Karang was full, another time a full meeting in Tiga Nderket. All the women from the villages would come. I invited my friends from Kabanjahé. My friends there were freedom fighters too, Roncah Barus, Madasa Berahmana, all of them came and they all gave speeches, but of course I was the head. Because no one disagreed, everyone was happy back then. Sacrifice whatever there was, it wasn't like there had to be rice there, with meat or a nice soup, there wasn't anything like that. Everyone brought their own meal. You'd bring your own fish if you had any, if not some boiled vegetable, maybe eggplant or whatever, that's how it was.

In addition to inspirational speeches, recruitment efforts, and solicitations of material support, village rallies often featured such forms of entertainment as patriotic songs and didactic dramas. "Everybody came," said Terang beru Singarimbun of Tiga Nderket. After all, she added, there wasn't much to do for fun in the village. "You felt sorry for the villagers, they never had any entertainment." Sometimes there would be a *sandiwara* (M., play). Occasionally this would be a Javanese *kuda képang* trance performance or some other exotic show, but more often it would be an agit-prop drama by a government-sponsored troupe or by local youngsters, like the Pesindo Theater group that 'Cik Muham organized in Batu Karang. The group traveled around to the nearby villages, telling "stories about loving independence, how we ordered our children to join the struggle, how fathers struggled, how mothers too took part in the struggle. Lots of stories, but the essence of all of them wasn't 'love,' not marriage, not a fashion show or whatever. No. It was all so that they would struggle for independence, only that."

The *sandiwara* was less a dramatic narrative than a series of simple didactic scenes or tableaux. Scenes alternated with musical interludes of Karo or Malay love songs or more commonly *lagu gurila* (I., guerrilla songs). Roncah beru Barus, the daughter of the Christian *sibayak* of Barusjahé, was also an active participant in the *saranen* campaign.

> RONCAH BERU BARUS: We . . . made dramas. Village *sandiwaras*. Then there would be speakers who could explain things to the villagers. And I sang, everyone came. We'd make a show, they would watch. Every night. Just little short things, just light stuff, so there would be someone who watched, nothing of quality. It was just, how a girl fought for freedom, died, like this, how she helped the youth who was her sweetheart, yeah, stuff like that. That kind of story. We told about how a family, the child was shot because that child died as a freedom fighter, that's just what the story was. There were all kinds of songs.

In Tiga Nderket, an all-girl *sandiwara* group was organized by Nandé Katana, who had also headed the public kitchen there. "That was my auntie," said Terang beru Singarimbun. "My auntie's house was where we all gathered at night for *saranen*. I was still small, but because they got together in her house, my mother let me go, so I could listen there.

> TERANG BERU SINGARIMBUN: At the beginning, there were meetings every night. *Saranen*. I was still small at the time. And there they started to teach the girls a little about what politics was, what the meaning of *merdeka* was, you know? We were taught to march. And at that time we put on a play in the villages. The curtain was just some sheets hung up there. And I had an older sister who was really tall, we made her play the Dutchman because she was so tall. In Tiga Nderket. The play was just short. We attack this Dutchman. We carried a long knife—we did like this [she mimes slipping the knife blade between her arm and torso]—the Dutchman fell with a crash, people shouted, you know. That's all we did in the villages. After that we sang. For a *sandiwara* you have to have songs as well as scenes, you know.

Sometimes they sang "Indonesia Raya," the national anthem, or "Erkata Bedil" (K., Rifle Reports), the love song that served as an informal theme song of the *saranen* campaign, but the song women remembered best was "Mariam Tomong" (I., Mortar Cannon), a Toba Batak composition in the jaunty "Opéra Batak" style, to which humorous or patriotic verses could be added infinitely. Nandé Marlina beru Ginting and her friends in the north Karo village of Mardinding still remembered several verses, in mixed Karo-Indonesian, which they sang for us one afternoon: *Dalan motor ei, jalanna Polonia, erdame Nippon e, merdeka Indonesia* (On goes the bus / on the road to Polonia / peace for Japan / independence for Indonesia), or *Man kai bunga kacar, la kap banci man sembur, man kai babah mekacar, la kap ia pang bertempur* (What's the use of the balsam flower / it's no good for medicine / what's the use of his sweet talk / he's scared to go to war), before returning to the bouncy chorus, "Oh , the mortar cannon, *dainang* [Toba, mother], oh, the machine gun." "'Mariam Tomong,' that was really popular in the villages," said Terang br. Singarimbun. "'Erkata Bedil' too, but 'Mariam Tomong' was best because it was fun, easy, and cheerful. That's what we sang there." Nandé Marlina chuckled, "We always raised a ruckus out in the yard with that one."

"NO ONE MUMBLED AND NO ONE GRUMBLED"

"At the beginning of independence, everything was tough," 'Cik Muham told us.

> 'CIK MUHAM: There was no money, nothing. Even bullets, you know, the only way to get them was by stealing. There was just nothing. Only spirit that was brimming over. In terms of spirit, there was no one who mumbled, no one who grumbled, everyone was happy, even if their rice all went to feed the soldiers. Tomatoes, peppers, whatever there was in the village, they gave it all to feed the soldiers. Yeah, all of them helped like that.

For Nandé Madasa beru Ginting, from the north Karo village of Berastepu, the beginning of independence was a time when food was given freely to strangers. "At the beginning of this independence, there wasn't an army yet, they made it up from just, just boys like you [meaning Jabatin], since the year of our independence took us by surprise."

> NANDÉ MADASA BERU GINTING: Back then there wasn't even any rice. We'd all beg for rice at all the houses, one would give two *tumbas*, three *tumbas*, like that at the beginning of independence, to feed those who fought the enemy, so.[20] Then, pound it at night, even at night you'd pound it. So then, when someone came, called, the ones who were to be fed, you'd ask for rice at the houses, there wasn't any husked rice, there wasn't a mill. Pound it, pound it like that, then cook it. We wouldn't get to sleep before dawn if someone came who had to be fed. So then, what to fix to go with it? If nothing was cooked, you'd go get something from the houses again. Well, pound the rice, make the stew. Nothing was off limits. You'd catch somebody's chicken, or somebody's pig, they weren't off limits.

"Did you know these soldiers, Granny? Were they from around here?" Jabatin asked. "They were from other places," she replied sharply. "If they were from around here, well, wouldn't we know them already, know how we were related to them?" She meant that if the soldiers had been related, however distantly, to anyone in the village, then it would have been up to their local kinfolk to feed and house them. "Sometimes they said that the ones to be fed came from Medan. We didn't even know them, we didn't have the chance to find out how we were related. What else could you do? Soon they'd move on to someplace else. That was the problem. Tomorrow others would come too."

Berastepu, where old Pa Tongat welcomed the Dutch troops with the *Merdeka!* salute, may have been the most *un*harmonious place in the Karo highlands, and strangers were not always welcome there. The entire Empat Teran (Four Ridges) subdistrict, of which it was one of the largest and most prosperous villages, had long been known for trouble-making and conflict. During the independence struggle it was probably the area least effectively integrated into a unified military command structure. In Nandé Madasa's account, however, the flood of transient and undifferentiated freedom fighters—"those who fought the enemy"— becomes the narrative condition for an idealized depiction of communal harmony and generosity. Karo are obliged by social practice and by custom to take care of even the most distant of kin, but here kinship doesn't matter, and no one's livestock is "off limits"—whoever comes should be fed. Nor is the feeding of soldiers from elsewhere an occasional or extraordinary occurrence; it is what happens, seemingly, every day. "Tomorrow others would come too." The designation of these soldiers as neither relatives nor nonrelatives marks them as extraordinary and the food they receive as freely given.

Why had Karo responded so eagerly to the call of *merdeka*? I asked 'Cik Muham. It was, she said, "because the Karo spirit is a patriotic spirit."

'CIK MUHAM: Because from long ago the Karo people lived in a true style of mutual assistance *[gotong royong]*, you know? Back then, just to build a house, Karo would have to cooperate with the whole village to cut down the trees. Drag the logs from the forest to build a house in the village, back then. So that spirit was overflowing, not to mention the love of independence *[cinta kemerdekaan]*. I think some may have had as much, but definitely no one had a greater love of independence. The point is, the Karo people truly have an independence-loving spirit that is truly patriotic. . . . The reason was that basic, that fundamental: love for homeland, love for the nation.

'Cik Muham was of course speaking as a propagandist, for there is no particular reason to expect that the intimacy of this Karo love for homeland would translate to a love for the unimaginably distant nation. That aside, what is interesting about her statement is the way it associates the spirit of nationalism with an idealized picture of "long ago." Whether located in the immediate past of personal recall or, as here, in the deeper, fictive "pastness" of tradition and ethnic character, the evoked memory of home is what provides the emotional ground upon which national aspirations are built.

Self-sacrifice is a common idiom of nationalist discourse, and memories of a shared past are easy to invoke. Whether they take the form of Sukarno's vision of grand precolonial kingdoms or the pan-Indonesian spirit of *gotong royong*, such imaginings offer points of departure and collection for more localized, intimate expressions of national belonging. When 'Cik Muham spoke of Karo patriotism embodied in traditional house-building practices, she was linking a vividly local expression of social participation to a translocal idiom of communal virtue, at once asserting the special place of Karo as "the most patriotic people" and situating them within a political discourse of mutual assistance that served as the cultural justification for Indonesian nationhood. When Nandé Madasa of Berastepu talked about feeding the unfamiliar soldiers from somewhere else, she was likewise placing mutual assistance and self-sacrifice at the heart of the project of independence and finding locally salient (and gender-specific) ways of extending the social value of generosity, beyond the personalistic ties of kinship and familiarity, to encompass the broader, invisible community of the nation.

"REVOLUTION IN KAROLAND"

At the other end of the spectrum of communal imagining is Frantz Fanon's invocation of the transformative power of violence: not to die for one's country but rather to kill for it. Fanon, who approached the question of nationalism from the angle of a colonized peasantry, regarded popular violence as a source of national unity as well as of personal liberation from the psychic scars of colonial subjection: "The mobilization of the masses, when it arises out of the war of liberation, introduces into each man's consciousness the idea of a common cause, of a national destiny, and of a collective history." For Fanon, memories of the past had little value—the deep past of tradition being little more than a record of atavism and superstition, and the immediate past of colonialism an experience of failure and humiliation. But in the grass-roots revolt of the colonized, "each individual forms a violent link in the great chain, a part of the great organism of violence which has surged upwards in reaction to the settler's violence in the beginning." In this confrontation between colonizer and colonized, the past is redeemed and "the future nation is already indivisible" (Fanon 1963:93).

Neither the harmonious spirit of mutual assistance, nor the violent Manichaean face-off of colonizer and colonized, nor even a combination of the two, captures the full scope of nationalist action and imagination in Karoland at the beginning of independence. What both fail to acknowledge is the capacity for violence *within* the national community itself. This is what my Karo informants meant by *repolusi*, a condition of intermittent but pervasive fear and indiscriminate brutality, a "war of us against us," as Rasi beru Ginting called it, in which *anyone* could become a victim.

For Nandé Rikson, the daughter of a ward chief in the north Karo village of Gamber, the violence of *repolusi* had been foreshadowed by a song:

> NANDÉ RIKSON BERU TARIGAN: There was this song. I didn't like it. In fact I despised it. It burned me up! But then things really did turn out that way. It was, I remember it was before Independence. It was approaching independence, though, OK? Sing, we'd sing like this, all the kids. "Battles *[pertempuren-pertempuren]* in Java-land," it went. "Revolution in Karoland," we'd say, "*garetek garetek* [the sound of teeth gnashing]." That went on all the time, you know. Kids. "Battles in Java-land," it went, "Revolution in Karoland." Then: *garetek garetek*. It meant that when there was fighting in Java there would be a revolution in Karoland.

The first phase of the independence struggle, which indeed coincided with the start of fighting in Java, was marked by extreme volatility throughout East Sumatra. Xenophobic rumors, the overwrought rhetoric of nationalist propagandists, and the lack of directed activity for armed gangs of young men contributed to what Patricia Spyer, in a contemporary context, refers to as a "climate" of violence: an atmosphere that is "mobile, dense, and murky . . . built on spirals of information, misinformation, and disinformation, on the revamping of criteria of credibility, customs of trust and accountability, and on knowledge forms that blur the boundaries between what is seen and what is heard, what is known and what is suspected, what is feared and what is fantasized, what is fact and what is fiction" (Spyer 2002:24). Impatient to begin the military action for which they were being prepared but without a clear enemy in sight, militia groups clashed with one another over arms and ideology and, in the case of more radical groups, directed their attention to those members of the local elite "whose movements," in Surbakti's (1978:91) memorably choreographic phrase, "were too slow to follow the rhythm of the struggle." In lowland towns, young self-styled freedom fighters engaged in turf wars and borderline acts of social banditry; suspected Indonesian "feudalists," collaborators, and reactionaries were kidnapped or threatened; Japanese soldiers and European civilians were attacked; and Chinese homes and businesses were plundered. Mob justice, in the name of popular sovereignty (I., *kedaulatan rakyat*), traced and intensified old grudges, personal vendettas, political antagonisms, ethnic resentments, and lineage feuds.

Ideological and personal conflicts at the national level fed into, enabled, or in some cases exacerbated these tensions, so that petty resentments and longstanding antipathies might suddenly explode into violence. Conflicts could thus have roots both deep and shallow, as affiliations with a range of external powers were deployed by or foisted on local actors. These sometimes contradictory alliances were inherited, continued, transformed, discarded, or reactivated by successor groups, over time. Power shifts at the center could reconfigure the local balance of power, transforming even chance connections with unexpected, sometimes deadly, consequences.

The Wild Tiger Brigade offers the most dramatic, though by no means the only, illustration of this kind of "joint production" (Kalyvas 2003) of political agency. Part of an underground guerrilla network established in the last months of the Japanese occupation, it was formed by an unlikely alliance of conservative elements in the Japanese military, the provincial leadership of the leftist Gerindo Party, and lowland Karo land-rights agitators. In 1938, a series of protests over the distribution of use-rights for fallow plantation land had been organized by SETIA (Serikat Tani Indonesia, Indonesian Peasant Union; the acronym means "faithful"), a Karo peasant organization in the Deli area. Their cause was taken up by Gerindo at a time when the party was looking for a way to build a mass base beyond its small urban constituency. In the process a lasting relationship between Gerindo and some of the rural Karo activists was formed.

In the first months of the Japanese occupation, an overlapping but more extreme successor group to SETIA, known as the Aron, emerged in the Karo villages of upper Deli. The movement quickly spread to the highlands, especially in the *urungs* of Batu Karang and Tiga Nderket, where land grievances had been particularly acute in the last years of Dutch rule. Aron groups there attacked pro-Dutch officials, moneylenders, and land speculators and took over wet-rice fields held by some wealthy villagers. Several people were killed or injured in the fighting. The Japanese forcefully cracked down on the movement, imprisoning or executing a number of its members. Among those arrested were Gerindo leaders Jakub Siregar and Saleh Umar, who were assumed to be involved with the Aron actions. This was, somewhat ironically, the beginning of an alliance of the two Gerindo leaders with the enigmatic Japanese head of military police, Lt. Inoue Tetsuro, a military hardliner with a background in agricultural organizing.[21] Together the three men established TALAPETA (Taman Latihan Pemuda Tani, "Peasant Youth Training School") in the Karo piedmont zone of upper Serdang. Ostensibly a school for farmers, TALAPETA indoctrinated its students with Inoue's own sense of military discipline, "romantic ultranationalism" and "almost mystical belief" in the peasantry as the soul of the nation (Reid and Oki 1986:79). The school's graduates formed the basis for a politically indoctrinated underground guerrilla network known in the Karo area as the Mokutai (J., wild tigers). After the Japanese surrender, the group, renamed in Indonesian Barisan Harimau Liar, became a quasi-autonomous militia organization affiliated with Napindo and the Indonesian Nationalist Party. Yet BHL actions on the ground seem to have been motivated less by ideology or by top-down strategic imperatives than by a range of local issues: personal animosities and lingering resentments, perceived slights, prior acts and allegiances, alleged sympathies, and old battles.

The Japanese occupation had provided a range of opportunities and resources for nationalist mobilization, from TALAPETA and the BOMPA indoctrination campaigns to the Gyugun and Heiho military training programs and the weapons that passed from Japanese hands to the newly forming popular militias. But it also left behind a profound residue of fear, suspicion, and resentment, much of it directed against officials who had been called upon to implement Japanese policies. Wealthy landowners and officials who had cooperated with the Japanese or profited excessively under the Dutch were targeted by youth militia groups or by their fellow villagers. Sometimes victims of these so-called *daulat* (sovereignty) operations simply "disappeared in custody." Nandé Senantiasa beru Bangun of Payung Village described it this way: "Say you're the headman. 'Come on, we have to go do a job for the army,' they'd say. You'd go out with them. Then you'd disappear." Bapa Rajamon, a "bold" headman under the Japanese, was called to the militia post in Pernantin to "stand guard" and never returned, said Nandé Tabonal beru Karo. In Juhar, Nandé Rosali beru Ginting recalled going to the house of the district head and finding there a strange young man wearing his clothes; the headman was never seen again. Nandé Karina beru Ginting of Kidupen described how the village's former headman was arrested:

NANDÉ KARINA: Back then he was the headman when it was still Dutch Time. After independence he was arrested. They were supposed to take him to [the district seat of] Tiga Binanga. He didn't even make it past [the nearby village of] Raja Berneh. I don't know if they killed him there or if he was still in custody. Maybe [they buried him] under the house. So then all his clothes, and even his wife's clothes were taken by the soldiers. So he was dead. They made his house their headquarters. It was the command post for the village youth, their guard post. So if somebody passed by that they didn't know, they'd capture them and hold them in the headquarters. They had a lot of grain. It was supposed to go to feed the soldiers in Lau Perimbon. "Why should we take it to Lau Perimbon?" [the youth asked]. I don't know how it was settled, I guess they settled it by sending part of the grain to Lau Perimbon. It was supposed to be to feed the soldiers. The husband was dead, and then they took all the grain.

Within militia organizations little attention was paid to the chain of command, and village guards, local volunteer groups, and fighting units acted largely on their own initiative. Popular militias kidnapped members of rival units, stole weapons from one another, and fought over territory, resources, and pride. Among the most troublesome areas were the Tiga Nderket and Empat Teran (Four Ridges) subdistricts, which had been the scene of flare-ups of Aron violence. There, according to Surbakti, "the activities of the pengulus who had governed in their villages for generations had been taken over by the youth brigades, in fact among those pengulus there were some who were arrested, held in the [local] headquarters, and there were even some who were 'pacified' [I., diamankan, i.e., killed] by the people, because they were considered unwilling to adapt to the developing situation" (Surbakti 1978:93). Finally, after a series of unauthorized arrests of members of rival militias by village-level Pesindo units in the two subdistricts, the army implemented a retaliatory "cleansing" of some of the organization's branch units there. About fifty Pesindo members were arrested and held in the district prison in Kabanjahé. As a result, for the first months of 1946 popular militias in that troubled area were, for good or ill, without effective leadership.

Even the independent-minded militias recognized the need for greater cooperation among the various fighting forces and for a greater degree of control over their own fractious members. Repeated efforts were made to establish a viable umbrella association to sustain and coordinate militia activities. Most were short-lived and ineffective. The strongest of these was the Persatuan Perjuangan (I., United Struggle), a coalition of some 140 political groups formed in January 1946. With its "minimum program" of "100% Merdeka" and rejection of diplomatic negotiations with the Dutch, the PP expressed the national aspirations and impatience of most militant youth.[22]

In February 1946, republican representatives met with the rajas, sultans, and *sibayaks* of the former native government in East Sumatra to exhort them not to interfere in matters such as taxation and military organization, which were now prerogatives of the republic. This demand was largely ignored, and rumors began to circulate that members of the "feudal class" were in secret contact with the Dutch. In these circumstances, the PP insisted that it was necessary to "overthrow the fortress of violent autocracy, the fortress where the sultans and rajas had governed for generations, and to replace it with the fortress of democracy" (Surbakti 1978:100).

On March 3, 1946, popular militias in East Sumatra began a coordinated assault on members of the Malay court. Armed youth gangs attacked the lowland sultans of Deli, Serdang, Langkat, and Asahan and their extended families, as well as conservative Batak heads of upland districts. The acting governor Dr. Amir quickly hailed these actions as "a tremendous social revolution . . . to change the structure of government and the style of government in a radical way, in accordance with the will of the people" (Mansjur 1976:271–72). As Dr. Amir's (perhaps coerced) statement suggests, the express aim of this action was to replace the "feudal" aristocrats who had governed under both the Dutch and the Japanese with democratically appointed representatives of the republic. What this "social revolution" came to in the end was, as one local journalist put it, little more than "butchery and seizure of property" (Said 1973:174). The palaces of Malay and Simalungun Batak aristocrats were looted; expensive cars, gold, jewels, and regalia of office were taken, ostensibly to support the nationalist militias. Many members of the royal families were arrested, injured, or killed. In a case that seems to have shocked even the most antifeudal of the nationalists, two daughters of the sultan of Langkat were raped.

In little over a week, as news of the extent of the violence emerged, a backlash set in. The army commander Lt. Col. Achmad Tahir unilaterally declared martial law. His action was largely disregarded, however, by the youth organizations that were the effective power-holders in much of the province. Nevertheless, East Sumatra was nominally under military rule until April 9, when the state of emergency order was rescinded. Governor Hasan confirmed the appointments of district heads "chosen by the people in their respective districts" retroactively to the date of their election (Reid 1979a:241), thus not only ending but in effect erasing the short period of military rule.

Karoland was one of the few areas where this transfer of authority was accomplished efficiently and without bloodshed. Selamat Ginting, who had recently been elected to head the Pesindo militia in the Karo area, called a compulsory meeting of all district and subdistrict officials, at which they were informed that they were being removed from power. They were then arrested and moved to guarded camps, where they remained until the evacuation of the highlands in 1947. The district apparatus of government was reorganized under the leadership of the PNI head Rakutta Berahmana.

There were three main reasons for this comparatively smooth transition. The first is that the socioeconomic divisions and resentments that drove the violence in the lowland plantation zone were not as extreme in the less prosperous highlands. The *sibayaks* and *raja urungs* of Karoland were the least privileged of the native rulers of East Sumatra; the lateral stretch of affinal ties created an expansive and closely knit system of kinship relations and customary etiquette that further mitigated the effects of colonial class formation. Second, the leaders of the most radical of the youth militias, the Japanese-trained, vehemently antifeudal Wild Tiger Brigade, were in custody at the time as a result of prior violent actions. Finally, the youth leaders who stage-managed the social revolution in Karoland were themselves of fairly elite background, in most cases close kin of the men they arrested and replaced.

The social revolution in Karoland may have been a "model operation" (Reid 1979a:230), but the violence did not end there. At the time of the Dutch invasion of the highlands in 1947 there were unauthorized mass executions of political prisoners who had been held in "protective custody" since the social revolution. Refugees fleeing the fighting in the lowlands, who were suspected of harboring collaborators and spies in their midst, were interrogated, tortured, and even killed by village guards in the highlands. A range of acts of banditry and assault were rendered imaginable—if not legitimate—in the wake of attacks on the native aristocracy. Some of the violence was opportunistic or unguided, but it could also be authorized by those in positions of power. Thus, one of the first acts of the Karo district's new republican leaders was to "export" the social revolution to the adjacent province of Tapanuli. P. S. Ginting (in figure 11, he is the young man holding the kitten) described to us what happened:

> P. S. GINTING: There was news that in Tapanuli the government wasn't running smoothly, the transition to the republic, because the direction was taken by the former rajas. Meaning the rajas in Tapanuli, Samosir and Silindung weren't too enthusiastic about receiving [the republic], or let's say, not too optimistic. So that Governor Mr. Tengku Muhamad Hasan . . . commanded the troops from Taneh Karo to arrest the rajas in Tapanuli. Now I can see that in addition to us not being very rational, just following orders, you know, we took on the task in a simple-minded way.

The arrival of Karo troops in late April led to fighting between local militias and the unwelcome outsiders. After a rough comedy of arrest and counterarrest, the chastened and beaten Karo volunteers were sent home, where they were welcomed as heroes. Soon thereafter, intervillage warfare incited by party-based ethnic militias broke out in the border zone between Karoland and Tapanuli. The army intervened, and two months of sporadic fighting ensued. By the time peace was restored in the region in late June 1946, some three hundred people were reported killed and another seven hundred injured (van Langenberg 1976:510).

REVOLUTION TIME

Repolusi in Karoland took a variety of forms. Its targets and motives changed or reversed themselves in convoluted dramas of reprisal and counterreprisal; it drew in the incautious and unfortunate, spun out mimetic chains of terror and brutality, and charged the euphoria of independence with a darker energy. It was inspired at times by motives of revenge, family feuds, fear of outsiders, moral panics, orders from above, sheer criminality, misplaced patriotism, or, as Nandé Ndapet of Payung Village put it flatly, for no reason at all: "Lots of people disappeared who were killed for no reason. They were tied up in sacks, still living, dragged off, and tossed into the Dog River [K., Lau Biang] over there." "*Repolusi*," said Rasi beru Ginting of Batu Karang, "you know, those [Dutch] people weren't our enemies anymore. We were our own enemies."

NANDÉ RIKSON BERU TARIGAN: There was a revolution in—there was a war, you know. We were at war with the Dutch, there was a revolution. All of the [political] parties, whatever, they took all the evacuees, and a lot of them were victims. They were tied up, all of them were arrested, all of them. So once I heard them say, "How many," you know, "How many goats do you want butchered?" they said. They meant, people. Say, four, they'd take four of them away. . . . They tied all the people up under the wild coffee trees. Sometimes two tied to one tree. Wouldn't you feel sorry to see that? I was sorry seeing them. But if you said you pitied them, if a man said, then "You're a traitor too," they'd say to him. Then you couldn't say just anything at that time, the time of the revolution.

The violence of *repolusi* permeates certain sites, such as the ravines of Lau Biang and Lau Borus, where the bodies of victims were dumped, and the Lau Melas hot springs, where suspected spies were tortured. Karo stories were quite specific about concrete details and sites of violence—places that could be seen today, village landmarks, the manner of deaths, the words of killers—even when these could be presented only speculatively. Our informants recalled to us the fate of the *raja urung* of Gurukinayan, who was "arrested" and sentenced to death: when the executioner was slow in arriving, he hanged himself in the market hall; villagers then stoned his body. No one told us when this had happened or what he had done to excite such a desire for vengeance, but they were very clear about where and how it had happened. Several people mentioned the headman of Payung Village, who was arrested by armed youths, stabbed, and thrown into the Dog River. (In one version of this story the headman survived this grisly attempt at execution. Naked, he managed to crawl home, where he was discovered and then executed again, this time in front of his family.)

NANDÉ RIKSON BERU TARIGAN: The path going to the fields in our village, no one went that way. Near the river you couldn't pass by there. You couldn't stand the smell of the water. Fish in the Borus [River], I don't know how many years it was they weren't eaten. Because they threw the corpses into the river. Who'd want to eat that? Even when we came home after the evacuation [in 1948] no one ate the fish. It was like they still smelled. That's so you'll know how miserable it was. A lot of people died for no reason, butchered. Do you think that's wrong? Well, the Karo people were all crazy then.

Most stories of *repolusi* were difficult, if not impossible, to place chronologically. The term itself evidently derives from the social revolution of March 1946, but *repolusi* exceeded that brief phase of violent excess in both time and targets. Attacks on collaborator village heads and officials began in late 1945 and continued at least through the first half of 1946. The killing of lowland refugees and political prisoners that Nandé Rikson described occurred around the time of the first Dutch "police action," between the fall of the Medan front in late July 1947 and the initial assault on the highlands in early August of that year. Many of the lowland detainees from the time of the social revolution were also killed during the 1947 evacuation of the highlands. Beyond this, Karo accounts cannot do much to clarify either the timing of particular events or the actual extent of the violence.

Karo recalled *repolusi* in strange signs and vivid images, like the blood-splashed rocks in ravines and the imagined flavor of corpse-fed fish. Terror is encapsulated in a euphemistic word: "How many goats do you want butchered?" someone says, and you know that *goat* means "person." Such are the small signatures of what John Keane (1996) calls "uncivil war," political violence aimed not at the state but at the community itself and conducted without regulation or remorse. "That's how bad it got back then, in the revolution," said Nandé Senantiasa of Payung Village. "We were our own enemies. Holland wasn't our enemy anymore. *Repolusi*, you know, that was all just people hating each other. Friends didn't understand one another anymore."

Bapa Ruth Ginting, an occasional member of our research crew, was one of the few people who spoke of a connection between revolutionary violence and the patriotic aspirations of Independence Time. He had been an employee of the district civil administration under Japanese, interim, and republican governments; at the time of our research he was writing essays and serialized romances set during the independence struggle for the Karo cultural journal *Tenah*. His theory was that the violence was caused by the singing of "imported" French revolutionary anthems like "Darah Rakyat" ("the blood of the people is still flowing . . . the people will judge") and equally sanguinary Japanese fighting songs at village rallies and in marching drills, so in a sense even his explanation detoured around Independence Time's inspirational core.

BAPA RUTH: Like this Japanese air force song: "Powerful hero, restore the destiny of Holland's colonized people. Let me be carried on a tide of blood"—now, that's cruel, there—"so long as we are free." That's how it went. Now that's a cruel song. "Though corpses be spread o'er the field of battle. . . . Annihilate the nation's traitors, though they be our fellows and brothers." Well, this influenced the spirit of the troops. Whoever opposed their wishes was seen as a traitor. Just kill them. . . . So all of this I reckon was precisely on account of the influence of these songs, which destroyed the spirit until there wasn't any feeling of comradeship anymore. That's the danger of these songs.

Repolusi, as most Karo described it, was a discrete and dangerous force, something that could "step forward" at any time. It appeared like a preternatural, almost sentient being: something that existed—like a ghost—outside the realm of ordinary time and space but could burst into that reality at any moment. Sometimes they referred to it as Zaman Repolusi, as if these scattered outbursts of internal violence could be contained in a time of their own, set off from the euphoria and patriotic inspiration of independence. Nandé Senantiasa and her friends in Payung, for instance, argued about how long it had lasted. Though her friends thought it must have gone on for a year or more, Nandé Senantiasa insisted that its duration couldn't have been more than two weeks. "During Revolution Time, you know, there was no government for two weeks," she said. "For two weeks, there wasn't any government to complain to. So the revolution came forward. If this revolution had gone on any longer than that, there wouldn't have been anyone left alive."

Notice how this explanation aligns itself with the authoritarian claims of the state: the *absence* of government is what accounts for the occurrence of violence. "It wasn't just ignorance," commented Mulih Kwala Sebayang, a former sharpshooter from the highland village of Kwala. "Usually, if the nation is in 'chaos,' anything can happen [biasana adi 'cawes' negara, apapun bisa terjadi]. Now this is a modern nation, but if the situation was confused, anything could happen. Like: robbery, murder, rape, whatever, arson, it could happen. Look at Rwanda today. It was like that back then."

For Nandé Senantiasa and her friends, and for many others we spoke to as well, all the terrors of "us against us" coalesce in the mysterious signs and songs of Revolution Time. The stories of spies and collaborators, the rumors of danger that threaded through the routines of daily life, the traces of death, and the fears of betrayal—all these happenings, as if under a kind of narrative quarantine, are sheared off from the popular enthusiasm of independence and the orderly trajectory of the struggle, to be refigured as links in a transhistorical chain of violence, a submerged counternarrative of criminality and treachery that could "come forward" at any moment. In Karo memory and in national history, *repolusi* draws to itself all forms of gratuitous violence and criminality, all resistance to the ordering power of the state. Whether framed by ignorance, foreign influence, musical inspiration, or governmental vacuum, *repolusi* offers itself to the imagination as independence's dark alternative: it is both an anterior sign of subsequent betrayals—the 1948 uprising in Madiun, East Java; the conspiracies of 1965; and all the disturbances of the national status quo attributed by the Suharto regime to communism and its "synonyms"[23]—and a repertoire of conventional images that are used again and again to convey, for different historical moments, the uncivil commonalities of political violence.

DELICIOUS FREEDOM

On the cover of the February 1947 issue of the Karo district government's official magazine *Kebangoenan* (I., Awakening) is a drawing by the Karo artist Roegoen Sembiring.[24] A pastiche of images—a farmer, a soldier (rather Japanese-looking) carrying a rifle and bayonet, the distinctive rooflines of Minangkabau and Karo houses, an airplane, a train, factory smokestacks, the rising sun (also rather Japanese-looking), and, in the top center, a radio tower sending forth communicative lightning bolts—suggests that independence is a vital force merging present and future, action and aspiration. Despite the crudeness of the workmanship, the picture is urgent and dynamic. Everything appears to be in motion except the soldier, who is poised as if on guard. The lines of the train engine echo the form of the Karo house, the swooping rooftops push the viewer's eye upward to the towers of industry and communication (figure 13).

Merdeka may have started out in the hands of nationalist leaders and local intellectuals like Rakutta Berahmana and Selamat Ginting, for whom it meant national self-rule pure and simple, but to the young men and women whose coming of age coincided with the effervescence of independence it came to have more immediate personal implications. In Java this might have meant escaping family responsibilities, or the restrictions of birth in a profoundly hierarchical society, or something as banal as riding the trains for free (Reid 1998:156). In Karoland it meant having new options, a new sense of purpose and personal worth. In sensuous imagination, *merdeka* was articulated through invocations of pleasure, ease, and fulfillment and by promises of a future without limits, in which no opportunity would be lacking.

Against the hardships, humiliations, and limited options that defined "how it felt to be colonized," nationalist propagandists introduced the idea of independence in a series of sharp, vivid contrasts to the brutality and privations of the Japanese occupation. Nandé Sri Arihta captured the contrast precisely when she imagined a movie about the Japanese occupation: "If they made a movie about it they'd call it 'Suffering

KEBANGOENAN

NOMOR 6   PEBROEARI 1947   TAHOEN 1

FIGURE 13. Cover art, *Kebangoenan* 1, no. 6 (February 1947), by Roegoen Sembiring. Wasson Collection, Cornell University Library.

Brings Enjoyment' [I., *Penderitaan membawa nikmat*]. It was because of the suffering that we dared to fight, isn't that so? The result was, independence, right?" Government propaganda kept this vision fresh in popular memory until the fall of the New Order in 1998, when a history of more vivid and immediately encountered forms of unfreedom *within* independence—the 1965 massacres, the "mysterious shootings" of the 1980s, the "killing fields" of Aceh, the tragedies of East Timor and West Papua, the 1998 shooting of student demonstrators at Trisakti University in Jakarta, not to mention the routine forms of oppression and state violence that permeated people's everyday lives during the New Order period—came to be more openly recognized and acknowledged.

The political rhetoric of the New Order was dominated by the intertwined themes of stability and economic progress. Once a heartfelt if inchoate expression of political aspiration and personal yearning, *Merdeka!* was replaced as national watchword by the New Order mantra of *pembangunan*, "development." Nowhere was this shift from *merdeka* to *pembangunan* more vividly displayed than on the billboards and gateways that annually celebrated Independence Day. Drawing on an earlier idiom of political art that Roegoen Sembiring's cover illustration represents, these posters and wall paintings mostly take the form of historical diptych: the left side depicts the struggle for national independence and the right displays the idealized present of a modern, disciplined, and technologically advanced Indonesia, in which natural abundance is harnessed through technology and citizens enthusiastically conform to the disciplinary ideals of the state. Balancing the disorder and violence of the left side's ragged guerrillas, burning houses, and fleeing refugees are today's happy, uniformed students, white-coated scientists, and planned families (with the slogan "Two children, that's enough!"). Gigantic, overflowing cornucopias of fruits and vegetables rest beside tiny images of tractors and harvest combines. There are airplanes, trains, radio (or television) towers, laboratories, factories, and urban skylines as well as the standard signifiers of tourism and regional identity—a couple in ethnic wedding attire and the distinctive rooflines of traditional houses.

A 1995 billboard in Medan showed scenes from the independence struggle there (labeled "Bali Street," "Serdang Street," and "Tembung Front," in case viewers did not recognize the events depicted); the flag-bearing main figure points toward an imaginary cityscape (his future, *our* present) of diligent "Friday cleanups," construction projects, a

FIGURE 14. "Once the sails are unfurled, we cannot retreat." Independence Day billboard, Medan, 1995. Photo by the author.

housing development of tidy, identical homes, and (least plausible of all) clean, uncrowded streets and orderly flows of traffic. In the center, dividing the picture's halves, is a great boat with golden sails, inscribed with the message "Once the sails are unfurled, we cannot retreat." Lest the picture's overall meaning be missed, a huge yellow banner proclaims, "We struggled to achieve independence, now we [must] struggle to fill in independence by improving national discipline" (figure 14). On another 1995 billboard (on the campus of a state teacher's college in Java), a massive, smiling, blue image of President Suharto's head floats in ghostly benevolence above and between a scene of battle (in which a younger, unsmiling Suharto also floats above the fray) on one side and a bird's-eye view of a hypermodern city of skyscrapers on the other; between these and beneath the president's godly blue visage are school children, a well-dressed teacher, and a gowned college graduate, diploma in hand.[25]

In the mid-1990s, the things that Karo remembered best from the *saranen* campaign were neither its entertainments and instructions nor the "chaos" of revolutionary violence with which it was entwined, but rather its promises for the future, once independence had been won. These mostly took the form of modernity's material signs.

MADASA BERU BERAHMANA: One time I remember, I gave a speech to the army cadets at Bukit Kubu [the officer training school outside Berastagi]. I remember well what I said, but I don't know where the idea came from. "Later on, when we have an airplane and that plane roars above Kabanjahé, surely we'll be great too, even though there are many challenges today." To this day I ask myself, how could I say that, where did I get it from? How could I know, I didn't understand this independence stuff, I didn't even know anything about politics. I was just a teacher. Here I was as an Indonesian, in fact a Karo Batak, and I knew just a little bit about how politics works. "Later, when we're independent, we can have our own armada, when we have our own planes, and they roar over Karoland, then we will be great. How could I say that? That's what they call the Karo spirit, in short. They didn't care, they wanted to participate in the struggle of the Indonesian people even though they didn't know anything at all. Like me, I didn't know politics. What a war was. I figured this war would never end. Ah, this is what it'll be like from now on, I thought. Apparently it had an end too.

In Jakarta in 1995, at a conference on the independence struggle in the Karo area, one man mimicked Rakutta's orotund speechmaking, to the great amusement of his audience: "O mothers and fathers, uncles and aunts, sisters and brothers, when we're independent you'll have electricity in every village."[26] Madasa Berahmana also recalled the speakers' promises: "'Later, when we're independent,' they said, 'this is how it will be. We won't pay taxes anymore, all the appliances in houses will be automatic, we'll have telephones, electricity, and so on.' All this was explained to them, and I joined in, explaining it in the villages."

Bapa Mul Sembiring from Gurukinayan echoed Madasa Berahmana's account. A middle school student at the time of independence, he had learned "a bit" about independence himself, he said, but most people only knew what they were told at the *saranen*. "At most, just if you're independent later, you won't pay taxes anymore, we'll all be happier, the roads to the villages will be improved, now it's just in the city that there are radios, but later we'll have radios too, now we use oil lamps but later there will be electricity."

Nandé Rikson recalled promises of an end to such tedious domestic tasks as husking rice and weeding the garden. "Oh, they'd say all kinds of things at these meetings. 'When we're independent,' they'd say, 'you won't have to hoe anymore. Someone will come to hoe the weeds for you. You won't have to husk the rice, someone will come to husk it for you." Nandé Rosali beru Ginting's vision of independence took the form of houses with glass windows and "real wood floors." For Terang beru Singarimbun, independence was the almost unimaginable prospect of portable radios.

TERANG BERU SINGARIMBUN: They told us about colonialism, and how deli-cious [I., *enak*] independence would be. "When we're independent, you'll be able to take a radio anywhere," they said. Even climbing a sugar palm you could take a radio. . . . We couldn't imagine it because we'd never seen a radio in the villages. That's how delicious this independence will be. So all our spirits were inflamed.

The word I translate above as *delicious* is the Indonesian *enak*. It might also be rendered as *delightful, tasty, pleasant, nice*—all connoting bodily enjoyment or pleasure. Nandé Senantiasa, from the village of Payung, used the roughly synonymous Karo word *ntabeh* (delicious) to describe the postindependence future.

NANDÉ SENANTIASA BERU BANGUN: We'd gather for a meeting, right? Knocked on the table, we all got quiet. . . . So, "When we're independent, you mothers, sisters, fathers all, it'll be delicious [K., *ntabeh*]. We'll all be able to go to Medan," he said. They'd never even seen it, only been to Kabanjahé a few times. We can order shrimp paste from the market. . . . When we're independent it'll be delicious. Now you all have to do the hoe-ing, he said. You won't have to hoe anymore, a tractor will come. All you'll have to do is carry the rice seed out to the fields, isn't that what he said? The tractor will come *gerdok-gerdok-gerdok*. What is a tractor? we thought. Airplanes will come, they said.

In an article titled "Ice Boxes Sabotage Colonialism," then-president Sukarno was quoted on the important part that the American film indus-try played in inciting the national revolutions of postwar Asia. Movies, he said, "provided a window on the world," through which colonized people could see the things they had been deprived of. "It is perhaps not generally realized that a refrigerator can be a revolutionary symbol—to a people who have no refrigerators. A motor car owned by a worker in one country can be a symbol of revolt to a people deprived of even the necessities of life."[27] Refrigerators and automobiles could, he thought, generate a kind of revolutionary consciousness, in the form of an aware-ness of deprivation. Karo imagined independence through objects that connoted visibility and openness (electric lights, glass windows), mobil-ity and connection (roads, radios, airplanes), because these were the pre-requisites of national belonging. They were what enabled people to think of themselves as (potential) members of a modern community made up of not-yet-known but equivalent others. Dreams of electric appliances, radios, tractors, and hired workers reflected more than a desire for a more luxurious lifestyle; they laid out the conditions necessary for rural women and men to think beyond the village. In concrete form, they expressed an inchoate yet profound recognition of the possibility of the nation and the wish for a future share in the world it promised.

Nande Marlina and her singing partners in Mardinding happily pictured today's roads and rural electrification as the "rewards" of independence.

> NANDÉ MARLINA BERU GINTING: Whoever would have thought that Mardinding here would have lights and electricity? Well, no one would have thought it. Who would have thought you could go all the way up Mount Sinabun on a road? That's how it feels to be independent. Roads everywhere, electricity in the middle of the forest. We've nothing to regret, now we've got our reward.

> NANDÉ BUNGAREM BERU SINGARIMBUN: They had *saranen* here, sonny. "There'll be electricity in the forest," they said.

> ND. MARLINA: It's not true, we said, not true.

> NANDÉ BAHAGIA BERU TARIGAN: Impossible.

> ND. BUNGAREM: Impossible. I got sick back then, and I thought, "If I die, what is this *merdeka*?" I thought, "Don't let me die. I want to see electricity in the forest."

> ND. BAHAGIA: It happened.

> ND. BUNGAREM: It happened.

> ND. MARLINA: You can put it in your fields.

> ND. BAHAGIA: There'll be rice mills, they said. We didn't believe it.

When ideals are embodied in mediating objects such as these, it is possible to get the things themselves but miss what they stood for. In 1994, before a plague of economic and political crises made Indonesian national integrity and economic progress look for a time more like a hope than a certainty, Mbeligai Bangun and his wife, Rasi beru Ginting, from Batu Karang measured the promises of Independence Time against the hardships of the Japanese occupation—"Blackout Time," they called it, when people burned castor beans because they had no oil for lamps.

> RASI BERU GINTING: They told us, they said, independence will be so delicious [K., *entabeh*]—

> MBELIGAI BANGUN: So be diligent giving rice to the soldiers, they said, treat them nice—

> R. BR. G.: We won't have to pound rice, they said, cooking rice we won't have to collect firewood, they said. That's exactly the way it is now.

> M. B.: Right, if you want to buy fish, then the fish will be delivered to your door.

R. BR. G.: We'll be happy then, they said.

M. B.: If you want to buy cloth, it'll be delivered to your door.

R. BR. G.: We'll be happy then once we're independent, they said.

M. B.: We won't be colonized by anyone, they said. . . .

R. BR. G.: Like pounding rice back then. Now we don't have to pound rice, there's a rice mill to do it. Isn't it nice to have lights? Back then the only lights we had were those lamps on the wall.

M. B.: Just a little oil lamp was considered pretty good.

R. BR. G.: If you look at life back then and you look at it now, we're pretty happy now.

M. B.: Back then even a little lamp with a wick was already nice. Castor beans, you'd skewer them on a string.

R. BR. G.: You know, that was back during the Blackout. During the Blackout, you know, there wasn't any oil to buy, no salt, not anything.

This dialogue's double comparison charts a direct line of material progress from Japanese Time to New Order, even as it bypasses the intervening ORLA (Orde Lama, "Old Order") years and the brutality of the 1965 regime change. The economic successes of the present confirm the truth of Independence Time's seemingly extravagant promises. "That's what they told us so we'd want this *merdeka*," said Nandé Senantiasa, an active veteran from the village of Payung, who cited her recently obtained government pension as proof of independence's offerings. "Now you see all those things have happened." One woman exemplified independence by a plane trip she'd taken to visit her son in Jakarta: "See, we can go anywhere now." Another saw the propagandists' promise that "someone will come to hoe the weeds for you" fulfilled in the influx of impoverished Javanese laborers to Karo villages. "Now we can hire these Javanese to do the work for us," she said with satisfaction. Selective recall or even downright retrofitting (as with Nandé Senantiasa's recollection of the promise of a pension) strained Karo recollections to fit the framework of such New Order "successes" as these.

In these statements of national enjoyment, independence is emptied of political content, then refilled with development's shallow rhetoric of money and goods. Yet even within that depoliticized space two readings are possible. In the first of these, the New Order is revealed as the embodiment of national aspirations—what independence had, all unrecognized, been about from the beginning. The cynicism such a reading should provoke was heightened, even before Suharto's fall, by the fact—rarely mentioned, but quite well known—that the roads, electricity, and running water that now appear as the rewards of independence were selectively bestowed, following national elections, on villages that filled the desired voting quotas for Golkar, the official party of the New Order regime.

The second reading might be called an "Old Order" interpretation. Recalling the frequency with which Karo informants referred to themselves as ORLA people, the ubiquitous portraits of Sukarno prominently displayed in their homes, and the pride with which they spoke of their contributions not just to the struggle itself but also to the national project during the brief heyday of Indonesian democratization in the 1950s, one might suspect that by identifying the material benefits of the present as "rewards" of independence, they were reclaiming them as things *already embedded* in the act of proclaiming independence and as *already earned* by their own efforts and sacrifices.

> RAJAI GINTING: Back then, the Bupati, Bupati Rakutta Sembiring was the one who spoke in our village. "Once we're independent this is how it will be," he said. Everything they said in the *saranen* came true. "Buses will come all the way to our village, there will be electricity, running water." It all happened. Some villages like ours, they just recently got water. The same with electricity, it's new in our village. Water's just been here for a year. That's the result of his words.

Fifty years after independence, the memory of *repolusi* continued to shadow the nation: in public reminders of the "great chain of violence" that linked nonconforming events of the struggle to an ongoing conspiracy of the left; in an army-dominated regime that recognized certain kinds of brutality but not others; in a political rhetoric that demonized those whose paths diverged from the smooth route to national unity and warned continually of "latent dangers," secret communists, and "formless organizations" working to destroy that unity. What *positive* vision of independence could have endured through thirty years of such heavy-handed propaganda and authoritarian rule? For Karo veterans of the 1945 generation, to speak about independence without bitterness or a sense of betrayal required that they celebrate the nation's successes in whatever constricted idiom they could find. Faced with the ordinary unfreedoms of life under the New Order, they imagined independence in the form of delicious objects—radios, glass windows, airplanes, tractors—and returned them, in memory, to their proper place, at the beginning of independence.

CHAPTER 4

Eager Girls

In April 1946 Rakutta Berahmana was appointed head of the republic's civilian government for the Karo district, with the newly created Javanese title of *bupati*. This is how his family found out about it. His wife, Nandé Berah, was staying with her in-laws in the village of Limang at the time. "All we knew," she said, "was that he was spending a lot of time in Kabanjahé." It was her maternal aunt Nandé Tékén who brought the news when she came to help with the rice harvest. "Oh, Nandé Berah," the old lady announced breathlessly (in Nandé Berah's laughing rendition), "Bapa Berah's become a *merpati*," meaning a dove. "It's kind of like a king [M., *raja*]," the aunt went on to explain. "He's the king of Karoland!"

On the face of it, this story seems to be a simple illustration of the conceptual gap in nationalist thinking that divides an urban leadership from its rural constituency.[1] Political leaders in the Karo district took their ideas of nationhood from an internationalist discourse of modernity and their cues for action from the republic's Javanese center. Villagers tried, not always successfully, to make sense of those acts in terms of local values, common experiences, and familiar concepts. So, in a chain of linguistic misrepresentations, Nandé Tékén renders the strange Javanese title *bupati* as the semihomonymic (and probably also unfamiliar) Malay *merpati*, turning Bapa Berah momentarily into a dove before he becomes, almost as inappropriately, a king. A raja is of course precisely what the *bupati* is intended *not* to be—that is, a hereditary lord—and yet it is the closest analogue to that position of general leadership in the Karo lexicon. It is this conceptual misfitting that is highlighted by the intrusion of *merpati* into the sequence of Rakutta's transformations.

To become a raja (or a dove) is to enter the realm of legend, a space determinedly local in its narrative conceits even when it contains the outside world within its storied domain. To speak of the "king of Karoland" is to replace colonial dependency with native sovereignty and to conceive of political authority as coterminous with cultural space. The title "raja" interrupts the flow of power at the edge of the Karo world—or, in this case, it might be more proper to say that it *extends* the flow of power to the edge of the Karo world, since one of Rakutta's first actions was to stake a claim to the predominantly Karo areas in the four adjoining districts. Yet it also echoes with foreignness. According to local histories, the honorific Malay title of *raja berempat*, "four kings," was bestowed on four Karo headmen by the sultan of Aceh in exchange for their (nominal) fealty. This largely forgotten title was revived by the Dutch to form the administrative capstone of indirect rule in the Karo district. The ironies and complications of Nandé Berah's story multiply further when you discover that her elderly aunt Nandé Tékén was the sister of Ngerajai Meliala, the *sibayak* of Sarinembah, who, as *primus inter pares* of the "four kings," headed the native government of the Karo subdistrict under the Japanese and transitional administrations—thus being, quite literally, the raja of Karoland—before he was so unceremoniously replaced by his nephew-in-law (K., *kéla*) Rakutta.

What makes this story both more and less than an illustration of the contradictions and miscommunications that plague peasant nationalisms is that it locates these in the heart of the family, along the lines of gender. The contrast between female naïveté and male ambition around which Nandé Berah constructs her story is a key feature of Karo thinking about gender and politics. Playing to this stereotype allows the narrative's humor to flow in two directions at once, gently mocking the ignorance of its female interlocutors Nandé Berah and Nandé Tékén, but also pricking the grandiose ambitions of men like Rakutta, who would be kings of Karoland.

Nationalisms, as Ann McClintock (1995:260) points out, are always gendered. The gendering of the nation may be obvious and symbolic, as in metaphors of motherland or heroic cults of military masculinity. Care for the nation may be enfolded with desire for one's beloved, in patriotic love songs or inspirational poems like this verse from the front cover of the PNI journal *Radikal* (October 1946), titled "Kepada Seri-kandi" (For a Heroine): *Are you not delighted-happy/to have for a sweetheart the nation's hero?/You are pretty, he's an officer./What great fortune in the world!*[2] Gender can be embedded in the promises of independence and in the objects and opportunities through which that freedom comes to be both imagined and desired. It can be embodied in the physical disciplines and practices of national participation, delineated in the allocation of social tasks, or inscribed in national space, as in the familiar separation of front lines from home front. It can be fixed in the active "forgetting" of certain forms of participation and the privileged remembering of others.

For moderate Karo leaders like Rakutta Berahmana and his PNI-Napindo comrade Selamat Ginting, a gender revolution was never really part of the nationalist agenda. Nevertheless, social programs put in place at the beginning of independence, when these men and others were constructing a new postcolonial order in Karoland, had a profound impact on women's lives. This was especially so for girls whose coming of age coincided with the repressions of Japanese Time. They had been sequestered, taken out of school, hidden away, disfigured, married off. Suddenly they were being called upon to take part in the collective struggle against colonialism, to enact a public role in the play of independence, to serve as romantic objects of soldiers' desire. School-teachers, nurses, and other young educated women found a public voice and, for some, a prominent role in nationalist associations; they spoke at public rallies, led village work groups, ran literacy programs, and organized agit-prop dramas and didactic entertainments. They saw themselves as contributing to the improvement of rural life, primarily through the inculcation of metropolitan standards of respectability: cleanliness, order, discipline, propriety, and the virtues of domesticity. Village girls, who were the primary target of their more cosmopolitan sisters' efforts, found occasions for learning, travel, work, and, above all, a measure of personal autonomy and a new sense of social worth, however brief its duration.

More so than men, Karo women—girls, I should say, because the kind of personal autonomy and spare time required in order to take part in nationalist activities pretty much ended for women upon marriage—were captivated by Independence Time's possible future. They seem to have taken to heart the encomiums and exhortations of the nationalist propaganda campaign, its expectation of cheerful sacrifice and promises of "delicious" freedom. They imagined this future through the electric lights, tractors, glass windows, radios, and air-planes that were modernity's visible signs and through the possibilities of mobility and visibility that these signs represented.

Looking back on the euphoria and excitement of Independence Time, Karo women sometimes described their younger selves as *meliar*. This term is generally glossed as "energetic, helpful, hardworking, showing initiative"; I translate it here as *eager*—though *feisty* might actually come closer to its nuances of self-assertion. Nandé Lina beru Karo of Mardinding was just reaching her teens at the time of independence; when it came to military training, she said, "I was so eager I wouldn't ever remember to cook the rice for supper. I'd get home and my mother would slap me. 'Why haven't you cooked the rice, why haven't you gathered the firewood?' she'd say. We were having so much fun I forgot all about my chores at home."

> NANDÉ SRI ARIHTA BERU BANGUN: In our village we were the most eager [I./K., *yang terliar*], just a couple of us who were the most eager, like that. Eager *[liar]* as all that, but I didn't talk much back then. It was just my spirit really—what can I do, so I don't have to hoe anymore?—something like that. If this happens, let me not have to hoe anymore, it's hard work. If we actually, if we truly are independent, I said, we won't have to hoe anymore. Because of my spirit, I wasn't afraid of anything. I actually wasn't afraid of anything, to this day I'm not afraid of anything, even if your uncle here [her husband] leaves me at home alone, I'm not scared. I can go anywhere by myself.

Meliar is etymologically cognate to the Malay *liar*, "wild," and this coincidence serves as the pivot of another of the many Karo jokes about cross-cultural miscommunication. In this story, a Dutch officer approaches a village headman and asks him if there are any *orang liar* (M., lit., "wild men," but in the Dutch-Malay patois meaning "rebels" or "outlaws") in the area. The headman, thinking that the Dutchman is looking to hire some hard-working porters or other willing laborers, responds with enthusiasm, "Oh, sir, believe me when I say that there are many of them around here. Take that fellow over there, he's *meliar*. Actually I too am *meliar*!" And so he was arrested. Fortunately someone explained the mistake in time; otherwise he would have been taken away.

Hardworking, industrious, curious, bright, energetic, busy, self-motivated, enthusiastic: these were the qualities that women indicated when they described themselves as *meliar*. But when I repeated their self-description to others, I was quickly corrected. When applied to women, I was informed, the meaning of *meliar* comes closer to the

Malay *liar*. A *meliar* woman is not industrious but wild, unruly, out of control, out of place, and above all promiscuous. Women could not possibly refer to themselves that way, I was told—and yet they did. They could have used instead the common Indonesian word *rajin* (hard-working, industrious) or the Karo terms *tutus até* (conscientious, serious, dedicated) and *mejingkat* (lively, diligent, nimble, willing). But none of these quite captured the edgy adolescent sensibility of the gender-inappropriate *meliar*, which indexed both masculine energy and feminine restlessness. And so I repeat it here, recognizing its ambivalent articulation of agency and desire, to suggest the contradictions and tangents, the opportunities, uncertainties, and dead ends of gender in a time of struggle, which are the subject of this chapter.

PARABLES OF COMMUNITY

For the eager girls of the Generation of 1945, neither the soldier's trope of progress nor the nostalgic "romance of the struggle" worked to explicate the experience of independence. Their stories ran instead to parables of community. They recalled the beginning of independence as an extended moment of collective endeavor, communal harmony, and hopeful energy, running from the end of the Japanese occupation to the evacuation of the highlands during the first Dutch military campaign in 1947. Sandwiched between two periods of privation and fear, this interval has taken on an idyllic quality in memory: if not a time of plenty, it is at least one of promise.

Women's stories of Independence Time often emerged dialogically, in the company of others. Family members or neighbors joined us to listen or contribute to our conversations. More than an audience, they served as a supporting chorus or as alternative interlocuters, asking questions, swapping stories, adding or correcting information, occasionally disagreeing. Sometimes our informants invited friends along to our meetings—to help them remember, they said. Some of our most successful and illuminating interviews were conducted with small groups of women, either arranged informally by our village "aunts" and "grandmothers" or set up for us by local officials.

Women recalled Independence Time for us in narratives of hard work and dedication. For them, the stories that mattered told of industrious selves responding to the special demands and responsibilities placed upon them by the call of independence. In this they echoed the inspiring rhetoric of the *saranen* campaign. They spoke of the beginning of independence as a time saturated with the delicious promises of freedom. They dwelt on curiosities and commonplaces: on new words that could be savored for their strangeness, like *bupati* and *merdeka;* on new skills and forms of knowledge, like shooting a rifle and reading a newspaper; and on ordinary activities that took on a new significance when illuminated by the spirit of struggle, like cooking and pounding rice.

Women's stories of Independence Time characteristically took the form of generalized events and shared remembrances. They dwelt on the typical rather than the exceptional and emphasized recurrence rather than divergence; they had less to do with dramatic occurrences and singular experiences than with the routines of life in an extraordinary time. They mostly steered clear of the grander political forces and forms of the struggle, remaining resolutely close to the local ground and the familiar details of shared experience. These stories were usually told in the first-person plural form *kita* (I./K., we all). More than just a politely inclusive way of speaking, this was also an expression of collective action and communal agency.

NGEREM BERU SINGARIMBUN: There were about ten of us from here, or maybe fifteen, who did the cooking. We took turns. Say this is our group's turn. Tomorrow it would be the Sukatendel group, then the next day the Tiga Nderket group, then the day after that the Mardinding group. Then it would start over with Kuta Mbaru. That's how we did it. What they called the public kitchen. At first it was at Nandé Katana's house in Tiga Nderket. What they called the public kitchen. Then it was moved to Kabanjahé, we cooked at the Bupati's office. We took turns there too, we all took turns, you know, several villages. We all cooked together at the public kitchen.

Accounts like these didn't fit comfortably within the frame of a ready-made chronology, nor could they easily meet the evidentiary criteria of pension verification. There was little in them that could be described as eventful at all. For this reason, some found them easy to disregard, like the Berastepu headman who commented that women just did the cooking, as they had done before and were doing still. "What kind of struggle is that?" he laughed.

Women tended to view the matter differently. When my "middle mother" (K., *nandé tengah,* FBW) in Berastepu invited a group of older women to her home to talk to us, the conversation soon turned to cooking.

NANDÉ MADASA BERU GINTING: During Independence Time women were really the most important.

NANDÉ RIKSON BERU TARIGAN: True. They did the cooking, they did whatever had to be done.

NANDÉ LIA BERU TARIGAN: Cook or whatever, they never got angry.

ND. M.: If men had to do it, like I said, begging for grain from the houses, how could a man do that? Or pounding rice, what man knows how to do that? As soon as we got the grain, we'd pound it. We didn't even dry it, no. As soon as it was pounded, cook it. How could a man do that? But [now] it's as if women had no part in the struggle, isn't it?

ND. R. AND ND. L.: Right.

ND. M.: Then we were the best, at the beginning of independence we were the best. But now there's no more meaning in being a woman.

ND. R.: No.

ND. M.: At first we were the most important ones.

ND. R.: Not even the leaders from around here [K., *si kepala-kepala arah enda ndai*, "the heads around here"] remember the women now.

Youthful exuberance and political rhetoric come together in the recollections of both elite and village women to generate a highly idealized, self-assured picture of the beginning of independence as a time when they counted for something: when "we were the best . . . we were the important ones." They said: "that's why we were so tired," or "there was no lack of tiredness," as if their remembered tiredness could serve as a legitimating credential, much as the names and dates of pension testimonials served for their male counterparts. So their accounts piled up tasks and responsibilities, training and travel. In Payung Village, Nandé Usman, assisted by her friend Nandé Senantiasa, condensed the remembered experience of Independence Time in a series of shared labors.

NANDÉ USMAN BERU PANDIA: In the beginning, in the year of '45, we had training. Learning to handle a spear, stuff like that. Then, once that was done, we graduated. By then there was already fighting. There were people who were hurt. We were in the Red Cross. We'd treat them there, whoever was injured. When we were finished with that, the headman came, well, you're not done yet. There's rice to be prepared. You all husk it first.

NANDÉ SENANTIASA BERU BANGUN: There's no rice for the soldiers, he said.

ND. U.: No rice for the soldiers. You all go to the rice mortars and pound it, he said. So we all went there.

ND. S.: We all went to pound the rice.

ND. U.: So after we went there, once we were done with that—

ND. S.: Take it to the supply storehouse, you should say.

ND. U.: Right. We took it to the storehouse.

ND. S.: To Pérés [PRS]. "Pérés" is what they called the storehouse.

ND. U.: Yeah, to the supply storehouse. Once we were done with that, then we'd start with the drills. It never stopped.

ND. S.: So then at night you had to go collect rice [contributions], once that was done.

ND. U.: At night too. Get the rice, cook for the soldiers, nonstop.

ND. S.: Yeah, if they came at night you had to cook.

ND. U.: We didn't go to the fields anymore, child, in getting this independence. So that's why, at the time, there was no shortage of tiredness for us. So, for instance, say there was a wounded soldier, right, friend? Go gather wild greens from the hillside.

ND. S.: That's for his dinner.

ND. U.: Oh, and grinding medicines. Grinding medicines for the soldiers.

ND. S.: Right. So say the injury is healed. Well, you're still not done. There aren't any cigarettes for our soldiers. Here's the tobacco, you all roll cigarettes for our soldiers to smoke, said our headman.

Accounts like this are hard to use for history. It's not just that the activities Nandé Usman and Nandé Senantiasa described were, by their very nature, mundane and repetitive—cooking, pounding rice, training— or that they transformed what can have been only occasional occurrences, like gathering wild greens for a wounded soldier, into generalized events, as if such things were part of an everyday routine. It's also that they depicted these activities as if they were all the work of a single, recurrent day. It didn't seem to matter that military drills were held in the first year of independence but began to wane by May 1946, when most of the militia recruits (and all of the carbines) had been sent off to Bandar Baru or the Medan front, or that caring for injured fighters would have been necessary only during the first military campaign in 1947. The collection of foodstuffs for Pérés (PRS, Pertahanan Rakyat Semesta, I., Total Popular Defense, an agency established in January 1949) must have taken place during the second military campaign, when guerrilla units set up bases along the northern side of the Karo plateau.[3] The activities Nandé Usman and Nandé Senantiasa described are not concurrent, but they are conceptually linked to the idea of independence as something to be earned through hard work and sacrifice.

GENDER LINES

Total popular involvement in the independence struggle did not mean that everyone was expected to participate in the same way or even at the same time. Gender was the primary means through which responsibilities and expectations were channeled and defined. This was the message of the song "Erkata Bedil," in which the trope of a lovers' parting dialogue separated and delineated the complementary responsibilities of young volunteers and their female counterparts. Its catchy melody and simple storyline, in which a young man is called to report for duty at the front while his sweetheart remains at home, faithfully tending the fields and preparing the rice to feed the soldiers, made it a cathectic node of nostalgic remembrance for male veterans of the '45 generation. Sempa Sitepu, a former TRI company commander from the village of Ergaji, on the southeastern side of the Karo plateau, used the song to illustrate the wartime division of labor. "That's the point of the dialogue between the boy and girl in 'Erkata Bedil,'" he said, then broke into song: *Rifle reports in Medan city/calling us to report for duty.* Going to fight, that's the boy. So what's the task at the rear? To increase the supply of food. . . . There was a public kitchen, at the rear lines, to supply food during the fighting."

The song's bifurcated logic of gendered space and double mobilization suggests, but does not fully cover, the social division of wartime labor, which surpassed both the conventional generational fixation on "youth" as nationalist actors and the standard military sexualization of space in terms of (masculine) front lines and (feminine) home front. Mothers were asked to permit or even encourage their sons to go fight the Dutch. Parents were required to contribute to the upkeep of their soldier-sons by paying for their uniforms, shoes, weapons, and, of course, their food. Wives were expected to support and sustain their families in a husband's absence and to supervise the collection and preparation of food in public kitchens. Unmarried girls were called upon not simply to continue their work in the fields and home and to inhabit the romantic fantasies of young men at the front. They also served as propagandists, teachers, nurses, cooks, laborers, and— perhaps someday—as a reserve military force. They delivered food to the front, made bullets, rolled cigarettes for the soldiers, acted in plays, and tramped from village to village attending political rallies. They were an enthusiastic audience for the star turns of celebrity orators or for the local stardom of uniformed soldiers and new recruits and a mocking chorus for young men unwilling to volunteer for military service. Some even became celebrities themselves, for a time.

A "tireless speaker for the struggle" was how Encik Kumpul beru Muham described herself. "Of all the female orators," she said with pride, counting off her friends Roncah beru Barus, Madasa Berahmana, and a few other educated girls, "I was probably the one who gave the most speeches. . . . There's probably not a single village where I haven't spoken." She had gotten her start as an orator during the BOMPA campaign in the final year of the Japanese occupation, during which she headed a branch of the official women's association, the Fujinkai. "*Fujin* means 'women,' *kai* means 'organization,'" she explained. "So, Fujinkai is 'Women's Organization.' Yeah, at the time we only had one organization. . . . it was just like a women's association, so that there was unity and secondly so that women as a whole were conscious of their duty and responsibility in the household and in the nation." 'Cik Muham was a language instructor at the local teachers college, and her conversations, though primarily in Indonesian, were routinely larded with foreign phrases. Switching momentarily into English, she continued: "*To be a good wife, to be a good*—whatever—*member of* society. Yeah that's it, right, first a good wife, a good mother, and then a good member of society. That was the goal of our indoctrination to women as a group. It went on, too. That's what we continued after independence in women's organizations."

Her *saranen* speeches, as she recalled them, went beyond such conventional sentiments of female domesticity; instead, they bristled with the conflicting terms of a gendered nationalism. "If it was in a big public rally," she said, "what they called giant rallies, if the *bupati* was there, when it was his time to speak, he'd always stand up. 'Before I speak,' he'd say, 'I invite my sister here to speak.' So I always spoke at the giant rallies. Invite the youths so they'd dare to fight, and the mothers so they'd give their sons permission and their daughters to join the struggle. So we truly succeeded I think, there was no one who didn't want to join the struggle. They all joined in." In these speeches she asserted a sexual division of labor while invoking the essential "sameness" of men and women and played on such gender stereotypes as military masculinity, maternal nurturance, and feminine morality.

'CIK MUHAM: To the men, I'd say this: "Hey you men, don't be scared, if you're afraid to fight to defend our nation, then you're not men. You're a waste of the mother's milk you drank." That's what I said. There were even some men who threatened me for talking like that. "What's that you said?" they said. "Yes, that's what I said, a waste of the mother's milk that nursed you. She raised you to be a good child. If you don't love independence your mother will regret that she gave birth to you," I said. Well, at the time we were all inspired, Mer, we were all inspired, no one was scared.

"What was your message for the women?" I asked.

> For women it was even more intense. "We're all the same," I said. "Woman and man were created the same by the Lord God. Now, if men have the responsibility to defend our nation and to struggle for independence, must women just stay at home? No. If it's not yet necessary we needn't pick up weapons. But if it's necessary someday, we'll do that too. Right now we don't have to go, because it's not needed, yet let's work hard. Give us rice to feed our soldiers. Otherwise, how will our soldiers eat? If there are tomatoes, peppers, vegetables, onions in your fields, bring them here. So I can give them to the battalion commander, so I can give them to the militia commander. So our soldiers at the front lines don't have to go hungry."

Much of the gendering of nationalist discourse is done through idioms of family and kinship. Tropes of kinship provide a familiar idiom of social differentiation. This makes them useful in justifying and, indeed, in constructing the forms of inequality that precede as well as underwrite the "deep, horizontal comradeship" of national belonging (Anderson 1991:7). They also function rhetorically to invoke a sense of social connectedness, organic unity, and moral obligation. If, as Benedict Anderson asserts, the family is understood to be a "domain of disinterested love and solidarity," it can serve as an apt mode for expressing "political love" for the nation (1991:143–44). 'Cik Muham's accusation that a man afraid to defend the nation was "a waste of the mother's milk [he] drank" perfectly illustrates this point.

As fundamental principles of social ordering and as felt reality, the patterns of kinship and family are woven into the practices of everyday life through actual relationships with familiar others. This is what gives them their compelling power in the national imaginary. Putting this slightly differently, you could say that it is through avenues of social identification such as gender and kinship that people approach the nation and their place within it. This is not a simple moment of recognition, in which one suddenly becomes aware of oneself as part of an imagined community of equals, theoretically interchangeable and simultaneously present yet never entirely knowable. It is a historical process of subject formation through specific, repeated, sometimes contested, and always mutable patterns of gendered action.

This gendering of nationalist practice can also be seen in its accommodations to the routines and schedules of daily life. Take for instance 'Cik Muham's explanation of why the *saranen* didn't start until after nine o'clock at night:

'CIK MUHAM: We'd get home in the middle of the night. Because the *saranen* didn't start until nine o'clock over there. That's how Karo are, right, Mer? They go to the fields [in the daytime]. Home from the fields, they cook. Slop the pigs. Feed the chickens. Then the village head comes by, the little gong calls them—*poong!*—to assemble. You know the small gong [K., *penganak*]? *Poong*, this house. After they've eaten, we all come out. *saranen* tonight, he says. So after eating everyone goes to the soccer field or to the meeting hall, so we can hear the *saranen*, so. Starting at what time, nine o'clock at the earliest, and sometimes ten even, finished up at midnight. Go home to Batu Karang. Just imagine, no wonder I came down with bronchitis.

This is not, of course, a description of "how Karo are"; it's a description of how Karo *women* are. The activities 'Cik Muham describes were typically women's—and particularly married women's—work. Both before and after marriage, women were responsible for all aspects of the rural household economy. Karo women, said Sempa Sitepu, are the "backbone of the family. . . . You could say that men, when there's no danger, their work is just playing chess in the coffee shop and so forth, but as for women, they are the ones who satisfy the needs of the family." Men might help with seasonal agricultural work, tend their oxen or buffaloes, or watch the children while wives were out in the fields; they might make money (or lose it) through such typical masculine occupations as long-distance trade and gambling; but the daily agricultural labor of planting and transplanting, weeding, harvesting, and storing the crops was principally women's work. Women slopped the pigs and fed the dogs and chickens, husked and winnowed grain, prepared meals, cared for children, hauled water, washed dishes and clothes. They wove the mats, storage bags, and baskets that served as the main articles of domestic furniture in rural dwellings. Women's domestic work in effect defined who they were, and where they belonged: *si rukat nakan*, "the one who stirs the rice," or *si mere babi*, "the one who feeds the pigs," are polite terms a man used to refer to his wife (Kipp 1998). Rallies were held at night so that women could attend them too.

"Nation-time" may be gendered in another sense as well. Nationalist thinking, McClintock argues, tends to veer between nostalgic imagining of an idealized, traditional past and impatient movement toward an equally idealized, modern future. This "temporal anomaly" is often managed by posing it as a "natural division of *gender*," in which women are identified as representatives of the "atavistic and authentic body of national tradition" and men as "the progressive agent[s] of national modernity" (McClintock 1995:92).[4]

Karo thinking about gender followed only partway along these lines. As in many other upland societies of island Southeast Asia in which public influence and authority are seen as effects of mobility, spheres of gendered activity were mapped onto an opposition of "home" and "away." The relative mobility of men and women was shaped by local assumptions about their character and appropriate conduct. Using a somewhat circular logic, Karo argued that because women lacked worldly knowledge and experience, they should properly stay at home and direct their efforts toward sustaining the household economy; these domestic responsibilities in turn meant that they had neither the need nor the opportunity for wider experience. Their soft and sympathetic natures (K., *keleng até*, roughly "compassion" or "sense of pity") suited them for this domestic role but put them at risk in the outside world.

Karo girls as a rule stayed close to home until marriage, when they were expected to move to their husband's parents' village. After marriage, household responsibilities left them with little time for going places. Travel beyond the range of known kin and familiar landscape was considered quite dangerous for women because of their vulnerability to the attentions of spirits that haunted river fords, ravines, forests, crossroads, and other wild places. Young girls who ventured into such places would have their faces mottled with red betel juice to imitate smallpox lesions or painted with magical designs to render them unattractive to lonely and lovelorn spirits (or, later, to Japanese soldiers), who might otherwise accost or kidnap them.

If women's lives were circumscribed by the requirements of domestic labor, men's were measured by the extent of their travels. Terms of reference for Karo wives associated them with the work of the household; the equivalent term for husbands, "the one who returns to this house," implies the opposite. Because they were seen as "harder" and more self-interested than women, men were considered to be more capable of worldly engagement. With fewer responsibilities at home, they were relatively free to engage in such typically masculine activities as long-distance trade, livestock herding, gambling, political reputation building, and—most of all—just talking.

But despite their identification of women with the household and the domestic economy, Karo did not associate women with traditional values in need of protection from the influences of a foreign modernity, for the simple reason that in the 1940s they did not see tradition and modernity as antithetical conditions. Nor did they associate traditional values with the domestic sphere. Upholding customary lifeways and preserving an essential Karo identity were not thought of as responsibilities for women. These were understood to be located in the wide network of kin relations constructed and performed through public rituals, customary negotiations, and formal oratory—in other words, in the male-identified world of kinship and politics. Nor was the gender of the agents of national modernity clearly marked. If women were naturally atavistic and socially conservative—or soft and inexperienced—then special efforts of education and indoctrination were needed in order to bring them, too, into the state of national modernity.

In the last decade of Dutch rule, new educational programs for girls, in the form of finishing schools and home economics courses, underscored the conceptual divide between female domesticity and male mobility at the same time that they created opportunities for some girls to both travel and work outside the household. Girls learned to knit and sew through the CMCM (D./M., Christelijk Meisjes Club Madjoe, "Modern Christian Girls Club") (figure 15). Private institutions like the Kabanjahé Meisjeskopschool (D., Girls' Finishing School) promoted European-inflected notions of feminine skill and virtue as distinctively modern attributes and cast educated girls in the role of social vanguard in their communities.[5]

Benedict Anderson (1991:121–22) argues that Indonesian national consciousness was fostered in part by the colonial education system, a "colossal, highly rationalized, tightly centralized hierarchy" in which young scholar-pilgrims encountered others who, despite differences of origin, culture, language, or religion, shared the same experience of schooling. This shared experience "gave the maps of the colony which they studied . . . a territorially specific imagined reality which was every day confirmed by the accents and physiognomies of their classmates." Instead of the "educational pyramid" that Anderson describes, what Karo students, male and female, encountered was an array of truncated, relatively autonomous educational pathways. Even by provincial standards, Karo leaders were modestly educated, and the great majority of the population had no more than a year or two of vernacular schooling at best. They were part of a multilingual educational world, of Karo, Malay, Batak, Acehnese, Dutch, Arabic, and Japanese, among other languages; of trade institutes and business schools, home economics courses, vernacular religious instruction, teacher training and nursing programs, classes for farmers—each of which was intended to slot its pupils into a specific socioeconomic role and status. Some of these schools were part of the colonial public education system, but many

FIGURE 15. Mrs. Van den Berg with a group of CMCM girls, c. 1935. Reproduced with permission of the Utrechts Archief.

were mission-sponsored or privately supported. For all but the most privileged Karo students, educational opportunities were effectively cut off at the fifth- or sixth-grade level. At the time of the independence proclamation, only two Karo men were enrolled in tertiary education programs—one in a German mission-run Lutheran seminary in Tapanuli and the other in law school in Java. As far as I know, no girls had progressed beyond the eighth or ninth grade, and most went no further than the vernacular *volksschool* (D., village primary school), which ended with the third grade.

"Not many people were educated back then," 'Cik Muham pointed out to us. "Not many had graduated from HIS [Dutch-language elementary school]. Not many had graduated from the Meisjes Normaalschool [school for midlevel female teachers, in West Sumatra, which 'Cik Muham had attended]. It was just us, we were considered the bright ones, everything depended on us. Like me at the time, lots of tasks were heaped on me. So automatically I came to love nationalism, to love independence." The logic of coming to love independence automatically as a result of "lots of tasks heaped on" is not as obvious as

'Cik Muham seems to suggest, although surely the sense that everything depended on them must have been seductive, especially for a girl privileged by birth and education.

For Karo nationalists, the concept of "instruction" went beyond the propaganda of the *saranen* campaign. It included a range of disciplinary projects intended to improve the general standards of village life. These too tended to target village women. Social reformers took it upon themselves to contribute to the "uplift" of women and the improvement of rural life. In the following passage, 'Cik Muham characteristically brings together the value of education, the love of independence, and the need for progress, using "Karo people" synecdochically to mean "Karo women," whose inappropriate attire is a sign of rural backwardness.

> 'CIK MUHAM: At the time, there weren't many educated people yet. The small bit of knowledge I had, had to be given to my people [I., *bangsa*, "nation, people, kind"]. But Batin, you asked what moved me. Yeah, to tell it straight, that spirit of independence. People loved independence, I loved independence too. Not to mention that, don't be offended, but people at that time didn't know anything yet. Karo people [i.e., women] at that time, you see, they just wore blankets, they didn't wear blouses, just a cloth wrapped around tightly [above the breasts].[6] That's how Karo were back then. What can you do? They were just a little too late progressing. As far as progress is concerned, the Bataks were a little ahead of Karo people. The reason for that is that the Christian religion came to Tapanuli earlier than to Karoland. So you asked why I was active, right? Love of country, Batin! And because there was some education already. . . . Give them a little knowledge, teach them. Because you know, Meri, truly Karo people back then—I'm Karo myself, why would I want to insult Karo people?—but they were really not yet advanced. They didn't know anything. Even their way of dressing was still very *simple*. That's what we taught in Fujinkai. How they could be, uh, a little better.

Educated young people like 'Cik Muham were particularly sensitive to the double standard of Karo nationalism. On the one hand they celebrated and endeavored to reproduce an inclusive, kinship-based ethos of equivalence—of "all the mothers and fathers, all the same, equally beloved"—and on the other they accepted a colonial hierarchy of value, in which emulation of a European standard marked one as superior to those whose lifestyles were more identifiably "native." This was not a dilemma that they could entirely resolve through the application of gender or even class distinctions. Instead they pitched it energetically into the future, across Sukarno's golden bridge of promises. Their own (present) superiority could be displayed by teaching modern ways to others, thus extending to them too the signs of (future) modernity. This was why universal literacy was so important to young Karo nationalists. The literacy campaign was one of several areas in which villagers'—and especially village women's—failure to be sufficiently modern was addressed and, the hope was, rectified.

TRAINING

Soon after the official announcement of independence in Medan on September 30, 1945, the TKR set up military training programs throughout the province, mostly led by ex-Gyugun officers. Demand for military instruction soon exceeded the army's limited capacity. Volunteer militia groups became a conduit through which young men's enthusiasm and aspirations could be channeled. Village Pesindo branches were charged with providing the first level of military training for village recruits. "First the young men went into training," said A.R. Surbakti. "Before the enemy got to Taneh Karo, everyone had been trained, even the women had been trained."

"They taught us to fight like the men," said Nandé Senantiasa and her friend Nandé Usman of Payung Village.

> ND. SENANTIASA BERU GINTING: This is what our leader said. "If we don't have enough soldiers someday then women will be called to the front," he said.
>
> ND. USMAN BERU PANDIA: "You'll all go to the front," he said.
>
> ND. S.: So that's why they taught us to fight like the men. We even learned to shoot.
>
> ND. U.: We did. They taught us how to shoot.
>
> ND. S.: Carbines and all. They taught us.
>
> ND. U.: They taught us. So that's why we were so tired here.
>
> ND. S.: Our hands were all rough and cracked from crawling through the weeds.

"Everyone got training," agreed Mbeligai Bangun of Batu Karang.

> MBELIGAI BANGUN: Old folks and girls trained, young men and husbands, all of them trained. Only at different times. For example, you know, like with parents coming home from the *juma* (dry-rice fields), the young men couldn't go out there while they were training. They divided up the time, starting at four o'clock, stopping at five, just one hour so they could still cook the rice [for the evening meal].

Here "parents" [I., *orang tua*] is a polite euphemism for "mothers." The time frame that Mbeligai Bangun presents, in which training is slotted into their daily routine between work in the fields and preparing rice for the evening meal, makes that clear. The prohibition against young men's presence during the training sessions is an adaptation of local standards of propriety to novel, and sometimes embarrassing, circumstances, such as the one that Nandé Madasa beru Ginting of Berastepu pointed out to us:

NANDÉ MADASA: So finally they formed the army, I don't know what it was called, maybe it was TKR back then. They trained us too. That's how hard it was to get independence back then, you see. Training, we had to carry rifles, and—pardon the expression—we didn't have any underpants, so you'll know how hard things were. You couldn't do anything else. There wasn't even any cloth. How do you think we could crawl carrying a rifle if our clothes weren't—you know? There weren't even any towels back then, jackets, sarongs. That's how hard it was chasing this independence.

In the village of Mardinding, girls attended military training on the village soccer field three afternoons a week; two other afternoons they spent pounding rice to feed the soldiers. "We wrapped vines around our heads, at practice, so we wouldn't look human," said Nandé Bahagia beru Tarigan. "Wrapped it around all our bodies. Then we'd have to crawl through the weeds. Then they'd say, retreat, we'd retreat like that. We girls, you know, we'd be wearing a dress or a skirt, you'd get all scratched up underneath."

I'd heard stories about women trainees dressed in pants; in fact I'd seen a picture of Selamat Ginting's wife, Piah Manik, wearing a military uniform (figure 6) so in one of our first interviews I asked my "Granny Tigan," Nandé Rikson beru Tarigan, what they wore for training.

NANDÉ RIKSON: A sarong. Where would we get a blouse? Just a sarong, [because] there wasn't any cloth. You'd tie it up tight, like this [under the armpits]. So even when we marched it would be all right. Because all we did was to learn to carry a spear and to go like this [she mimes crawling]. So you'd squeeze your legs together tight, because we were so modest. Then you'd grab the spear, and you'd go like this [thrusting]. Your head couldn't go up or they'd rap it.

In Selandi they had training every day, said Nandé Marlina beru Ginting. Likewise in Kidupen, where Nandé Karina beru Ginting headed the girls' drill program, the trainers were waiting when the boys and girls got out of school at noon every day.

NANDÉ KARINA: What we studied: First, marching. Then we learned about the Red Cross Corps, we learned how to bandage wounds, things like that.

Or how to catch someone who'd been swept away [in the river]. Or how to carry a person [who had been injured]. That's the kind of thing we studied. Or say there was someone who died, how to carry them so you didn't have to walk upright. So you're not seen by the enemy, you'd have to crawl and drag the stretcher like that. That's the kind of thing we studied. Or to bandage a wound, maybe an eye was hit, how to bandage one side, or both, how to bandage it, that's the kind of thing we studied. We didn't even know the alphabet. . . . In this village I was a trainer for girls. Here they'd have training in the afternoon. Say they got home [from school] at noon, we would already be lined up and we'd continue till late afternoon. Then: learning how to carry a spear at the ball field. That's how we did training around here. How people wage war.

The BHL militia established a training station at Lau Kawar, modeled after the Japanese TALAPETA program and supervised by the former Japanese chief of military police Inoue Tetsuro. Nandé Rikson beru Tarigan, who grew up in the BHL stronghold of Gamber, described—with a little help from her friends—the training they got there.

NANDÉ RIKSON: We had a leader who trained us. For us in Gamber, well, didn't I say that the one who trained us was Bapa Inomi? The one who escorted us to Kawar was Bapa Reken, from Gamber. He was the actual head. The head of the Wild Tigers [in Gamber]. He took us to Kawar frequently. Bapa Inomi trained us there. . . .

JABATIN BANGUN: What all did you study there?

ND. R.: We learned how to carry a spear, how to put it on your shoulder.

NANDÉ LIA BERU TARIGAN: Lifting it up like that was the hardest thing.

ND. R.: Then how to put it down.

ND. L.: If you didn't get it right, you'd have to do it the next day.

ND. R.: If you didn't get it this time, repeat it tomorrow. Marching, so your steps are all even. Left-right, left-right, they said. If they weren't even, tomorrow repeat it too.

ND. L.: That's how it was all the time.

ND. R.: Like that all the time. Because it was hard to keep your steps even, yeah, if you'd never done it before.

ND. L.: Never swung your arms, like, step to the right, swing to the right.

ND. R.: There were some people who couldn't do it like that, couldn't do them together. They got really mad at them.

ND. L.: March right they'd say, they'd march left. We were tired out.

ND. R.: Yeah, left face right face, they said. We didn't know. Now I don't know, back then, you know, right face they'd say for instance, you'd bring your right foot to the back, then move it there. Pick up your right foot, they'd say. Then, left face, they'd say, pick up your left foot, move it there, move your left foot from the back to the front, they'd say. We were always getting mixed up.

For women, training provided neither experiential continuity nor trajectory to national inclusion. With no meaningful context and little practical utility, "training" mainly signified to them the novelty and excitement of Independence Time. Many women humorously emphasized the incongruity of their experiences, like Nandé Madasa acting out for us her efforts to crawl, carrying her rifle, in a sarong without underwear. They told us about learning left face–right face, *push up* and *jot-jot*, "spear practice."

NANDÉ MARLINA BERU GINTING: We'd make bamboo spears, put them on our shoulders like that. . . . That was in Selandi, they called the field "Clove Hill." We'd march in two lines. The little ones in front, the tall ones in back. So then after we'd done the marching drill, they'd put up some poles, like tree trunks, but they'd give them hands, make a head, make legs. They made it from bundles of razor-grass. They made it look just like the image of a person. So we had the bamboo spear on our shoulder, that's what we'd stab with. Wherever they told us to stick, that's what's we'd do. "*Huuh jot!*" they'd say, and "stab the head." Bull's-eye! So then, "stab the eye!" Bull's-eye again. We took turns like that, until the leaves were shredded. Then we'd go home.

Women delighted in repeating to us the strange, sometimes foreign names that things acquired in Independence Time, like *sandiwara* or *saranen*, *jot-jot* or *push up*. Training they most often called *kyoring*, a Japanese-derived term that seemed to be specific to women; men recognized its meaning but rarely used it to describe their own activities, which they described instead as *latihan* (I., practice) or sometimes *trénen* (from E., training). "Before the evacuation we all had training *[latihan]*," said Ngerem beru Singarimbun from Kuta Mbaru. "We called it *kyoring*." Nandé Tabonal beru Karo from Pernantin said, "First we had *kyoring*, study, our training back then. We studied 'push up,' crawling, all like that. 'Push up,' that was like military practice." Nandé Marlina said, "When we got to Independence Time, I wasn't grown yet, but I always wanted to go. Whenever they said '*kyoring*,' I went too. We'd go to the soccer field, we'd all line up there, they called it *kyoring*." They described the special wartime skills that they were taught: basic nursing skills; how to carry a stretcher; how to thrust a spear; how to bandage an injured eye; camouflage; how to tell how near cannon fire was.

NANDÉ MADASA BERU GINTING: This soldier came, he said, "If there's mortar fire, auntie, don't you retreat," he said. "If it falls beside you, go forward. Don't retreat," he said. So if we were working in the field, you know, say we'd hear the mortar go, *jup!*—stop hoeing. If it went *ngiing*, it's still far away, he said. But if it went *gebeg . . . gebeg*, well then it was getting close. So that was right, we got a lot of lessons like that. So then, hoe all together, like that, if it went *ngiing*, together like that. When you hear that, wait till it stops. If it stops after three hoe strokes then you'll know how far away it fell. Then when it goes *ngiing . . . gebeg . . . gebeg*, over there, then run to the mountain, don't even stop to rinse off your hoe. Then it's near, when it goes *gebeg-gebeg*.

Nandé Madasa went even further, dramatically contrasting the "hardness" and inspiration of women during Independence Time and the femininity of women before and after.

NANDÉ MADASA BERU GINTING: Yeah, that's how it was back in our time. Everyone was inspired, to achieve independence, truly, now no one understands, they're afraid to even look at a rifle. Back then, no. Women back then were all hard. God must have arranged it so that they were so hard, otherwise, don't you think we'd have been scared to hear gunfire? As for me, I reckon my blood is different. If there's no sound of gunfire, I feel lonesome. So. I feel lonesome, because back then, starting around eight in the morning there was a code, *tek . . . tor . . . tek tor*, it went, then I'd start to feel excited. If there wasn't any, no. Then I'd feel lonesome. That's how it is if you're used to hearing gunfire all the time. That's how crazy this *merdeka* was, that's the truth. "Crazy," I mean "inspired." I feel lonesome if there's no sound of shots. So I, you know, if you're already old, your memory isn't anymore. . . . I don't have recollections anymore.

Village training programs formed the basis for mobilizing female labor for a range of auxiliary tasks, from collecting food and cooking in the public kitchens to carrying supplies for the soldiers. 'Cik Muham, who headed the Barisan Pemudi Indonesia, the Indonesian Girls' Brigade, in Batu Karang, described some of their tasks:

'CIK MUHAM: You know, there was the [Indonesian] Youth Brigade [Barisan Pemuda Indonesia, BPI], well this was the Girls' Brigade [Barisan Pemudi]. Their duties were just about the same as the militia volunteers. It went like this. I was the head, sometimes I'd be called by the commander, yeah, the commander of BHL, or Pesindo, or the commander of Napindo. This is what they'd say—back then all of us teachers were called "*encik*," so the commander would say, "Encik Muham," he'd say. What? "Call out your troops today, thirty of them," he'd say. Where? "To collect rice from the fields that are being harvested today." The wet-rice fields there, in Batu Karang, they were extensive. So I would take thirty girl recruits, each of them carrying their own rice basket—now, this is the women's role, you see.

Each one would carry a basket and they'd go to Mr. A., Mr. B., Mr. C., Mr. D., and ask for some rice. We'd get thirty *pelgan*, or sixty *kaleng*, over here forty *kaleng*, that's how much we'd get.[7] What was it for? To feed the soldiers in the struggle. Otherwise how would they eat? Ah, that was one kind of work we did, gathering rice in the fields that were being harvested.

We were the ones who managed the public kitchens. The ones who managed the public kitchens, because you know the volunteers who went to war, well, they had to eat. So, we made a public kitchen. So this public kitchen, it was really dirty. *You can imagine*, yeah, there wasn't a river, there wasn't any flowing water, they'd slaughter an ox there, slaughter a water buffalo, and they'd cook it to feed the volunteers for two or three days. If you butcher an ox, it's enough for two or three days. Some of it was made into *dendeng* [dried spiced meat], just dried overnight, then seasoned for the volunteers' food in the future. I did all of these things for a year.

Another time they'd call on me again, "Encik Muham." What? "Today take thirty women *laskars*," or maybe it would be forty. To where? "To Singgamanik. To fetch *pelor*." *Do you know what* pelor *is*? Bullets. Carry little sacks, because bullets are heavy. We'd all carry them on our heads. So we'd go in a line. Without a guard. That's why I'm truly amazed, at the time we were all brave. So we'd go to Singgamanik, I'd take the girls, thirty women, to get the bullets and those bullets would be carried to Batu Karang or to Selandi or to the nearest front.

Women's stories of Independence Time celebrated their new freedom of movement. "We didn't even notice" that most of the young men in the village had gone off to fight, Terang beru Singarimbun recalled. "There wasn't a feeling of fear, like at the beginning of Japanese Time." 'Cik Muham echoed her sentiment. As a *saranen* speaker, she traveled widely: "Today to Sukatendel, tomorrow to Nageri, tomorrow to Jandimeriah, another time to Bintang Meriah, another time to Rimo Kayu, all the villages. There wasn't a car, Meri. And when we got there we weren't treated to coffee or sweet tea, never! Going on foot. Getting home at three in the morning." Yet she didn't feel afraid, she said, even when walking in isolated areas. "Luckily everyone was nice, there wasn't anyone who was bad at that time. No one was bad, there wasn't anyone who bothered us. We'd get home in the middle of the night."

Even training took them places. Women enthusiastically recalled the group runs they made from village to village or even to the subdistrict market center. Nandé Karina from Kidupen led group runs to the market center in Tiga Binanga. "We'd have to run for half an hour along the road past the market," she said. "We'd have to [run] into the market three times in a week. They taught us. Starting from here." Girls in Kuta Mbaru ran the three kilometers to the Tiga Nderket market.

NGEREM BERU SINGARIMBUN: We went to Jandimeriah, we went to Tiga Nderket for training, we went up the mountain, we went over by Nandé Ermalam's orange grove, what was the name of that place? Makam. When we got to the training, we wrapped ourselves in passion-fruit vines [for camouflage], then we had to lie flat, like that. Say there was an enemy over on that side, we were over here. Then we all had spear practice. Our spears were bamboo. Yeah, all bamboo, sharpened bamboo or whatever. That's what we used for spears. We had *kyoring* on the village common. First training, then running. Then marching drill. . . . So finally we joined up with the people from Tiga Nderket. We went on, straight on the road through Genting, you know, not stopping the whole way, in our troop, we marched all together with the people from Jandimeriah, the people from Tiga Nderket.

"Erkata Bedil" may have placed women's home-front efforts on a par with the front-line struggles of their male counterparts, but its conventional division of labor, in which young men go off on lowland adventures while their faithful sweethearts stay at home tending the rice fields, must have sounded more like continued drudgery than new opportunity to the eager girls of Independence Time. They were more for going places than for staying at home. They reveled in strange words and new activities, took pride in their fearlessness and their freedom. They relished the chance to exceed conventional expectations, whether by giving a speech about airplanes and the future greatness of Indonesia or by just running down the road to the next village. Perhaps for this reason the song "Rifle Reports" didn't make much of an impression on them, however much it may have appealed to masculine sensibilities. What they liked best were the marching songs, like the cheerfully foreign "Mariam Tomong," with its heavy beat and happy refrain, *Oh the mortar cannon, mother, oh the machine gun,* which sounded like it might take you somewhere.

GOING PLACES

One of the most important military training programs for women was the Srikandi Corps. Established by the Indonesian army in the first months of independence, it took its name from the warrior-wife of the heroic Arjuna, of Javanese *wayang* shadow puppet theater. Srikandi is one of *wayang*'s best-known female characters, but she is an ambivalent figure: brave and competent, yet flawed by her lack of womanly submissiveness. She characteristically lifts her head boldly, like a man, rather than bowing with downcast eyes. She carries a bow and arrow and delights in the arts of war. The epitome of *meliar* ambiguity, Srikandi is sometimes depicted as a virago or a bold and willful vamp. For Karo girls, though, *srikandi* was just another of Independence Time's many foreign words, like *merdeka, kyoring*, and *push up*.

The Srikandi Corps was modeled on a like-named scouting program for adolescent girls set up on Java by the Japanese under Fujinkai auspices. Both the Japanese and nationalist programs provided some basic military training for girls, but neither seems to have actually been meant to prepare them for combat roles. Srikandi girls performed drill demonstrations at public events; they displayed the ideals of discipline, conformity, and patriotic participation and extended these to others through a range of activities and training programs. In practical terms, they served as an auxiliary labor force—transport, kitchen work, first aid, and the like—to support the soldiers.

Although the army's resources were already stretched thin by the flood of male volunteers seeking basic military training, a provincial-level Srikandi program was started in Medan as early as November 1945. Girls admitted to the first small cohort were expected to become instructors for subsequent groups, whose members would in turn expand the program further by setting up Srikandi programs in their own home areas. The first Srikandi volunteers in Medan were urban girls with family connections to the TKR or nationalist political leadership.[8] After they finished the six-month course, a second group of trainees was admitted. This second cohort aimed for broad regional representation. It was made up of about a hundred girls, ten from each district in the province. To accommodate this larger group, the program was moved from the shop district of Asia Street to more spacious quarters on Duyung Street in an old residential section of the city, and the program was shortened from six to three months.

Fourteen-year-old Piahmalem beru Sembiring, the daughter of an orange grower from Berastepu, was the youngest of the ten girls selected from the Karo district for this second Srikandi cohort.

PIAHMALEM BERU SEMBIRING: They sent a letter, to every village, from the Bupati. So we came to Kabanjahé. Maybe three or four people from each village. There's where we were chosen, who wanted to go to Duyung Street. It so happened that from our village all three of us were chosen. The rest were Kabanjahé people, all of them. . . . I was still young, around fourteen, so I felt proud. I was the youngest one who was chosen.

Major Djamin Ginting, who commanded TKR Regiment I, was in charge of the selection process for the Karo district. He contacted his wife's best friend, Roncah beru Barus, the daughter of the *sibayak* of Barusjahé. Roncah was teaching in Kabanjahé at the time.

RONCAH BERU BARUS: He said, "Roncah, there's a training program in Medan now, the Srikandi training program. So I'd like you to get together some of your friends, about ten people, go there to the training program, we'll pay your expenses," he said. So I asked my friends, how about going to the training program there? What kind of training program? Military. A military training program. So these friends said, if this is military training, does this mean we're going to be soldiers? But I'd already talked to Djamin Ginting about this, what's the real purpose of forming this Srikandi? This is what he said. "It's not to fight, but for preparation, just so you can defend yourselves, meaning, so you all know how the situation is, so, for example, if you had to, you could defend yourselves. . . . When we're in difficulty, or whatever, well then, you can help us, that's the point, we can ask you for help."

Like Roncah, most of the girls selected for the Duyung Street training program came from the "aristocratic circles" of Karo village society or from prosperous entrepreneurial families with an urban orientation. This was partly a matter of schooling. Because of the program's multiethnic composition and urban setting, Malay/Indonesian was used as the vehicular language of instruction. That limited the pool of candidates in the Karo district to girls with some postprimary schooling beyond the vernacular instruction offered in village classrooms. It was also a form of protection for elite families. Sending a daughter to train with the army was both a (fairly risk-free) indication of support for the nationalist cause and a way to remove vulnerable girls from a dangerously volatile political situation.

PIAHMALEM BERU SEMBIRING: That's why, back then, if we were invited to join the struggle, we agreed right off. See, if we're thought to be *pro*[-Dutch] then this is what will happen, so when you're invited—ah, let's join the struggle, I thought. Even though we didn't actually understand. [Roncah Barus was] the child of a raja. That's why all of them joined. They were all rajas. That was how it was, generally. So, let's join the struggle, let's join the struggle. My father was like that.

These rural schoolgirls found conditions on Jalan Duyung unexpectedly harsh. "At first we thought it would be fun to go to Medan," Piahmalem Sembiring recalled. "But there was nothing there, you had to line up for the bathroom unless you wanted to use the gutter beside the building. Only three outfits, you had to wash them and wear them." Sanaria boru Silalahi, whose family moved to Kabanjahé from western Tapanuli, was the only non-Karo girl chosen from the district.

SANARIA BORU SILALAHI: At first, where do we sleep? [we asked.] Here [they said]. But we were told there would be a mattress, a pillow—we didn't understand, apparently it was a real training program, we didn't understand. You don't use a pillow, there wasn't even a mat to sleep on. The funniest thing was bathing. One open tank [for bath water]. Queue up. Oh, we're as good as dead, I thought. In Kabanjahé there's a lot of water, here we didn't have enough. But that's how it was at the time.

The girls were taught how to clean a pistol, load a gun, and use a bayonet. "We learned how to march, how to shoot," said Piahmalem beru Sembiring. "When we fired, it really hurt my shoulder. I was just fourteen, and not very strong." They wore baggy "Gurkha trousers" and carried real rifles, "just like the soldiers," Sanaria said, not the wooden guns and bamboo spears that village girls (and often boys) used in training. They studied first aid and learned about political and military topics from "all the big people of the time." If there were evacuees to be fed, they worked in the public kitchen. "Then if there wasn't anything else to do, we rolled cigarettes [for the soldiers]."

Once their military training in Medan was done and the girls had returned home, Roncah proposed that they start their own Srikandi course for village girls.

> RONCAH BERU BARUS: I conferred with all my friends. How about if we make the Srikandi here? "What is the purpose?" [they asked.] This is what I said. For me, it's to open the way for development.[9] We're going to be independent, so there's sure to be a lot that we have to be able to do, not just fighting. . . . Actually we've learned how to fight, so if it's necessary we'll already know how. We already know. But nevertheless we're not to be used by the government for fighting. We won't. Because we—yeah, our soldiers are sufficient, and as for weapons, there aren't even any weapons. My goodness, why would we women be fighting when the young men don't even have enough weapons?

With the blessings of Djamin Ginting and the army, the Karo Srikandi Corps soon set up shop in Kabanjahé. Letters were sent to each subdistrict and village head inviting them to nominate likely girls to represent their community. "They were supposed to have finished school," Sanaria said. "At least third grade, know how to read. If they didn't know how to read, how could they take notes? And also, they chose the pretty ones to send, and the smart ones. That's usually how it is. They were all really pretty. Yeah, all the soldier boys were tempted." Roncah's criteria were somewhat different. "I wanted to teach people who were illiterate," she said. "Even the ones who couldn't read or write, I took them too." For her, character was what mattered most.

> RONCAH BERU BARUS: I was the one who had to go to the villages. I went to the villages, I told them the requirements are like this: you have to be brave, and not hope for wealth, you can't. This is what I required, all the Srikandis

weren't allowed to ask for money from their parents. Not to mention the leaders, the ten of us. I said, "Whoever asks for money, go on home. You can't do that."

Five or six cohorts of 60 to 150 girls each completed the three-month Srikandi course in Kabanjahé. The program's basic expenses for food and housing were covered by the army and the district government; participating villages contributed to the girls' upkeep as well. But Roncah wanted to reduce their dependency on others and to increase the girls' self-reliance and sense of social participation, so they grew vegetables and raised chickens to supplement their rations. They rolled cigarettes to sell for some extra cash. They joined the ceremonies of mourning for volunteers killed in the fighting. Some evenings they walked to nearby villages to help with literacy and training programs or to take part in political rallies. Most days they dressed in ordinary clothing, but on special occasions they wore their uniforms, shirts and culottes of unbleached cloth.

Roncah was in charge of the educational aspects of the program. "We studied in the morning," she said, "studied about how to act in war and all that. Srikandi stuff, you know, studied fighting and all, whatever the soldiers wanted, how to do this and that, we studied all of it, just like soldiers." After that, the girls attended classes on a range of topics. "We taught them all kinds of things," she said. "Culture, history, in the mornings. Before they went home, they studied Red Cross. They were taught to hold weapons. Basic. As women, how to take care of the body."

Piahmalem beru Sembiring, Sanaria boru Silalahi, and two other girls handled military training. (Even though she held the rank of major, Roncah was no good at training, they confided.) "Marching. How to form a unit," said Sanaria boru Silalahi. "And we taught them military discipline. Like if anything happened, we would make the sacrifice, we would replace the men." Piahmalem beru Sembiring elaborated: "We were the ones who were out in the sun every day. We applied the same training [as on Duyung Street]. We took them to the forest, ordered them to cut a passion fruit vine, put it around their heads, that's how we did it. Then we'd walk to Kacaribu. [The vine was] so we couldn't be seen by enemies passing. We were doing like in war. Hiding."

Sometimes the girls were sent to the Medan front to assist the soldiers. There they helped prepare and distribute meals of rice with stewed vegetables or perhaps a bit of meat curry. Occasionally they took food to the troops at the front lines.

NANDÉ SENANTIASA BERU BANGUN: We were sent to the front at Barung Ketang. With Selamat Ginting and his wife. . . . So our work there, we weren't the ones who cooked, we just wrapped the meals. There were these Javanese in the *dapur umum*, the public kitchen [who did the cooking]. Once we'd finished wrapping [the meals], we carried them to the front. The Padang Bulan front. At four o'clock we'd already left Barung Ketang. The Dutch often shot at our truck. Sometimes the truck caught fire. Because they hated us the most. "If it wasn't for you bringing food to your soldiers, they wouldn't be able to go on," they said, isn't that right?

Other times they were put to work making bullets for the army or gleaning grain from deserted rice fields.

RONCAH BERU BARUS: Now our work at the front, we made bullets, gunpowder, all that. That was our job. Now the front, we were behind the lines, that's where we were. What do you call it, that stuff that's like tin [lead], then you fill it up, that's what we did. At the front. Sometimes we'd steal. Steal what? Food at the front, rice, sometimes the grain was ripening, so. During the battle, we'd steal cassava, for all our soldiers. You know, no one dared to go [to their fields] anymore, people were fighting. The soldiers would advance, we'd steal whatever there was. . . . Once the soldiers advanced, if there was any rice or whatever, we'd take it. Whatever there was. In the daytime you couldn't do it. Daytime there were soldiers, planes. When the *moment* came when we could do it, well, that's what we did. Sometimes at night, depending on the situation. The point is, if the army advanced, everything behind them would be empty. We, couldn't we do whatever we wanted? The people who lived there had already run off. Whoever dared could take it, mostly for the soldiers.

Going to the lowlands was a thrilling experience for the eager Srikandi girls, most of whom had never traveled farther than Kabanjahé. They were brave at the front, Roncah said proudly.

RONCAH BERU BARUS: There was one time in what they called the Medan Area. I took them along. They weren't afraid of mortar fire. If a plane flew overhead, they just stared at it. "Hey, airplane! Airplane!" they'd say. They'd never seen a plane before, "Oh look, an airplane!" they'd say. They'd see the plane, "Eh, an airplane," they'd shout. Oh, I was scared. That's our responsibility, isn't it? But they weren't, they'd never seen a plane. They thought it was weird. Villagers, they weren't scared. The trouble is, they didn't understand what planes could do. Until finally Selamat Ginting said to me, "Watch out, those Srikandis of yours are going to get killed!"

Fortunately, none of them did, though they did see soldiers who had died in battle, and they escorted the bodies home for burial. Rather than frightening them, the sights and sounds of war seemed to confirm the usefulness of their labor, by showing that they were important enough

FIGURE 16. Going places: Srikandi girls *(left to right)* Roncah beru Barus, Piahmalem br. Sembiring, and two unidentified friends. From the collection of Nandé Lidia br. Barus.

to hate. That was the point hyperbolically expressed by Nandé Senantiasa: "The Dutch often shot at our truck. Sometimes the truck caught fire. Because they hated us the most. 'If it wasn't for you bringing food to your soldiers, they wouldn't be able to go on,' they said, isn't that right?"

For these girls and their instructors, the Srikandi Corps was both more and less than a military training program. Roncah made it clear that political indoctrination was not in her mind, though she saw the program directed toward Indonesia's future through education.

RONCAH BERU BARUS: I'm not bragging, you know, it's just that with us Srikandis the education was complete. Only we Srikandis were oriented to education. The others were just: struggle, struggle, struggle. That's why they were all the same. Struggle, public kitchen, public kitchen, that's it. Because that's all they had, that's all it was. Join the struggle, if necessary help the soldiers, if there's a battle, go along with the public kitchen. But on regular days, there was nothing to do. Because we were in the dormitory. I was afraid they'd get bored. They'd go home if there was nothing to do. Put people in dormitories for months, what are they going to do? So, let's start some activities [I said]. Let's go to the villages, we can teach there, the soldiers can accompany us to the villages. On foot. For example, to Buluh Raya, Rumah Kabanjahé, you know where that is, don't you? Kacaribu, Lingga, yeah, the ones around here, not too far away. Sometimes there were five of us in a group, or four. We all spread out, we taught in the villages too. So these people we'd trained, they taught in the villages too. That's how it was at night.

When they had completed the program, some of the girls set up Srikandi branches in their home villages. Others continued their first aid instruction through nursing courses. Many eventually became involved in local civil defense efforts or joined militia groups as staff medical personnel.

> RONCAH BERU BARUS: After the training, we returned them to the leaders in their village. They had the same training, but it was up to them what they wanted to do with it, it depended on what they needed in that village. . . . The point is, we returned them to the village. They went back to the village, we turned them over, here are the ones that we've trained. Now it's up to you how to use them here. Those kids, they were all capable and energetic. . . . Sometimes there were a few who after they entered training, they didn't— But the point is, we had trained them. I'm truly proud of that.

GENERATIONS

One of the things I was struck by in women's stories of Independence Time was how thoroughly they were cast in a generational frame. Parents, elders, and nationalist leaders were for the most part missing from these accounts or insignificant to the narrative action. With the exception of passing mentions of "our parents" or "our leaders" or the enabling affirmation of political figures like Djamin Ginting (in the case of the Srikandi Corps), Rakutta Berahmana (who introduced 'Cik Muham as a speaker at the public rallies), and Nandé Katana (who organized the *sandiwara* in Tiga Nderket), the narrative focus throughout was firmly on the girls themselves and what they did. Parents were mostly mentioned to approve the girls' actions or, in a few cases, as an obstacle to their participation, like Nandé Lina, who was slapped by her mother for neglecting her chores in her "eagerness" to take part in the struggle. Nandé Bahagia's stepmother wasn't understanding, either:

> NANDÉ BAHAGIA BERU TARIGAN: Me, at the beginning of independence there was practice in the village. Practice in the village, every day at four o'clock we'd practice marching on the soccer field. Practice, back then they called it *kyoring*, now they'd say practice *[latihen]*. . . . "Don't make me go," I'd say, "I've got a stepmother, and her baby is tiny," I'd say. "If you keep making me practice, I won't get anything to eat at home," I said. "Well, you have to go," said the village headman and the militia leader. So there was practice every afternoon. Well, I asked again, please don't make me go every day,

how about twice a week? My stepmother has a little baby. "You won't get any rice to eat at home if you don't husk it" [stepmother said]. There wasn't a grain mill there yet. "All right, twice a week," they said. So I went along. Then after the *kyoring*, for several months we had to run to the market [in Tiga Nderket] for training. "I can't do it," I said. "You know I have a stepmother, don't make me do that," I said. "I'm willing to go anywhere, if it's at night, but not in the afternoon," I said. . . . It was like that all the time. Practice, make a drama, go to a meeting, they'd say. Go to a meeting in Batu Karang, in Juhar, in Tanjung, Bintang Meriah. The militia leader had meetings all the time. Come home from there, "There's no rice left," my [step] mother said. That's how it is when your stepmother has a tiny baby. "Your chores aren't done," [she said]. That's why they call it a struggle, you know, because it's hard. You had to struggle at home, and you had to join the struggle with the village too. Wasn't that exhausting? It's not good to divide the village's defenses, but if you go along, you don't have a place at home.

The *idea* of maternal sacrifice is deeply embedded in the everyday affect of Karo kinship. It certainly held a central place in nationalist propaganda, as a review of excerpts from 'Cik Muham's speeches quoted above will demonstrate. Why, then, did we hear so little in our interviews about the actual contributions and enthusiasm—or the hardships and suffering—of mothers and older women? For one thing, we didn't talk to that many of them. The passage of nearly fifty years meant that most of our informants had been in their teens at the time of the struggle. Many of the older generation were no longer alive or were frail or in poor health. Some of our elderly informants, men and women, were forgetful or uninterested in talking about the past in general or about Independence Time in particular. The memories of a few of our older informants seem to have been reduced to a single idée fixe, obsessively repeated, or scattered, as if scenes or images from the struggle had been preserved but the links and sequencing that joined them had been lost.

The absence of older women from our informants may have been due to other factors as well. We had to depend on the guidance of others to identify interview subjects. Many names came from pension registration rolls, which were skewed toward the better educated and better off, toward those with government connections and no family history of left-wing political affiliation, and toward those who could construct a certain kind of legitimating account of their participation in the struggle. Some we met through friends and relatives, who led us to well-known local figures like 'Cik Muham, Nandé Menda, Piah Manik, and Roncah beru Barus or to grandmothers and aunts who had regaled (or bored) audiences for years with stories of their adventures and activities during the struggle. As a result, our informants tended to be those who were recognized by their families, their communities, or the state as having something interesting or valuable to tell us. Although we were aware of this limitation and actively sought informants outside the circles of official and local recognition, a certain predictability was nevertheless built into the selection process itself.

Much of this had to do with the prominence of the Generation of 1945 in Indonesian national consciousness. Especially during the Suharto years, the '45 generation as a cohort was seen as embodying the independence struggle both as its agents and as the continuing guardians of its spirit of struggle (I., *semangat juang*). The historical centrality of their experience, generalized and celebrated in the heroic terms of passion and sacrifice, was reflected in the notion of youth (I., *pemuda* [m.] and *pemudi* [f.]) as a national vanguard. While youth was understood more as an attitude than as an age group, it nevertheless conveyed a sensibility not limited by personal social attachments, parochial interests, or the demands of family life. Older men—political leaders especially—could continue to represent themselves as *pemuda* well into middle age if they had a wife at home to take care of household responsibilities. But for most women, youth and marriage were mutually exclusive categories. Nandé Berah, the wife of Bupati Rakutta Berahmana, made this gender distinction most clearly: "I had to work in the fields. That was my struggle, feeding the family. He didn't even know how we were doing. He was gone, I don't know where, with the struggle."

When we did talk to older women, we often found they had little to say. Some were reluctant to talk or insisted that they didn't know anything about the struggle. Others deferred to their husbands' experience or, like Nandé Berah, downplayed their own contributions as merely domestic obligation. The eager girls of the '45 generation, who were for the most part unencumbered by husbands, children, or family obligations, threw themselves into the struggle with enthusiasm and zest. But for women with families to support or young children to care for, this was not such a good time. The ones who fed the pigs and cooked the rice, they were required to attend political rallies and meetings after working in the fields all day; were asked to contribute their sparse provisions to support the soldiers, even if their own children went hungry; and were expected to send their sons as armed volunteers and their daughters as workers for the nationalist cause. Not for them the jolly stories of marching to neighboring towns, cheering at rallies, learning *jot-jot* and *push up*. In their accounts, the claim of "tiredness" took on a different significance, signaling not the extent of women's collective contribution to the struggle but rather the excessive nature of the demands placed on them individually.

So it was with Nandé Ndapet beru Perangin-angin, who was one of a group of four women we interviewed in Payung Village. While her younger companions Nandé Senantiasa and Nandé Usman held the floor, reminiscing breezily about shared work, training, Japanese songs, and "no end of tiredness," she and her friend Nandé Namali waited patiently for their turn to talk. Finally, Nandé Ndapet could wait no longer. Once she'd started talking she didn't seem to be able to stop. Fueled, it appeared, by decades of suppressed resentment, her account looped back on itself, obsessively returning to the day she had to contribute half of her family's harvest of chili peppers to feed the soldiers. Like so many others that we heard, Nandé Ndapet's story turned on the trope of tiredness. But for her, this was not an assertion of common experience, shared effort, or patriotic "eagerness." It was, instead, a sign of difference and inequity: "You all had it easier, *we* were tired back then," she said, speaking to her friends not in the inclusive first-person plural of collective agency, *kita*, but rather in the exclusionary address of *kami*, "we-not-you."

At the beginning of independence, Nandé Ndapet already had three children. She was living in the village of Selandi, which was a BHL stronghold. She referred to the BHL leader Payung Bangun (alias Pa Berontak, K./I., "rebel's father") as her maternal uncle (K., *mama* [MB]), and it may have been on account of this relationship that she was chosen to lead a work group there, against her own wishes.

NANDÉ NDAPET BERU PERANGIN-ANGIN: In Selandi I was the Selandi head. You all had it easier, we were tired back then. "Go clean up Tokih's field," say. "Not me, if our leader isn't there," they said. Planting corn, it was the same thing, why was it that way? Then rice had to—"Dried chilis, get us a sack of them, a gunny sack full," they said. There weren't any. Our own chili peppers, we took them, when the bag was full we said we'd collected them. Every month they checked the rice. "Take three *tumbas* from each house-hold," they said. As for me in Selandi, you all had it easier.

I wasn't sure what to make of all this. The story itself was hard enough to follow, what with its self-interruptions and recurrences, its cast of characters mostly unfamiliar (to us) and unexplained, and its still-raw emotional punch. Even more than usual, I felt as if we were listening in on a conversation whose target audience did not really include us. Even the excluding *kami* (we-not-you) didn't take us into consideration, being directed against her fellow veterans Nandé Senantiasa and Nandé Usman. It was as if she was stuck in the frequently rehearsed recollection of one specific occasion, when a sack full of chili peppers seemed to hold all the injustice of the struggle. Her account circled back obsessively to those peppers, spiraling out with each return to fill in more details, deepen the complaint. Did she contribute her own chilis once or several times? How many times was she elected the "Selandi head"? Should we interpret her account via a recursive poetics of condensation and intensification or as a variant form of the gendered idiom of generalized events and industrious selves? Was her memory caught in the looping paths of dementia or the narrowing window of age? Was her anger a reaction to the overly cheerful tales of her companions? If so, then why?

At once enigmatically elliptical and maddeningly redundant, Nandé Ndapet's account calls for an alternative practice of listening and reading, one attuned to lyrical as well as narrative modes of expression and sensitive to the weight of its recursivity as well as to the bitter resentment that haunts its ironic refrain: *"The homeland calls," they said*. It defies summary, and I translate it without commentary below in full, including interruptions from her friends, as they, unsuccessfully, attempted to move her monologue in a more socially acceptable direction ("We all made sacrifices back then," they reminded her. "Everyone was like that back then.") For the sake of clarity, I have added some brief explanatory material in brackets, and for readability, I have broken the narrative into short paragraphs.

"THE HOMELAND CALLS," THEY SAID

In Selandi I was the Selandi head. You all had it easier, we were tired back then.

"Go clean up Tokih's field," say. "Not me, if our leader isn't there," [the work crew] said.

Planting corn, it was the same thing, why was it that way?

Then rice had to—

"Dried chilis, get us a sack of them, a gunny sack full," they said. There weren't any.

Our own chili peppers, we took them, when a bag was full we said we'd collected them.

Every month they checked the rice. "Take three *tumbas* from each household," they said.

As for me in Selandi, you all had it easier.

The reason I say you had it easier, we had a quota. If you didn't meet it, they'd come for you.

Then, "You have to plant corn," they said in Payung-Selandi.

Amé Pilih was my friend here,[10] I was the leader there. I didn't want to be the leader, I didn't want to join the cooperative work [I., *gotong royong*], my childen had to go hungry.

I already had three children at the time.

This is how they treated you then.

The soldiers came to the house from the direction of the irrigation canal; it was secluded there.

Pa Berontak himself always came to Simpang Lau.

"Let's go," they said.

"I don't want to go unless the leader goes too," said the boys and girls [in the work crew].

I had to carry my children there. Over by [the nearby village of] Toraja.

I wept.

You boys and girls, you all have it easy. I'm the one who's had the bitterest [experience].

I wept, then, how did it go? "Don't always make me [the leader]," I said.

"The homeland calls," they said.

Bapa Berontak from Batu Karang and . . . who else? There were Nampé, Kerani, from Batu Karang, from Bapa Berontak.

The chili peppers, finally I took half a bag of my own peppers. Well, what else could I do?

They said, "Everyone gather up two, three *tumbas*, take them to the rice mill."

"Take half a bag of mine," I said.

I'm not making this up. I wept.

Nande Senantiasa broke in at this point. "We all made sacrifices back then," she said, trying to get the conversation back on the appropriate track of collective agency and shared action.

"Everyone was like that back then. Not just you," agreed Nandé Usman.

"I had three children then," Nandé Ndapet retorted. "You, you know, you all were still unmarried girls. I already had a family."

"We were still free (I., *bebas*)."

"It's like, you were already getting old, we were still girls. You know, you . . ."

"That's not it," said Nandé Ndapet, and returned to her story.

"Now, if you have anything, take it," said Kerani and Nampé, for Pa Berontak of Batu Karang. I remember all this.

Then, "Plant corn," they said.

"*Ya ah*, don't make me join in, I was the one who had to gather watercress from Toraja," I said.

"The homeland calls," they all said.

"If you don't go, we won't go either," said all the girls [in the work crew].

In the time just before the evacuation, no one had more difficulties. No one had a harder time.

We wept.

I already had three children.

"Then, don't be like that," I said to Uncle Pa Berontak of Batu Karang, "I'll die—"

"You aren't going to die," he said. "You can't say no, you have to gather two *tumbas* of rice from every household," he said.

There were some who had no rice.

So then, when some didn't have any, "If they don't have any, never mind," they said.

This was Pa Berontak Batu Karang, yeah?

Then, "What else can be done, let someone else be the leader," I said.

"You're the only one who can [do it], you're the chief leader," they said.

I wept, I'm not lying.

So after that, [I went]with the girls to there. *Ih*, came [back] from there.

Word came from the village headman, "Gather up a bag of dried peppers," he said.

"*Ih*, where can I get them, I don't have any," [I said.]

"Just get them," he said too.

I gathered them, each of us gave one kilo, two kilos, I had fifty kilos, so I gave ten kilos.

I was already skinny because I had three children.

Then I wept all the way down the road to get them, carrying the baby.

Because it was, "Boys and girls, you all go there," I said.

"If the leader doesn't go, I won't either," said the boys and girls. "We're scared," they said.

I had to carry my baby.

You'd think my littlest one would have died.

You'd think that even the moon wasn't enough. It was hard because it was always war.

Then, finally word came from the government. "In Selandi collect two sacks of chilis," they said.

We had a leader for twenty [families], I had one assistant.

We asked then, people gave us two kilos, one kilo.

"Three more days [before mine are ready]," "Four more days for me," they said too, that's what happened when we collected them.

Got half a sack.

My own dried peppers had been bagged up because that was my work, none of them had been sold. That's what I gave, a bag and a half more to Pa Berontak.

"You can't refuse," they said. "Our soldiers will all die," they said.

So there, give them all to the soldiers.

Then, once that was all done, "Plant corn," they said, give it all to the soldiers.

"If the leader doesn't go, I won't go either," said all the boys and girls.

I had to, my little baby was half dead with all that.

And why not? Carried around like that everywhere.

The journey was long, back then there wasn't a bus, no lie. You had to walk there.

I'll just die. If I'm the leader.

I don't want to be the leader anymore.

"The homeland calls," they said.

So even as sick as I feel now that I'm old, I was sicker then with those three children and I was the leader. I cried all the time.

"Don't make me," I said,

"If you don't go, we won't either," they all said.

I had to carry my baby.

Half dead I carried him, I'm not lying, maybe four months after this was all over, the little one died.

What do you expect, carried around like that?

I wept, if this is what being a leader is like, I don't want to.

We have to choose a leader, all the Payung-Selandi people went there and decided.

Everyone who was there, they met with the Selandi headman and the Payung headman, my uncle [Pa Berontak], Nampé, and Kerani.

"OK, we've decided," they said.

Oh, this is dangerous, I thought. I didn't know what to say. What else can I do, I thought.

"Nandé Ndapet," they said. The gavel rapped, and it was done.

Iyah, this is bad, I thought, but I didn't say anything. I'll finish this, I'll force myself, I thought.

Choose again, one more time.

Another election. "Now the most important thing," they said, "we have to gather a bag of chilis."

"Ask your followers for them," they said.

Ask for one kilo over there, ask for two kilos here.

Where else can I go?

Actually our field of chilis was wide.

Because I, because it had been hard all along, [some] people didn't do anything at all, I worked all the time.

I took half a bag of my own peppers, then they asked for the rest.

For the soldier's food.

That was Pa Berontak, no one back then dared to oppose him. He was strong in Batu Karang.

After that, where—"Here is a new school," they said too. "The leader has to go to school," they said.

"Yeah, PBH [adult literacy classes]," chimed in Nandé Namali, the fourth woman who was present.

Ih, this is dangerous, what else can I do? I thought.

"When is this school?" I asked.

"Three in the afternoon," they said.

"Then that's all right," I said, [because the chili peppers had to be delivered to another nearby village, Tanjung, before then].

Because it was hard to go to Tanjung carrying those peppers. I looked, and it was almost two o'clock.

I ran [all the way] to Kité Kambing there to get to that school of ours in Selandi.

There we read like children.

"Make a school," said the village head. So that's why I know how to read a little bit.

Really, it's a good thing, but it was bitter back then. I can read and write a little bit.

So for instance if I'm selling, I know a bit.

They gave me a certificate. Really it was fortunate, but it wasn't half bitter at the time.

"Really bitter," confirmed Nandé Senantiasa.

Tired. Three children to take care of. Not one of them big.

Then, I was always the one who was chosen. Chosen by the boys and girls, "Me, if our leader doesn't go, I won't go either," they said. I had to be there.

They all chose me. Even the old folks. I was the one who was chosen. How do you think that feels? There were lots of people [who could have done the job].

"*Ih*," I said, "what is this?" I said.

Kerani and Nampé and Pa Berontak said, "Our homeland calls, is there no answer?" They said it firmly.

I bowed my head. I carried it all. I'm not lying.

Until the evacuation was finished, I carried it always, nonstop. That's what I did.

After working I went to Selandi, I had to go to school.

"School," they said, I already had three children. Actually I didn't know anything, I didn't know. I studied too.

"I'll die if I don't know [the lesson]," I thought, here it was already night. I'm not lying, I studied halfway through the night, I repeated [the lesson] over and over.

I learned how to write *a-i-r* [I., water], and all. Finally I could do school. I finished too.

After that, after I'm old like this, I haven't received anything [as compensation]. I don't mean to beg. I reckon my feelings are hurt.

I carried all the tasks.

All of you who were still youngsters, you all were really tired. As for me, I had to carry a baby too. What do you think that was like?

"Everyone was like that, everyone," said Nandé Senantiasa.

"Everyone," echoed Nandé Usman.

Nandé Ndapet would have none of this. "Meaning, you wanted to look nice but you didn't have a chance to beautify yourself, isn't that right?"

"Yeah, not even a dress," said Nandé Senantiasa.

My child was hungry there, I'm not making this up. God heard what I said, I'm not making this up.

"That's really how it was," Nandé Senantiasa acknowledged. "This whole village knew."

I wept, what have you done? Don't choose me again, because I've already, yeah, that's enough, I thought.

"You can't not do it"—the kids—"I won't do it if our leader doesn't," they said. They chose me again. I was always the leader in Selandi. Just two hundred people, that's all.

"Every village actually had to have a leader," said Nandé Senantiasa.

Yeah, that's why I was so tired.

So I think, why was I the one who was chosen, I'm not even pretty, I'm not lively either, but it was always me.

Sometimes I thought they were taking advantage of me, but that's OK. It's OK because now there's someone to lift me up. God, I mean.

I think that's really true. Truly God was with me.

. . .

Nationalism's gendered framework in Karoland may have been taken from that of family and kinship, but, as Nandé Ndapet's account makes clear, the two frames were neither entirely congruent nor fully compatible. Both depended on the productive and reproductive labor of women. As a result, women's work was doubled—"you had to struggle at home, and you had to join the struggle with the village too," as Nandé Bahagia put it—or one was forced to choose between them, a choice that, for reasons of scale at least, was weighted heavily in favor of the nation. *Our homeland calls, is there no answer? They said it firmly*, and the threat implicit in those words is clear. *I bowed my head. I carried it all.* Efforts to accommodate the *saranen* campaign to women's work schedules; to celebrate their domestic roles and their household labor; to reckon them as equal to men and as targets of programs of social improvement; to demand their active participation, in ways that were explicitly gendered, like the spatialized division of labor of the song "Rifle Reports" ("you'll stay behind, sweetheart . . . tending the fields, cooking our rice, O sister dear"), as well as in ways that aimed to create the illusion of gender neutrality, like the various paramilitary programs, from village *kyoring* drills to the Srikandi Corps, which trained women to fight "like the men" but insisted they would not be expected to do so, or to make their contributions appear identical to their ordinary domestic responsibilities ("before the struggle they cooked the rice too . . . what kind of struggle is that?")—these cannot disguise the fact that the nationalist infrastructure in Karoland was parasitical, both materially and symbolically, on the family form, which is to say that it depended on the extraction of an extra surplus of women's economic and social value to sustain itself. This was a burden unequally shared by married women and unmarried girls, mothers and daughters, elite and village women. Nandé Ndapet's complaint, with its emphatic repetitions and spiraling narrative form, insists on recognizing this, above all in her rejection of the inclusive *kita* of Nandé Senantiasa's pious "we all made sacrifices back then" in favor of *kami*, we-not-you, or the singular maternal "I," who "wept all the way down the road . . . carrying the baby."

FAMILY FOUNDATIONS

I like to think of the eager girls of the '45 generation marching to Tiga Nderket or Tiga Binanga, carrying bullets to the troops or collecting cabbages for the public kitchens. I imagine them singing at rallies, crawling through the brush, or learning "right face–left face" in training, having the time of their lives. I laugh at their jaunty self-depictions, their "inspiration" or "craziness," their fearlessness and "hard" demeanor. I thrill at the excitement of airplanes and the promise of a future thick with possibilities—even after those possibilities had shrunk to disappointing meagerness, unevenly distributed.

Despite such exuberant imaginings, it is worth noting how much these women's accounts, with their emphasis on self-sacrifice, collective action, and the willing performance of delegated tasks, seem to conform to a New Order ideal of mass citizenship, in which "the people" were celebrated as compliant followers of generalized orders from above but also recognized as a potential source of disorder and danger. This is why Nandé Ndapet's account, with its own version of the trope of "tiredness" and its own unsequenced narrative, seems so transgressive. Its insistence on difference, its contradiction of the ethos of *kita* and the spirit of the willing masses, not only refused the rhetoric of Karo communalism, of "all the mothers and fathers, all the same"; it also dissented from the prevailing ideology of national citizenship.

Under Suharto's New Order regime, the concept of citizenship was fundamentally bifurcated, consisting, on the one hand, of an agentive, military "supercitizenship," in which the army and its adjuncts took on the obligation to preserve and guide the nation and received the privileges and perquisites to which this action entitled them, and, on the other hand, of a passive mass citizenry of compliant but apolitical supporters. While this dualistic model of citizenship was not explicitly referenced to gender, its gendered dimensions are clear enough, especially when viewed in the light of the New Order's so-called *azas kekeluargaan* (family foundation). The family, according to this proposition, is the moral foundation of the nation-state, which functions properly only when it replicates the structure of the ideal domestic unit, under the undisputed guidance of the president as paterfamilias.

Motivated by what the Suharto biographer R. E. Elson (2002) calls a "fear of the people" as a potential source of danger and disorder, the New Order regime implemented policies and actions ranging from the so-called floating mass principle, which prohibited political activity at the village level except during the rigidly circumscribed periods of election campaigning, on the presumption that such popular depoliticization was necessary to prevent unanticipated or untoward occurrences; to the regular and brutal application of state-sponsored violence against sectors of the population that threatened to deviate from this passive norm (Elson 2002; cf. Pemberton 1994). Mass citizenship was thus ideally figured in terms of collective responsibility, docile support for the actions and guidance of others, and acceptance of a hierarchy of political authority explicitly derived from a particular (Javanese, colonial, elite) notion of patricentric domesticity.[11]

The idea of the family as the foundational model of and for the Indonesian nation-state can be traced back to the beginnings of the nationalist movement. Perhaps its fullest early political articulation came in a 1945 speech by the Javanese aristocrat Supomo, one of the framers of the Indonesian Constitution, in which the anti-individualist "family principle" was presented as an alternative to the guarantee of individual rights.

> We want the spirit of family covering all aspects of human life, not only in social and economic fields, but also in the fields of politics and government in the sense that the relationship between the government and its citizens should be based on the family principle. Thus, there should be no question as to whether we have a right to association. It is an individualism. . . . In our system the attitude of the citizen is not *what is my right?* but *what is my duty as a member of this family?* (cited in Lubis 1993:78–79)

Supomo's "totalitarian" or "integralistic concept," in which the state is "integrated with the whole people, transcending all groupings" (Lubis 1993:86ff.), was influential in the original shaping of the constitutional debate, but it was not until the New Order period that it came into its full strength as a fundamental principle of government. In 1967, President Suharto defined what he called "Pancasila democracy" in terms of the "five principles" *(panca sila)* of state ideology, arguing that these are in turn based in *kekeluargaan* (family feeling) and *gotong-royong* (mutual cooperation, working together). Following Supomo's earlier critique of individual rights, Suharto insisted in a later (1975) statement that the implementation of democracy in Indonesia "must be directed for the collective interests" rather than those of individuals and that the "application of democratic rights must be in accordance with responsibility" (Lubis 1993:174).

The concept of the family foundation of the New Order state took as its starting point the mutually reinforcing assumptions that the relation between the state and its citizens should follow the hierarchical model of the paternalistic family and that the family should replicate the model of the patriarchal state. It assumed that the family—and particularly the nuclear family—was the basic unit of national life and that the state's primary responsibility was thus to ensure the security and well-being of families. This formulation led in two directions, both of which have been discussed in much detail by scholars both inside and outside Indonesia.[12] The first was that the kind of family it supported and idealized was middle-class, urban, nuclear, permanent, small ("two children are enough," according to the family planning campaigns), patricentric and paternalistic, and heteronormative—which is to say that it established a standard of domestic organization that was quite at odds with the variety and flexibility of actually occurring family forms. These included not only the extended, multigenerational family common throughout Indonesia but also the laterally expansive dispersed family characteristic of Karo and other clan-based societies, the polygynous family accepted in Islamic practice (though officially discouraged for civil servants), "blended" families of divorce or remarriage, female-headed households, large families, childless families, corporate families, same-sex domestic partnerships, unmarried adults living alone or together, dual-career families or family businesses, and a range of other options. As Suzanne Brenner (1998:237) points out, New Order ideologies of domesticity "reconceptualized the family in a way that [was] intended to drain it of its local significance and to gear it toward the fulfillment of national goals." In the process, female domesticity was fetishized in such a way that being a good citizen largely depended, for women, on qualities of "wifeliness"—the ability to manage family life and the domestic sphere properly.

The second direction was to assert that the welfare of the family, as the fundamental constituent element of society, required the guidance and protective intervention of the state. As Brenner (1998:226) notes, "There is no question that the remarkable staying power of the [New Order] regime . . . depended in large measure on its ability to insert itself deep within the domestic sphere." Much of this effort to preserve and protect the family was directed specifically at women, in their fundamental role as wives and homemakers (Suryakusuma 1996). Of particular significance here were "voluntary" organizations such as Dharma Wanita (Woman's Duty), an association for the wives of (male) civil servants, and the Family Welfare Guidance program (Pembinaan Kesejahteraan Keluarga, PKK), which targeted women in rural and low-income urban neighborhoods. Both organizations, which were led both locally and nationally by the wives of civil servants, operated as parallel structures mirroring the hierarchy of governmental authority and were specifically intended to enhance domestic harmony and engage households in the social project of development (Newberry 2006).

With programs ranging from family planning implementation and public health instruction to the promotion of literacy and household management skills, the PKK played a highly visible role in village life during the New Order period. Its promotion of domestic responsibility as a national obligation was underlined by the PKK posters displayed in every village head's office, which listed the "five duties of women": to support her husband's career and responsibilities, to bear children and care for them, and to be a good housekeeper and community guardian. Pronouncements like this echo 'Cik Muham's Fujinkai-inspired indoctrination speeches: "so that women as a whole were conscious of their duty and responsibility in the household and in the nation . . . *To be a good wife, to be a good*—whatever—*member of* society. That was the goal of our indoctrination of women as a group. It went on, too. That's what we continued after independence in women's organizations." Muham's efforts to instruct women in cleanliness, etiquette, and good household management could clearly be traced to colonial domestic instructional programs as well as to the Japanese Fujinkai, but these also resonated with late New Order fixations on domestic harmony, order, and well-being. In a somewhat different register, so too did the pride that women like Nandé Senantiasa and Nandé Usman took in doing what was asked of them, even if it was "just cooking," and in sacrificing their own desires and energies for the good of the soldiers. Their reiterated "tiredness" thus staked a specifically female claim to national belonging, in an idiom that had taken on increasing prominence in New Order self-imaginings.

"Eagerness" was what muddled this model of generalized acquiescence and passive mass citizenship. It retroactively reinstated a form of feminine agency under the auspices of a willing performance of tasks and responsibilities but at the same time suggested a kind of perturbed overinvolvement, in which girls could be accused of doing too much and going too far. It signaled a feisty hypercompliance that risked slipping into excess, bringing to mind the unruly potential of the unguided masses,[13] and served as a reminder that female sexuality was not just a symbolic marker in the repertoire of nationalist rhetoric but also a competing site of desire and responsibility that potentially brought the family and the nation into conflict and drew energy away from the struggle. This was the secret that was exposed by Nandé Ndapet's bitter complaint, the same secret that ran through the romantic fantasy of the song "Rifle Reports." The double meaning of *eagerness*—at once enthusiastic participation and promiscuous disorder—catches this contradiction, and the impossibility of its resolution, precisely.

CHAPTER 5

Sea of Fire

"They talk about the Bandung sea of fire [Bandung *lautan api*]," said Nandé Timur beru Ginting, the widow of the former Sektor III chief of staff Ulung Sitepu, "but if you want to talk about a real 'sea of fire,' actually compared to our villages, the sea of fire wasn't there, *here* was the real sea of fire." She was referring to the burning of the city of Bandung, West Java, in March 1946. It was one of the most famous events of the independence struggle, one of the handful of incidents that all Indonesian schoolkids would know, at least as a song, "Hello Bandung," and as a slogan, "Bandung sea of fire."

Following a series of escalating clashes with nationalist youth groups, Bandung's British occupiers demanded that Indonesian forces be withdrawn from the southern side of the city. The republican government, wishing to avoid confrontation with a superior military force, agreed, but nationalist militias refused to comply. In a strategic compromise, the decision was made to withdraw not just the army and militias but the entire population and to burn the city behind them.[1] It was a dramatic gesture demonstrating the strength of popular support for the cause of independence, and it became a model for last-ditch defensive action by nationalist forces in Java and Sumatra during the first Dutch military campaign of 1947.

Nandé Timur continued:

NANDÉ TIMUR: I'm not just bragging. We've seen it all. Because they [in Java] are better at promoting themselves, it's as if the struggle was greater there, you know. Just ask how many villages were burned there. Here, you know, it's just about all of them. We can take pride in that because we burned them with our own hands. Our ancestors built them in a proper manner. You couldn't do that now, but back then there was cooperation [I., *gotong roy-ong*]. Hundreds of people had to raise [the logs]. Without nails or anything. Because of their love for their homeland.

It wasn't the soldiers who burned them, it was the villagers themselves. Burn your village so the Dutch won't be able to stay there, they said, and they burned it right away without much thought. In our village, Sukanalu, there wasn't a single house left standing. Although there are still some in Barus Jahé. In Sembahé there are two or three, but in Sukanalu they're all gone. Tiga Binanga, because it was surrounded they didn't have the chance [to burn the town], that's where the [Halilintar] headquarters was. In Kuta Bangun they had time to burn them, but not Tiga Binanga. All of Kabanjahé. Actually we were almost trapped there [in Kabanjahé], so there wasn't time to get them all.

. . .

Dutch troops swept through the Karo highlands in July 1947, quickly taking control of the district's main towns and roads. Over the six months of fighting that ensued, nationalist forces engaged in an ill-conceived and ineffective "scorched earth" campaign that Karo today refer to as the "sea of fire." Villages and towns were burned, bridges destroyed, and crops left to rot in the fields. As the army and militias retreated, nearly the entire population of the highlands joined an evacuation that left them dependent on the unreliable, capricious generosity of strangers and vulnerable to marauders, xenophobic village guards, and armed bands of self-styled freedom fighters who preyed on refugees under the guise of seeking out collaborators and spies.

The terror and confusion of these events have been condensed into an iconic image of sacrifice for the nation. The burning of Karo villages is celebrated in songs and stories and annually iterated by Karo schoolchildren in Independence Day poster and painting contests. Young artists depict the old houses with their steep thatched roofs aflame and inhabitants—tiny figures with their oxcarts and bundles, hanging on to children's hands—fleeing in panic (figure 17). Gateways are decorated with images of ragged freedom fighters armed only with bloody bamboo spears. Poets and singers describe the aftermath of burnings in formulaic images of "foundations higher than roof beams" and "dark billows shading our charred villages."[2] In the magnitude of their sacrifice, not just of property, but of a whole, irrecoverable way

FIGURE 17. *Dark billows shading our charred villages.* Detail, Independence Day billboard, Kabanjahé, 1994. Photo by the author.

of life represented by the distinctive old houses, Karo see a demonstration of their uniquely powerful commitment to independence, a commitment that, according to Nandé Timur and many others, has gone unrecognized within the national community as a result of the superior public relations skills and political dominance of the Javanese. Independence Day parades and posters, painted gateways, pension testimonials, and obsessively repeated itineraries of evacuation are all attempts to claim a local space for national imagining by envisioning events in Karoland in tandem with but *otherwise than* the official histories of the nation.

This chapter and the two that follow are concerned with that turbulent period of war and displacement. Here I provide a general overview
of its events and circumstances and consider the narrative strategies of
blurred agency and displaced responsibility through which these events
are reconfigured as an assertion of national belonging and pride. Not
there, they say, but *here* was the real sea of fire.

"NOT ONE INSTRUMENT OF AUTHORITY"

The presence of British transitional peacekeepers in Medan following
the Japanese surrender did little to impede the breakdown of governmental authority in East Sumatra. The social revolution of March 1946
put an end to even the illusion of rule by the Malay sultans and demonstrated the weakness of the moderate politicians of the republican
Komité Nasional Indonesia. Contending forces struggled to fill the
power vacuum. Encamped around the city's periphery, militia groups of
varying degrees of legitimacy blockaded the roads, turning back or
appropriating shipments of rice, vegetables, and fruits and demanding
tolls from travelers.

British notes on the militia buildup around Medan give a sense of the
edgy, overexcited mood of the city's occupiers:

> TANDJOENG MORAWA: Expected conc. of 10,000 (Bataks). Hundreds of
> extremists with full military equipment are parading the village and Br.
> Indian soldiers (deserters) are joining them as well. If immediate steps are not
> take the situation will worsen.

> TWO RIVERS: Approx. 4000 Indonesians, 50 Japs, 5 Indian soldiers. Arms:
> more than 100 Jap carbines, 2 sten-guns, one case of hand grenades.

> TEMBOENG BATANG KUIS: Br. Indian soldiers assisting the extremists to
> search the Chinese shops, they have 2 MG's, here the extremists belong to
> the Black Buffalo org. A special group of kidnappers have been formed;
> straw hats, large brim, one side turned up.

> MEDAN: 60 pemoeda's [youth] from Temboeng arrived on the 16-4-46. 40
> spies from Langsa arrived the same day, to find out the whereabouts of the
> Sultan's family. . . . 23-4-46. 200 pemoeda's from Brastagi passed Arnhemia
> for Medan. Arms. Jap rifles and pistols. Race: Bataks and Achenese from
> Kota Tjane. Bataks and Achenese from Brastagi.

The Dutch intelligence report to which these notes were appended
described the city as a "besieged fortress," warning that "armed irregular bands now have an entirely free rein outside the protected sectors of
town. The republic is unable even by force to maintain a semblance of

order" (Indonesia Rapportage 1946). On April 25, in despair of "achieving anything amidst this bandit band," Lieutenant Governor Amir defected to the British. "The country is sliding towards chaos," he warned. "There is not the least unity in Sumatra. The TRI is of no account. There is not one instrument of authority" (cited in Reid 1979a:244).

Some accounts (e.g., van Langenberg 1976:517) suggest that the expansion of popular militias in the Medan Area was a result of the flood of individual volunteers drawn by news of the fighting. While the anticipatory excitement of battle is likely a "pull" factor in drawing rural youth into the militia organizations, the "push" factor is probably just as significant in accounting for the militia buildup around the city. For the newly appointed republican leaders in rural districts like Taneh Karo, the Medan front offered a quick solution for one of their most pressing political concerns: how to control and contain the armed bands that had played such a violent and disruptive part in the first months of independence. Karoland had avoided the worst of the turmoil associated with the social revolution elsewhere in East Sumatra, but idle, politicized young men with guns remained a serious threat to order and the new status quo in the district. In May 1946, the Karo Pesindo leadership instructed all its branches to commit their best recruits, and all their weapons, to the formation of the Combat Area Battalion (Batalyon Daerah Pertempuran, or BDP). Some five hundred Karo volunteers were sent on to Bandar Baru, a tea plantation and rest stop on the Medan-Berastagi highway in upper Deli, just below the steep final approach to the Karo plateau. Blockades and watchposts were set up along the road to the border of the Karo district. The volunteers continued their training, but without experienced drill instructors they could only repeat the same rudimentary drills they already knew. Food, cigarettes, money, and clothing were in short supply, as were weapons and ammunition. Before long the young men were asking permission to go home or simply leaving on their own (Surbakti 1978:120).

Toward the end of May 1946 the first Karo troops were sent to Pancur Batu, a market town on the edge of the plantation zone outside Medan. The idea was to familiarize the volunteers with the area around the city, which most of them had never visited, and to provide them with more advanced military training. Over the next month the entire battalion was gradually shifted to the Medan front. The Karo BDP was given primary responsibility for patrolling the important southwestern sector of the city's perimeter (Surbakti 1978:120). Units were rotated regularly between the forward observation post at the Bengali Bridge and the rear lines at Pancur Batu, an exchange that was "done in such a way that the weapons stayed at the front and it was only the men behind the guns who took turns" (127).

Shifting the militia presence out of the highlands may have alleviated some political tensions in the district, but it also created new logistical problems. How were the volunteers to be armed and provisioned? Unlike the government-financed TRI, the militias were largely self-supporting. A series of umbrella organizations were created to coordinate planning and supplies for the militias, all of them relatively ineffective.

"The militias back then," explained Eben Hezer Sinuraya, "they each had to find their own food, their own financing." Even bullets had to be foraged. "Bullets, we found the ones that had been thrown into the river. Lots of us hunted for bullets that had been thrown into the river. That the Japanese had thrown into the river. We dived after them, hunted, hauled them out, then dried them in the sun. Some of them actually fired, some didn't." Spent cartridges were collected and saved for reuse; village girls were put to work refilling them with gunpowder and shot.

Selamat Ginting, who took over the Pesindo command for Taneh Karo in December 1945, liked to quote Mao Tse-tung's famous maxim that the army's relationship to the people is like the relationship of fish to water: the fish need the water to survive, but the water can get along quite well without the fish. The implication of this adage was that the militias depended on the goodwill and generosity of local populations, but in practice they relied for support on a range of extractive measures, not all of which were likely to build goodwill. These included crop levies on peasant producers, taxes and tolls on travelers and traders, the sale of nationalist tokens such as paper flowers and flags, the solicitation of contributions—voluntary and otherwise—in cash or kind, and a wide array of labor arrangements, likewise ranging from voluntary to coerced. *Members of the Propertied Class!* one Medan graffito of the period exclaimed. *The struggle asks for the sacrifice of your wealth and property. Contribute!*[3] Militia units confiscated property belonging to suspected collaborators and "feudalists."[4] They raided houses and granaries in villages where the inhabitants had fled from the fighting, and they sometimes gleaned the grain from deserted fields.

The economic weakness and political fragmentation of the republic in Sumatra and the consequent self-sufficiency of the popular militias formed the basis for a pattern of territorially based command often described as "warlordism" (van Langenberg 1976:526–32). Militia leaders claimed and defended exclusive zones of action in which both civil administration and economic resources were under their control. Chief among these resources were the foreign-owned agricultural estates of the plantation zone. By the middle of 1946, some of the stronger militias in the Medan Area had taken over large estates and were selling or bartering their yield abroad. Working with local and Malayan Chinese trading partners, the "new military entrepreneurs" of East Sumatra were able to obtain weapons and equipment for their troops and in some cases to amass personal fortunes (van Langenberg 1976:560). Competition over these and other territorial resources led to frequent clashes between rival militias and TRI units, escalating in a few instances to near civil war.

The Medan Area was a patchwork of petty militia fiefdoms, with each unit guarding its own territorial authority from its fellows as well as from the enemy. In his account of a journey across the Medan front, journalist Muhamad Radjab describes the situation in late June 1947:

> Between Pancur Batu and Pangkalan Brandan we were stopped 14 times and our travel documents checked, and if we left two packs of cigarettes at the guard-post we were allowed to proceed on our journey. If we had not given them cigarettes—according to our driver—things would have been made difficult for us, we would have been ordered to open all our suitcases, they would have arbitrarily rummaged inside or tipped out the contents of the suitcases, because in this region they wielded the power. If they had shot us the police would not have dared to arrest them. . . . We were stopped and checked by Napindo, Harimau Liar, Pesindo, Mudjahidin and Banteng (Barisan) Merah, the distances between one roadblock and the next often being only one kilometer. It seemed that those guarding the post ahead refused to recognize those who had checked us previously. It appears that these checks were not aimed at investigating people's credentials, but rather at relieving travellers of money and cigarettes. (Radjab 1949:28, cited in van Langenberg 1976:568)

The Karo Batalyon Daerah Pertempuran was not one of the most powerful of the popular militias, but it did control some valuable territorial resources. The first of these was the Dolok Barus rubber estate, near Bandar Baru, at the border of Taneh Karo and upper Deli. Tons of sheet rubber from Dolok Barus were transported through the Karo district to the small port of Teluk Nibung, in Asahan. From there the rubber was exported to Malaya and bartered for such essential items as weapons, cloth for uniforms, machinery, radios, auto parts, and medical supplies (Surbakti 1978:149). Tokih Ginting, who started out as a BDP platoon leader and was later promoted to company commander in Sektor III's second battalion, described the weapons trade:

TOKIH GINTING: So even now there are—what do you call them?—arms dealers [I., *dagang perang*, lit., "merchants of war"]. Arms dealers, they know how to sell weapons everywhere. Back then the arms dealers were in Singapore. So whenever we'd give them tobacco or rubber, they'd trade for weapons. So on the shore, at Pantai Cermin, their speedboat would be waiting. The kind with two motors. They'd barter, exchange, like that. . . . Over there in Marike [in Langkat] there was lots of rubber, the tobacco came from the mountains. From Tiga Lingga [in Dairi], wherever.

The BDP's second major resource was the Medan-Berastagi highway, which it controlled with blockades and checkpoints at its upper and lower ends. All vehicles and their cargoes moving along the road were inspected and taxed by armed guards. Unauthorized individuals— suspected deserters, spies, collaborators—entering the highlands were subject to arrest, and any goods being transported to Medan without an official letter of passage might be confiscated. Similar inspections, authorized or unauthorized, could be repeated numerous times along the road by local militia units or opportunistic armed gangs, in each case accompanied, as Radjab describes above, by demands for "contributions" of cash or cigarettes.

A third major resource for the BDP was the Karo plateau itself. Harvests were good in the first years of independence, and after the hardships of the Japanese occupation it seemed a time of plenty. Villagers bought guns or donated old hunting muskets to arm their sons at the front. They put their daughters to work in the public kitchens. Farmers gave a portion of their harvest to feed the troops, though not always willingly, and collection units had to fill their quotas any way they could—by social pressure, threat, or, if necessary, force. Rice and vegetables like potatoes and peppers were stockpiled in Kabanjahé and periodically sent to the lowlands to supply the public kitchens there (Surbakti 1978:131–34). Truckloads of more perishable crops like tomatoes and cabbages were sometimes delivered directly to the front by Pesindo leaders, accompanied by local dignitaries and village girls bringing sweets, cigarettes, and cheer to the soldiers.

The growing number of militia volunteers posted to the Medan front soon strained available resources as well as the logistic capacity of Pesindo's support apparatus. To run the public kitchens, an adequate labor force had to be mobilized and maintained. This burden mostly fell on Javanese estate workers, who served both in the kitchens and on the plantations as "relatively passive (and sometimes victimized) providers of labor" for the army and popular militias (Stoler 1988:244). Seasonal foodstuffs had to meet the constant demand for soldiers' meals. Provisions had to reach the public kitchens in a timely and sufficient manner. Meals had to be delivered to soldiers posted at the front as well as in camps behind the lines. This meant that roads, bridges, and warehouses had to be minimally maintained and safety of movement along the roads ensured. Vehicles had to be kept in running order. The preparation and distribution of meals were further complicated by unpredictable fluctuations in troop strength in the Karo BPD. New recruits simply showed up or changed unit affiliation at will, and some volunteers quickly tired of life at the front and went home.

The republican government tried repeatedly to resolve these problems by placing the militias under a unified military command structure. However, neither the government nor the TRI was capable of exerting this kind of control, as the militias were in many areas stronger and more influential than either the civilian administration or the army (van Langenberg 1976:521–26). Militia units, even within party-affiliated organizations like Napindo, were no more inclined to cooperate with one another than they were to work with the army. Although the necessity of improved planning and coordination was widely recognized by the militias themselves, consolidation attempts were plagued by ideological differences, personal rivalries, corruption scandals, militia resentments over the favored treatment accorded the army, army irritation over the lack of discipline among the militias, and "childish" disputes over the relative rank of militia and army commanders (Biro Sejarah PRIMA 1976:431).

BROKEN PROMISES, SCORCHED EARTH

On November 15, 1946, Dutch and Indonesian representatives meeting in the West Javanese resort of Linggarjati reached a preliminary agreement regarding the future of the republic. This agreement, which was required by the British as a condition of their military withdrawal from Indonesia, recognized the de facto authority of the republic in Java, Madura, and Sumatra only. Four days later, British forces began pulling out of Indonesia, transferring their peacekeeping responsibilities, and most of their weapons, to the Dutch troops that had arrived in anticipation of the turnover.

Conditions at the Medan front worsened following the British departure, as Dutch forces took a more aggressive posture toward the armed insurgents camped around the city. Through the month of December, as treaty negotiations continued, the Dutch repeatedly complained of Indonesian attacks and border violations. They followed up these protests by bombing and shelling militia and TRI encampments.

The lack of an effective centralized command structure, continued difficulties with provisioning the troops, and conflicts between army and militia units over plantation resources and government funds resulted in a series of failures in coordinated nationalist assaults on Dutch targets. The province's republican capital was shifted from Medan to the town of Pematang Siantar, about a hundred kilometers to the south, and the BDP/Napindo Halilintar forward post was relocated to Titi Rante (Chain Bridge), in the midst of the tobacco fields beyond the city limits.

On January 2, 1947, Dutch troops began an assault on BDP positions, gradually forcing the Karo fighters back to Pondok Mangga, at Km. 10 on the Berastagi Road. Defensive fortifications, which had been constructed without regard for the openness of the terrain, failed to halt the advance of Dutch tanks and armored cars (Surbakti 1978:167). In February a major, coordinated attack on the city failed, in part because some of the disgruntled militias did not make a serious effort to cooperate with the army (172).

A month later, the Linggarjati Agreement was ratified by the republican legislature. It established a formal demarcation line between Dutch and republican territory in East Sumatra, crossing the Berastagi road about halfway between Medan and the town of Pancur Batu. By the time it went into effect, confidence in its measures had already broken down. Cease-fire violations on both sides were so frequent that it was referred to by Indonesians as Langgar Janji, the "broken promise" treaty.

On June 3, 1947, President Sukarno, in an effort to rationalize the structure of nationalist fighting forces, issued a decree ordering the integration of all armed forces, including both the popular militias and the TRI, into a single, unified military command, to be named the Tentara Nasional Indonesia (TNI). The plan was to take effect on July 22. Before this reorganization could be implemented, however, events took an unexpected turn. In the early morning hours of July 21, the Dutch launched what they called a police action (D., *politionele actie*), aimed at gaining control of economically and politically strategic areas in Java and Sumatra. Infantry units, with air and artillery support, began a broad attack on republican targets across the entire Medan front. Intense fighting continued for the next six days, in virtually every case with success on the Dutch side.

The Karo BDP had been entrusted with the defense of the strategically important Berastagi road, which linked the city with the agricultural heartland of the interior. Armed mainly with light rifles, they faced
Dutch infantry from Medan, which was supported by planes, tanks,
and armored cars. Focused on this frontal assault, the BDP troops were
caught by surprise when two Dutch units moved cross-country to take
the town of Pancur Batu to their rear. The Karo soldiers scattered, then
regrouped, exhausted and demoralized, on the outskirts of the occupied
town. Over the next few days, they sporadically attempted to dislodge
the Dutch from Pancur Batu while constructing emergency defensive
fortifications along the roadside beyond the town.

When Dutch soldiers entered Pancur Batu, they found the town in
ruins. Some areas had been damaged by repeated strafing by Dutch
planes, but much of it was burned by republican forces after the inhabitants had fled. This ill-advised action, which provided considerable
leeway for looting, was the prototype of a long-standing republican
defensive plan of tactical retreat in the face of an enemy superior in
arms and expertise. In the lead-up to the Dutch assault, Vice President
Hatta had called on the people to carry out a scorched-earth campaign
(Bangun and Chairudin 1994:154). Nationalist troops were ordered to
slow the Dutch advance if possible, then to withdraw after taking or
destroying whatever vital resources they could, to prepare for a long
guerrilla struggle (Reid 1974:113).

"We didn't know much about military campaigns or tactics," military historian A. R. Surbakti explained when I asked him why they had
resorted to these tactics. "Our leaders had read in the newspapers how
the Russians defeated the German Blitzkrieg with a scorched earth campaign. So the Germans would have no food or shelter. They thought,
let's do the same thing here."[5] Eben Hezer Sinuraya expanded on this
explanation:

E. H. SINURAYA: Now, regarding the scorched earth, ah, there were actually
lots of reasons why we ordered the scorched earth. Some of them recalled, or
they knew a little bit about it, how the German Blitzkrieg was opposed with
scorched earth. In Russia, they said, they can come in but don't leave them
even a single grain of wheat. Burn it all. But those men [the Russians], they
retreated to wait for winter. Actually the German army tactic of Blitzkrieg,
that's how they got supplies because they didn't bring enough supplies. The
Germans at that time. They created a battle system that was called Blitzkrieg,
lightning war, so the people wouldn't have a chance to evacuate, that's
where they would get their provisions. The Russians, the troops retreated as
rapidly as possible, but they wouldn't leave as much as a grain of wheat

behind. That's the term. So there were fires. When they got to Leningrad it was already winter, the Germans couldn't stand any more, they didn't have anything to eat, so that's where they failed.

A military strategy designed to take advantage of Russia's wide expanses and bitterly cold winters was unlikely to have the same effect in the close spaces and tropical heat of East Sumatra. With little in the way of explosives other than Molotov cocktails and Japanese hand grenades, the inexperienced sabotage units were unable to seriously damage important sites such as hospitals and warehouses. Instead, civilian populations became the campaign's main targets. As the republican forces were pushed back, they set fire to houses and shops, seizing whatever they could find of value as they went. Ethnic Chinese, rural Malays, and detainees from the social revolution were especially vulnerable, but the violence was widespread and relatively indiscriminate.[6] In the wake of the Dutch assault and the republican scorched-earth campaign, thousands of terrified peasants, plantation workers, and townspeople fled along with the retreating nationalist forces, "sometimes willingly, sometimes out of purely reflexive response at seeing their houses and farms disappear" (van Langenberg 1976:380). They packed up whatever of value they could carry—cooking pots, blankets, food, clothing, personal mementos, and the gold or jewelry that, in the absence of reliable banking, was the primary form of savings for the poor—and took to the roads and forest tracks heading toward the apparent protection of the highlands.

Within a week Dutch military reinforcements, aiming to crush the blockade around Medan, landed at Pantai Cermin, a beach southeast of the city (map 3). From there, they circled south into the interior. So rapid and unexpected was their advance that saboteurs had little time to destroy any of the main bridges and highways on their path. The Dutch quickly secured the bridge over the Snake River (Sei Ular) and launched an attack on the town of Perbaungan, in the Simalungun district. The town was taken "without meaningful opposition . . . in an atmosphere of a sea of flames" (Surbakti 1978:183). Over the next two days the town of Tebingtinggi fell, and soon after it the republic's provincial capital, Pematang Siantar. Recognizing that this trajectory would lead to Kabanjahé and Berastagi within a few days, Karo units scrambled to slow the Dutch progress and allow nationalist forces at the front and in the highlands to escape the enemy's closing grasp. A rifle squad was dispatched to Si Piso-Piso, a picturesque spot near the edge of Lake

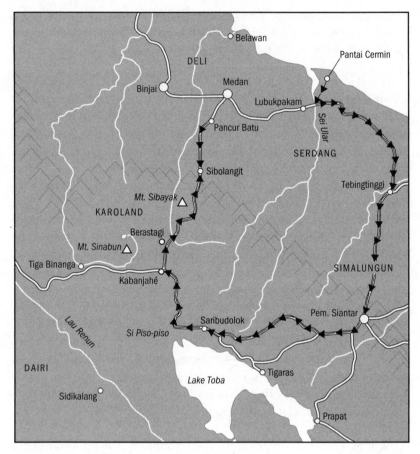

MAP 3. Dutch troop movements, July 27–August 3, 1947.

Toba, where steep cliffs and sharp switchbacks in the road created the ideal conditions for an ambush. But with limited ammunition, the sharpshooters could do little more than delay the Dutch advance.

THE FALL OF KABANJAHÉ

Selamat Ginting was surveying the situation of his Napindo troops around the lowland town of Pancur Batu on July 31 when he was called away to deal with the Dutch army's imminent move toward the Karo district. His wife, Piah Manik, remained in Batang Kuis, where she was in charge of the public kitchen on the eastern sector of the Medan front. "He left around four in the afternoon," she recalled. "So by ten o'clock we'd all gone to bed. The phone rang. 'Leave right away, the Dutch are already in Tebing[tinggi], if we don't defend the road with our men, by morning the Dutch will be in Mérék,' [he said].'' From Mérék, a crossroads village on the Karo-Simalungun border, it was a straight shot to Kabanjahé, only a few hours away.

At Napindo headquarters in Kabanjahé, plans to evacuate and burn the town were immediately put into effect. Essential supplies, including such items as writing materials, gasoline, radio and vehicle parts, medical supplies, and equipment from the public kitchen and weapon shop were collected, and documents were secured or destroyed. Prisoners were released from the town jail with a speech urging them to join the struggle (Surbakti 1978:190). Soldiers' families, medical workers, and members of the kitchen crew were sent to safer locations, and troops began to be shifted to the Halilintar battlefront headquarters near the Lau Simomo leprosarium. Government workers began to move their offices to the new provincial capital of Tiga Binanga, in the central region of the Karo district. The rest of the town's inhabitants were then advised to evacuate. That night, "The residents of Berastagi and Kabanjahé had no time to sleep at all. Everyone was talking about the Dutch attack while they packed to leave the city. The bustle of activity and feeling of apprehension that swept over the minds of the inhabitants also spread among the evacuees [from the lowlands]. Except for individuals of Chinese descent, everyone packed up and prepared to evacuate their belongings out of the town" (Surbakti 1978:191). By midnight the evacuation was complete. Meanwhile, Piah Manik and her crew were salvaging what they could from Batang Kuis, rushing to reach Kabanjahé ahead of the Dutch.

PIAH MANIK: So we arranged everything in the public kitchen, the medical personnel. . . . We had about six vehicles. Then the cooking equipment and the rice and the side dishes, we put it all in there. Then between Berastagi and Kabanjahé, there was an airplane. It was close, so we left the cars behind and we ran into a bamboo thicket. We hid under the bamboo. Because we were scared they'd shoot us, or bomb us. We left the cars, then once the plane was far away, "Come on, come on, let's go," we said. So we went on to Kabanjahé.

In the early hours of August 1, the Dutch army rolled through Mérék and into the Karo district. The road from Mérék to Kabanjahé had been crowded for days with evacuees, but ahead of the Dutch advance it was empty save for the remains of burned vehicles and abandoned oxcarts. "Nothing that moved on that highway could escape being targeted by aerial gunfire" from Mustang fighter planes that circled overhead (Surbakti 1978:194).

At 11:00 that morning, a sabotage unit using Molotov cocktails began to move through Kabanjahé. Napindo quartermaster Koran Karo-Karo "took the first bottle filled with kerosene, lit it and set fire to his own home. [He] had no opportunity to remove its contents. . . . He actually could not bear to see the house he had set fire to himself totally destroyed, but his sadness was not apparent to anyone else."[7] From there, the flames moved toward the center of town. Because of the rush of the evacuation, much of the town remained intact, including such strategic sites as two hospitals, the central market, the prison, and a portion of the Chinese section, where the residents had remained behind to guard their homes and shops. In Berastagi, an army sabotage unit managed to burn the Planters' School, which had served as the headquarters of TRI Regiment I; the Grand Hotel, "the largest and most luxurious hotel in Southeast Asia"; and several other important buildings, but little else (Gintings 1975:36).

NANDÉ TIMUR BERU GINTING: We evacuated from Kabanjahé, I forget the date, well, that's what happens when you get old. We evacuated from Kabanjahé, then everyone scattered. We didn't see our husband [K., *perbulangan kami*, "our husband(s)"] there, we left one by one, like so, they went one way, we went the other, like that. So when the Dutch had been seen in Siantar, we couldn't wait for our husband. We just left, like that, carrying the baby, we didn't take anything at all, just the children, and some basic clothing. Kabanjahé hadn't been burned yet. We left early in the morning. By nightfall Kabanjahé and Berastagi had burned down.

"When we got to Kabanjahé," Piah Manik said, recalling her flight from Medan, "it was almost like a ghost town. Most of the people had left already." She went immediately to the house where her parents were living. They were preparing to go to nearby Kandibata. Fearing that would soon be unsafe as well, she convinced them to stay instead with her husband's family in Kuta Bangun. She arranged a place for them on the public kitchen convoy, which would pass through Kuta Bangun on the way to Tiga Binanga. "I got them in the group from the public kitchen, my mother and father, and my little brother. I put them in the car. I told them to go to Kuta Bangun. I told them to go there. Then all the public kitchen vehicles left Kabanjahé heading for Tiga Binanga. I stayed behind. My older sister, Nandé Ramona, stayed behind too." By the time she left the city with her husband and sister, the planes were unbearable.

PIAH MANIK: They were shooting constantly. So we ordered the driver to go on to Kandibata. We didn't go in the car. "Wait for us in Kandibata," [we said]. "We'll take the car from there." You know where Kandibata is? We traveled in the direction of, um, there was a cow pasture near Kacaribu, then on to Kandibata. We cut through under the bamboo. Because of all the planes, maybe five of them sometimes. So we walked. I was really dumb. It was like this: This plane flew over, we were right in the middle of this, wide cabbage field, maybe a hectare. Well, it's a long way across, so I said to Pak Ginting—*eh-nnnnng!* went the planes—I said, "Get under me, so you won't be hit," I said. "If I'm hit it doesn't matter, just so you're all right." I thought I'd be his protector, whereas if I was hit, he'd be hit too. "*Eh*, you're out of your mind," he said. If I'm hit, it's not important, I thought, but if he's hit, our soldiers wouldn't know what to do. . . .

So then, we were running, we made it out of that field, we made it under the bamboo grove, there were oranges, maybe four truckloads dumped out there, they couldn't be sold anymore, there was no one to buy them. We picked them up, all these oranges. So, "Hey, look at the oranges," [we said]. We put them in our knapsacks, we put them in our pockets. I don't know where all we put them, the five of us. We carried off a lot of them. There were maybe a hundred soldiers there in Kacaribu, under the trees, they'd all gathered there. "Hey, here's an orange, here's an orange," we had enough to give one to each of them. "Here's an orange, here's an orange."

They picked up their driver and automobile on the road between Kandibata and Kacaribu, then continued to Kuta Bangun by car.

PIAH MANIK: Pak Ginting said [to the driver], "Be careful over by Lau Simomo. That's where our front is. From there we'll organize our battle for Kabanjahé." The Dutch were already in Tiga Panah then [about halfway between Mérék and Kabanjahé]. When we left. Well, wasn't that close? We went to Kacaribu, Kandibata. The soldiers, they didn't have any vehicles, they had to walk to Lau Simomo. We had a car. We had a car, we got to, um, past Raja Merahé, what's the name of the place? Past Raja Merahé, it was empty, there wasn't even any [cover] there, so we headed for Tiga Binanga.

[Farther on] we met up with Rokim's brother, he was in the medical corps too, Nandé Ruth's brother. I forget his name. He was on the ground with these three fellows. He was a medic. These fellows had been hit, in the legs. "*Eh!* What's going on?" we said. "Go on ahead, I'll take care of this," he said. They'd already been hit, shot. That was the plane that had tailed us all the way, but we weren't ever hit.

We got to Perbesi, the planes couldn't go that far. We got to Perbesi with Pak Ginting and all of them, they headed [back] to Lau Simomo, the soldiers and all. We went on to Kuta Bangun. Kuta Bangun, then we set up a hospital there, we set up a public kitchen.[8]

Among the last evacuees out of Kabanjahé was Sanaria boru Silalahi. The daughter of a Toba Batak man who had moved to Kabanjahé following a family dispute over political succession in his home village, she was one of the twelve Srikandi girls from Karoland who attended the training program on Jalan Duyung. When she and her family departed the sirens were sounding, but they didn't dare to look back. Everything was in flames.

> SANARIA BORU SILALAHI: By the time we got out of Kabanjahé, it was already burning. Already burning. Just imagine how our hearts were—Mom was already scared, my younger brother was still little. . . . *Wah*, it was really horrible. I think the clouds and the smoke from the fire had already combined. We didn't dare to look behind us. There were waves of people on the road. Leaving Kabanjahé.

In the panicked crowds along the way, her younger brother became separated from his mother and sister.

> SANARIA BORU SILALAHI: So when we got to Kacaribu I accidentally lost hold of my little brother. My mom was screaming, "You only have one little brother, what's the point of living [if he's gone]?" If it had been a girl who was lost, it wouldn't have been such a big deal.[9] But my little brother— "What were you thinking?" [she said]. I was confused. Where? It was dark. My mom was anxious. I didn't know what to say. My mom just wept. She didn't want to go on. "I don't want to, let me die," she said.
>
> The next morning she found my little brother. We met up again, my mom kissed him. Only then did we go on.
>
> My little brother had two kilos of rice. Apparently he'd dropped the rice, and he was scared. I was carrying [our belongings] on my shoulders, and I held on to my little brother's hand. My mom was carrying the rest of our things. So I held on to him. When the rice fell, he pulled loose to go look for it. When we met up the next day, we went on, but we didn't have any rice.
>
> We kept going, until Gurusinga or Kacaribu, I don't remember anymore. Whenever we saw a dragonfly above us we'd hit the ground. That's how horrible our evacuation was back then. And we were hungry too. What could we take along? We didn't have anything to carry, we didn't carry anything.

Dutch troops entered Kabanjahé at two in the afternoon on August 1, with a total strength of six tanks, thirty armored vehicles, and about a thousand soldiers (Djamin Ginting, cited in Bangun and Chairudin 1995:149–50). By then the town was virtually deserted. At 5:00 in the afternoon the bridge at Kandibata was destroyed by republican saboteurs, thus temporarily severing the connection between Kabanjahé and Tiga Binanga. Hearing the sound of this explosion, Dutch troops in Kabanjahé fired several mortar rounds in that direction, causing a panic among the inhabitants of several nearby villages, who quickly packed a few belongings and fled during the night (Surbakti 1978:196).

A few hours later, the town of Berastagi was also taken. This meant that the Dutch controlled both ends of the Medan-Berastagi highway, at Pancur Batu in the lowlands and Berastagi at the edge of the Karo plateau in the interior. Midway between them, the remnants of the Karo BDP struggled to maintain their defense of the road near the market town of Sibolangit.

Because of the chaos of the evacuation and the lack of working communications equipment, the Karo troops were not aware of the speed or direction of movement of the Dutch reinforcements. "The news from Kabanjahé, they just said the Dutch were there, that's all," Eben Hezer Sinuraya explained. Assuming that the Dutch assaults would continue to come from Medan, the remaining Karo defenders had built their fortifications facing the city, but when the Dutch troops unexpectedly came at them from the rear, these were rendered useless. Already exhausted from the intense fighting, the BDP soldiers were quickly routed.

Karo accounts of the battle of Sibolangit frequently cast it not as a failure but as a fatal misrecognition, in which enemies are taken for friends and allies. Often the misidentification is explained as a Dutch trick: the enemy's tanks fly the Indonesian flag or are painted with pictures of wild oxen, the symbol of the Napindo forces. In the version told by Eben Hezer Sinuraya, the Dutch forces are mistaken for reinforcements from India:

E.H. SINURAYA: [The Dutch] made a trick, they plastered red and white paper [flags] on the tanks. Then they moved toward here. So that's why we—well, as I said before everyone was illiterate, they didn't know anything, they thought India was, where? They didn't understand. So there was an expression that went around at the time, *bantuan kita dari India*, "our help from India." So. Because in the terms that our leaders used, India was supporting us. India supported our independence struggle. Well, when the tanks came, we never thought, Where in the world would *we* get tanks? Never thought of it. Just, the tanks came, all decked out in red and white, wow, this must be help from India coming. Yeah, they didn't know where India was, they hadn't been to school, how were they supposed to know? So they thought India was who knows where, help from India has arrived, they all came out, at Sibolangit. They all came out, *Merdeka! Merdeka!* Then these guys attacked them. We didn't know that in war anything's fair.

The remaining Karo defenders fled, singly and in groups, cross-country toward the highlands. Some were following a prearranged fall-back plan; others were simply trying to get home. Along the way they joined the flood of evacuees heading for the apparent safety of the highlands from Medan, Pematang Siantar, and other towns that had been touched by the Dutch attack and the nationalist scorched-earth program.

RETURN TO *REPOLUSI*

On August 4, 1947, less than two weeks after the war began, international pressure led the Netherlands and the republic to agree to a cessation of hostilities. Although the Dutch had little more than a toehold in the highlands, under this agreement most of the Karo district was ceded to their nominal authority. As they tried to extend their actual control over the six months that followed, the district became a no-man's-land of deserted, ruined villages and neglected fields. Journalist Hans Post, who followed the Royal Dutch Army's Fourth Infantry Battalion, reported that the Karo district, "which before the war counted around a hundred thousand inhabitants," was "almost totally deserted" when they arrived there; with the exception of the few areas held by the Dutch, it was a "wasteland" ruled by "bands of criminals" and "nationalist extremists" (Post 1948:41).

The *saranen* campaign had prepared Karo villagers for the arrival of Dutch forces but not for the sudden appearance of thousands of evacuees fleeing the lowland fighting. "The retreat of the soldiers and militia volunteers, the speed with which the enemy could take Kabanjahé and Berastagi, the flood of evacuees from every direction to Karoland, truly startled and generated anxiety among the population," writes Surbakti (1978:219). "The people were shocked that this could happen, and did not believe that the town of Pematang Siantar, the provincial capital and headquarters of the TRI Divisional Command, could fall to the hands of the enemy without opposition. . . . Their amazement grew when a number of officers withdrew to Karoland without their men." Retreating soldiers were mocked as cowards, and some who strayed into rival territory were captured, robbed of their weapons, or even killed.

As the fighting units struggled to collect and regroup their scattered forces, a corrosive mix of fear, uncertainty, and rage triggered a return to the uncontrolled violence of *repolusi*. Soon the lowland evacuees, many of whom were impoverished Javanese plantation workers or Malay peasants, were swept up in the violence. By the beginning of August 1947, stories of mass executions, robberies, and attacks on evacuees were circulating widely throughout the province. Rumors spread that collaborators had slipped in among the masses of refugees and that some were themselves secretly directing the Dutch aerial attacks.

Groups of refugees were "picked up" by village guards and renegade army and militia units, interrogated, searched for incriminating evidence, and in some—perhaps many—cases "pacified" (I., *diamankan*, the nationalist euphemism for lynching or other extrajudicial execution). Stories of the wealth of the deposed sultans provided a convenient rationale for arresting or robbing travelers carrying items of value.

> BAPA MUL SEMBIRING: Maybe it was because of valuables or gold, or jewelry or whatever. According to today's measures, the reasons don't make sense. For example, let's say maybe there's a little picture of a Dutch flag on someone's body, like an old tattoo, all kinds of things like that. They looked for an excuse. Sometimes they'd use a mirror, if there was a reflection like a rainbow, you know. There's the color red, there's yellow, now that's what the Dutch flag is like *[sic]*, right? Maybe on account of that, someone's soul would be lost.

A human life was worth less than a cigarette butt back then, remarked Nandé Marlina from the village of Selandi, as she described the torture and killing of a group of evacuees at the Lau Melas hot springs between Payung and Selandi.

> NANDÉ MARLINA BERU GINTING: Near our village was the Payung hot springs. There were a lot of Javanese, you know. *Kaki tangan*, they said—well, it was right at the stroke of noon, or anyway it was really sweltering. Led them to the hot springs, put them in the water, you know. They screamed because of the heat of the water, you can imagine. We'll only bathe in the hot spring there when it's cold. It was right at noon they pushed them in. . . . *Iyoh*, all the Javanese shrieked. "I confess, brother, I confess," they said. "I confess, I confess. I'm a spy," they said, because of the heat of the water.

Strangers were not the only ones who might have been taken for collaborators. In this situation of extreme volatility, a linen sheet laid out to dry, a red blanket, or a mirror could be taken as a targeting signal to Dutch bombers. The color of a dress, or even a bruised fingernail, might mark you as pro-Dutch. "I had this dress," said Terang beru Singarimbun. "It was red, white, and blue. But I couldn't wear it. I'd be yelled at. 'That's the Dutch army,' [they'd say]." Piahmalem beru Sembiring, of Berastepu, said, "It's the common people who suffered. So you'll know, if someone had a fingernail that was inflamed, just pull it out. This is red, white, and blue, the Dutch flag, the nail would be pulled out. Horrible!" Even an unintended expression of sympathy for the evacuees could be dangerous.

NANDÉ NDAPET BERU PERANGIN-ANGIN: In Selandi, there's a ravine there. This is what they did, they lined them up there. We watched from Selandi hill over there. "These are *kaki tangan*," they said. They made them turn around. We saw them get pushed. *"Aduh,"* I said, without thinking. They pushed them into the hot water, they hit them. *"Woi!"* I exclaimed. They threw them into the ravine. "Come on, let's get home," [I said], "or we'll be killed next," so we went home. Even so, it wasn't finished. The next day, four more people. They were like frogs. Back then, humans were like crickets.

Intellectuals, members of the Westernized elite, Chinese shopkeepers, and Christians were accused of being pro-Dutch. In one particularly tragic case, Dr. Saragih, a Simalungun Batak physician residing in Berastagi, was executed as a collaborator "because he was found with European-made medicines that were still new" (Vice-Governor Mr. S. M. Amin, quoted in a report reproduced in Bangun and Chairudin 1994:161).[10]

Nandé Titing beru Karo was among the evacuees from Kabanjahé. Her father, Mumah Purba, ran a flower shop in Medan's Indian district, Kampung Keling, and served as the *kapitan* (sheriff) of the city's small Karo community during colonial time. Educated in Java, he came under the influence of the Indo-Dutch journalist Ernest Douwes Dekker, one of the founders of the early nationalist Indische Partij. Nandé Titing's family was active in nationalist activities in Medan, and both her father and brother joined the TRI officer corps immediately after its formation.

In December 1946 Nandé Titing went with her mother and younger siblings to celebrate Christmas in Kabanjahé; they stayed on in the highlands to escape the hardships of life in the occupied city. Shortly before the Dutch invasion she married Roga Ginting, one of the leaders of the district Pesindo organization. None of these nationalist affiliations protected the family during the evacuation; on the contrary, they increased the danger, as Nandé Titing described in her account of the family's escape from Kabanjahé.

NANDÉ TITING BERU KARO: I'd just gotten married. But we weren't together. I didn't know where he was. I just went with my mother. Because they had all gone. My in-laws had gone ahead. They were in one group. I didn't want anyone close [because] I was the child of a soldier. I was active myself, so the people who wanted to run away, they didn't invite us [to join them].

First we ran to my mother's village, Lingga. We brought our things, you know? We had five suitcases, this big. We went there on a, not a bus, like that but smaller. A lot of suitcases could fit on the top. [The militia fighters] wanted to open them up to look for weapons. What for? My mother had a pistol in her hand. They didn't dare to take it. "Don't come any closer," my mom said. We didn't want to sleep in the house. There was a barbershop, it was empty, we slept there. My grandfather, my father's father, slept in one room, we slept in the other. At night we were scared. They wanted to search our things.

This was the funniest thing, a picture of Douwes Dekker was what saved us in my mother's village. They wanted to kill us. Because they said this album was full of pictures of Dutch people. "They're enemy spies," they said. Luckily there was an HIS [Dutch-Indonesian elementary school] student there. "What are you talking about?" [he said]. "This is Douwes Dekker, he was an adviser to President Sukarno." Then they were quiet. Luckily there was an HIS student there, in Lingga. This was in my mother's father's own house, that's how cruel it was during the revolution. What they actually wanted was those five suitcases.

At Kampung Merdeka near Berastagi, about a hundred detainees from the time of the social revolution were killed by a rogue BHL militia unit (van Langenberg 1976:581; Gintings 1975:42). Meanwhile, "the same sickness emerged to the east of Kabanjahé" (Surbakti 1978:221) in the Tigapanah subdistrict, where some family members and supporters of the *sibayaks* were being held. In the hasty nationalist retreat, the detainees were deemed an unnecessary hindrance. Unwilling to free them, their captors decided they should be executed. Surbakti's account of the incident is characteristically circumspect:

> Because of the difficulty of guarding and feeding [the prisoners] while they were imprisoned, they were forced to Lau Biang, [the river] near the village of Benuraya to complete their life stories. But the fate of men is truly in God's hands and death is not permitted before the ordained end. The guards who escorted the prisoners were not expert marksmen, so although the prisoners, with hands tied, were sprayed with bullets on the banks of Lau Biang, only one or two were struck by bullets, and the others pretended to fall into the river and let themselves be swept away, even though they were not hit at all. (1978:222)

When a squad of soldiers sent by Selamat Ginting to investigate reports of violence in the north Karo region went missing, presumably captured or killed, it became clear to the nationalist leaders that the situation had to be resolved, even if it meant diverting resources and attention from fighting the Dutch. A team composed of representatives of the TRI, Napindo, and the district civil administration, and backed by Halilintar troops, moved into the disturbed areas, freeing political prisoners, kidnapped soldiers, and other detainees. By August 22 the wave of internal violence was receding, at least for the moment. By then

Dutch forces were pushing deeper into the interior, and residents of many of the villages where refugees had been arrested or killed had themselves been forced to evacuate.

As Patricia Spyer (2002:33) notes regarding local journalists' accounts of recent sectarian violence in Ambon, cautious Indonesian writers tend to employ an "abstract lexicon" of culpability when describing violent incidents, speaking of "certain parties" [oknum-oknum tertentu] or "unknown persons" [orang-orang yang tak kenal] as a way of deflecting and dispersing blame. This may be done, she points out, "with the very best of intentions," out of concern that specifying responsibility for such acts may shatter the fragile harmonies of social life in the aftermath of internal violence. And yet, she argues, this elusive agency can "produce a sense of phantom danger, which lurks both nowhere in particular and therefore potentially everywhere in general."

In a similar manner, though perhaps for different reasons, Karo accounts routinely depict acts of internal violence as agentless, "wild and irresponsible actions" (Gintings 1975:38), a "sickness" that could "emerge" on its own, or attribute them to specific but unnamed agents: "some fighting units in several villages" (Surbakti 1978:222) and "other units whose actions could not be considered praiseworthy" (Selamat Ginting, quoted in Bangun and Chairudin 1994:149). In his account of the Lau Biang executions quoted above, Surbakti goes even further. His upbeat assessment, in which the murderous intent of the guards is fortunately negated by their incompetence, leaves the fate of the prisoners "in God's hands," in which "death is not permitted before the ordained end." He implies, but carefully does not say, that most saved themselves by pretending to fall into the river and letting themselves be swept away (I., berpura-pura jatuh ke sungai dan menghanyutkan diri). The verb form meng—kan diri (I., cause oneself to be) is sufficiently clear as to the intentionality of the action on the part of the prisoners, but the root, hanyut (swept away), leaves the outcome of that action in doubt. Hanyut is the term most often used when someone is lost in the currents of the deep and turbulent highland rivers or in the flash floods that occasionally have taken victims even in the shallow and slow-moving lowland streams. It is not a term that ordinarily implies survival. For Surbakti, however, the point is not to indicate whether the prisoners lived or died but rather to relieve the unnamed freedom fighters of responsibility for the killings.[11]

The usual estimate of civilian casualties in the Karo district during this time is two thousand (Reid 1979a:256). Figures like these—

"precise, yet extravagant" in their rounded-off simplicity—are indicative of the "persistence of rumor" in a discourse of truth (Pandey 2001:71). They are at most "best guesses," signaling the enormity of the event while remaining within the precincts of the bearable (Pandey 2001:91). The actual number of deaths, whether greater or fewer, is impossible to determine, in part because there is no reliable count of the number of evacuees who reached or passed through the Karo highlands in 1947–48.[12] Neither European observers nor those of the nationalist center, even in Medan, had access to much information other than the rumors that swirled within the highlands. Incidents of violence against civilians were clearly widespread, ranging from village executions and mob attacks to the robbery and rape of fleeing evacuees in isolated and unpopulated regions. Many other evacuees died of hunger, hypothermia, shock, exhaustion, or the accidents and hardships of the journey. While unwitnessed deaths such as these may have left little trace, local incidents may also have been magnified in imagination over time or fused in memory with later events, such as the traumatic violence of 1965–66, which was, at the time of these interviews, still literally unspeakable in the face of continuing state repression. They may have been overlaid with images and stories of violence elsewhere, from films and news reports, public art, and political rhetoric.

Official reports of the violence, both Dutch and Indonesian, are based in hearsay, rumor, and speculation, yet carry the aura of truth. As Pandey (2001:90–91) suggests, such "rumored statistics" may measure the extent of what one can bear to imagine in a particular instance, or they may demonstrate how extravagantly numbers can be called on to serve political or sectarian ends, but they can neither be dismissed nor taken as a literal measure of casualties. For Karo witnesses, not numbers but metaphors convey the emotional weight of the violence. A human life, we were told, was "worth less than a cigarette butt" back then; people were "like crickets"; they were slaughtered "like goats," their bodies left in the rivers as a warning to others.

BURN YOUR HOUSE DOWN

Immediately after the burning of Kabanjahé, military leaders in the highlands issued directives prohibiting further scorched-earth actions, but these had little effect. Over the course of the six-month military campaign, some fifty-three villages in the Karo district were burned (Gintings 1975:167). Some of the destruction was the result of Dutch bombing and artillery fire. Dutch soldiers set fire to a few villages in reprisal for harboring "extremists." Others were probably burned by their fleeing inhabitants. But most were torched by retreating nationalist forces after their inhabitants' departure.

Many of the old-style eight-family log houses, which Karo regard as the architectural epitome of a traditional way of life, were lost during this period. Of all the old houses in Barusjahé, only the residence of the *sibayak* was left standing (Gintings 1975:106). In the large and prosperous village of Batu Karang alone, ninety-five of the old houses and the "very elegant" office of the *raja urung* of Lima Senina were burned on November 25, "the day after the great evacuation of inhabitants from north Karo to the west, after the Dutch army broke through the [nationalist] line from Sibintun to Tiga Pancur, where a terrible battle between the two forces went on for five hours" (Bangun and Chairudin 1994:154–55).

One of the first houses to be burned was the residence of the *sibayak* of Lingga, on the road between Kabanjahé and Berastagi. Setianna beru Tarigan recalled the destruction of this grand house with the ambivalence of conflicted loyalties. She had been a nurse in the army medical corps, for which she was awarded the Guerrilla Star, the highest Indonesian recognition for military service during the independence struggle. She was a prominent member of both the Veterans' Wives Association and the North Sumatran Organization of Female Veterans. But she had also been related by marriage to the son of the old *sibayak* of Lingga.

SETIANNA BERU TARIGAN: I remember it well, because my oldest sister was married to the [younger] *sibayak* of Lingga. You'd call her his First Lady.[13] At the time the *sibayak* was still imprisoned [following the social revolution], you know? So it was ordered—yeah, we were really the ones who did the burning, not the enemy, OK? [I., ya, itu memang kitanya yang bakar, bukan musuh kan]. She was ordered to come out, the house was burned. *Our* house was burned too, but it didn't burn down, only one corner was burned, like. But my sister's house was totally destroyed. Totally destroyed. From there it began to be set in motion, *we* were the beginning of the scorched earth, where it started to spread.[14]

When Karo talked about the highland "sea of fire," they often used the first-person plural inclusive voice (I./K., *kita*, "we all"), as Setianna beru Tarigan does here, in which the "we" who did the burning merges with the "we" whose homes were burned. In part this was an ideological confusion intentionally introduced by nationalist propagandists. Villagers' participation in the republican military withdrawal from

Dutch-controlled territory was supposed to provide a lesson in the meaning of independence. By sharing the soldiers' travails, villagers would gain a stake in the struggle—whether they wanted it or not. The primary aim of the scorched-earth campaign, as Eben Hezer Sinuraya explained, was to keep strategic resources out of Dutch hands, but there was a secondary purpose as well:

E. H. SINURAYA: The second effect of the scorched-earth [campaign] was to ignite hatred toward the Dutch. See, what we were worried about at the time was that if the people turned back to the Dutch, we'd be in trouble, it would be hard to conduct a guerrilla war. If the people weren't our friends any-more, it would be harder. So we worked it so that the people truly felt like [the Dutch] were their enemies. And created suffering so that their hatred would increase.

How well did this strategy—assuming that it was a strategy and not just random violence rationalized after the fact—work? It certainly did not work for those who already saw themselves as marginal to the national community, such as the ethnic Chinese, or for educated elites who were again targeted as collaborators because of a supposedly Dutch lifestyle. Nor did it work for moderate and conservative nation-alists, among whom, as Anthony Reid notes, the "chaos and division left behind by retreating Republican [units]" confirmed the suspicion "that the Republic was incapable of ensuring the security which would make the goal [of total independence] feasible" (1974:115). But this induced suffering does seem to have produced a payoff in popular com-mitment where political indoctrination had already prepared the way for it or where a sense of solidarity with nationalist groups already existed, through kinship, friendship, principle, or cultural affinity.

Since the beginning of independence, *saranen* propagandists in the Karo highlands had been urging villagers to burn their homes and flee rather than to accept a Dutch return. Nandé Senantiasa and her friends in Payung described one of the meetings there:

NANDÉ SENANTIASA BERU BANGUN: This is what they said back then, let's gather for a meeting, isn't that right? They knocked on the table, *tok-tok*, and we were all quiet. "How about it, do we want to be colonized by the Dutch or do we dare to burn all of our village so the Dutch don't come here?" Isn't that how it was back then? Burn it down, it doesn't matter, we said. "Even if our houses are destroyed, won't we be glad to be independent?" they said. Glad! we all said. We'll be glad to evacuate, so that we aren't colonized by the Dutch. Even if our village is burned, we'll be glad.

NANDÉ USMAN BERU PANDIA: Yes, we were glad, even to burn down our houses.

NANDÉ NDAPET BERU PERANGIN-ANGIN: We'd rather be dead than colonized.

Of course, it's easier to be happy about burning your house down in anticipatory imagination than it is in the actual event, and the enthusiasm of this remembered response had been reinforced by a half century of celebratory nationalism. In his posthumously published memoir *Titi Bambu*, TNI regimental commander Djamin Ginting offers a classically heroic depiction of the scorched-earth action in Karoland. Written in the third-person plural of "the people," his account resonates with the we/*kita* of national remembrance.

> The scorched earth was not just carried out by members of the military units, but by every level of the population [I., *segenap lapisan rakyat*]. The people set fire to their homes, sheds, rice storehouses; they left behind all of their possessions, their gardens, wet and dry fields, to follow the evacuation, according to the summoning of the republic, in the direction of the interior. Not once did they tremble, nor were they frightened or terrified to face the new life that they would experience along with their Nation that was threatened with destruction by the colonizer. The people proved their determination at the beginning of independence for "MERDEKA ATAU MATI" [independence or death] with the fact of their deeds and attitudes now. (Gintings 1975:35)[15]

"A HOUSE THAT HAS BURNED CAN BE REBUILT"

Fighting quickly spread across the Karo plateau as Dutch troops pushed back the inexperienced and underarmed nationalist forces. Over six months of fighting, the Dutch gradually captured all the main roads through the district. Just ahead of the invading forces, villagers fled with whatever goods they could carry.

NANDÉ RIKSON BERU TARIGAN: One night it was announced, everyone work together to destroy the bridges here and there. What were their names? Tiga Pancur, and the bridge at Lau Lateng. In one night they destroyed them, men and women all went out to destroy the bridges so [the Dutch] couldn't break through to here. So then there wasn't a Gamber front anymore. There wasn't a front here, they'd already moved the front to the mountain. "Front," they said, meaning headquarters, our soldiers' headquarters. So for a long time they defended the front at Bakerah. . . . Tanks were coming from the far field over there. On the other side of our village. They'd already come through to there. So one night, around half past seven it started, they fired the mortar, their soldiers advanced, airplanes firing from above, they broke through here. They broke through here, they occupied Sibintun, they occupied Kuta

Buluh. We'd already spread out on the mountainside. After that, we had to evacuate. You couldn't not evacuate. Then everything was all mixed up. There was no telling what you'd eat, kids. Even hungry, you got what you could, the rice would come to a boil, *por*! The rifles would go, and you'd put the rice pot on your head [and run away]. The rice had already come to a boil but it wasn't done yet. Even half-cooked it tasted good because you were so hungry. You'd eat it half-cooked. It even tasted good. Why not, if you were hungry enough?

As the Dutch gradually "spread their wings" (Gintings 1975:152) over the highlands, the nationalists' supplies, money, and morale dwindled. Surbakti (1978:200) describes the troops as "in an exhausted condition, their clothing on average was only one set, and a large number no longer had any shoes." In evacuated areas nationalist soldiers could no longer pass incognito among the population, since those few who remained were presumed to be Dutch sympathizers. Nor could they count on the support of villagers for food and labor. Instead, they found themselves in the position of having to assist the now-homeless villagers who followed them.

From the Halilintar forward post at Lau Simomo, militia forces engaged in occasional forays into the enemy stronghold in Kabanjahé and struggled to repel Dutch advances along the northern fronts, but by October 11 the Dutch had gained control of the eastern side of the district. On November 19, TNI troops withdrew from the front at Suka, leaving the poorly armed Halilintar forces to defend the front alone. The Dutch were then able to quickly break through the nationalist defenses at Tiga Pancur, Sibintun, and Kandibata. On December 7, Lau Simomo was abandoned. Three days later the Dutch attacked and took Tiga Binanga, the market town serving then as the provincial capital-in-exile.

"In theory," writes Surbakti (1978:252), "with the Dutch army's success in taking Tiga Binanga, the Karo highlands were all within the area of their conquest. But based on the facts in the field, the enemy's victory did not yet mean that our troops had been expelled from the area. The enemy troops were not able to occupy every village they attacked, and as soon as they left our troops would return to occupy them." Nevertheless, with the Tiga Binanga–Kabanjahé highway under Dutch control, the district was effectively bisected; militia units could still operate on the southern part of the plateau and in the north but could not move between the two sectors. While the southern sector included the major rice-producing region of Juhar, the area north of Tiga Binanga, where the main Napindo Halilintar forces were located, was rugged and underpopulated with little arable terrain, making it difficult to provision the troops and their dependents.

From Tiga Binanga the Dutch were able to launch direct attacks into the heartland of Halilintar support. The field hospital and supply stores at Kuta Bangun were quickly moved to a remote site, but their precious short-wave radio, hidden near the village, was taken by the Dutch. Over the last two weeks of December the Halilintar Regiment gradually shifted its support personnel and accompanying dependents into the Taneh Pinem region of Dairi district. By the end of the year they had all been settled in the string of small villages that lay just across the Lau Renun River from Karoland.

If there was a bright spot in all this, it was a symbolic one. On January 1, 1948, Vice President Mohammad Hatta sent New Year's greetings addressed to "the Karo people whom I love."

> Merdeka!
> From afar we have observed your tremendous struggle to defend from enemy attack the sacred land where our blood has been shed. We are sad to feel the suffering of you whose homes have been burned down when your village lands fell into the hands of the vicious enemy whose aggression continues, and area of conquest widens, despite the cease-fire ordered by the U.N. Security Council.
>
> But we also feel the pride of people who are so willing to sacrifice to defend our ideals of independence.
>
> I am proud of the Karo youth who struggle to defend the Homeland [I., *tanah air*, lit., "land and water"] as faithful sons of Indonesia.
>
> A house that is burned can be rebuilt, a village that is destroyed can be built again, but the honor of a nation, once lost, is difficult to restore. And your suffering is most righteous, let everything be gone, as long as the nation's honor is protected and the ideals of independence continue to be defended until the end.
>
> The people who are so determined, and this is truly the determination of the entire people of Indonesia, the people who are this determined will not be swallowed up [I., *tenggelam*, drown, sink beneath the surface, disappear], but will certainly reach the victory of their ideals.
>
> Above your villages and lands that have been burned to the ground, the radiance of Indonesian independence will then shine, and the seeds of well-being and prosperity will sprout among the Karo people, as a part of the people of Indonesia that are one, indivisible.
>
> We conclude our praise and thanks to you with our slogan, precisely: Once Free, Always Free.
>
> *Your comrade,*
> *Mohammad Hatta, Vice President of the Republic of Indonesia*[16]

• • •

On January 17 and 19, 1948, representatives of the Netherlands and the Republic of Indonesia ratified a peace agreement aboard the U.S. troop ship *Renville*. The Renville Accord called for an immediate cease-fire and affirmed, as a temporary measure, the Dutch claim to territory captured during their first military campaign. Northern Sumatra was divided along Vice Governor Van Mook's proposed line of farthest Dutch penetration into two administrative entities, one a part of the Republic of Indonesia and the other the Dutch-supported State of East Sumatra (Negara Sumatera Timur, NST). The provinces of Aceh and Tapanuli and a narrow adjacent slice of the Karo plateau fell outside the Van Mook Line in republican territory, but most of Karoland was inside it and thus under the aegis of the NST "puppet state." All republican military forces and government offices were required to be withdrawn from this area, regardless of the actual control they may have exercised there. In exchange for these concessions, the Dutch agreed to hold a referendum within the year to determine the ultimate status of its occupied territories. Reversing their original policy of mass withdrawal from areas controlled by the Dutch, republican leaders urged Karo evacuees to return to their homes in anticipation of the promised referendum.

Over the year that followed, Karo made their way back to their homes and began the process of rebuilding them. Building materials were provided by the Dutch; village plans were designed to facilitate surveillance. If you travel through Karoland today you will see, alongside the ruins of a few of the remaining old houses, much evidence of this reconstruction. Low single-family houses or duplexes, small shops and cafés—mostly of unpainted boards and rusty zinc roofs—stretch along the roadside or encircle a central *losd* (D./K., a large open-air building where ceremonies and markets are held). Other more recent additions—a church or two, perhaps a mosque, a health clinic and a government office, a few houses of brightly painted cement built by city-dwelling children for their rural parents or grandparents, an array of political signs and notices, electric power lines and satellite dishes, gateways and guardposts, all of which would be at home anywhere in Indonesia—measure a continuing history of assertive state intervention, national incorporation, and global connections.

"The master saga of nationalist struggles, " writes Shahid Amin, "is built around the retelling of certain well-known and memorable events." The significance of such "celebratory accounts . . . lies in their elaborate and heroic setting down, or 'figurating,' the triumph of good over evil"

FIGURE 18. Ruins of an old Karo house, Mardinding, 1994. Photo by the author.

(1995:2). The Bandung sea of fire was an event that seemed to lend itself to such figuration because of the self-contained, dramatic, and highly visible nature of the incident itself as well as the apparent unanimity of support for it among Indonesian nationalist actors—the republican government, the TKR, the militias, and the civilian population of south Bandung. (That the "enemy" in this case was the British peacekeeping force rather than the Dutch seems to have been easily disregarded.) By contrast, Karoland's own sea of fire seems obscure and confused, dispersed and drawn out, and largely unnoticed beyond its immediate precincts.

Even at the time of Karoland's sea of fire, there seems to have been little knowledge or understanding among republican leaders in Java, or locally in Medan, of what was going on in the Sumatran hinterlands. This was partly because of weak lines of communication and authority between the city and the countryside and partly because of the "urban bias" of observers, whose interpretive standards were set in the metropole (Kalyvas 2006:38–48). Secondary sources, both academic and journalistic, have been largely shaped by these views as well. Most emphasize the acts and decisions of a small group of national leaders. Grassroots actions are interpreted mainly in terms of how well local actors align with these central figures, how well they do or do not follow directives from above. As a result, nationalist histories have tended to reproduce the invisibility or irrelevance of events on the nation's outskirts, in Karoland and elsewhere, depicting them, if at all, as a "blur of rustic excesses, fueled by local political machinations" (Amin 1995:192), or, like the Karo sea of fire, as unoriginal repetitions of events that have already happened elsewhere. Hatta's New Year's greeting transmutes all of this unclarity into a symbolic expression of "good over evil," not by drawing it into a triumphal narrative of heroic struggle or figuring it as a second Bandung, but rather by celebrating the "most righteous" suffering of the people in defense of the nation's honor and by obscuring the agents of that violence.

The legitimation of collective, organized violence by the Indonesian state has been historically effected by the moral myth of the struggle, in which the army appears as the sole active force responsible for generating and protecting national independence—as opposed to the people (I., *rakyat*), who appear as merely passive recipients of military action. This dyad has conventionally taken the form, in public display and in popular memory, of a ragged, long-haired youth carrying a blood-stained bamboo spear, ready to attack an unseen enemy (figure 19). This image, inscribed on book jackets, comic books, and ceremonial arches, reenacted by costumed schoolchildren on national holidays and in television miniseries and museum dioramas, encapsulates a heroic vision of the struggle against Dutch colonialism. Its counterimage is of a group of women, often clutching infant children, running in fear from the scene of violence (figure 20). The gendered logic of these representations is obvious. Equally significant, however, is the way that actions and effects are detached from each other in these images. Notice how, in the first, the object of violence is removed from the field of vision altogether; in the second, the agent of violence is present but separate, placed in a different cell and in fact moving *away* from the clustered victims.[17]

A similar separation of cause and consequence was repeatedly effected in stories Karo told of the sea of fire. They employed an "abstract lexicon" of undisclosed responsibility in which acts of internal violence were carried out by unknown or unnamed miscreants: "certain persons," "irresponsible individuals," or "other [military] units." "No need to say who was responsible" for the killing of refugees or political prisoners or collaborators, they told me repeatedly, "just

FIGURE 19. Cover illustration, *Medan Area* comic book (Arry Darma 1993).

SUNGAI ULAR

GERAKAN MENGHINDAR DARI KEPUNGAN MAUT INI BER-
LANGSUNG HINGGA PAGI HARI. PASUKAN KITA BERBAUR
DENGAN PARA PENGUNGSI BERJALAN MENUNJU ARAH
SUNGAI ULAR DENGAN MELALUI LADANG-LADANG DAN KAM-
PUNG. JEMBATAN SUNGAI ULAR DIJAGA OLEH MUSUH
SEHINGGA HARUS DIHINDARI. SEBAGIAN MENUJU KE ARAH
BAGIAN HULU DAN ADA YANG MENUJU KE BAGIAN HILIR.
SAAT ITU SUNGAI ULAR SEDANG BANJIR SEHINGGA
MERUPAKAN RINTANGAN ALAM YANG SANGAT BESAR.
RAKIT YANG ADA TIDAK MEMADAI UNTUK MENGANGKUT
ORANG BEGITU BANYAK. TIMBUL LAH RASA PANIK DAN
CEMAS, TAKUT KALAU-KALAU TERBURU DIKETAHUI OLEH
PIHAK MUSUH. DAN APA YANG DICEMASKAN MENJADI
KENYATAAN. TIBA-TIBA MUNCUL BEBERAPA PESAWAT
MUSUH YANG LANGSUNG MENEMBAK KAN SENAPAN
MESIUNYA DARI UDARA KE ARAH RAKIT DAN KE ORANG-
ORANG YANG MASIH BERADA DI TEBING SUNGAI. BANYAK
DIANTARA MEREKA YANG TERJUN KE SUNGAI DAN
LANGSUNG TERBAWA ARUS YANG SEDANG GANAS. TER-
JADILAH TRAGEDI YANG MEMILUKAN. TAK TERHITUNG
BANYAKNYA KORBAN. TAPI MEREKA ITU JUGA MERUPAKAN
BAGIAN DARI PADA KORBAN-KORBAN LAIN YANG TELAH
MENYUMBANGKAN NYAWANYA DALAM PER JUANGAN ME-
NGUSIR PENJAJAH DARI BUMI TERCINTA INDONESIA.

FIGURE 20. Indonesian refugees at Sei Ular (Arry Darma 1993).

say, 'such-and-such happened.'" They claimed, "We burned the houses
ourselves," disregarding the military coercion that in many cases lay
behind those actions or blurring the inclusive stretch of the first-person
plural *we*. Does *kita* here represent the inhabitants of the houses or villages that were burned, or is this a form of collective agency shared by
civilians and soldiers, neighbors and strangers, alike?

In these representations of the Karo sea of fire, the verbal as well as the visual, there is no recognition of agency beyond the inclusive we/ *kita* of intertwined responsibility and sacrifice, the anonymous culpability of "certain persons," or the blurry representation of the idealized nationalist subject, "the people." Proximate causation is not important here, because the burnings are understood as a general condition of struggle and, above all, as a claim to national belonging. Like the violence of *repolusi*, which could "step forward" at any time, independent of human agency, the sea of fire simply "spreads" through the highlands, its destructive flames uniting soldiers, peasants, politicians, and evacuees in the passion of independence.

CHAPTER 6

Letting Loose the Water Buffaloes

If I'd understood back then, if I'd understood from the beginning like I do now, I truly would not have dared to go to war.

—Eben Hezer Sinuraya

"Every war is ironic," writes Paul Fussell in *The Great War and Modern Memory*, "because every war is worse than expected" (1975:7). The incommensurability of means and ends, the "dynamics of hope abridged," the disjuncture of optimism before and despair afterward, the "benign ignorance" of those at home and the horrible recognitions of those who fought, the frailty of human flesh and the deadly power of metal and machinery—all these are figures of a tragic irony that, according to Fussell, has come to be "an inseparable element of the general vision of war in our time" (35). It is through the "mechanism of irony-assisted recall," he argues, that a narrator is able to "locate, draw forth, and finally shape into significance an event or a moment which otherwise would merge without meaning into the general undifferentiated stream" of wartime experience (30).

Karo soldiers' recollections of the independence struggle have little of the vivid, nightmarish horror typical of Fussell's World War I battle stories, but they are steeped in irony nonetheless. Their "satire of circumstance" is gentler and more self-mocking. Karo men charted the trajectory of their wartime progress in the verifiable evidence of pension testimonials and displayed their incipient patriotism in nostalgic recollections of the romance of the struggle, but it was above all in ironic tales of "ignorance" that they dramatized their wartime experience. This is irony in a comic mode, which dwells lightly and with laughter on the contrast between perception and reality, between what soldiers should know and what they had not yet learned, between what they expected and what actually took place.

Cults of sacrificial heroism are a common feature of official nationalisms, exemplary deaths serving as the ultimate model of subordination of self to the aspirations of the community or the will of the state.[1] In Indonesian nationalist iconography, the fallen heroes of the struggle for independence were memorialized as "flowers of the nation," like a bunch of jasmine (I., *serumpun melati*), which remains sweet even after it has dropped from the vine. But Karo veterans wasted little time on death, exemplary or otherwise. Instead of battlefield heroics, they drew attention to the comical, everyday "ups and downs" (I., *suka-duka*, lit., "joys and sorrows") of military life. When they spoke of death, it was in the matter-of-fact tones of the pension testimonial, with its straightforward body counts and names of casualties. What they mostly told were survival stories, which hinged on missed connections, failed encounters, and lucky escapes.

Their stories played humorously on the raw recruits' lack of military competence—like the one about the soldier who accidentally fired his gun straight up in the air and found when the bullet came back down that he had shot himself, or about the volunteer who fell asleep while smoking and set his bed on fire, so that his mates, startled awake by what they thought was the smoke of any enemy attack, jumped out the window (fortunately incurring only minor injuries and some embarrassment). Even scenes of battle were mined, with self-deprecating humor, for their foolish mistakes and military incompetence. One soldier described his attempt to arrest corpses—"I shouted as loud as I could: 'Hands up! Hands up!' while aiming the barrel of my rifle at them. Not a one of them would move, because they were actually already dead." Another, ordered by his commanding officer to find the cartridge box for a captured machine gun, came back with "the box holding the Dutch solders' bread ration" instead (Surbakti 1979:249).

One of my favorite survival stories had to do with the invulnerability charms (I., *jimat*) many of the volunteers wore. Much has been written about the use of these amulets by *jagos* and other "social bandits" in Indonesia, but this was actually the only story I ever heard about them. It was told by Eben Hezer Sinuraya, a Christian company commander in Selamat Ginting's Napindo Halilintar Regiment/Sektor III. Eben Hezer's father, who was one of the Dutch mission's early converts, composed many of the hymns that were still included in the Karo church hymnal and served as a catechist (K., *guru agama*) in the subdistrict seat of Tiga Nderket, on Mount Sinabun's southern slope. This was one of the most enthusiastic, and unruly, areas of mobilization in the first months of independence, and Eben Hezer was among the first volunteers.

EBEN HEZER SINURAYA: There was even one of my men—eh, we, at the time there were still lots of *perbegu* [K., spirit-keeper] people. As a rule they were mostly *perbegu* at the time. So at the front we all wore amulets. I didn't, actually, because my father in Dutch times was an evangelist, a Protestant religious teacher. So, no way [I said]. But I was influenced. This friend of mine said, "It's like this," he said, "they're shooting at us. Since you don't wear an amulet, sir, all the bullets will run to you," he said. "For example, suppose the men on your right and your left are wearing amulets, and you don't wear one, sir, the bullets will all skew toward you. So you should get an amulet," he said.

Finally, I went to get an amulet from this [Acehnese] man. The best time for an amulet is during the dark of the moon. So it was exactly the right time. "Eh," I said, "let's go, Dad, it's the dark of the moon." "Well," he said, "come on, come on, I'll make it," he said. He made it, Arabic writing. He wrapped it up, I don't know what with, used a string, tied it up here. He gave it to me, now wear this. I remember it well, what he said. "Wear it. Death is forbidden before the end." Oh yeah, so I wore it.

So then they ordered us to fight. It was the second time I'd been ordered into battle. The first time we didn't meet [the enemy], this time we didn't meet either. But I chased around there, lots of coconut trees were broken off because they'd been hit by cannons. Chase, chase, chase, we didn't meet up. They were in vehicles, I was chasing them on foot, right, so we didn't meet. I was really pissed off thinking about it. Ah this, this thing, it's probably this amulet that's making us not meet, I thought. I thought a long time. He said before the ordained end death is forbidden. Ah, I pulled it off, that's no charm. Even without a charm there's no death before the ordained end, I thought. I threw it into the rice field here, I don't know which field it was. I threw it away and I never wore another amulet.

Eben Hezer was one of the most thoughtful military ironists that I knew. In the special form of generational etiquette that still held among veterans of the struggle, he was mostly known by his personal name, and though I addressed him as Bapa (K., father, as a senior man of my patrilineal clan, Karo-Karo), this was how I always thought of him. We first met at Selamat Ginting's funeral, where he delivered a memorial speech on behalf of the Sektor III troops on the themes of leadership and its responsibilities. Maybe that had put him in a particularly elegiac frame of mind. Bits of that speech filtered into his conversation with us a few weeks later, giving his stories a serious edge despite their comic motifs and frequently farcical tone.

One of the things that made his stories so entertaining was that he told them (to us, anyway) in Indonesian. Instead of the poetic elegance and intricate wit characteristic of Karo storytelling, his narration took on the pared-down awkwardness of a nonnative speaker. This had the paradoxical effect of drawing attention to their "Karo-ness." Their tone of ethnic self-parody would have been quite impossible to render in the Karo language. As his monologue went on, his accent thickened and his rhythms and phrasings became increasing Karo-ized. Common Indonesian stereotype holds all Bataks to be backwoods rubes, and this played perfectly to Eben Hezer's overarching narrative theme of the perils of ignorance. (Dialect humor, which Karo enjoy greatly, is virtually untranslatable, but to get a similar effect, imagine his stories spoken in an overdone American southern accent.)

"I'm a little odd," he told us, explaining that he'd gone from being a schoolteacher to farming to serving as a militia commander and then on to a career in the army, from which he had recently retired, with no previous military training other than his brief service in the civil air patrol before the Japanese occupation. It may have been his Christian background that made him dislike the Japanese so much, because most of the teachers I knew spoke of them more sympathetically; at least the Japanese respected teachers, they said. Eben Hezer was teaching at a Christian primary school near Kabanjahé when he had a run-in with some Japanese soldiers. They made him load oil drums onto a truck for a daily wage of only three Japanese cents. Offended by this treatment, Eben Hezer quit his teaching job and returned home to Tiga Nderket. Because military press gangs would often show up unexpectedly, looking for Heiho volunteers or laborers for the salt works at Tanjung Tiram—duties from which few young men ever returned—he hid out in a field hut, where he spent his time shredding local tobacco to be sold for cigarettes. When he popped up again after the Japanese surrender, everyone assumed he'd been off serving as a Heiho in Burma all this time. "That's why they made me an officer right off," he said. "Whereas actually I'd never been a soldier at all. I guess it was from being a teacher, the others didn't catch on as quickly as I did. I'd watch them do something, I'd study it, then I'd try."

Eben Hezer was sent to the Medan front in May 1946, part of the first wave of Pesindo volunteers from Taneh Karo. Not long after, he was ordered to take a troop of fifty recruits three kilometers cross-country to Bekala, where a militia unit under attack by a British patrol had called for reinforcements. "The thing is," he said, "why did they ask me? I was, like I said, this was the first time I'd fought. I didn't know how to do it, but I was determined."

All he knew from his brief military orientation was the run-and-drop maneuver, which was intended as an evasive action for troops under enemy fire. "When you ran and when you dropped, our instructor himself didn't know, because he'd never done it before, he didn't understand it either." So Eben Hezer had his troops running and dropping all the way to Bekala, over fields of coarse, knife-sharp *lalang* grass. "Run and drop, it was cat-and-mouse the whole way, run and drop, till my men's faces were just shredded, where that *lalang* grass swiped them." By the time they arrived in Bekala, the British patrol had fortunately retreated. While his men were resting, Eben Hezer reported to the local commander.

> E. H. SINURAYA: He was the one who'd asked for help. That's why I came. "Wow!" he said, "the bullets were zinging and all"—and really I could see the teak trees there had been struck by bullets, they were all torn up. Eh! I thought. I never knew that bullets zinged. Well, I'd shot a carbine maybe three or four times before I came to the war. I didn't know that bullets whistled. Apparently they whistle, like: *nging-nging-nging.* I'd heard this while we were running and dropping. I heard them, *nging-nging.* But I didn't know that was bullets.
>
> So I went back. I met my men. "What's up, sir?" they said.
>
> "Ah," I said, "they've already gone.'
>
> "So we can go back?"
>
> "Right."
>
> "If we have to go back, let's not go the way we did before, sir," one of them said.
>
> "Why?"
>
> "You know, there were all those bees," he said. "That *nging-nging-nging,*" he said.
>
> Now I took action, because I already knew the score. Whereas I hadn't known it before. "Ah, you're an ignoramus," I said. "That's why I ordered you to run and drop. Those were bullets, not bees," I said. He was surprised, too!
>
> "Wow," he said. "You're a real champ, sir!"

. . .

Veterans' nostalgia thrives on this sort of comedy of errors, which can be seen as a theatrical denial—to themselves, to others—of their own capacity for violence. In ironic tales of ignorance and folly, Karo veterans suppressed the brutality of warfare in favor of its ludic possibilities. They celebrated their former innocence in uncannily morphing objects like the bullet-bees of the Medan front and commemorated their youth in the vivid details of everyday life during wartime. Self-portraits of the narrator-as-naïf enabled a storyline of incremental awareness, as these Karo citizens-in-the-making learned, however partially, what it meant to belong to the national community. In the process, their stories enlivened and supported an official narrative of routinization, in which the republic was transformed from a "state of mind" to a state "strong enough to establish authority over its most troublesome subjects" (Cribb 1991:192).

"Ignorance" was how the Sektor III veterans defined their relation to the nation-state in its early years.[2] This was more than a simple acknowledgment of the things they hadn't known: the sound a bullet makes, the political meaning of independence, the nature of modern warfare, even of the nation itself. It also implied something positive. It was a *natural* condition of belonging: a spontaneous, visceral recognition of the national community and an intuitive desire to defend it. In their view, knowledge and bravery were antithetical attributes. "From what I saw," said Eben Hezer, "all of [the volunteers], they were really all equally ignorant, all of them. But because of that spirit, that spirit was what made them [into soldiers]." Mulih Kwala Sebayang, a member of the Halilintar/Sektor III sharpshooter squad, had this to say:

MULIH KWALA SEBAYANG: All the men of Sektor III, 85 percent of them were ignorant people. That's why they were daring. The ones who had a little bit of schooling, they all stayed in the rear, they became staff officers because they weren't daring. The others were the ones who went to the front. They didn't know yet about bullets and all, that they could kill, they didn't think much about it. They were daring. The ones who'd been to school, they thought about things, bullets are like this, or that. Maybe they'd read about them in books, maybe from experience, from other people's stories, maybe they'd seen movies. They were scared. That's it. So 85 percent ignorant people, that's us in Sektor III. Ignorant in the field of knowledge but invulnerable in spirit.[3]

"Strong desire, bravery, that was all [we had], just that," said Tokih Ginting, who had also been a Sektor III company commander. "That was the capital, only that was our capital for this independence." These men depicted their ignorance of warfare as a kind of accidental gift to the nation, but you could just as easily see it as the nation's first tragedy, this lethal mix of terror and violence, of popular justice and military impunity. Ignorance situated even the most heinous acts—village burnings, the murder of refugees—within the framework of an organic nationalism, if not to condone them, then at least to make them comprehensible.

More than most of the people we talked to, Eben Hezer allowed his account to echo with darker ironies of fear and fortitude, nationalist fervor and moral uncertainty, tragedy and farce, exploring in the process the despair and responsibility of leadership and, above all, the ambiguities of ignorance that underlay both the heroism and the failures of the freedom fighters. Taking his stories and those of some of his fellow freedom fighters as a guide, this chapter follows the fighting from the fall of the Medan front in July 1947 through the temporary ceasefire of the Renville peace accord in January 1948, then picks up their military experience after the war, as they learned to "fill in independence from the inside."

SIGNS AND RUMORS

When the provisional republican capital of Pematang Siantar fell to the Dutch on August 1, all official radio and print communication with the Karo district was cut off. Telephone and telegraph lines were down as well. To nationalist historians like Surbakti (1978:220), this "governmental vacuum" and the lack of communication media that could "convey to the masses what must be done" were major factors in the mass panic that ensued. But as James Siegel (1997a:194) notes, the danger was not so much the lack of information as it was too much communication. Rumors filled the expanding spaces of uncertainty and dread. Marks were taken for signs, and objects were endowed with an excess of meaning. Texts, like the propaganda pamphlets dropped by Dutch planes expressing their friendly intentions, might mean the opposite of what they said, or they might encode secret messages within seemingly inconsequential expressions. The sudden and unexpected appearance of masses of lowland refugees added to the atmosphere of fear and suspicion. Warnings about spies and collaborators (kaki tangan), confused stories of conspiracies and acts of sabotage, the sounds of explosions and distant mortar fire, and reports of village burnings and evacuations elsewhere produced a stunned incomprehension as Karo awaited the arrival of the Dutch army. As Dutch planes began bombing highland targets, villagers unfamiliar with the technology of aerial surveillance or bombsights speculated that the pilots must be receiving signals from the ground—the flash of a mirror or a white sheet laid out to dry—telling them where to strike.

Stories circulated that *kaki tangan* had slipped in among the refugees. Some said they bore a special identifying mark (I., *cap*, "stamp, brand")— a rainbow, a tattoo, a code word. "Back then there was a post, you know, they caught everyone with a mark, all the Javanese people," said Rasi beru Ginting of Batu Karang. "They said it was the mark of a *kaki tangan*. 'You're a Dutch spy,' they said to all of them. 'I see the mark right there.'" Of course you wouldn't know whether there was actually a mark on your back at all, as Terang beru Singarimbun pointed out, but if someone claimed they had seen it, there was nothing you could do.

> PIAHMALEM BERU SEMBIRING: We saw this ourselves. "Come sit here, you," they'd say. "Look at your back, look at your back, there's a Dutch mark here," then wham-wham, they'd hit it. Whereas there wasn't really any sign on their back. "Here it is, here it is," they'd say. Because the militias were still ignorant. If they were educated, how would it be possible for them to do this? They didn't even know the letter *A*, so—what do you think?—he could get his revenge now, to his heart's satisfaction.

Some said that *kaki tangan* were stamped with the letter *F* (for the Fujiwara-kikan, a radical pro-Japanese organization) or the number 5 (for the conservative Pasukan V, "Fifth Force"). Others mentioned PADI, which was the acronym for Persatuan Anak Deli Islam, the Association of Muslim Sons of Deli, a royalist Malay militia that had been formed by a group of rural Islamic students in 1938.

> E. H. SINURAYA: All these ignorant people, plantation workers, Javanese contract workers, lots of them went to the villages in our area, they went out to the fields and all. I don't know where they all came from. They called themselves freedom fighters too. So they stamped them. This is when there were all those killings, they had stamped these people. They said, if you want to be a freedom fighter you have to wear a stamp. This PADI stamp, for example, lots were put out with that term.

Eben Hezer explained that a document had been discovered that gave PADI a different meaning: "Partai Anti-Demokrasi Indonesia. They made it out like it stood for the Indonesian Anti-Democracy Party, like they were all anti-independence, the ones who had that stamped on their backs, that stamp. . . . They left it like it had been accidentally dropped, sort of like they'd lost it. '*Wah,*' we said, 'this is a Dutch code that's been lost. The collaborators' code has been dropped. It must be this . . . this . . . this . . . oh, this is all a disaster!'" Eben Hezer now believed that the document was just another dirty trick of the *kaki tangan*, part of a disinformation campaign intended to mislead the nationalists, but at the time that stamp meant disaster for the refugees.

Eben Hezer was one of the few people we met who owned up to any part in the killing of refugees. Wounded during the fighting at the Medan front, he had been sent home to Tiga Nderket to recuperate. There he was assigned to teach literacy classes, which he did for about three months, until the Dutch military campaign began. At the time, not many Karo knew much Indonesian beyond the keywords of nationalist sloganeering, which is probably why Eben Hezer, who had more education than most, was chosen to do the interrogating. Few of the refugees knew the Karo language, and Javanese laborers might not even know any Indonesian beyond the functional commands required for their jobs.

> E. H. SINURAYA: Lots of the Javanese we examined had been stamped like that. "What are you doing?"—I went along with it, I was still a part of the inspections. "I was ordered to attack." "Attack where?" "Sukatendel Village, over there." "What are you supposed to attack?" "Don't know." "Wow, so why are you wearing that stamp?" "Well, it's the sign of the freedom fighters." But in the report we'd seen, it was Partai Anti-Demokrasi Indonesia. That stamp meant disaster! Those were the ones who were slaughtered. You see, this was a "psywar" inside the war. Because the Dutch were really smart, they already knew, we didn't know anything yet, did we? We didn't understand any of that yet.

"I had doubts back then," he admitted, "but if I'd said don't kill them, maybe I would have been killed too. Because they'd have thought I was helping [the *kaki tangan*]. At the time there wasn't a commander. Meaning, even the commander, if he was considered mistaken, he could have been taken to the river over there [and executed]." So Eben Hezer kept his doubts to himself, even when the work of "collaboration" was something that seemed as harmless as hoeing or letting water buffaloes out of their stable.

> E. H. SINURAYA: There was one fellow I interrogated, I was truly amazed. "What are you supposed to do?"
> "Let the water buffaloes loose."
> "Hah! What are the water buffaloes let loose for?"
> "Don't know."
> That's how it was, these people were all ignorant, the plantation people, Javanese contract workers, they were all ignorant back then. "What's your job?"
> "Let loose the water buffaloes."
> "What water buffaloes?"
> "Yeah, water buffaloes."
> "Why do you let them loose?"

"Don't know."

So I thought, What's the point of all this? What's the point of letting water buffaloes loose? But I ran into them later, and that's when I found out. . . .

PSYWAR

In writing about this phase of the independence struggle in East Sumatra, nationalist historians and memoirists consistently emphasize the role of *kaki tangan* in a psywar aimed at demoralizing the population. In these accounts it is the *kaki tangan* who is to blame for the violence against evacuees and political prisoners. As "news spread from mouth to mouth, it was readily spiced up and supplemented along the way, and sometimes, all unrecognized, infiltrated by enemy collaborators in a war of nerves. This *psywar* [English in original] launched by the enemy readily influenced thoughts and general opinions, until anxiety and panic surfaced among the people" (Surbakti 1978:191). In a similar vein, TRI commander Djamin Ginting insists that unauthorized killings (I., *pembunuhan-pembunuhan liar*) were the result of "individual sentiments and . . . 'the spread of enemy poison' that whispered the news that many enemy collaborators had slipped into the midst of the community and among the evacuees" (Gintings 1975:37). Such "provocations and poisonous circulations," Ginting concludes, "certainly came from Dutch collaborators" (40).

But why would collaborators spread rumors about the presence of collaborators? This sort of circular reasoning, which shifts the responsibility for extralegal violence from the perpetrators to their victims, is a familiar feature of contemporary Indonesian political rhetoric. Perhaps the most egregious case of the denial of culpability through reverse attribution is the military-supported slaughter of alleged communists and fellow travelers in 1965–66. Decades later, New Order propaganda still fervently condemned communists for provoking the massacre, in which as many as a million lives were lost. Similarly, the "Petrus Affair" of the early 1980s, in which several thousand tattooed recidivists in Java and Sumatra were said to have been executed, was at first depicted as the work of rival gangs and "mysterious marksmen" (I., *penembak misterius;* "Petrus" is an acronym). Later, when these not-so-mysterious shooters were publicly acknowledged to be members of army death squads, responsibility was turned on their victims. "If there are killings," a government representative explained, "that is because of the presence of crime."[4]

Another common strategy of displacement has been to blame acts of mass violence on secret agents or provocateurs like the *kaki tangan*—mysterious, often invisible strangers who incite violence within communities for their own secret, nefarious purposes. Conspiracy theorists—a category that includes virtually every Indonesian citizen—readily point to shadowy figures such as the mysterious marksmen of the 1980s; ski-mask-wearing "ninjas"; strangers whose military-issue shoes or "handy-talkies" reveal their army affiliation; mystical burglars who can turn themselves into cats to evade capture; hired thugs and urban gangsters; foreign jihadists; dangerous ghosts bearing grudges; as well as the "all-purpose" *provokator*. However accurately some of these may (or may not) identify the instigators or ultimate sources of violent acts, blaming them also deflects culpability from more proximate local actors caught up in the rush of violence. This could be seen as a form of moral evasion, a refusal to accept responsibility for one's own actions, or an attempt to make sense of what must be the most horrifying and inexplicable of circumstances, the eruption of violence in the midst of ordinary life. It could be a recognition of how easily, and fatally, both victims and perpetrators can become caught up in events that they neither understand nor control. Like the "abstract lexicon" of unspecified agency, it is certainly an attempt to find a way to go on living in the wake of communal violence (Spyer 2002: 33).

The enigmatic, perhaps apocryphal, document of Eben Hezer's account, which identifies the *kaki tangan* as both secret conspirators and innocent victims, knits together these techniques of scapegoating and displacement in a densely ambivalent exploration of the perils of ignorance. The Javanese victims are ignorant; they call themselves freedom fighters but they are actually pawns of a royalist organization. The militia volunteers and village guards are ignorant; they are fooled by the false letter identifying the evacuees as collaborators, members of the "Indonesian Anti-Democracy Party." And all of them are victims of the "real" *kaki tangan* and their Dutch masters operating smoothly and invisibly behind the scenes. How else could such things have happened?

WAR IN THE HIGHLANDS

On August 4, 1947, just two weeks after the start of the military campaign, Dutch and Indonesian representatives accepted an internationally brokered cease-fire agreement. By then the Dutch controlled the main roads and towns of East Sumatra and of East and West Java but not the rural areas beyond them. Nevertheless, they claimed authority over all intervening territory up to their most forward points of progress, linked by the unilaterally declared demarcation line that came to be known as the "Van Mook Line" (or, in republican parlance, *impian* Van Mook, "Van Mook's fantasy"), after the Dutch lieutenant governor-general Hubertus van Mook, who designed it (Reid 1974:113). This meant that much of the Karo district, though actually in Indonesian hands, was claimed by the Dutch. "Policing" and "mopping up" operations within this zone of imagined authority provided a cover for continuing Dutch military actions.

Anthony Reid (1974:114) describes a "fitful war" going on inside the Van Mook Line from the time of the nominal cease-fire until the January 19, 1948, signing of the Renville peace accord, which officially recognized Van Mook's territorial claim. This description underestimates the intensity of fighting in the Karo area, where Dutch and nationalist forces struggled to exert control over the contested hinterlands. To illustrate: the following incidents were reported by Halilintar and TNI sources in the days leading up to the declaration of the Van Mook Line.

- August 20—Dutch attacks on Napindo troops in Kandibata, Cinta Rakyat, and Lausimomo and on TRI units in Suka and Benuraya
- August 21—TRI troops attacked in Samura and near Katepul, on the Lau Biang
- August 23—fighting in Samura, Tiga Panah, Seberaya, and Sukanalu
- August 26—ditto Suka, Kuta Kepar, Kacaribu, Naman, Perteguhan, Kuta Tengah, Bunuraya, and Pertumbukan
- August 27—Kutatengah, Gambir, and Sukandebi
- August 28—Sukandebi again, also clashes between Dutch and BHL units in Cinta Rakyat, Gambir, Kuta Tengah, and Sukanalu II
- August 29—Deram; Dutch fighter planes fire into the market plazas of Tiga Binanga and Tiga Nderket; in Tiga Nderket eight civilians, including one child, were killed and the BHL headquarters (formerly the home of the Raja Urung) burned.
- August 31—fighting in Semangat, Gurusinga, and Kuta Gadung (Surbakti 1978:217–19, 226–27; Gintings 1975:53–88).

Over the next several months, skirmishes and battles continued at nearly this pace, especially in the northwestern Karo area, where the main Napindo forces were deployed, and in the southeastern area around Suka and Seberaya defended by TRI Regiment I. Hans Post found the fighting there during this period "harder, tougher, and more dangerous than in the 'police action' itself." No one here realizes, he wrote to his Dutch audience, "that the 'police action' was a pleasure trip compared to the titanic work that had to be done in the months of August and September." Across Indonesia, 58 Dutch soldiers were killed and 234 wounded between August 5 and 26, a number only a little lower than the casualty rate during the police action itself. Of these, the KNIL Fourth Infantry Battalion stationed in the Karo district sustained a total of 76 losses (including dead and wounded), the highest of any Dutch unit anywhere in Indonesia (Post 1948:59).

These figures say more about the energy of Dutch efforts to root out "extremists" in Karoland than they do about the military prowess of the poorly armed and inexperienced Karo fighters. Despite their losses, says Post, the enthusiastic "KNIL-lads" went about the "hunt for extremists [D., *extremistenjacht*], as if it were a kind of sport" (Post 1948:43). But neither their enthusiasm nor their superior weaponry and tactical skill were enough to establish control over the territory. Patrols routinely searched villages said to harbor nationalist fighters, but the Dutch did not have sufficient personnel to maintain a dominating presence throughout the highlands. Nationalist forces, despite their superior numbers, had neither the expertise nor the weapons to repel the Dutch. Instead the combatants engaged in brief, usually inconclusive clashes that frequently ended when the Indonesians ran out of bullets. "You'd only have two bullets for one carbine," said Mulih Kwala Sebayang, recalling his time as a sharpshooter.

M.K. SEBAYANG: Even those were made in the forest, "Wait-a-minute" [brand]. When you fired, they'd go *sssshhhh*, you had to hold it tight before it would go *"tarr,"* like that. They weren't like automatic weapons nowadays that go *tar-tar* like that, no. So, for us guerrillas—let's say I was the leader of a squad of guerrillas—we'd look for a strategic place, so if we got hit we could run. Because we couldn't stand up to a battle. There weren't even any bullets. So we'd wait, shoot at them, then run. So we could do it again the next day. That's it. Run. Defend it, what for? Just to die. Tomorrow, there'd be nothing left [of you], and for what? You didn't know if the War for Independence would be over tomorrow or the next day. Plus, your weapon would be lost. So, we were trained to shoot once. Scare them, then run off. Because if you didn't run, they'd strike back. That was my tactic back then.

DIFFERENT FIELDS, DIFFERENT GRASSHOPPERS

Once the fighting spread to the uplands, the burden of supplying food for the fighting forces became increasingly unbalanced, weighing most heavily on communities nearest to the command centers and shifting fronts, where the troops were clustered and where most of the fighting took place. Some villages were subjected to almost daily demands to feed passing militia and army units. Major Djamin Ginting, the commander of TRI Regiment I was stating the ideal when he described the generosity of Karo villagers: "The people were willing to give their rice, their vegetables, for the good of our troops. The people were willing to eat corn instead of rice, as long as the soldiers who were fighting with all their strength could have rice" (Gintings 1975:81).

Eben Hezer put a somewhat different spin on the relation between food and fighting. "If we happened to spend a week in one place, [the villagers] would give us food," he explained.

> E. H. SINURAYA: But if we didn't fight a single time, they would get stubborn, and finally they wouldn't give us anything to eat. So, back then, at least minimally, once every three days we had to fight. If you weren't being a guerrilla over here, then over there, we had to run around looking for fights. For units that didn't ever fight, [villagers] didn't want to take care of them. . . . But there weren't many like that. They were called silik [K., from I., selisih, "to miss the way"] soldiers, simbel soldiers. You know what simbel means? Simbel means to pass by. Simbel soldiers were "bypass soldiers." If the Dutch came from here, they moved over there. So they'd never meet. Bypass soldiers got nothing.

This may have been one reason that TRI units, which were subject to a more rigid command structure and so were less prone to engage in random skirmishes, were sometimes seen as unwelcome intruders in Karo villages. For instance, when several TRI officers entered the village of Berastepu to arrange a midday meal for their troops, they were not fed but rather disarmed by "a group who thought they could put the weapons to better use." The weapons were returned only after the soldiers threatened to burn the village to the ground (Gintings 1975:41).

The TRI's tendency to identify with the abstract power of the republic rather than the intimate connections of kinship, as well as the presence of non-Karo "foreigners," urbanites, and Muslims among them, cannot have helped matters. Village hospitality, however well-meant, was not always considered suitable by the troops, especially those who were not familiar with Karo foodways. Cipera, a kind of toasted corn-meal gravy that Karo serve as emergency rations, "looked just like your morning shit," one Acehnese soldier recalled, a similarity that was enhanced by its being served in a vessel that resembled a chamberpot (Sjahnan 1982:360). And teritis, a stew made of the partly digested grass contained in a cow's rumen, "absolutely could not be eaten."[5] Another Karo specialty, *bohan* (seasoned congealed blood roasted in bamboo tubes), provoked the bemused response, "Different fields, different grasshoppers, there certainly are a variety of traditional foods that can be found in our Nation" (Sjahnan 1982:134).

More serious was the kind of dietary misunderstanding that led to a "bitter experience" for the former butcher P. S. Ginting from Kabanjahé. When Pesindo was forcibly disbanded in 1947, he joined the Napindo Halilintar militia. His decision was based more on provisions than on ideology, he explained. "I was given two alternatives. One was to join [TNI] Regiment IV under General Djamin Ginting, and the other was to join Sektor III under the leadership of Selamat Ginting," he said.[6] "I thought, if I choose Regiment IV, the headquarters are in Sarinembah, whereas my troops are in Kubu. If I choose Sektor III Regiment Halilintar, the center is at Lau Simomo, it's closer and they had already sent us rice." Another incentive was the presence of a herd of cattle pastured in nearby Ujung Suka. "This is probably silly, Margaret, but I'm more interested in those sorts of things."

The responsibility for providing meals for his unit rotated among the nearby villages: Bunuraya, Kacinambun, Manukmulia, and Kuta Mbelin. Every day they butchered one of the cows from Ujung Suka, "that was for our food," until "after two months they were all gone."

P. S. GINTING: After two months all the cattle were gone, all the chickens were gone, but there were still pigs loose in Bunuraya. So I said, if everything is finished, just find whatever there is. Pigs. They took the pigs but I forgot that some of my soldiers were Muslims. So for a day or two it didn't matter, Margaret, they didn't say anything. But after a few days, I received a report, I got a report from Tunas Purba, yeah, those men didn't want to return [to Kubu], they didn't want to be rotated [from the front lines]. They were offended. Why? Because we offered them that pork.

Yeah, I thought, this is dangerous. So I gathered up my courage, I went to the front without a weapon. I left them all behind. Aman was their leader's name. Aman, I'm coming, your commander. "Don't come, I'll shoot," he said. This was an experience that left a permanent mark. You can shoot, Aman, but hear me out first. I kept coming forward. "I'll shoot," he said. Don't shoot first, let me talk, Aman. So I came close, closer, he embraced me. Wept—he wept. I even wept too. We wept. Understand, Aman, this is revolution, struggle, we don't always know what is going on. I myself as commander don't [always] know what's happening, I don't know Islamic law, I don't know what I have to say. But we didn't run the kitchen, it's run by the people. So I apologized and asked him to advise all our subordinates that this was not my fault as commander. So finally they started to quiet down, started to calm down, because it was all unintentional, they probably could forgive it, right? Then a week later, it happened again.

Apparently because it was the turn of another village to work in the public kitchen, they prepared pork again. Another time. So that night without my knowledge as commander, those sixty men vacated the front, the front was empty. If the Dutch had entered, we'd all have been done for. They just took off. . . . I was called directly by Selamat Ginting to Lau Simomo. "Arrest him! Shoot him!" [he said]. I was to be shot, because my troops deserted, the front was empty and it was dangerous, right? They wanted to sentence me to death. So before I went into Selamat Ginting's office, the Sektor commander Netap Bukit, who later became the *bupati*, whispered to me, "*Iyah*, you'll be going to the wall for this, watch how you answer that Pa Kilap." Pa Kilap, that was [Selamat Ginting's] nickname, Pa Kilap, Kilap Sumagan.[7] "Whatever the sentence, that's up to you, but this is the story," I said. "I absolutely had no intention of doing this. But our public kitchen is run by villagers who don't know, and in fact the food was served several times. So they left not because they were scared or whatever, but because of their religion."

So then I saw inside, Tama Ginting and Selamat Ginting, the two of them. I went in, and I was chewed out immediately. I saw his eyes were really red and his face was red. "Commander *Hau-hau* [I., joke, ridiculous]," he said, all kinds of things. "I'll have you executed, shot!" he said. May I speak? "Say anything you want, but you're fucked for sure this time," he said [K., "Kai atem, kataken, gelah munggil kau şendah," nina.] That's about how rough his language was. *Munggil* means "to be beaten to death."[8] I told them my story. You can shoot me or whatever but it wasn't my fault, it wasn't the fault of this commander, I said. You can shoot me, I said. The fault was the villagers' not understanding. I told the story. "In that case, you're transferred. You'll be reassigned," they said. That's how I became the assistant to Eben Hezer Sinuraya, his second-in-command. They reduced my rank by one grade.

LEADERS

When Karo men talked about the independence struggle, they rarely had much to say about politics. Mostly they denied any knowledge of the ideological bases upon which the various groups stood and by which these groups differentiated themselves from one another. "At the time we didn't know PNI, we didn't know Murba, PKI, and all that yet," said Riano Perangin-angin, listing some of the main political parties of the period.[9] "It was just, you know, the common people wanting independence." This resolute refusal of politics may have been, for the rank-and-file volunteers, a simple statement of fact. It was probably also an effect of the New Order regime's denigration of anything that "smelled of *politik*"—a term equated with mass violence, social disorder, and self-interested duplicity.

So it is not particularly surprising that character routinely displaced politics in stories about leaders. Good leaders were remembered as tough and daring, as well as "fatherly" and "loving." Selamat Ginting's men spoke with affection of his hot temper and robustly profane language and of his propensity, which went beyond rudeness to border on eccentricity, for addressing everyone (even the president, they said) by the condescendingly familiar second-person pronoun *engko*.[10] "He was so bold and so loving too that the rules of military hierarchy sometimes got lost," said P.S. Ginting. Mena Pinem, who signed up with the Thunderbolt Regiment after a brief stint in the navy, disagreed. He quickly "saw through" Selamat Ginting's bluster and switched his allegiance to the Wild Tiger Brigade. Why did he choose the BHL? "I was drawn to his personality," he said of the Wild Tiger's commander, Payung Bangun.

MENA PINEM: The man was courageous, he didn't have a lot to say, more action than talk. As a speaker he wasn't too—well, he just wasn't an orator. But he was a writer and if we look at his writings and all, he was an artist. He was a kind of artist, this Payung Bangun. But it was his attitude as a commander that was so admirable. If he said yes, it had to be yes. No if it was no. He was a person who took a stand. . . . And I was one of the people he trusted until the day he died. Because a follower, as a soldier, wouldn't want to betray his superior and wouldn't want to confuse the thoughts of leaders like that. A man who's "loyal."

Above all, leaders were hard (I., *keras*, also "harsh, cruel"). "This Pa Berontak," said A.R. Surbakti, referring to the Wild Tiger leader Payung Bangun by his teknonym "rebel's father." "People said he was hard. A hard man"—a statement he qualified by shifting from conversational Karo to stiff, bureaucratic Indonesian: "Did not hesitate to kidnap one person for the good of many" (tidak segan mencuri orang demi kebaikan orang banyak).

"All the leaders back then, they were so hard, so hard," said Eben Hezer. "We'd think, *merdeka* but what this *merdeka* actually was we didn't know yet, we didn't understand independence." His words wrenched ambivalently between the spontaneous patriotism of ordinary folk and the rough coercion of leaders:

E.H. SINURAYA: Those who were half-hearted, well, some were carried off, even though they actually didn't understand it all yet. At the time, I think, if I'm not mistaken, the Indonesian people, just a few percent had become [politically] conscious. So whatever, if they said *merdeka*, what were the politics, they didn't know. But one thing they knew about *merdeka*, it was not colonized. Whatever was independent was not colonized, don't let the

Dutch back in again. Other than that, they probably didn't know anything about it. It was just the outcome of pressure from the leaders, the leaders' indoctrination. They just went along.

Actually one thing that's extraordinary I think, at the time in Taneh Karo, it was just about everyone. The Karo people, if we just look at it, truly the Karo people were all freedom fighters. If we think about it, it's extraordinary. The thing that was extraordinary was this, if they said, your father's a traitor, kill him, they'd kill him. Your father's a traitor, kill him to show that you're a real freedom fighter, they'd kill him. Now, that's how it was at the time, they didn't know all kinds of things. Actually they didn't know anything at all about war and all, that's why we had all kinds of experiences during the war.

We were talking at the time about Selamat Ginting's notorious hot-headedness. "He'd curse you out in a flash," Eben Hezer recalled. "That's how he was. I was the only one he never swore at. He'd nick-named me Preacher. Maybe because of that he was sort of reluctant to swear at me, because of my nickname." In his eulogy to Selamat Ginting, Eben Hezer invoked his legendary toughness as a leader:

> E.H. SINURAYA: In one fight our troops from the Halilintar Regiment retreated after being repeatedly hit by the Dutch army. As soon as [Selamat Ginting] got the report, he showed up carrying a piece of bamboo. He chased down and beat the members of our unit that had retreated and forced them to advance again to attack the Dutch. . . . From that time, the expression was commonly heard around the Napindo Halilintar Regiment: Better to advance to face the Dutch than retreat to face Pa Kilap Sumagan. (E.H. Sinuraya, in Bangun and Chairudin 1994:420)

There had been a time, he admitted, when he'd had some doubts about Selamat Ginting's leadership. It was when Kuta Bangun fell to the Dutch and Selamat Ginting's long-time Javanese comrade Muhammad Nuh was killed. "That's when I thought, oh he's human after all, he doesn't care about being a leader. Because in a situation where everything was confused, I saw how shortsighted he was."

Muhammad Nuh had been with Selamat Ginting since the early days of street fighting in Medan. Nuh handled what Eben Hezer called "logistics," which seemed to cover just about anything from sabotage to fundraising to kidnapping. But he'd never gone into battle, because he was a great favorite of Selamat Ginting's. "One time this Nuh, he said to me," Eben Hezer recalled, "he said, 'If the Old Man' [K., *parang mbelin*]—that's what they called Selamat Ginting—'if the Old Man tells me to go into battle, I'm sure to die. And my death will be drenched with blood.' Sure enough, that's what happened."[11]

By December 1947 the highland front at Lau Simomo was under heavy assault by Dutch troops. Kabanjahé, Berastagi, and the other main towns of the province had already fallen, and Tiga Binanga, the market center a few kilometers from Kuta Bangun, was serving as the provisional capital of both the Karo district and the province of East Sumatra. A regimental field hospital had been set up in Kuta Bangun; the command staff was quartered there as well, along with their families, and the whole area was flooded with refugees looking for military protection. At the time of the Dutch assault, Eben Hezer's company happened to be in Kuta Bangun for training exercises. No other troops were stationed there, and most of the regiment's working weapons were in use at the front. Twenty rifles and a few pistols were all they had for a company of 250 men, and those guns were what the soldiers called "Wait-a-while brand" weapons *(senjata cap tunggu dulu)*, which might fire or might not. So when the Dutch took Tiga Binanga, and Kuta Bangun became their next target, the troops there had virtually no guns with which to oppose them. Eben Hezer and his poorly armed soldiers were ordered to delay the enemy's advance as long as they could, to cover the evacuation of the regimental staff and their families, medical workers, and patients in the field hospital. Under heavy fire, they were forced to retreat, and Nuh, who had at the last minute been ordered to accompany them, was killed by a machine-gun fusillade.[12]

E.H. SINURAYA: When he found out Nuh was hit, the Old Man wept. I thought to myself, apparently even a leader like this can give up hope. Because of what he said, and these are his words: "Better I should be dead. If I were dead my part would be played out," he said. ["Ijem si madin kuakap aku mate, lah nggo sai panggungku," nina.] So I thought, wow, he's given up, I thought. But because I'd seen his anger every day, this isn't a regular human being, I thought. . . . Wow, it's that easy for this human, that easy to give up, that's what I thought. Here was Selamat Ginting, the man I feared and respected the most of anyone in the world. And he could say in that situation, "Let me die, so my task, um, my responsibility will be ended." That's why I asked him later, because I was thinking about these things, I asked him, How far does a leader's responsibility to the people go in the War for Independence?

The day after Nuh's funeral, Eben Hezer talked this over with the Old Man at his new quarters in Lau Tawar.

E.H. SINURAYA: Like I said, I was a leader at the time. A small leader, sure, but it would still be considered leadership. My understanding of independence was still far from perfect. I didn't understand. That's me, far from perfect. Let alone the ordinary people. But if we said to them, Burn your house, they'd burn it. That's why I said, well, don't the leaders have to take responsibility? Leadership involves responsibility. So how far does a leader's responsibility go to people like this?

This is what he said to me: "We could gain independence four hundred more times, son," he said to me, "but if you're ignorant, you'll always be a coolie," he said.

I thought, I'm still ignorant but I'm a leader. I still hadn't yet plumbed the meaning of independence. How things would be later, I had no idea. But I'd mobilized the people. So I thought, if we've mobilized the people, there's a responsibility. If I said, Burn your house, they'd burn it. What does it mean to burn your house? There should be restitution later. If we succeeded in this struggle, there would surely be restitution for that burned house. That's why I asked. But the Old Man up and answered, "You can be independent four hundred more times but if you're ignorant you'll always be somebody's coolie.

Wow, what a mess, I thought. . . . Yeah, now it can be seen that not all leaders were, in the true sense of the word, responsible in the struggle. Some of the people are satisfied, but the ones who helped us back then, who counseled us in the struggle, are increasingly burdened. That's what I meant. How far does our responsibility go? His answer, at the time I thought it was pretty mysterious.

THE KIND OF THING THAT HAPPENED

The Indonesian word *bodoh* is usually translated as "stupid," but Karo ordinarily use it as I have here to mean "uneducated" or "without knowledge, ignorant." It is frequently qualified as *masih bodoh*, "still ignorant," indicating that this is a condition that can be expected to improve over time, as in a child who hasn't started school or a militia leader who hadn't yet "plumbed the meaning of independence." In contrast, Javanese, unless they are national leaders like Sukarno or faithful comrades like Nuh, are liable to be characterized as permanently *bodoh* by Karo, who are shocked by the apparently willful ignorance of those Javanese they are most likely to meet: house servants, beggars, peddlers, prostitutes, highland sharecroppers, and plantation laborers. The most disturbing thing about Javanese, from the Karo point of view, is that they are willing to work as paid laborers, "coolies."

"Terror strikes the heart of every right-minded Batak who hears the word coolie," missionary Wijngaarden wrote in the early days of the Karo mission. "For the Batak, being a coolie is the lowest form of existence. To have to work hard, and also to be beaten or kicked occasionally, the Bataks won't swallow it. They look down on coolies with boundless contempt, they are beasts of burden. A free Batak will never become a coolie; and for this reason he will not follow the missionary" (Wijngaarden 1894:170–71).

This attitude hadn't changed much by the time of the independence struggle. That was what gave so much weight to Selamat Ginting's bitter words, "If you're ignorant you'll always be somebody's coolie." Eben Hezer later interpreted this to mean that "independence is the struggle to oppose all forms of ignorance and backwardness, in order to free oneself from the shackles of suffering" (Sinuraya, in Bangun and Chairudin 1994:423). The kind of responsibility to the people that he himself had espoused could easily turn to paternalism or xenophobia and become enmeshed in the perilous snares of ignorance itself. This was the lesson that Eben Hezer took away from his second encounter with the man who was supposed to let loose the water buffaloes.

It was during the first months of fighting in the highlands. Eben Hezer hadn't yet rejoined his unit, but, as he explained, he "couldn't stand it anymore after the enemy came," so he put together a unit armed with bamboo spears and decided to attack the Dutch base at Berastagi.

> E. H. SINURAYA: I took this spear unit of about six hundred men from Tiga Nderket. We walked from Tiga Nderket toward Berastagi. By midnight we'd reached Simpang Empat. From there on we had to be careful. I put a scout out in front, what the Japanese call a *ceko*. We started down the road, and on the right side and the left side there was a ditch. It was a major road. We started down the road, we'd gone on there for a bit, so here he comes running, who? The lookout, my scout from out in front. "Tank!" he said. "Tank," like that.

Simpang Empat, "Four Corners," is about halfway between Tiga Nderket and Berastagi. It is not a settlement but only the intersection of the two major roads on the north side of Kabanjahé. It was a terrible place to be caught. No villages were nearby, only open fields with no cover for the troops other than the shallow ditches on either side of the road.

> E. H. SINURAYA: He didn't report to me, no. He just blurted it out like that, "Tank!" Wow, when my men heard that, they all took off running, all running. Six hundred men, *gerbak gerbuk*—now that was it! I was already used to this kind of thing, but my men—they ran here, they ran there. That's when I saw, there really was someone whose job was called "letting loose the water buffaloes."
> Back then, if you had twenty or thirty buffaloes in a field, you'd make them a corral, right? Make them a corral out in the field. He let them out, let loose those water buffaloes, the buffaloes in that corral, he whipped them out. So these buffaloes ran, the buffaloes ran, we were running around,

everyone was running around, finally we were all mixed up together. The buffaloes were scared because they saw humans running, running every which way. My men were startled too, running here and there chased by the buffaloes, but luckily not one of them got speared. They were carrying spears, but not one of them was wounded. But lots of my men fell down the ravine.

I wasn't in command anymore, how can you command human beings who are in that state? They were running, all scattered. Six hundred running, I didn't even know what to do anymore. I was just silent. Because I was thinking, what kind of humans are these, all this because someone said, "Tank!"

I waited and waited. These guys were really smart. They got horses, two of them. I guess they'd heard rumors that we were going to attack. But, you know, they didn't take us seriously, like this term "letting loose the water buffaloes." That was enough to fight us, apparently. That's how smart they were.

They took these two horses, tied this zinc, zinc roofing to their necks, so they were dragging it. The horses were dragging the zinc roofing. *Rerrr* . . . it went, and the horses were spooked. Because they were spooked, they ran right off. Ran right along the road. The two of them chasing one another, then my man on account of this *Rerrrr* . . . noise, hearing it off in the distance, he thought it was a tank. Thought it was a tank. He ran right to me, "Tank!" he said.

Then everyone was running, they met up with all those water buffaloes, chasing around with those buffaloes, that night was when I realized, "Oh, so that's what he meant by letting loose the water buffaloes."

When I asked him why they let the water buffaloes loose, "Don't know," he said. He probably didn't know, either. They told him to let them loose, so he did it. If he'd known, he could have resisted them. "Oh, I can't do that," right? Because he said he was a freedom fighter too. What are you fighting for? *"Merdeka,"* he said. . . . "What's your job?" "Let loose the water buffaloes, let loose the oxen over there, attack over there." "What are you attacking?" "Well, I don't know," he said.

What a mess! On account of that lots of people were killed. Because we didn't understand, after all, we didn't understand either. . . .

But it didn't make any sense at all. Let loose the water buffaloes? What is this, what is this job? But there really was this, letting loose those buffaloes. We were chasing around with the oxen, with the buffaloes, because of all the humans, well, they were scared too, right? They ran, then the men heard the buffaloes running, like *gerdek-gerdek*, finally they were all like that. At the crossroads they went into the ravine, rolled down, it was total chaos! I didn't find all my men till noon. But finally I waited there, then I met—those horses came. Wow, horses dragging that zinc roofing. They were spooked too because it made a noise like *Rerrrr*. . . . At that time the road hadn't been paved, it was still gravel. So if it made a noise like that the horses would be spooked. They'd run faster and faster. The faster they ran the louder it was. The other one was the same way, both of them. They were chasing after one another. They just let them loose like that. This is the kind of thing that happened in battle.

MISRECOGNITION SCENES

The burlesque humor of Eben Hezer's story masks its serious intent. It is a demonstration of how horribly wrong things could go, despite all the best intentions—the kind of thing that could happen when people were ignorant, or acted without thought, in simple reaction to unexpected circumstances. In a chain of mishaps reminiscent of the slapstick chase of the mules, the cow, the chickens, old Het, and I. O. Snopes around Mrs. Hait's front yard in William Faulkner's comic masterpiece "Mule in the Yard,"[13] the sound of the terrified horses dragging zinc roofing along the unpaved road is misidentified by the scout, whose shouts of "tank!" in turn frighten Eben Hezer's inexperienced soldiers; the Javanese man lets out the water buffaloes, which tangle with the already panicked soldiers; everyone is running around in the dark; and the only knowing actors in the drama are not even present: the (unnamed) Dutch, presumably the invisible hands manipulating the action. "That was all it took to fight us, apparently. That's how smart they were."

Events never escape the transformative energies of storytelling. Even as they occur they are conditioned by prior stories, other accounts of the "kind of thing that happened" in this or that circumstance. Events are experienced within the interpretive framework of narrative, and as they are performatively recalled they are cast and recast in new forms, honed and polished in retelling by skill and time. They are saturated by the demands of genre and ideology, inflected by subsequent happenings, other stories, present concerns and cares. Images and idioms are borrowed, repeated, recycled, deformed; after all, as Bakhtin says, it is not from dictionaries that speakers—or tellers of tales—take their words but rather from "other people's mouths [and] other people's contexts" (1981:294).

Storied events are built not just according to factual or causal sequence but also by rhythm and tempo; by repetition, digression, distortion and citation; by intention and interpretation. They spin off into other stories or slip into inconclusiveness. Attention shifts from foreground to background: a minor element in one account becomes the focal point of another; a narrative arc is stopped halfway on or extended into other storied domains. Stories poach from one another: tag lines, poetic images, dramatic vignettes, motifs, and themes all float freely from place to place and version to version in a "cultural poetics" of memory and experience (Stewart 1996:78). Recurrent motifs and themes weave them together, heightening their familiarity and intensifying their effect.

Take, for instance, the moment in Eben Hezer's story of the buffaloes when things suddenly go wrong: *So here he comes running, who? The lookout, my scout from out in front. "Tank!" he said. "Tank," like that.* The misidentification of the tank is the narrative knot with which scattered recollections are tied together to form this particular story: the interrogation of refugees and the mysterious work of the Javanese man who lets loose the water buffaloes (at whose command?), the heroic ignorance and fragile daring of the Karo volunteers, and their near-fatal intersection at the midnight crossroads. There's no way to know how much of this actually happened or whether any master hands really were behind the scene. What is important is the way the ironic structure of the narrated event, as it is generated by this moment of misrecognition, opens up an avenue for Eben Hezer to explore the fatal ambiguities of agency, leadership, and ignorance.

Yet we expect such stories also to bear witness to a literal truth. This is perhaps asking too much of them. Reading *Titi bambu* (I., The Bamboo Bridge), the posthumously published memoir of TNI regimental commander Djamin Ginting, I came across a "misrecognition scene" remarkably similar to Eben Hezer's. Embedded in an entirely different sequence of events, it highlights soldierly esprit rather than military incompetence and provides a moment of comic relief in an escalating arc of pathos. In one of the few graphic descriptions of fallen Karo soldiers that I know of, Ginting describes the aftermath of the tragic ambush of a squad of TNI soldiers at the book's eponymous makeshift bridge over the Lau Biang. The account is drawn from his wartime diary:

> I examined one by one the corpses of the nine soldiers from headquarters company Regiment I, and the 6 soldiers who had suffered serious wounds. The fallen, in addition to being torn and penetrated by gunshots, the bodies that now lay without breath were evidently full of bayonet wounds, and the guts of some poured out. The faces of the soldiers who had already returned to the side of Almighty God appeared to be speaking to those of us who stood around them, urging that the struggle for independence continue until our aspirations were realized. . . .
>
> While I was in this atmosphere of extreme emotion, suddenly a shout was heard: "Watch out, a tank is coming!"
>
> Hearing this shout, the situation became panicked. But fortunately it was quickly calm again because in a moment we discovered that what was meant by the word *tank* was the oxcart of a farmer who had just returned from his fields.
>
> In a situation so emotional and sad, some of our soldiers could still crack jokes. After I realized this, I turned quickly back to look again at the corpses laid out on the earth. (Gintings 1975:62–63)

How can I account for the similarity of the two incidents? Is it a matter of sheer coincidence or of imitative borrowing? Both events purportedly took place around the same time, in places not far apart. Neither comes from an entirely reliable source—a well-polished yarn, fifty years old, on the one hand, and a ghost-written, reverential memoir on the other. Did Karo recruits frequently misidentify livestock as tanks? Was this just a commonplace soldier's prank, already narrativized before the fact? Is the "tank" motif a free-floating element tacked on to transform "what happened" into "the kind of thing that happened" or to create a good story—in one instance farcical, in the other sentimental—out of the raw material of circumstance? Does this imitation/duplication cast doubt on either version or on both? Questions like these, unanswerable, shift attention from the matter of evidence to the context and artistry of the story's telling.

While such indeterminacy is a standard feature of narrative, it is most troubling in the case of traumatic events, in which the need to determine what actually took place may be crucial, yet an excess of horror seems almost to demand recourse to formulaic depictions and stereotypical memories. Violent or terrifying incidents seem almost literally to bleed into one another, both in the mimetic structure of the event itself and in the re-creation of events in memory and in narrative. That is why so many acts of mass violence in Indonesia have been represented in the same condensed, stylized images of blood-red rivers, their courses clogged with the bodies of victims.

It is difficult to unstitch the fabric of violent memory. Were the ironic comedies of Eben Hezer and other former soldiers a cover for painful or humiliating experiences, a denial of complicity, or an attempt to construct a moral message from the circumstances of war? What can we make of the compelling potency of "rumored statistics" of violent death (Pandey 2002) or the recurrent appearance of such shadowy exculpatory figures as "collaborators" or "provocateurs"? Perhaps because events like these are so far outside the moral realm of everyday experience, because their effects are so extreme, they seem to be especially prone to conventionalizing or mimetic modes of representation and remembrance. Were my informants' accounts of *repolusi* a screen memory for the internal violence of the 1965 massacres, or did the earlier killings serve as a model—in narrative or in action—for the latter? Did newspaper accounts of the German-Soviet Winter Campaign of 1941–42 inspire East Sumatran freedom fighters to replay it in their failed "scorched earth" campaign, or was this analogy simply an after-the-fact attempt to rationalize or explain a failed campaign of terror? Are stories of battles with water buffaloes or of freedom fighters falling like spent jasmine blossoms attempts to redeem, through humor or pathos, what might otherwise appear as humiliating defeat? To ask such questions is not to undermine the evidentiary power of these accounts but rather to apprehend them differently, as densely layered, sometimes conflictual negotiations with the passage of time.

POSTINGS

When I began thinking about the ubiquity of "ignorance" in the stories Karo veterans told, I took it as a simple description of the experiences of their past selves caught in circumstances that wildly exceeded their understanding. Ignorance thus seemed to be a relatively uncomplicated measure of the gap between "what we know now" and "what we knew then"—or, to paraphrase Selamat Ginting, between being a citizen and a coolie. But it would be incorrect to assume that ignorance was merely an inert category of difference and that what it covered, not to mention its choice as an expression of ironic contrast, was not conditioned by intervening social and political factors. These included, among other things, the postwar incorporation of many Sektor III volunteers into the TNI and their ambiguous position therein; the high value placed on education in postindependence Indonesia, especially by the army; the military's understanding of its own role in establishing and protecting the republic; and perhaps even the powerful transformative rhetoric of Christian conversion and the generational transfer of power underway in Indonesian social and political life in the mid-1990s.

Ignorance and daring may have been enough to carry the militia volunteers through the war, but afterward the state required more docile subjects, more responsible citizens. For many of the Karo freedom fighters, the process of simultaneously coming-to-understand and coming-to-belong that Eben Hezer described as "filling in independence from the inside" extended beyond the period of the struggle itself through continued military service. At the war's end Selamat Ginting resigned his commission and returned to civilian life, but about a third of his men, including most of the officer corps, were absorbed into the reorganized TNI structure as Battalion 114, also known as the Halilintar Battalion, under the leadership of former Sektor III second-in-command Ulung Sitepu.

From the beginning, the army had tried to contain and control the popular militias, which were considered to be troublesome, disruptive, and unruly, their loyalties shaped by partisan concerns and personalistic ties. The territorial command system, established at the end of the first military campaign in 1948, was a major step toward bringing these independent fighting units under the authority of the army. Granting the militias autonomy of action within designated sectors was intended to reduce the potential for internecine conflict and to enable units to support themselves by "taxing" local resources. After the transfer of sovereignty, this territorial system was again revised by creating "regional" units within the TNI, like the all-Karo Battalion 114. Because of their militia origins and uncertain allegiance to the Javanese center, such units retained a second-class status within the military chain of command. It is not surprising, then, that they were quickly shifted out of their home districts, where their political affiliations and personal relationships made them a potential threat to order.

In April 1950, after brief postings in the Dairi and Karo districts, Battalion 114 was sent to Makassar in South Sulawesi, to face the first of the series of local rebellions and separatist movements that flared and smoldered across the archipelago during the next decade. Tokih Ginting, who had gone on to lead a company in the TNI Battalion 114, described the departure of his ragtag soldiers, who were still without uniforms, shoes, or even adequate weapons:

> TOKIH GINTING: So back then, pardon the expression, we were kind of ignorant at the time. But we wanted to learn. Especially when we were sent directly to Sulawesi. Yeah, taking a ship the whole way, even though we'd never even seen the ocean before. Never even seen the ocean. Taking a ship all the way from here, the Wewerang, a cargo ship, the largest size. So it went to Sabang [on the northern tip of Aceh], then through the Indian Ocean to Jakarta. From Jakarta on to Sulawesi. Two battalions went. When we got there, everything we saw, we'd never seen before. But after a while we could manage.

Over the course of their turbulent careers, the men of Battalion 114 learned the nation firsthand, as an itinerary. They moved around the trouble spots of eastern Indonesia, across Sulawesi and the Moluccas, then back to Sumatra in 1952 at the onset of the first Darul Islam (DI) rebellion in Aceh. While stationed in Aceh in 1952–53, many of them converted to Christianity, following a religious instruction campaign organized and supported by several Protestant company commanders.[14] In the late 1950s they had to deal with a rebellion closer to home, when Colonel Maludin Simbolon, the commander of the North Sumatran TNI Regiment I/Bukit Barisan, sided with the PRRI (I., Pemerintahan

Revolusioner Republik Indonesia, "Revolutionary Government of the Republic of Indonesia") and declared martial law in the province. After the PRRI revolt came to a negotiated conclusion in 1961, some of them went on to take part in the military campaign to annex West Papua, which had recently declared its independence from Dutch colonial rule, or were posted to Borneo, where Indonesia was engaged in a dispute over sovereignty that culminated with the 1963 border confrontation with Malaysia.

Through these military trajectories of violent territorial consolidation, they came to recognize the nation and to identify themselves fully with it. Tokih Ginting described this process of recognition as if it were a military walking tour of archipelagic hot spots:

> TOKIH GINTING: Well, if I look at my experience, here's how it was. Experience as a guerrilla, I traveled all across Taneh Karo, all on foot. I traveled all over Aceh during the DI war. All the villages . . . to Sulawesi, South Sulawesi, all the way to Central Sulawesi, Palu, Donggala, all of them. After that, Menado, Tomohon, Tondano, I've traveled to all of them, on foot, not by automobile. Then to North Maluku, the islands of Ternate, Tidore, Jailolo, the island of Obi, Sanana, I traveled to all of them by *perahu* [outrigger canoe]. A year and a half there. That's my experience. To Java, West Java, with the DI, to Aceh with the DI in Lau Berek. In South Sulawesi with the DI people there. That's it. Then with the PRRI [in 1958], experience in North Tapanuli, Sidikalang, Balige, all of that already, all the way to the mountains, on foot. In short, the villages, by now I know every village. All the way to South Tapanuli, to Ujung Batu near the border of Riau. Natal in South Tapanuli. Only not to Nias yet.

In a review of developments in the Indonesian armed forces since independence, Ruth McVey (1971, 1972) noted the emphasis placed on education, both philosophically and practically, by the army's high command. Themselves generally from less elite backgrounds and with less exposure to Western-style schooling than their civilian political counterparts, military commanders both valued education as a modernizing force and distrusted it as a softening influence on military vigor.[15] From the mid-1950s on, formal training programs were seen by the army "as a means of enhancing [its] ideological unity and hierarchical discipline" (McVey 1972:162). Partly shaped by the disciplinary rigor of Japanese and Dutch colonial military training and partly inspired by the American model of military professionalism, a pyramidic system of military instruction was established, targeting not just the elite officer corps but soldiers at all ranks. Exposure to "new ideas, skills, and central control" was a means to enhance discipline and expertise but also to foster "a nationalism deemed to be above partisan politics . . . and a sense of pride at being part of a vital and highly trained organization" (166). This emphasis on military education meant that those who had little formal schooling, like the Karo soldiers of Halilintar Brigade 114, were both disadvantaged in terms of advancement in rank and subjected to repeated programs of training and indoctrination. Ignorance thus defined and restricted their place within the military hierarchy. "The story was about the same for all of us," said Tokih Ginting. "Because for most of us, understand, at the time there wasn't even a middle school. Usually just primary school. Some had finished the third grade. Some hadn't finished at all, or were illiterate. As long as we were in service, we had to study, like that."

Since independence, the armed forces have claimed a dominant role in Indonesian political life. This claim derived from a deep suspicion of party politics and civilian leadership and from the TNI's perception of the key part it played in the independence struggle. "In their eyes," Ruth McVey wrote of the officer corps, "the army had borne the brunt of the struggle against the Dutch, while the politicians had quarreled among themselves, negotiated concessions to the Netherlands forces, and even rebelled against the Republic itself" (McVey 1971:131). The experience of the independence struggle gave them an almost obsessive sense of the value of national unity and an equally extreme distrust of potentially divisive forces. These were intensified by the political and regional conflicts of the 1950s, during which the TNI again claimed the mantle of "responsibility for saving the nation." Its political role and autonomy of action were enhanced under the 1957 state of emergency and the subsequent period of "Guided Democracy" and were consolidated after General Suharto's rise to power in 1965 on a bloody wave of internal violence that crushed the TNI's main rival for power, the Indonesian Communist Party.

Under the army-dominated New Order regime, both the nation's present and its history came to be understood through an incremental narrative of vertical integration and centralized power. In this frame, bureaucratic rationality and economic development appeared to oppose the unruly and dangerous forces of *politik* and primordialism. Mass political action and indeed virtually all forms of political dissent were ruthlessly suppressed in the name of national stability and economic development, and the political role of the military was explicitly expanded through what came to be known as the "dual function" (I., *dwifungsi*) principle. In a 1966 seminar on the role of the military in society, participants argued that "the army does not have an exclusively military duty but is concerned with all fields of social life" (Crouch 1988:345, quoted in McGregor 2005:222). This principle provided the justification for military participation in politics at every level. It was subsequently elaborated in a 1972 TNI seminar on the "transfer of 1945 values," which were defined as "the values for which those of the 1945 generation . . . had fought." In this context, as McGregor suggests, "1945 generation" refers specifically to the armed youth, military, and paramilitary, who led the struggle, and the phrase "1945 values" was "essentially . . . a code for promoting military values and for acceptance of the military's political role" (222).

Nationalist mythologizing of the heroic freedom fighter and the army's fetishization of its leading role in the independence struggle contributed not only to a generational mystique that dominated Indonesian political life until Suharto's 1998 resignation but also to an unreflective continuation of colonial legacies of military force directed against the civilian population and of state collaboration with agents of extrajudicial violence. Over time, these congealed in what has been described as a "culture of violence" within the Indonesian armed forces, based on a "barely disguised military contempt for civilians" and an "overbearing military triumphalism" (Cribb 2002:238). In its worst aspect, this attitude supported corruption, exploitation, brutality, repression of popular dissent, and even mass killings. At best, it authorized a kind of antipopulism, in which soldiers functioning as "supercitizens" acted with impunity "in the name of the people"—and often against the people—rather than as an "arm of the people."[16] Karo, who had never been in a position to reject the demands of citizenship, seemed by and large to accept this order as natural or at least unavoidable. This does not mean that they could not imagine (or remember) a time when other outcomes were still possible.

By the time of President Sukarno's fall from power in 1966, most of the men of the old Halilintar Battalion 114 had either left the army or were on the cusp of retirement. Some, like their former commander and subsequently provincial governor Ulung Sitepu, had fallen victim to the 1965–66 purge of communists and fellow travelers. As they rose in the ranks and especially following retirement, they began to take on positions of leadership in their home communities, religious institutions, and political organizations. Privately and through veterans associations they supported development and social welfare projects in their home villages. Especially during and after the mass conversions to

Christianity that followed the violent turmoil of 1965–66, they came to hold positions of authority in local congregations and in the Karo Protestant Church Synode (Sitepu, n.d.).

You could see this history displayed on their living room walls, alongside the usual family memorabilia of children's graduation photos and diplomas, wedding portraits, and funeral pictures. Framed certificates of veteran status, letters recognizing military service and rank, and statements of appreciation from the Karo Protestant Church hung next to the souvenirs of their various tours of duty: Acehnese swords, carvings from Borneo, elaborate textiles from eastern Indonesia. Religious images— tapestries depicting the Last Supper and the Sermon on the Mount for Christians or Koranic verses for Muslims—sometimes shared wall space with portraits of the young "Bung Karno," Brother Karno, the familiar term by which President Sukarno was known to his followers.

By the 1990s, Sukarno's reputation had been partly rehabilitated, from alleged communist cat's-paw of the 1960s to flawed but charismatic leader of the independence movement. His children were taking prominent, though necessarily subdued, oppositional political roles, and there was a thriving market in cheap prints, decals, and posters of his image. These served as a mildly transgressive alternative to the staid official portraits of President Suharto and his vice president of the moment, which graced most every public space and many private spaces as well. But the dusty frames and faded images of many veterans' pictures of Sukarno suggested that they had predated his recent return to popularity. "We're ORLA people," they said, taking on the anachronistic term Orde Lama, "Old Order," with which the Suharto regime labeled its predecessor. They meant by this that they were old fashioned, out of sync with the New Order and its crisp military professionalism, rampant corruption, and narrowly Java-centric preferences and policies.

Just as ignorance was a measure of boldness and national belonging in the context of the independence struggle, it also had a double face in the context of late New Order militarism, signifying both the marginal position of Karo soldiers within hierarchies of state power and influence and their critical stance regarding the relation between the Suharto regime and its ordinary citizens. Ignorance intertwined the passion of the freedom fighters and their claims to national belonging. It acknowledged the marginality of their position within the armed forces and in society at large, as well as their efforts to overcome that marginality. Like Djaga Depari's song "Sora Mido-ido" (Voice of Appeal), which I quoted in the introduction to this book, it asserted a moral claim on the state, for themselves—not to be forgotten or their actions trivialized—and for their children and grandchildren—to be allowed to grow in knowledge and understanding rather than in fear and narrow-mindedness.

> Listen! you who guide the sails,
> avoid greed and triviality,
> our breath and blood were the price of this freedom,
> don't squander our nation's sacred gift.

CHAPTER 7

The Memory Artist

News from afar sometimes seems to bear an uncanny resemblance to one's own remembered past. This is not because of the banal redundancy of events but because of memory's interpretive reach and its inclination to refurbish itself in contemporary designs and novel images. In 1994, when I was collecting these stories, horrifying pictures of ethnic violence from around the world seemed to appear nightly on the television news. In central Africa, roadways were filled with thousands of starving, desperate people traveling toward unknown destinations. This made a big impression on my Karo informants. "That's exactly how it was here," they told me over and over. "I saw it on TV last night. I told the kids, 'We were just like that during the evacuation.' Nothing to eat. No clothes. We were living like animals."

What they were recalling was the 1947 evacuation of the highlands. Having been prepped by the propagandists of the *saranen* campaign to expect the worst, virtually the entire population fled the Dutch troops' advance. In the process, more than a quarter of a million people were displaced. Thousands may have died, either at the hands of village guards and quasi-outlaw bands or of exposure, starvation, and disease. The civilian population was at risk from both sides. Farmers working in their fields were strafed by Dutch planes on the lookout for "extremists" and "terrorists." Some villages thought to be rebel enclaves were bombed as well. Others were burned by retreating nationalist militia units. Inhabitants who remained behind were liable to be taken for collaborators and executed. Those who fled were at the mercy of armed bands only loosely subordinate to a military command structure.

Even before the start of the first military campaign in 1947, lowland villagers had begun to move away from the conflict zone of the Medan Area, shifting first to the relative safety of their rice fields, then to the rough, forested hillsides of upper Deli and Langkat, and eventually, as the fighting intensified and spread, to the Karo plateau itself. This flood of refugees, composed mainly of Javanese plantation workers and Karo and Malay villagers from the outskirts of the city, was soon joined in the highlands by the first wave of internal evacuees, mostly townspeople and military families evacuated from Kabanjahé and Berastagi, like Nandé Titing, the wife of Pesindo Leader Roga Ginting.

> NANDÉ TITING BERU GINTING: We didn't know yet whether we would be gone long or not. We went to the nearest village, yeah, the nearest village. When it seemed that things were getting dangerous, we were picked up again. A youth met us, took us to a village that was farther away. We didn't know anyone there. The people there were scared of us. The *pemuda* there took care of us. Everyone [else] was scared of us. It was hard. The Dutch are going to be looking for her, they said. Then we were picked up again, we went to Tiga Nderket. Tiga Nderket and Sarinembah are close, and my father was in [the TRI Regiment IV headquarters in] Sarinembah. Then it was safe, but we were all jumbled up. Scattered, you know. We were picked up again on horseback from there. We went on, and from there we arrived in Kota Cane.

As fighting spread across the highlands, villagers near the receding front lines of engagement hid in the forests near their homes, returning surreptitiously at night to collect food and supplies. Even these forest hideaways soon became uninhabitable, and they too were forced deeper into the interior. Usually traveling in small groups of one or two families, the evacuees began to move away from the fighting. Some followed the retreating soldiers; others sought out kin in villages where the war had not yet reached. At first they were politely welcomed by the villages they passed, but as the stores of these ran low or their inhabitants fled in turn, the evacuees were forced to hire themselves out as day laborers or to steal from villages they passed in order to feed themselves. Two women (whom I won't name here for obvious reasons) described some of their hardships to us:

> NANDÉ A: Then we went back to Mardinding, we were staying just below there. Buluh Belangké was the name of the place. So, to get food, we pounded rice [for the villagers]. We'd pound a whole *pelgan* of grain, all we'd get in return was a *tumba* [two liters; a *pelgan* is twenty *tumbas*].

That's how hard it was. So finally our thoughts turned to stealing. I've stolen. Who can say they haven't?

NANDÉ B: I did it all the time.

NANDÉ A: We'd poke sticks into the ground in their gardens [hunting for buried grain caches]. If we found rice there, take it. During the evacuation, we stole, that's no lie.

NANDÉ B: You know [the village of] Temburun? They hung someone there, Auntie. There was rice right underneath him. We held our breath, then we scraped up that rice, what could you do?

Gradually most of those who survived the trek reached the territory of Aceh, one of the few areas still under the control of the Indonesian republic, or the rugged border zone between the Karo and Dairi districts held by the Napindo Halilintar Regiment. Evacuees who followed the Wild Tiger Brigade were pushed even farther, on what they described as a *long march* to South Tapanuli, where the BHL had become embroiled in a violent internecine conflict involving two rival TNI units. There they remained, in camps and scattered field huts, under conditions of extreme privation, until the temporary cease-fire initiated by the signing of the Renville Accord in January 1948. Forty-seven years later, the televised tragedy of Rwanda seemed to replay their experience of displacement and terror. "Those poor people," they said. "Just like us." ✳

. . .

This is a good illustration of the "mobile and unforeseeable relationship between mass-mediated events and migratory audiences" that Arjun Appadurai (1996:4) locates at the heart of global modernity. In the last several decades, Appadurai argues, there has been a dramatic transformation of the social imaginary, as "moving images meet deterritorialized viewers." The work of imagination has become despecialized; self-fashioning and radical reinvention have become a part of everyday experience. Events from another time and place, in this instance halfway around the world and half a century later, are seen through the autobiographical screen of recalled experience. This may generate a momentary sense of closeness or solidarity with a diasporic community of suffering (as with my Karo informants' insistence that they were "like that too") and a reinterpretation of local events as cases illustrating some universal principle of evolutionary predation or progress. In other contexts it may inspire new attention to cultural differences or to group identity, provide material for a reconfiguration of the sense of self, generate aspirations for democratic reform or reactionary violence, or promote a desire for the glamorous signifiers of an international consumer elite: Nike shoes, Italian designer fashions, Japanese or German sedans, the English language, cell phones, computer literacy, American movies.

Appadurai (1996:10) identifies this globalized modernity as "postnational," because both the electronic mass media and their diasporic audiences have "broken the monopoly of autonomous nation-states over the project of modernization." Nevertheless, in much of the formerly colonized world, the project of modernity is still closely tied to and indeed often synonymous with the nation-state.[1] Indeed, middle-class pressure for democratic reform in Indonesia and elsewhere has been largely motivated by the desire to *detach* modernity from the state. Globally disseminated images of violence and victimization play largely on stages set by the state, where these images displace other, more immediate possibilities of solidarity-in-suffering: Rwandan refugees may have made it onto the (state-controlled) nightly news in Indonesia in 1994, but the East Timorese victims of the Indonesian state's extreme violence never did. And while imagination may exceed the bounds of state control, this does not mean that bodily experience does—a point graphically demonstrated by the harrowing entanglements of Rwandan refugees in the politics of neighboring (as well as distant) states.

The nation form depends upon, as well as produces, such effects of social and territorial dislocation, which find expression in the complementary idioms of home and homelessness. Patriotism, as Benedict Anderson reminds us, most often addresses its object in the emotion-laden vocabularies of kinship or of home—as motherland (I., ibu pertiwi), *vaterland, patria, heimat,* homeland, birthplace—all of which simultaneously naturalize and domesticate one's connection to the national community, yet leave the patriot essentially *outside* the imaginary space of home (1991:143). "Transcendental homelessness" is how Georg Lukács described the modern condition: individuals and actions, he argued, are alienated from social relations and values, and the world is experienced as "a prison instead of as a parental home" (Lukács 1971:61–63). It is precisely this contradictory sense of naturalness and of inevitable loss that makes the idea of home so powerful a symbol of national identity and so potent a source of national inspiration under modernity. One of the "most powerful unifying symbols for mobile and displaced peoples," the idea of home is where the deterritorialized ethnoscape of postnational modernity meets up with the territorial project of the modern nation-state (Gupta and Ferguson 1977:39).

This chapter examines three interrelated, characteristically modern themes—the break with the past, the idea of home, and the biographical trajectory of self—in a Karo text that situates the diasporic imaginary not in the experience of postnational mobility but instead in an account of national origins. It is a sung narrative of the 1947 evacuation, composed and performed by a woman ironically named Sinek (Silent) beru Karo. It was probably recorded in the late 1950s and has been sporadically available since that time in bootleg cassette form in radio shops catering to a Karo clientele.[2] The work of imagination, I want to suggest, is not merely an effect of modern displacements and fragmentations but is instead the core around which the experience of modernity itself is built. Memory artists like Sinek instigate and propel this work, by creating "recognition scenes," public dramatizations of personal experience that become both pattern and stimulus for popular imagination.[3]

modernity through imagination

Sinek's song doesn't have a name, being generally identified by its type, the quasi-improvisational Karo genre of blessing song, *katoneng-katoneng*, or, alternatively, as a "song of the evacuation" (I., *lagu mengungsi*), a descriptive appellation it shares with similar works by other performers. Sinek herself calls it a *turi-turin*. This Karo term can be translated as "story" or "history" but more broadly refers to any meaningful sequence of linked events or concepts.[4] By so describing it, she emphasizes the song's narrative line over its musical form or social function. The name *katoneng-katoneng* derives from the Karo/Malay word *tenang*, "calm." This indicates its purpose in ceremonial performance, which is to soothe and bless its audience. This aim is implicit in Sinek's song, but it is subordinate to the narrative exposition of sequential events. At once collective history and singular testimony, literal chronicle of events and fabulated personal narrative, Sinek's narrated recollection is more than a persistent mourner's lament for a lost past; it is also the history of her present. The story she tells is of her own coming to subjectivity as an artist through the travels and travails of modernity.

BREAKING INTO MODERNITY

"One of the most problematic legacies of grand Western social science," Appadurai (1996:2–3) writes, "is that it has steadily reinforced the sense of some single moment—call it the modern moment—that by its appearance creates a dramatic and unprecedented break between past and present." Appadurai acknowledges the deeply fictive and distorting nature of this view of historical transformation, but then adds ambivalently that the present time does seem to involve just such a "general break with all sorts of pasts." When modernity is taken to be an objectively given world-historical phase, the desire to fix its moment (and, it should be added, its *place*) of rupture/origin seems almost inescapable. Whether this takes the form of modernization theory's fetishizing of technological development, the Eurocentrism of Habermasian serial modernities, or the global mass-mediations of Appadurai's "modernity at large," the effect is of a discourse dizzyingly intent on recognizing itself out in the world: interpellation in reverse, as it were. But if we think of modernity instead as a structure of feeling, a way of thinking about time that is predicated on the idea of historical rupture and steeped in the consequent inevitability of loss, it becomes possible to comprehend this need for a break with the past as itself a symptom of the modern condition.

Freed from the constraints of tradition, temporality seems to accelerate. The present loses its connection to the past; experience, which is what is learned from the past, loses its value. In this time of constant transition, at once real and imagined, traditional forms of memory— myth, epic, custom—appear to be breaking down; history, which concerns itself with change rather than continuity, is the "sign of the modern" (Dirks 1990). "Things tumble with increasing rapidity into an irretrievable past," writes Pierre Nora (1996:1), in a pitch-perfect rendering of the modern state of mind: "They vanish from sight, or so it is generally believed. The equilibrium between the present and the past is disrupted. What was left of experience, still lived in the warmth of tradition, in the silence of custom, in the repetition of the ancestral, has been swept away by a surge of deeply historical sensibility. Our consciousness is shaped by a sense that everything is over and done with, that something long since begun is now complete. Memory is constantly on our lips because it no longer exists."

In Nora's terms, the modern moment is "a turning point in which a sense of rupture with the past is inextricably bound up with a sense that a rift has occurred in memory" (1996:1). What comes after this point— that is, the new, modern age—appears to be entirely unlike what preceded it. If modernity is characterized by novelty, invention, progress, mobility, fragmentation, instability, uncertainty, and unending possibility—if it is, to invoke Habermas (1980), an inherently "incomplete project"—then what came before must be stable, "ancestral," rooted in space and time, self-assured, unified, its horizon of possibilities inherently limited: in short, a completed project.

Stepping into modernity thus means crossing a historical divide. In popular imagination, this transition is often marked by the violence of war. The brutal periodization "before the war" and "after the war" holds past and present in vivid conceptual tension as objects of reverence and repudiation. Walter Benjamin, in his famous essay "The Storyteller," associated Europe's coming to consciousness of its own modernity with the cataclysmic circumstances of World War I:

> Was it not noticeable at the end of the war that men returned from the battlefield grown silent—not richer, but poorer in communicable experience? What ten years later was poured out in the flood of war books was anything but experience that goes from mouth to mouth. And there was nothing remarkable about that. For never has experience been contradicted more thoroughly than strategic experience by tactical warfare, economic experience by inflation, bodily experience by mechanical warfare, moral experience by those in power. A generation that had gone to school on a horse-drawn streetcar now stood under the open sky in a countryside in which nothing remained unchanged but the clouds, and beneath these clouds, in a field of force of destructive torrents and explosions, was the tiny, fragile human body. (Benjamin 1969b:84)

Benjamin's purpose in this essay was to trace and diagnose the "decline of storytelling" in the modern age of information. This is given dramatic expression in the contrast between the proliferation of books purporting to explain the war and the silence of soldiers returning from the front. In fact, the Great War did not render its generation speechless, but it did produce a vigorous discourse of incommunicability. As Paul Fussell shows in *The Great War and Modern Memory*, among the flood of postwar publications were works of poetry, fiction, memoirs, drawing, photographs, plans, and screenplays that concerned themselves precisely with delineating the unspeakable experience of war. These works put on display what Fussell calls the "modern 'versus' habit": the oppositional structure of then as opposed to now, before versus after, ignorance versus experience, we who were there versus you who were not (1975:79). Fussell's argument is that this ironic structure of opposition is the "dominating form of modern understanding" and that it was realized by the "application of mind and memory to the events of the Great War" by a generation of war writers (35).

Plenty of wars and disasters, before and after World War I, have been recollected or reimagined through idioms of temporal and experiential rupture. My interest here is not in which (if any) of these should

trauma +
popular
imagination

be recognized as the original source of a distinctly modern sensibility. What does interest me is how these moments of communal trauma and transformation are reproduced in memory through the work of popular imagination. For it is through the preservation of the moment of loss that a modernist history anchors itself most firmly in social consciousness. Think of Benjamin's image of the "tiny, fragile human body" dashed by torrents and explosions, alone in a "countryside in which nothing remained unchanged but the clouds." How memorably this scene crystallizes the moment of loss and, with it, the sense of modernity's "before" and "after" coming into view!

Karo, too, locate the historical watershed of their collective move to modernity in the experience of war. Nationalist propaganda, which went a long way toward preparing the ground for the evacuation of the highlands, was explicit on this point. Independence was about local economic autonomy and social advancement. It meant the promise of new technology—radios, tractors, and electric lights. It meant education, social mobility, an end to farm labor, an appreciation of modern hygiene and domestic virtues. For some it meant a break with the "feudal" system of colonial rule as well as a (selective) rejection of old ways and local practices. For others, it meant dressing properly, wearing shoes instead of rubber sandals. Even the language was new: Indonesian, with its magical keywords like *merdeka* and *rakyat*. The rewards of modernity required a sacrifice, however. Villagers were instructed to demonstrate their commitment to the nation and its promises by withdrawing from Dutch-controlled territory, after destroying their own homes, crops, and anything that might be of value to the occupying army.

It is in the light of this dazzling vision of the new world their sacrifices would, somehow, bring into being that Karo nationalism should be understood. To many Karo, the independence struggle was a chance to step beyond the prosaic and often oppressive limits of everyday experience and to count for something on a grand stage of collective self-fashioning. If Karo peasants imagined modernity in such material objects as tractors and glass windows, their vision was no less modern and no less profound for that. In these concrete forms they represented a willed break with the past, a choice of national progress over the colonial status quo. More than a forced displacement or a tragic and rather pointless destruction of life and property, the evacuation could be imagined as a departure on Sukarno's "golden bridge" to the future, even if the destination of the journey remained uncertain and the goal unreached.

THE STORY OF A SONG

"All beginnings," says Paul Connerton (1989:6), "contain an element of recollection. This is particularly so when a social group makes a concerted effort to begin with a wholly new start." Like Benjamin's storyteller, those persons that I call "memory artists" transmute the materials of personal experiences into the story of a community, but their vocation is not to embed narrative in the familiar cycles and rhythms of everyday life. Nor is it to return like Job's messenger, bearing the news of disaster to those who were not there to witness it. Instead, the memory artist renders the experience of loss in graspable, personal form, to a primary audience of those who were there too. The memory artist incites in her audience the desire to remember and gives them something to recall.

The work of the memory artist has an easy affinity with the elegiac genres of mourning and lament. Indeed, *katoneng-katoneng*, the improvisational song form in which Sinek's story is composed, is melodically and stylistically close to the mourning chants of Karo funeral rituals and spirit séances. This gives her performance a mood of sorrowful recollection. As she announces in the song's opening passage,

This is really
to freshen the dry, withered leaves
to reopen old, healed wounds
. . . .
digging up a history of heartache
when we went on the long evacuation long ago. (1–2)

Katoneng-katoneng is a highly formulaic song of praise, advice, and benediction honoring the host or sponsoring group at a Karo ceremony. It can be performed by one singer or by a male-female duo, who sing and dance by turns. Musically, *katoneng-katoneng* performances are constructed around a set of relatively fixed but unsequenced melodic motifs that the singer arrays improvisationally in extended vocal solos. These solos alternate and occasionally overlap with musical interludes played by a five-piece *gendang* ensemble, composed of a *saruné* (an oboelike reed instrument), two small drums *(gendang)*, and two gongs (figure 21). The musical accompaniment, the tune "Simalungun Rayat," consists of a different set of melodic motifs likewise improvisationally combined; the two melodic sets, *katoneng-katoneng* and Simalungun Rayat, are linked by a shared tempo, tuning, and drum-gong pattern.[5]

Conventional *katoneng-katoneng* texts build upon a relatively stable repertoire of metaphors, descriptive images, and stock phrases of

FIGURE 21. Karo *gendang* ensemble, 1994. Photo by the author.

blessing, endearment, and praise. They may be sung at weddings, for a son's or daughter's departure for college, at the opening of a new house, for a harvest dance festival or a church anniversary, or on any occasion where praise, blessings, and advice seem appropriate. In most *katoneng-katoneng* performances, the narrative potential of the genre is subordinate to its blessing function, but its structural flexibility makes it also adaptable to other purposes, such as political speech making, lovers' repartee, and storytelling. During the Karo cultural renaissance of the 1950s and 1960s, *katoneng-katoneng* singers flourished. Performances were commissioned for government ceremonies, union rallies, and political events, as well as in the more traditional context of village festivals, family rituals, and showpiece ceremonies of the postindependence elite. Today few younger singers can perform them well, and instead of intricate and often witty on-the-spot improvisations tailored to the occasion, you are likely to hear an abridged imitation of one of the generic blessing songs put out commercially by an enterprising local cassette company. The kind of enjoyment that comes through in the background of the old recordings is rare today; the audience usually fidgets impatiently through these brief, half-hearted renditions while awaiting the more exciting *kibord* (i.e., electronic "keyboard") part of the program.[6]

Sinek beru Karo was one of the most popular singers of *katoneng-katoneng*, the only real female star in a male-dominated field. She was generally considered to have been the first—and arguably the only—singer to develop fully the autobiographical and historical possibilities of the genre (Sitepu 1977). Especially in performances with her sometime partner Malem Pagi Ginting, Sinek invented classic comic turns on the melancholy themes of Karo love poetry. But her most famous composition was the story of the evacuation, which she performed regularly, often in tandem with her protégé Malem Pagi, the "sweet brother" *(turang si besan)* or "beloved" she addresses in her song. Malem Pagi also contributed his own sung history of the evacuation to the act. After Sinek's retirement, he went on to record and release his version commercially as a three-cassette blockbuster (M.P. Ginting, n.d.). Bristling with the ornamental stock phrases of Karo poetic convention, padded with pious sentiment, and longer on pathos than plot, this was the song of the evacuation with which Karo were most familiar.

My first encounter with Sinek's song was a complex transnational, multilingual engagement with the recorded word. This was during my dissertation fieldwork in the early 1980s, when I was living in the Karo neighborhood of Padang Bulan, in Medan. One afternoon a Karo acquaintance, Terbit Sembiring, showed up at my house with a typescript titled "Mengungsi ibas Revolusi Fisik thn. 1947" (K., Evacuation in the Physical Revolution of 1947). It was the text of a recording of Sinek's *katoneng-katoneng* performance that had been transcribed in the Netherlands by a Dutch legal scholar, Herman Slaats. Terbit asked for my help in polishing the grammar in his English translation, which he had previously presented at an international conference in Germany and was now revising for publication. I did, at the same time using the transcript to improve my Karo vocabulary by discussing the nuances of unfamiliar words and phrases with my Karo friends and informants. Not long afterward, I came across master recordings of this and other *katoneng-katoneng* performances in a dusty cardboard box in the back room of a local radio shop. Once I could bring together sound and sense, I was hooked. I did my own translation of several *katoneng-katoneng*, including Sinek's story of the evacuation. I spent time with musicians and singers and finally in 1994 met Sinek herself.

What first attracted me to Sinek's song was its similarity, in both structure and content, to the stories I was hearing from other Karo women of her generation. These stories, which routinely popped up, unsolicited, in conversations and interviews, were what first piqued my interest in the independence struggle. Sometimes they were little more than recitations of place-names: where a family's journey took them, where they stopped to rest along the way, for how long, where they went next, and so on—as if the listing of names could somehow moor the experience of dislocation in a knowable terrain.

> ND. WATY BERU PERANGIN-ANGIN: The evacuation—I don't remember the year anymore. During the evacuation we went to Susuk, went from Susuk to Perbesi, Perbesi to Tiga Binanga, Tiga Binanga to Kuta Bangun, Suka Julu, what was that other one—Lau Peranggunen, Sulu Balen, Lau Baleng, and on to Perbulan. From Perbulan on to Lau Baleng, that way to Tiga Lingga.

> BAPA PRISMA TARIGAN: Oh, from Perbulan you went back to Lau Baleng then into Tiga Lingga.

> ND. WATY: Yes. We didn't dare cross that bridge. What was that, that bridge? Lau Renun. You saw people carrying children across.

> BP. PRISMA: A cable, the bridge was just a cable.

> ND. WATY: It swayed, we didn't dare.[7]

These chronicles of travel were often interspersed with vignettes of bare-bones intensity, which condensed the experiences of exile and fear into stereotypic scenes of displaced domesticity. Their subject matter was endurance, not heroics; they depicted ordinary, daily acts transformed by the startling circumstances of war: tasteless food eaten without salt; a lost cooking pot or a blanket given away; an unexpected reunion with relatives or neighbors; the construction of a makeshift lamp; a crying child quieted so as not to reveal its family's hiding place to planes flying overhead; above all, the terror of moving outside the familiar space defined by kinship and local custom, into unknown and sometimes uninhabited territory.

One of the most poignant stories of the evacuation came from Nandé Namali, one of a group of four women we interviewed together in Payung. Her husband had been wounded and sent home in the early days of the Dutch military campaign. They had no doctors or medicine, and the wound did not heal. When Payung was evacuated, she was forced to take charge of the family.

> NANDÉ NAMALI BERU GINTING: *Iya*, then leave now, said the government. Well, we left, we went toward Tepas, the road to Nageri, you know? We went that way, about twelve o'clock we got to Tepas. Go to the ravine, sister. I wept, I had to carry him. The road was difficult. The bridge was already destroyed. You know, even now I cry when I think about it. It was so hard. So then, there were the two kids, you know. I took one child across, "Here,

my child, stay with our rice basket," I said. I took the other child across. Then, "I'll get your father now," I said. I took their father across. So it was almost dawn, we hadn't yet arrived at Nageri, Nageri that's across from Batu Karang. So, when we got to Nageri, we saw it had already been burned down. They burned the houses upstream first. So Bapa Layari's house was already burned. Downstream from it was our house, that's when I said, "Our house is burned," I said. So then, well, Batu Karang was burned. Everything was dark from the smoke of burning houses in Batu Karang. I screamed, he couldn't walk, I had to carry him all the time, hold one's hand, there was the basket to be carried too, the rice container. Then the cannons [*béréng*, anti-aircraft guns] roared under us. The cannon fire broke the rice dikes.

More mundane but equally vivid were the recollections of Nandé Petrus, my adopted Karo mother. She was a third grader in her home village of Kuta Mbaru at the time of the evacuation. Her father owned a bus line, so they had some cash for traveling expenses and traveled with a large group of kin, including her maternal grandmother, Nini Ribu, and her infant cousin Mimpin.

NANDÉ PETRUS BERU GINTING: At the beginning of the evacuation, we didn't know who ordered us to evacuate. But there was news that we should evacuate now, evacuate now, get out of this village, they said. We didn't know where it came from, we went along. We all evacuated. So we first went from Kuta Mbaru on to Serembané, the forest across from Kuta Mbaru. That's where we went first. That night, we made shelter from *cekala* [torch ginger] stalks. We made shelters. We planned to stay there. Then news came again that we couldn't stay, go on and evacuate from here, they said. So there were some who left there, there were some who stayed. We were among the ones who left. We left—this very night, yeah, we left—so we didn't have the chance to spend a single night in the Serembané forest. We left right away. We walked from Kuta Mbaru to the main road, Sukatendel. Then we followed the road toward Kuta Buluh. So the bridges between Jandi Meriah and Tanjung, there were three bridges. There was the Lau Jering plank bridge, the Lau Perira plank bridge, and one more plank bridge that I don't know what it was called. So this bridge had already fallen in, it had been destroyed. When it was destroyed I don't know. But it must have been fast. When we got there it had all fallen in. So we were forced to go down, go down to the bottom before we could go on from there. . . . From there we went on to Kuta Buluh. At Kuta Buluh we crossed to the rice fields and hills on the other side. So we stayed on the hillside, with the rice fields below. We stayed there for three nights. Because we were waiting for my aunt [K., *bibi nguda*, youngest FZ, Mimpin's mother] from Kuta Mbaru. She didn't come so we went on anyway. So from Kuta Buluh we went out from Simbelang Perbesi. Out from Simbelang Perbesi on we followed the big road straight to Kota Cane. On the way, wherever it got dark, that was where we spent the night, all the places from Simbelang until we got to Kidupen.

We spent one night in Kidupen. That was where it seemed that the people were really stingy. We couldn't even borrow a grinding stone. So we went to the bathplace, there were lots of stones, that's where we ground our chilies. That's how stingy the Kidupen people were.

So after that we went on our way, we spent the night in Harimas. This Harimas they said was a haunted village. Because Mimpin was still little and he was away from his mother, he cried all the time. That's where I told you how we tied him outside and the Harimas people got mad. Don't do that, they said, there are lots of ghosts out here, they said. After that we didn't tie him outside anymore.

We stayed in Harimas for a while, I guess four days. After that we went to spend the night in Mardinding. There were some others too, but I don't remember anymore, I just know the big ones. So in Mardinding we stayed in the schoolhouse, that's where we spent the night. After that on to Lau Peradab, Lau Perbunga—that's where we spent the night wherever it got dark, that's where we slept. But we always carried, what—in each village if it was still sort of light but not worth going on, we'd work. We'd help pound their rice. Because we were scared we'd run out of supplies. We'd help. They'd give a payment of one cup, like that, for one can for instance. So for that evening it was enough to cook. So we didn't bring that much rice. That's how we looked for food.

. . .

One of the exceptional things about Sinek's song is that it brings a story much like these accounts of the evacuation, told from a woman's perspective and in a woman's style, into the space of public discourse. Karo public speech is largely dominated by men, both in the formal arenas of oratory and customary deliberation and in informal venues of coffee shop yarn-spinning. Evacuation stories, to the contrary, were told almost exclusively by women. These stories came up casually in conversation with friends, neighbors, and relatives, on bus rides, at work, and during marketplace encounters. They are often (and repeatedly) told to children. Sinek retains the domestic focus and place sequencing that is generally characteristic of these stories and refines them through the simple poetry of everyday speech. Take, for instance, this short passage from Sinek's song:

Our plan
was to make it to Jinabun in one day's time.
In the middle of the forest
halfway across Mount Palpalen darkness had already fallen,
so we spent that night on Mount Palpalen,
the thick earth for a sleeping mat,
the numerous tree roots for pillows,

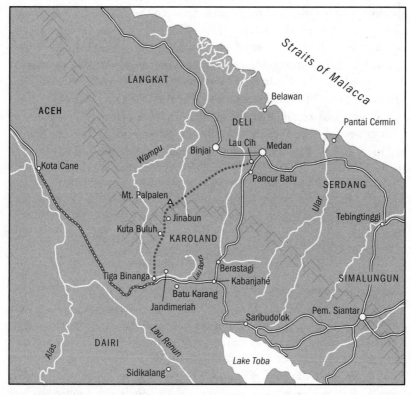

MAP 4. The journey told in Sinek's song.

the thick fog for a blanket,
the high heavens our roof.
The cold was incalculable,
we couldn't stop shivering. (31)

This brings me to the second thing that appealed to me about Sinek's song: I could understand it without much trouble. It had little of the poetic ornamentation typical of *katoneng-katoneng* and so was easier for me to follow than most such performances. The autobiographical framework was familiar to me. There was a central protagonist-subject, whose progressive development was the song's theme. The story was built around dramatic scenes and surprising reversals of circumstance. There was even a happy ending, of sorts. The plot line was simple; it could even be drawn on a map.

. . .

Speaking of the politics of translation between third- and first-world languages, Gayatri Spivak (1993:188) remarks, "The person who is translating must have a tough sense of the specific terrain of the original." This means more than just knowing its geographical setting. The translator must appreciate the artistic field in which the text is situated. She must be able to make an informed judgment about the aesthetic value of the original. Questions of standards and quality are more complex than this suggests at first glance, as feminist and postcolonial literary critics, Spivak included, have taken pains to point out. By conventional Karo literary standards (which is to say, by Karo *male* standards), all the things that made Sinek's song so appealing to me are artistic weaknesses: its strong narrative line; its lack of the ornate metaphors, elaborate phrasings, obscure terms, and formulaic praise that characterize fine Karo oratory; its relatively economical use of kinship references; its emphasis on individual rather than collective experience. I prefer to think of this as Sinek's special genius: a hybrid, self-confident aesthetic sensibility creatively and subversively engaging with the limits of genre.

In keeping with Sinek's straightforward style, I have resorted to a free, relatively colloquial translation. This choice requires some comment. Translated poetry, especially sung poetry, where the musical accompaniment is not also a part of the re-created text, is likely to lose much of what makes it poetic. The rhythm may be wrong, or the combination of sounds and vocal inflection, distorted. Vocal pitch and timbre are lost altogether. Equally important in this case is what happens to the tempo. As sung, the narrative spins out slowly and patiently, with long rests between lines and musical interludes for dancing in the intervals between verses. Phrases are repeated, stretched, padded. Toward the end of the song the pace gradually picks up, the lines get longer, and narrative momentum builds. This is how a skilled performer creates suspense and anticipation, while also making room for audience members to engage digressively with the song: chatting with their neighbors, offering criticism or praise, recalling personal experiences, comparing the singer's style with that of other performers. The written word, spoken or read, is apprehended more rapidly and monologically. This gives an entirely different feel to the narration. To get some sense of how the slowed-down tempo affects the feeling of the story, try reading aloud the passage quoted above, allowing about ten seconds per line.

When working across radically different languages, aesthetic traditions, social contexts, and bodies of knowledge, the translator's risks are great. As Walter Benjamin (1969c:69) says, "Any translation which intends to perform a transmitting function cannot transmit anything but information—hence, something inessential. This is the hallmark of bad translations." In that sense, what I'm presenting here is an intentionally bad translation. For even if it were possible to reproduce all the formal features of the original—its intonations, sound, rhythm, tempo, the precise nuances of words and images—the translation would still fall short, lacking, as it necessarily must, the historical and cultural contexts of performance, the individual and collective resonances the song draws forth from a Karo audience, the rich weave of intertextual references and connections it offers to that audience, the social knowledge and values that an informed listener brings to bear on the performance. These form the basis for aesthetic pleasure in the work. Lacking that basis, the reader's attention may at least be drawn to its absence by a translation that insists on restricting itself to the narrative framework around which such pleasure would, for a knowledgeable audience, have been entwined.

One of the pleasures that a Karo audience finds in *katoneng-katoneng* is the complex web of kin terms that decorate the song. Karo social relations are always understood as relations among kin—agnates, affines, cousins you marry, those you don't marry, siblings-by-extension, cross-cousins and double cross-cousins, in-laws of in-laws, and so on. Terms of address, rules of discretion and indirection, metaphoric references, and playful inversions make everyday conversation, let alone the refined language of poetry, seem blindingly complex to the novice. So, for instance, even in the stripped-down frame of Sinek's song, she refers to her performing partner Malem Pagi not by his name, as she does in ordinary conversation, but by (among other things) his patriclan (Ginting mergana), by the nickname of his mother's (patri)clan ("beré Biring [Sembiring]"), by the name of his eldest child (Pa Sabar, "Sabar's dad"), as mother's brother (*mama* Ginting, simultaneously a term of respect and romance), and as opposite-sex sibling *(turang)*. To take just the last of these, *turang* literally refers to a category of kin with whom marriage is absolutely prohibited as incestuous, but it is also, in a logic of inversion, a "term of endearment" used between lovers, which is how it is (fictively) meant here.[8]

In presenting Sinek's story of the evacuation in translation, I have chosen to simplify and reduce this armature of kinship even more. This is intended to echo Sinek's foregrounding of the narrative line by her own restrained use of the vocabulary of kinship. It is not an attempt to facilitate a cross-cultural empathy or identification, like the solidarity of global victimhood that my Karo informants discovered in televised images of Rwandan refugees "just like us." To remind you of what is missing here, I occasionally draw attention to this elision by interjecting Sinek's addresses to her partner, Malem Pagi, rendered uniformly as "brother."

THE LONGEST JOURNEY

Karo often speak of Sinek's song as the definitive account of the 1947 evacuation. They don't mean that it was the first *katoneng-katoneng* on the subject (although, according to Sinek, it was), or even that it is the best (although I think it is), but rather that it covers the most territory. *Of all the widespread Karo people*, Sinek sings, *we were the ones who traveled farthest* (5). It was as if her journey, by virtue of distance alone, encompassed the lesser travels and alternative experiences of all other Karo refugees. Such a claim to authority is utterly contrary to Sinek's own view, at least as it is presented in the text of the song, in which "we traveled farthest" is a simple statement of (dubious) fact, not a claim for representational privilege.

Her story begins in Lau Cih, a small settlement about halfway between the city of Medan and nearby Pancur Batu, a train depot on the main road to the Karo highlands. Sinek lays out its coordinates precisely:

> At the beginning we left from the land of Lau Cih,
> founded by the Karo-Karo clan, so many living together,
> in the Twelve Villages Federation,
> on the outskirts of Medan, the turnoff to Binjei.
> The Dutch were already there in Medan, it seems.
> We were farming at Kilometer Eleven, dear brother,
> on the outskirts of Medan. (7)

The eldest child of the family, Sinek attended the local Taman Siswa school, one of a Java-based network of private elementary schools combining modern secular education, moderate nationalism, and a culturally conservative orientation with a strong emphasis on traditional arts. She finished the fifth grade before the Japanese occupation interrupted her education. This was a rather high level of achievement for a girl at the time. When she was about fifteen years old, she began taking part in nationalist activities, such as selling flowers to raise money for the BPI. Even as a child she had been known as a fine singer and dancer, but she was too modest to perform in public. Her first appearance before a large audience was at a celebration of the anniversary of the independence proclamation, at which she sang patriotic songs to entertain the soldiers stationed at the Medan front.[9]

> No, before the evacuation, brother,
> even though I'd learned to sing a little,
> if I was called to a festival,
> if it wasn't to entertain the militia or our soldiers,
> I didn't want to sing. (68)

After the British turned over command of the Medan Area to the Dutch army in November 1946, retaliatory and preemptive strikes on nationalist camps on the city's perimeter increased. Villages near the front, like Lau Cih, were sometimes in the line of fire.

> They came by land,
> bringing all their tanks,
> shelling first with mortars,
> and they came from above in airplanes,
> firing down constantly
> with lots of big dumdum bullets. (8)

Ordered by the militia leaders to take cover, they hid at first in the nearby forest during the attacks:

> I thought, if we could stay here for a while,
> long enough to build a field hut, so I thought,
> but we couldn't stay long, brother,
> because the Dutch army kept advancing. (10)

Soon they were ordered to move farther away from the fighting. Sinek's family went to stay with relatives in the small hamlet of Barung Ketang. This was still within walking distance of their fields, and they could go back to harvest what remained of their rice crop when there was a pause in the fighting. Sinek makes special note of the generosity of the people of this overcrowded village:

> We were asking for pity from our mothers and fathers in Barung
>   Ketang,
> founded by the Karo-Karo clan.
> There, because of the goodness of the people of Barung Ketang,
> they moved to the fields, we stayed in their houses, brother. (14)

About six months after Sinek and her family moved to Barung Ketang, Dutch troops in Medan began a full-scale attack on the republican camps on the city's perimeter. Under this pressure, the Indonesian lines quickly collapsed. Within a week, Dutch military reinforcements landed south of Medan and cut overland across the Karo plateau to approach the city from its southwest margin, striking from behind at the relatively unprotected rear lines at Sibolangit and cutting off retreat for the already scattered nationalist troops.

Sinek's moving description of the battle of Sibolangit emphasizes the unexpectedness of the assault and, in a conventional poetic idiom, the transmutation of the human body in death to its elemental constituents.

> We really thought no one would come from upstream, brother,
> so all the militias and soldiers who were stationed around Sibolangit
> who defended homeland and our nation,
> there the breath of many returned to wind,
> blood to water, brother, bone to stone,
> because they came from upstream.

Karo accounts of the battle of Sibolangit frequently heighten and dramatize the irony of this scene by casting it as a fatal misrecognition, in which enemies are taken for friends and allies. Recall, for instance, Eben Hezer Sinuraya's account (in chapter 5, p. 225), in which the Dutch troops are mistaken for "our help from India." In Sinek's version, the Dutch tanks are decorated with images of *bénténg*, wild oxen, the Napindo symbol and a traditional icon of Karo homeland defense.

> Thinking they were reinforcements from Taneh Karo,
> because they had put pictures of *bénténg* on their tanks,
> our brothers and fathers gave a great cheer:
> "Here come our reinforcements from Taneh Karo!"
> That's what they said, but apparently it was the enemy, brother.
> Then when they shot, brother,
> when they fired,
> that's when our brothers and fathers knew
> it was the enemy that had come. (18–19)

One of the striking features that Sinek's song shares with many women's evacuation stories is the absence or invisibility of the agents of terror. In an empty terrain, violence takes its victims by accident or by surprise. Even in her account of the fall of the Medan front and the battle of Sibolangit—the one third-person passage and the only battle scene in her story of the evacuation—Sinek stresses the random and unexpected nature of violent events.

Then many threw themselves into the Sungsang River,
Sibolangit's bathing place, brother.
The scattered became more scattered,
like *cingkeru* [Job's tears] when it's beaten, brother.
The breath of some returned to wind,
the broken became more broken.
Many were the ways of death
for those we call brothers, the defenders of our nation. (20)

. . .

Like the other refugees, Sinek's family moved toward the interior, but
they did not follow the roads. Instead they traveled overland through
the densely forested slopes and across the sharp ridges to the Karo plateau. In Sinek's song they move not in the midst of violence but rather
in its silent wake. Sinek recalls the hunger, thirst, and cold, the children
crying, and the fear of encountering the always-unseen Dutch troops.
The difficulty and terror of the journey are vividly depicted in repeated
invocations of movement through unknown and uninhabited territory.

We went where no one had gone before,
the path never traversed by humankind
on the slopes of Mount Palpalen.
We climbed the terrible slopes.
What roots can I tread upon
so I won't roll down?
What aerial roots can I hold on to
so I won't fall off with my little brother?
That's what I thought
as I carried our belongings in my hands and on my head, and my little
    brother on my back. (27)

It is instructive to compare Sinek's pared-down, laconic account with
the rather more florid, sentimental description of a similar journey that
appears in *Titi bambu*, the posthumously published memoir of Lt. Col.
Djamin Ginting, the commander of TRI Regiment I. From Cinta Rakyat,
near the border of the Karo district and upper Deli, he and his escort
unit accompanied a group of some four hundred evacuees to Kineppen,
a village in the central plateau region, where he planned to make contact with the main body of his troops.

Thus the party that consisted of the commander of Regiment I and his escort
moved very slowly, followed by hundreds of children and women and only
a few men, carrying the belongings that they had managed to save. This was
a journey of great sadness, in which mothers, while cradling and nursing

their babies, carried packages in their hands and baskets on their heads. Children who were able to walk, accompanied their mothers at their side. Such was the situation on the journey, crossing rivers full of stones, climbing up and down steep valleys at the foot of mountains—penetrating the forests at the edge of steep cliffs terrifyingly agape. As you can imagine, it was impossible for this journey to be done with "full speed"—indeed often more slowly than an ordinary journey. Here and there the weeping of a child could be heard, both those who were being carried in their mother's arms, and those who were walking, because their feet were swollen or they were exhausted or hungry or thirsty. Many members of the unit could not bear this situation, and while being continually on guard, as they progressed toward their destination, also tried to lighten the burden of the evacuees by helping carry or quiet the children from time to time. [The evacuees] were guarded in the front and rear so that no one was left behind. Indeed there were some who were supported or held when crossing steep mountain slopes and deep canyons with great care because with a tiny mistake a soul could take flight, fall to the bottom, dashed on the great rocks. Although the journey was so difficult, none of the evacuees were left behind, unless they requested it themselves with a promise that they would follow later. They also felt it would be a loss if Regiment I was prevented from carrying out its duty because of them. The situation in this journey was increasingly anxious and heart-pounding primarily among the evacuees, all the more so after they heard the news, brought by other evacuees who had taken a different path from [our] party's, that wild and irresponsible behavior was increasingly violent and arbitrary, in fact had already taken victims in the form of human souls. (Gintings 1975:39)

imagination

While both accounts call upon their audience to imagine the terrors of the journey, Sinek does so in a spacious style that allows the work of imagination to take its own shape. That may be an artistic choice on her part, but it is an option because she can assume an audience familiar with the terrain as well as the tropes of her story. Images of evacuees fleeing along "paths never traversed by humankind" and in forests "wide and lonely as the sea" recall the conventional poetics of Karo songs of praise and exile, but they also evoke a known landscape. Writing in Indonesian and thus potentially addressing a national rather than a local audience—and writing as well with an eye on posterity—Djamin Ginting fills in the spaces of the narrative by telling the reader *what* to imagine, both pictorially and affectively. The motives and sentiments of the evacuees as well as the soldiers who accompanied them are spelled out; the dangers are clearly explained. The entire passage is designed to heighten the pathos of the evacuees' circumstances, as well as their patriotic resolve, while highlighting the soldiers' care for these vulnerable representatives of the national community—a dramatic contrast to the "wild and irresponsible behavior" of other fighting forces toward the evacuees.

In Sinek's song, even moments of high drama and horror seem to have an emotional flatness to them. Here she describes awakening after a night spent in the midst of the forest on Deleng (Mount) Palpalen:

> When the day grew light
> we looked around our sleeping place.
> We glanced to the left, to the right,
> we looked in front of us,
> we glanced behind us.
> To our surprise, right around the place where we slept,
> innumerable corpses, brother, in the forest.
> Many were those whose breath became wind
> from exhaustion and hunger,
> because of their strenuous climb
> up the terrible slopes, brother.
> Breath became wind because of exhaustion, brother,
> or from hunger and lack of food.
> "So then, let's not stay here any longer.
> If we stay, you know,
> the children will be scared,"
> so said the mothers and fathers of our group.
> We left before breakfast
> and covered tens of kilometers that day. (32–34)

Vivid signs of violence stand out against the empty landscape, as when they approach the ruins of Batu Karang:

> So brother, then we saw
> that the houses of Batu Karang had burned,
> an area as wide as the sea, the land of the Five Brothers (Lima Senina),
> founded by the Bangun clan, a single bloodline,
> with its wide wet-rice fields, brother.
> Its foundations were higher than the roof beams.
> We saw the black smoke rising, brother. (36)

Sinek traces her journey in search of safety from one village to another: Jinabun, Kuta Buluh, Tiga Binanga, Lau Baleng, Tiga Lingga. At each stop the group hopes to have time for a short rest but is ordered to move on:

> After the second night
> a command came for us
> saying, please go from here,
> that's what he said, the subdistrict officer of the Kuta Buluh subdistrict.
> So we went, brother,

toward the Gendaholi hills around Perbesi
heading for Tiga Binanga.
. . . after the second night there,
a command came for us
saying, no use for you to stay here long,
that's what our leaders said, brother.
So we left again, brother,
heading for the land of Lau Baleng,
wandering along the long straight road and the winding road,
not knowing where else to spend the night
till we came to the land of Lau Baleng. (40–41)

Finally, in the refugee camps of Kota Cane, in republican Aceh, their journey comes to a temporary halt, in a land of unfamiliar customs and unknown languages. Exiled among strangers, Sinek is reduced to *foraging like a goat*, shrinking in the heat *like a banana blossom, that gets smaller the older it grows* (47). The family gradually sells off their stock of blankets and clothing to buy rice.

So then, brother,
after all the blankets we'd brought were gone,
all our clothes were gone, traded away,
then a command came down,
then there was news.
We could leave now,
return to our birthplace,
that's what our leaders said.
Everyone went home, brother, going home to the place of their birth.
Only we did not. (51)

With Lau Cih still firmly under Dutch control, Sinek's father decides they should stay instead in the highland village of Jandimeriah, on Lau Borus. Shifting between the first-person plural (K., *kami*, exclusive "we") and the autobiographical third-person *beru Karo*, which is the polite formal manner of self-reference, Sinek complains that she was *stuck fast in Jandimeriah* (52) for nearly two years, unable to go home:

For twenty months beru Karo cursed her fate
because all her things were used up.
All her blankets had been cooked up, and all her clothes had been
    cooked too.
To go home like that to Lau Cih,
founded by the great Purba clan
on the outskirts of Medan,
the turnoff to Langkat,
going home now,

after all the clothes had been eaten up, all the blankets cooked,
surely beru Karo would be disregarded.
Surely we'd be left out
if the others had gotten home first,
if we didn't even have clothes to wear, so we thought—
we didn't go home to Lau Cih. (54)

PROSPECTS AND DEPARTURES

Going forward also means leaving something behind—another time, a
way of living, a home. For a Karo audience, what made Sinek's performance so compelling was the profound sense of loss she evoked. In the
following passage, for example, the refugees, having reached the peak
of Mount Palpalen, look back toward their lowland home for one final
time:

Then we all gazed down at the hot Karo lowlands,
wide and lonely as the sea, brother.
Our gaze drifted heavily down to the wide unbroken flatness;
there weeping gave way to more weeping for those who gazed.
Tears flowed and flowed,
spattering on faces, drying on laps,
and suddenly the day
was covered in clouds, nothing could be seen of the lowlands.
So we thought,
"Maybe here we aren't allowed to weep."
That's what we concluded, as we comforted one another,
the companions of a single group. (30–31)

The refugees' flight through empty space would end with a chance—a
command really—to return home. Yet there is the kind of ironic coda we
have come to recognize as distinctly modern: home regained but no longer
habitable; independence defended but no longer heroic; and a new struggle to recover what seems, in retrospect, to have been a livable past. Sinek's
farewell to the lowlands has all the poignancy of a tragic nostalgia, as her
own view of home is lost quite literally as a result of grief—because, she
surmises, the spirits of the place don't allow weeping there. This stun-
ningly concise delineation of modernity's chronic condition of homesick-
ness has the uncanny feeling of a moment trapped in its own aftermath.

This tableau of loss-made-visible completes the move away from
home initiated by an earlier scene of invisible danger and imminent
departure. This occurred at the time of the fall of the Medan front,
when Sinek's family and the other refugees had already moved away

from Barung Ketang to a safer camp near Lau Tengah. Sinek, who had been drafted to help in the militia's public kitchen, stayed behind. There, like the young soldiers taken by surprise in the Dutch assault, she too was caught in the unseen scope of violence.

> I was hoeing in the field;
> Mother, my little brothers and sisters, even my father had gone on to
>   the banks of Lau Tengah.
> I should go too, I thought.
> A plane was firing from above.
> How I ran I don't know.
> I was all alone, brother,
> not knowing where the plane was
> or what it was shooting at.
> I don't know if I was seen or not.
> This may be the time my breath turns to wind.
> Never again will I converse with my father, brothers, and sisters.
> That's what I thought. (22)

The same sense of human frailty and isolation in the midst of war that Walter Benjamin depicted in his scene of the figure on the battlefield echoes in this passage. Violence is at once everywhere and nowhere. There are the unseen plane and its unknown target, and, also visible in the naked landscape, the frightened, solitary girl. Although she is soon reunited with her family, this scene marks a change in Sinek's narrative. From this point it becomes a story of their journey and the struggle to survive in unknown, foreign territory. From here on, displacement is a permanent condition.

Benjamin represented in his vignette the end of the traditions of storytelling: soldiers returned from the front silenced—"not richer, but poorer in communicable experience" (1969b:84). Sinek begins as "Silent" (to recall the meaning of her name), but her story has a different ending. For as much as her song is about loss, it is also situated within a particular local aesthetic of mobility. It tells the story of an extraordinary time in a woman's life, a journey that provides not only the material for storytelling but also the occasion for it. From her experience she gains a new capacity to speak and a tale to tell that becomes the inspiration and basis for her postwar career as a professional entertainer. It is a story of departures . . .

. . . WITHOUT HOMECOMING

One of the many marvelous things about Sinek's song is the way it enfolds the history of its own production in the story it tells. This is what makes it more than just a personal narrative and also more than an official history: it recalls her recognition of herself as an individual subject and extends that work of introspection to her audiences. Introspection is not a quality ordinarily found in Karo literature; in fact, Sinek's story of the evacuation is the only instance of it that I know. This introspective turn begins in the marketplace of Tiga Nderket, not far from Jandimeriah. There Sinek meets an older woman, whom she addresses politely as *bibi*, "auntie." Looking for sympathy, Sinek begins to tell the woman about her predicament. Instead of offering comfort, the auntie replies with a story of her own. *I too went along to the land of Kuta Cané*, says the auntie:

> I took along your three little cousins, auntie's friend.
> Because it's not very warm here,
> and Kuta Cané is sweltering,
> they all passed away,
> your three little cousins that I took on the evacuation.
> They left us behind,
> so only their father and I came home
> to the place of our birth.
> Then we moved on to here
> from the evacuation.
> For what's the use of going,
> what's the use of returning to your birthplace
> if the mother's sons and daughters are all gone?
> I left them all behind,
> their breath turned to wind.
> Maybe that was the fate they requested,
> but memories are all that remain for me. (60)

What Sinek records here is the communicability of incommensurable experience, the uniqueness of *all* the fragmentary accounts inscribed in the history of the evacuation. Her own story is a traveler's tale of sorts, but it evokes an entirely different kind of story from the auntie:

> And so we two wept together,
> and my heart eased a bit.
> It seems we weren't the only ones who suffered,
> it seems we weren't the only ones who experienced difficulties.
> That's what I thought, brother. (61)

This is not a mutual healing through shared grief, Sinek insists. Rather it is a kind of self-recognition achieved through what Kathleen Stewart (1992:411) calls the "exchange of stories":

> No longer could I speak from my heart
> to give comfort, brother,

because it seems to me that for trouble and heartache
there is a remedy,
but the death of your children, the boys and the girls,
it strikes to the bone.
For that, there may not be a time of healing,
that's what I thought,
and maybe beru Karo will be stuck in this Borus until she's old.
That's what I thought. (66)

But Sinek isn't stuck there for long:

That's when I got the idea for all this traveling around, brother.
That's where my travels began,
far and wide.
Jandimeriah was where it all began. (67)

As she explained to me later, one day Sinek happened to meet a soldier, Kabun Sembiring, who had been her schoolmate at Taman Siswa.
He remembered her from local talent shows, she said, and so invited her
to entertain the troops at a dance festival in Tiga Nderket. She had sung
a few times around Jandimeriah, but this was the first time she was paid
to perform. "I didn't want to do it anymore, I was embarrassed," she
told me. "But he called on me, he paid me in advance. 'Tell the story of
the evacuation,' said Kabun. So I told it, I guess it just flowed out of my
brain, just as it was in my memory I told it. From then on I started to
sing all around. Before that my father wouldn't let me sing."

For a girl like Sinek, well educated by the standards of the time and
with a good family background, the life of a professional performer would
ordinarily have been considered shockingly inappropriate, which is why
her father objected to her singing in public. Indeed, the idea of a career of
any sort would have been nearly unthinkable had it not been for the opening of alternatives to marriage for women of her generation by the disloca-
tions and privation of the war. The nationalist impetus and often patriotic
tone of Sinek's performance gave her a somewhat "classier" reputation
than most female singers enjoyed and lent an aura of respectability to a
lifestyle that might otherwise have appeared scandalous.

From then on, brother,
I traveled far and wide,
stopping here and there.
The homes of all my mothers and aunts
were not enough for all my stopping places.
The platters of all my mothers and aunts weren't big enough
to feed my entourage. (69)

Karo stories begin with a departure, and they usually end with a homecoming—and, frequently, a wedding. In this sense Sinek's story doesn't really end; it only expands into other, more congenial travels, into a career as a professional singer and indeed to her meeting with Malem Pagi Ginting, the singing partner and "sweet brother" to whom her song is ostensibly addressed.

> So, brother,
> many and various were the trials we underwent in the evacuation,
> which is the beginning of my wide travels
> and the path to our meeting,
> as we travel together,
> sweet brother. (69)

Sinek's song of the evacuation concludes with an array of beginnings—of a voice, a career, a lifetime of departures and meetings and journeys. And an opening into other stories, too, as Sinek invites her listeners, present and future, to remember for themselves:

> So that we may all be a little healed
> of our troubled thoughts,
> may all your thoughts be like this.
> We weren't the only ones who felt the heartaches
> during our journey of the evacuation.
> Think about it,
> compare yourselves to beru Karo. (70–72)

Then, in a final gesture of narrative continuity, she passes the thread of the telling to her partner Malem Pagi:

> You, brother, where did you go back then?
> Where did the evacuation take you?
> Did you go on the evacuation or not?
> Please tell it for our mothers and fathers assembled here
> to hear and to listen, sweet brother.
> So then—
> I can tell it too, you say, my traveling companion.
> Tell the story, brother. (74)

AN AESTHETIC OF TRAVEL

Modernity, James Clifford (1997) says, is about "routes" rather than "roots." The same could be said for most traditional forms of Karo literature, which are shaped by an aesthetic of travel. Folktales and myths tell of journeys and quests and successful returns; local histories are stories of migration and dispersal, in which lineage fissioning leads to village founding, forgotten relationships are reactivated and new ones formed. The framing conventions of Karo poetry are departure and farewell. Even contemporary pop songs, as a Karo friend once joked, are mostly about leaving home. Walter Benjamin (1969b:84) quotes approvingly the German saying, "When someone goes on a trip, he has something to tell about." Karo might say that's because nothing worth telling happens to people who stay at home.

Before the struggle, Karo women had few opportunities for going on trips, and so they had little material for the making of stories and little reason for the composition of poetry. Both as literary producers themselves and as characters in the literary productions of men, women figured in literature mostly as those who stayed behind. This may in part explain their enthusiasm for talking about the evacuation, when they *did* get to go on a journey.

modernity + loss

What makes Sinek's story a modern one is thus not that it takes the form of a journey but that it dwells so insistently on the theme of loss—and, further, that this loss becomes the ground for personal growth and reflection. In other Karo stories a home is always there to return to, a sweetheart waiting, or else a new household or village to establish, just like the one left behind. Here, however, what is lost cannot be recovered or replaced. With its repeated departures and never a return in sight, Sinek's song tracks the record of incremental loss that is a consequence of thinking through the rupture: We wanted to rest, we had to go on; the view of home was blocked because "here we weren't allowed to weep"; we arrived in a land where we didn't know the language, we had to adjust ourselves to the ways of strangers; the others went home, only we did not. The only person who makes it home at all in Sinek's song is the bereaved auntie, who soon departs again—for what's the use of going home, she says, when your children are gone?

In such circumstances, travel becomes habitual. Returning to burned villages with "foundations higher than their roofs," to ruined crops, and, too often, to shattered families, the possibilities at home suddenly looked too cramped. Highlanders migrated downstream to the coastal lowlands, establishing squatters' claims to fallow plantation land on the outskirts of Medan, where Sinek's journey had begun. Some moved to the city for work or to send their children to school. Soldiers were sent to distant parts of the archipelago to put down local rebellions. Students went away to college. Even those who stayed behind seemed to be in motion. Bus lines crisscrossed the highlands, connecting traders to the local market circuits, bringing highland travelers to see family or friends in the lowland cities and city dwellers for nostalgic visits to the old home place, or taking performers like Sinek to sing about the evacuation in villages all over the highlands.

> This is the story of hardship
> when I traveled far and wide,
> when my resting places were uncertain,
> when we all went on the long evacuation.
> So then all of you who are listening
> to this story of the evacuation, mothers, fathers, brothers, sisters,
>   friends,
> weeping in memory of the heartaches back then
> or the difficulties when we went on the evacuation,
> compare yourselves to beru Karo. (70)

This reflexive turn occurs, remarkably, in a genre that would seem wholly unsuited to it. Unlike the stories of traveling heroes that make up most of the corpus of Karo oral narrative, public oratory and its associated genres such as *katoneng-katoneng* subscribe to the poetic ideals of collective subjectivity and social stability. The *katoneng-katoneng* is supposed to reflect as well as produce harmony and accord in public discourse by downplaying dissent, conflict, and contest (these being, not surprisingly, common features of Karo social life). It is supposed to call down blessings of wealth and happiness on its entire community of listeners. The following passage, which is taken from the conclusion of Malem Pagi's recorded *katoneng-katoneng* of the evacuation, is, except for the sales pitch at the end, characteristic:

> So may we all have good fortune, watched over by God.
> Watched over by God, our mothers whose love for us is unwavering,
> according to the faith of each.
> May all increase their wealth and ability
> and all add to their good fortune and the unity of their hearts from now
>   into the future.
> May our thoughts be united in seeking the good.
> . . . .
> So then, Karo clan, Sembiring clan, Tarigan clan, Perangin-angin
>   Sebayang clan, Ginting clan,
> let's not add to the feeling of suffering:
> if our feelings suffer, so too our wealth and prosperity will suffer.
> May the words that are lacking in my story
> bring a lack of disasters, bad dreams, troubling dreams,
> a lack of trouble in our hearts.

All of our clanmates, our wife givers, and wife receivers, and even the
    wife receivers of our wife receivers,
and all the mothers, none preferred above the others,
may we be more united in our speech.
Once again I'll remind you,
mother, don't forget to buy the cassette we've recorded at the Teen
    Shop.
Come in and buy a tape recorder, mother.
Whatever you want, they have it there, mother.
May you be able to earn a living,
may we all find good luck,
all my mothers, as I end my song may all the bad dreams, troubled
    dreams, come to an end.
The danger is over, the soul returns home.
May our hearts arise healed, mother.

Conventional *katoneng-katoneng* performances like this one speak of *nandé bapa kerina, si la erndobah si la erpilih*, "all the mothers and father, without difference, without preference," of "hearts and souls once divided now become healed," and of "all our conversations as one, one in step and one in style." Sinek's song offers none of these. What healing she provides comes from the recognition of difference. Think about it, she tells her audience; we weren't the only ones who suffered.

Compare yourselves with me: The modern sensibility depends on reflexive encounters such as these, in which subjectivity is produced and maintained by simultaneous identification with and denial of other possible life narratives. This move, in which another's experience displayed becomes a mirror for self-reflection, is where I began this story of the evacuation, with Karo television viewers in 1994 comparing themselves with the mass-mediated images of Rwandan refugees. In it is embodied a central feature of modern identity, which Anthony Giddens (1991) calls the "reflexive project of the self." To Giddens, this refers to the individual's capacity to maintain an autobiographical narrative, to keep a story of one's self going over the course of a lifetime. But it also refers to the capacity to recognize different stories in progress, to imagine other possible "trajectories of self." By placing the individual at the center of her story, Sinek effects a dramatic transformation in the image of community: not a single group, unified and harmonious, but a collection of individuals of differing, yet equally meaningful, life experiences. In her story of suffering measured in perseverance and cooking pots, Sinek places a woman's experience on public view as, literally, comparable to that of men. Extending the uncertain resting places of the evacuation into the journeys of a professional career, she raises the possibility of profiting from homelessness, while recognizing that for some—those for whom nothing but memories remain—there may not be a time of healing after all.

AT HOME WITH THE MEMORY ARTIST

Sinek did, of course, eventually get home. In the mid-1960s, when she was well past what Karo consider marriageable age, she retired from the music business and married a prosperous local businessman. Back in Lau Cih, where I met her in 1994, she told me that her *katoneng-katoneng* performance was a straightforward account of her experience, told from the heart, just as it had happened. Later she conceded that she had left some things out, such as the names of a few of the places her family stopped along the way and the leeches that plagued them in the forest. Nothing important, she said.

One of the things she left out did strike me as important, though. It seems that the "companions of a single group" with whom she traveled were not, as I had assumed and her song implies, the Karo villagers of Lau Cih and Barung Ketang but rather some three hundred political prisoners, many of whom were not even ethnically Karo. Her father had been entrusted with the task of escorting these accused enemies of the republic across the Karo highlands to a safer detention site in nationalist-held Aceh. Accompanied by a military guard and supplied with sufficient provisions for their journey, the group traveled according to official directions and carried official safe-conduct passes. These would not have protected them from Dutch aerial bombing but would probably have prevented what was in fact a more pressing threat to the evacuees: assault by predatory Indonesian militia groups or army units patrolling the highlands.

By omitting these details, Sinek creates an autobiography that resonates with the common experiences of Karo refugees: displacement, terror, radical uncertainty, the heartache and the freedom of modern homelessness. This is why her performance, as a work of art, still captures the Karo imagination. What is *lost* in her performance is the opportunity to recognize certain forms of violent agency on the nationalist side itself. The killing and robbery of evacuees; the scapegoating of "feudal" leaders and of ethnic groups deemed insufficiently committed to the nationalist cause; the social and economic devastation that resulted from the militia's scorched-earth policy; the continuing brutality inflicted on local populations precisely by those *brothers and fathers who defended the nation*—all these disappear from Sinek's account. In their place are the sound of distant bombers, the charred ruins of burned villages, the invisible dangers of forest and mountainside, the bodies of the dead, but with no indication of how they died or by whose hand: the signs of violence but not its agents.

I don't mean to suggest that Sinek's selective reconfiguration of past events is good art but bad history or that an ethnographic interview is a more truthful genre than a song. The issue here is not truth but memory: not what *really* happened in 1947 Karoland, but rather why the evacuation has come to be recalled and retold in one particular way and not another—why, in other words, Karo have come to think of it as a progress rather than a panic, a break with the past rather than another step in the long history of Karo journeys—and what might be at stake in this particular staging of national experience. In this instance, one of the stakes is a Karo share in the nation's future.

As Dipesh Chakrabarty (1992:21) has written, "histories that either implicitly or explicitly celebrate the advent of the modern state and the idea of citizenship" must necessarily downplay the "repression and violence that are as instrumental in the victory of the modern as is the persuasive power of its rhetorical strategies." Heroically reinvented as a unanimous, patriotically inspired, voluntary withdrawal from enemy-held territory, the evacuation establishes a Karo place in Indonesian national history and on the progressive track of modernity that the state still claimed as its own. In making the case for an inclusive model of Indonesian citizenship, Sinek's song suppresses evidence of the violence that was directed against its subjects by the state itself. This is the price paid for the work of imagination within the precincts of the modern nation-state.

Sinek's song of the evacuation was composed in the immediate aftermath of the struggle and performed (no doubt with considerable revision) during the 1950s and '60s, when artistic works aimed at local ethnic audiences, whether in traditional forms like the *katoneng-katoneng* or in more innovative works like the Karo-language popular songs of the composer Djaga Depari, were encouraged as local expressions of the national spirit. Although state censors increasingly policed the limits of artistic freedom, the arts were supported as a fundamental means of political communication, serving the aims of the government as well as those of the various political parties. This was a time of intense patriotism and regional pride, coupled with a restricted sense of the acceptable limits of historical inquiry. Historical orthodoxy in this period, as Anthony Reid (1979b:298) puts it, "acquired a somewhat brittle quality which did not invite too rich an elaboration" of local pasts, particularly those pasts that did not fit the mold of patriotic national commitment.[10] Sukarno glorified and idealized the events of the struggle as a golden bridge to Indonesian modernity but did not tolerate any moral ambiguity regarding the nationalist cause. It is, I think, telling nevertheless that the only explicitly nationalistic passage in Sinek's song is expressed as if in the voice of her singing partner, Malem Pagi:

> "Well, mother Karo,
> what's to be done, O sister,
> if our desire is for independence,
> Indonesian independence, sister?
> We have to suffer, sister,
> in order to gain the fruit of independence.
> So tell it clearly, sister, tell it,"
> That's what you say, brother,
> my traveling companion. (46)

Looking back on the Old Order time when Sinek's song was recorded, I'm tempted to imagine a time less vacuous, richer in public speech, than the New Order, with its pinched pieties and casual brutality, or even the slick commercialism of the neoliberal present. Unexpectedly recovered like an excavated artifact of former days, the recorded song encourages this desire. I want it to tell me not just what happened during the evacuation but also about the now-vanished time in which this patriotic but intensely local recollection was imagined and performed, when it was possible not just to remember but to remember *something*. It is important to recognize this recuperative range in the recorded song, which is shaped not just by its composition but also by its reception: in multiple contexts, live in performance or on tape at home; by various people at various times, including its audiences both anticipated and—like ourselves—unexpected. If Sinek's song, by dwelling in the moment of loss, does incite in its audience the will to remember, it does not specify where remembrance will lead: whether to crisis or acceptance—or to nostalgia.

For Nandé Petrus, my adoptive Karo mother, the song brought back happy memories. She accompanied me when I went to Sinek's house for a second visit, in 1995. Nandé Petrus too had been in the evacuation, as a child of about seven, and so she and Sinek swapped some tales about their various experiences. Sinek's story about crossing Mount Palpalen, carrying *our belongings in my hand and on my head, and my little brother on my back* (27), put Nandé Petrus in mind of the time during the evacuation when she was climbing down a steep slope with her family's rice pot balanced on her head. "That pot got to the bottom before we did!" she laughed, repeating a well-worn family joke about how the pot fell off and rolled all the way down. She told us about her crying cousin, who was tied outside at night for fear that their unwelcoming hosts would ask them to move on, about the villagers who refused to even lend them a grinding stone. But what she recalled most insistently was not the experience of the evacuation and its stories of hardship or adventure. Instead, it was Armed Forces Day, October 5, 1960. There was a grand Karo cultural festival in Medan on that occasion, and Nandé Petrus was the festival queen (Nandé Aron). She got to ride on an enormous float through the Karo district of the city, along with all the important dignitaries.[11] That was when she met Sinek for the first time.

What Sinek's song evokes for me is a perfect moment of my own, an evening in 1994 when I was visiting friends in Kuta Gamber, a community of the southern edge of the Karo plateau. Kuta Gamber is a small, clean, quite friendly village where another anthropologist, the late Masri Singarimbun, had done fieldwork in the early 1970s. At that time he had to come in on horseback or on foot, following the route of the evacuees who had flooded into the area in 1947. By 1994 a paved highway passed nearby, and there was a gravel road all the way to the village, but it still had the tranquil, slightly out-of-touch feeling that I imagined the best sort of field site would have. This was largely, I now believe, because there was no local school, and so all the village's school-age children boarded away. That night I played my tape of Sinek's *katoneng-katoneng* for my hosts. Neighbors began to drop in to listen. At first they were disappointed that it wasn't the better-known evacuation song that Malem Pagi had recorded, but soon they were enthralled. Place-names in the song called forth other stories of the evacuation; incidents of sorrow or terror brought silent sympathy. "That's just how it was," they said, and someone probably mentioned the Rwandan refugees once again. After the tape was done we talked for a while and the visitors drifted off again. I find it hard now to separate Sinek's song from that moment of exquisite comfort, when I truly, briefly, felt at home in the field.

The Sense of an Ending

The evacuees' return to their homes after the Renville Accord was not the end of the struggle, though it does provide a convenient stopping point for my story of Indonesian independence. The events that followed had more to do with the consolidation of the state than with the idea of independence. During the yearlong hiatus in the fighting, Indonesians turned their attention to matters of administration and governance, political routinization, and military reorganization. The army set up new training programs emphasizing guerrilla warfare, clarified and strengthened its chain of command, and endeavored to enhance the discipline and esprit of the corps. Idle fighting units were put to work on village projects, such as digging irrigation ditches and improving roads and bridges; they helped with the rice harvest in nearby communities and planted their own gardens to reduce their dependence on already hard-pressed villagers. They contributed to the support and protection of those evacuees who remained in the field huts and forest camps in republican territory.

Under the leadership of professional officers imported from Java, northern Sumatra's independent militias were absorbed into the TNI through the creation of a self-supporting territorial (Sektor) system. Intransigent armed groups were dissolved or hived off into separate zones of command. The hard-line Wild Tiger Brigade was relocated to South Tapanuli, where they became embroiled in a violent clash between two rival TNI factions. This was one of a number of regional rebellions

that were faced down by the army during the period, the most significant of these being the September 1948 "Madiun Affair," in which a
leftist uprising in the Madiun district in East Java was violently crushed
by the TNI.[1] Whatever energies the army directed toward winning
hearts and minds at the grassroots level, it was these unflinching demonstrations of force exercised against internal enemies that have, to this
day, most profoundly shaped perceptions of military power by
civilians and soldiers alike (McGregor 2005, 2007; McVey 1971, 1972).

Reorganizations were also under way on the civilian side. A network
of village-level economic organizations known as the Pertahanan Rakyat
Semesta (PRS; I., Total Popular Defense) was created, first in the south
Karo area of Sektor III, then extending into parts of the western and
central plateau where the Dutch presence was relatively weak. These
local organizations not only managed the collection of rice and other
foodstuffs for the troops but also acted as a shadow administration and
reserve force (I., *tentara cadangan*) on the ground in occupied Karoland.
The republic's provincial government began issuing its own currency,
known as ORIPS (Oeang Republik Indonesia Propinsi Soematera) or,
more commonly, *uang putih*, "white money," so called because it was
printed on plain, uncolored stock.[2] Tax-collecting trade offices and
checkpoints were set up along the border between Dutch and republican
territory. Luxury items like soap and cigarettes were heavily taxed, and
products for which there was an international market, like rubber and
benzoin, were diverted entirely to finance the war effort.

Trade offices and inspections, currencies and letters of passage,
brought the power of the state into the life of the people at every crossing of the border, but it was the PRS that embedded the republic in the
everyday experience of Karo villagers. "With the birth of the PRS,"
write Selamat Ginting's official biographers Tridah Bangun and Hendri
Chairudin (1994:268–69), "the guerrilla war was no longer just a war
between the TNI and the enemy, but a war of the army together with
the people in opposing the enemy." PRS groups provided guides for
guerrilla units, passed information about enemy troop movements,
delivered supplies to the troops, sabotaged roads and bridges, kept
an eye out for collaborators and spies, and assisted in the everyday
governance of their communities (Surbakti 1979:53–60).

On December 19, 1948, the Dutch, citing continued harassment by
nationalist forces, launched Operatie Kraai (D., Operation Crow), the
code name for its second military campaign against the republic. They
took the republican capital of Yogyakarta, in Central Java, with little

effective opposition and arrested Sukarno, Hatta, and most of their cabinet. Within a week, Dutch troops in northern Sumatra had surged across Lau Renun into Tapanuli's Dairi District, the heart of Selamat Ginting's Sektor III command. Instead of retreating, his troops responded by moving back onto the plateau, where they established guerrilla pockets (I., *kantong-kantong gerilya*) in areas of limited Dutch presence. With the assistance of sympathetic villagers and local PRS organizations, guerrilla squads engaged in roadside ambushes and cat-and-mouse attacks on outlying Dutch posts. These proved more effective than the frontal assaults and scorched-earth tactics of the first military campaign. By the end of the following year, when the formal transfer of sovereignty was completed, the entire Karo district, with the exception of the main towns and major roadways, was already under de facto republican control (van Langenberg 1976:745–46), even though it was technically a part of the Dutch-supported State of East Sumatra (NST). On August 17, 1950, following mass anti-NST demonstrations in Karoland and throughout the province, the State of East Sumatra was dissolved and Karoland became a part of the unified Republic of Indonesia.

. . .

We know about past events through the stories that have been told about them: stories calibrated in numbers and charts; tracked on maps and grids; visualized in paintings, monuments, and photographs; passed on in old men's yarns and well-worn jokes, scholars' books, and official records; inscribed in testimonies, travelogues, memoirs, and lists; told and retold as nursery tales, folklore, and family memories, in poetry and song; congealed in artifacts and archives or recalled in place-names, everyday objects, and cherished mementos. To begin to grasp the nature and significance of these storied forms—the meanings they hold or that they held for those who told, and lived, them—we need to comprehend the manner in which they are cast. The historian's causal sequencing and the state's simplified iconography, the demographer's calculations and the *lieux de mémoire* of public as well as personal recollection, track their own pathways through the thickets of past time. Both the comic-heroic stories of military ignorance told by Karo men and the matter-of-fact lists of place-names through which Karo women plotted their travels during the evacuation array events in straightforward sequences that make them memorable to narrator and audience alike. The evidentiary demands of the pension testimonial forgo considerations of motive and agency altogether in favor of the specificity of (already known) details that can confirm or refute claims of military service. The generalized accounts of women's activities, their eagerness and enthusiasm, offer much in the way of motive and sentiment but little of sequence or verifiable proofs. Each of these narrative styles frames past events according to particular demands of genre and emplotment, making of uncertain circumstances a story that can call up and, if it is good enough, satisfy its own audience. To unstory the past is to erase it, not to preserve it as history.

Events are shot through with stories even before they begin. The hardships of the Japanese occupation provided the raw material that nationalist propagandists in Karoland wove into a story of "how it felt to be colonized," revising in the process the experience of colonization and enabling a narrative of liberation embodied in the cry *Merdeka!* Sukarno's passionate rhetorical invocation of the "golden bridge" to independence inspired young men and women of the '45 generation to step forward, even if they were unsure where they were going. The felt injustices and betrayals of Dutch and Japanese rule, or perhaps of even earlier rivalries and feuds kept alive in lineage histories, family memories, and village myths, fed the violent retributions and preemptive assaults of Revolution Time; later, *repolusi* itself served as part of the backstory of communist betrayal and revenge that was used to incite—or justify—the killings of 1965–66. The Karo sea of fire replayed and, in local accounts anyway, exceeded the burning of the city of Bandung; both took their inspiration from news reports of the Soviet scorched-earth defense against the German blitzkrieg (itself perhaps a recapitulation of Napoleon's devastating failure in Russia a century before). The mass exodus that followed the Dutch invasion of the highlands was inflected with terror and violence, much of it provoked by stories of collaborators and spies, of codes, "marks," and secret documents. Later on, these same events were recalled, with some parts obscured and others highlighted, as a patriotic story of collective sacrifice for the nation.

But however much these stories—these rifle reports from another time and place—may be about the past, they also participate in deeper and more complex chronotopologies. Narrative time, as Paul Ricoeur argues, is more than a "linear succession of instants." This "episodic dimension" of narrative is joined by a "configurational dimension," in which "the plot construes significant wholes out of scattered events" (1980:178). A story's meaning thus arises out of the dual operation of sequence and pattern by means of the plot. Narrative emplotment requires a complex temporal engagement in the realm of memory: even as it moves toward completion, the narrative simultaneously scrolls backward from a now- (or soon-to-be) foregone conclusion. "The plot's configuration," Ricoeur says,

> superimposes "the sense of an ending"—to use Kermode's expression—on the open-endedness of mere succession. As soon as a story is well known— and such is the case with most traditional and popular narratives as well as with the national chronicles of the founding events of a given community— retelling takes the place of telling. Then following the story is less important than apprehending the well-known end as implied in the beginning and the well-known episodes as leading to this end. . . . The recollection of the story governed as a whole by its way of ending constitutes an alternative to the representation of time as moving from the past forward into the future, according to the well-known metaphor of the arrow of time. It is as though recollection inverted the so-called natural order of time. By reading the end in the beginning and the beginning in the end, we learn also to read time itself backward, as the recapitulating of the initial conditions of a course of action in its terminal consequences. (179)

What Ricoeur calls the "thought" or theme of a narrative is what unifies it, generating a meaningful pattern out of the episodic time of "mere succession." This can be a moral lesson ("suffering brings enjoyment"); a condition or state of mind ("tiredness" or "ignorance"); a punch line ("so that's what he meant by 'letting loose the water buffaloes!'"); or the attribution of a proper name or concept to a historical period, phase, or kind of event (Independence Time, *repolusi*, police action, ORLA)—names that "allow us to apprehend a set of historical events under a common denominator." Yet tellings accumulate not just as repetitions but as reconfigurations as well. These sediment and thicken, they veer into strange courses, set out for new territories, find novel patterns, new themes, other endings. Each repetition embeds the story in the particular circumstances of its telling. A place, a time, an audience: something happens that alters the story's significance or shifts the correlates of its meaning; these press it toward a future in which seemingly foreclosed endings may unexpectedly reopen.

The choice of an ending thus determines the meaning of the story. That is why I chose to conclude this story of Indonesian independence with the Renville Accord, holding open both its sense of future possibilities and the military failures and follies in which these possibilities were both embodied and derailed. Other stories might have traced the arc of military rationalization, as the popular militias were first absorbed into the TNI and then demobilized at the war's end, returning home with nothing to show for their service, or taken a biographical approach and concluded with Selamat Ginting's resignation of his military commission in solidarity with his demobilized troops and out of concern for the future role of the army in national life. A story of gender and war could have told how a few women, like 'Cik Muham, parlayed their wartime experience into exceptional social roles, in higher education and the church, while most others found themselves back in familiar domestic roles after the war's end. A story of national tragedy could tell how Karo were gradually caught up in the violence of 1965, how some chose the wrong side and were "done for" or chose the winning side and were not.

By way of conclusion, then, I offer one more story, in the hope that the various reopenings and reconfigurations it reveals may inspire an equal sense of narrative possibility among the readers of this book. It came from Eben Hezer Sinuraya, the Sektor III company commander who so memorably encountered the water buffaloes at the midnight crossroads on the way to Kabanjahé. Toward the end of our conversation, he embarked on a long soliloquy that brought together the themes of ignorance and leadership, his own version of the "values of 1945," and the somewhat unexpected course of events in (what turned out to be) the last years of the New Order regime.

LOOKING BACK ON THE "VALUES OF '45"

In 1994, when most of these interviews were conducted, the New Order's hegemonic grip was beginning to weaken. Modes of social control that had been maintained though coercion and fear were increasingly ineffective. Corruption in the military and indeed throughout all reaches of society had reached a level that made centralized state authority difficult to sustain. The temporary easing of censorship restrictions in the early 1990s and the emergence of new media technologies enabled a florescence of political journalism, which, if timid by international standards, was refreshingly transparent to Indonesians who had become fluent readers between the lines of highly censored news reports. The press gleefully reported on cases of government corruption, scandals of the rich and powerful, and the criminality of organized *preman* gangs, thugs for hire who supported and were supported by institutions ranging from political parties and religious associations to the army. The ongoing military and paramilitary violence in nearby Aceh was rarely mentioned in the mainstream media but was commonly known anyway in Medan. Political protests and military crackdowns in predominantly

Christian provinces of Irian Jaya (now Papua) and East Timor (now independent Timor Leste) brought antigovernment prayers, only thinly veiled, in Karo churches and Christian homes. The activities of legal aid and labor NGOs were spotlighted in the press, and human rights (I., *hak asasi manusia*) were a topic of public conversation. Everyone could see the environmental degradation caused by illegal logging operations supported by corrupt officials and their cronies. Urban intellectuals and coffee shop pundits knew which corporations, plantations, and businesses were controlled by the army or by the president's friends and family members and were familiar with the strategies by which army and police units provided "protection for pay" to international companies. A newly visible ethnic Chinese business elite was identified (and resented) as the local face of increasingly rapacious international conglomerates. There were sporadic reports of church burnings and religious conflicts in North Sumatra and elsewhere, and Karo Christians watched the emergence of Islamic political organizations, both moderate and extreme, with concern. Crime reporting became a cover for political criticism, and scandals, major and minor, fed an insatiable public appetite for rumors, gossip, and jokes pointedly targeting the Suharto family and other political celebrities. Still, there was considerable hesitancy about addressing these issues directly, especially to a foreign researcher with a tape recorder. Eben Hezer was the only person we interviewed who drew an explicit, critical connection between the time of the independence struggle and Indonesia's present situation.

Coming back to Medan the day after Selamat Ginting's funeral, we discovered that we had missed a huge workers' rights demonstration. A protest march sponsored by the unauthorized labor organization SBSI (I., Serikat Buruh Sejahtera Indonesia, "Indonesian Prosperous Workers' Union") had turned violent when demonstrators began to direct their frustration toward Chinese businesses along their route. Many shops were vandalized and looted, and in a separate but related incident one man was killed. This was the first of what John Sidel (2006:1) has described as "deadly ethnic riots" that occurred across Indonesia in the New Order's waning years, a "certain pattern of disturbances," usually directed against ethnic Chinese, that "seemed to crystallize in riot form." Although Sidel argues that these incidents usually emerged "without provocation," the looting and destruction in Medan were widely believed to have been instigated by undercover army provocateurs, wearing civilian clothing but identifiable by their short (military) haircuts and black (military) boots.[3]

"Medan in Turmoil" read the cover headline of *Tempo*, the national news magazine, later that week, but by the time we got back to the city things were quiet enough.[4] There were few signs of trouble, other than closed businesses and some boarded-up shop fronts along the route of the march. The event soon disappeared from the press, and from local conversation, with hardly a ripple. But it was still on Eben Hezer's mind when we met two weeks later.

E. H. SINURAYA: Here's where I see the collapse of the values of '45. I say that now, the values of '45 have collapsed, and nationalism has eroded. That's just me. As for me, I feel that nationalism has eroded too. Otherwise, it wouldn't be possible for things to be this way. Think about it: in the prologue to our struggle we were anticapitalist. But what's the difference between capitalism and conglomerates in practice? Only the terms are different, the behavior is the same. Are we being consequential in holding up the values of the struggle of '45? I think not. We were anticapitalist at the time. America was said to be capitalist, but America now gives stock to the workers in its factories. Now, as for us, workers hold a demonstration just because they don't have enough, we forbid it anyway. Where are their fundamental rights [I., *hak azasinya*]? It's difficult, isn't it? So that's what I mean. Are we still consequential with the values of the '45 struggle like this? I think not. . . .

Now, the government is wrong. Also not wrong. On the one hand, education has been improved. People are getting smarter. On the other hand the people are still being made into fools [I., *diperbodoh-bodoh*, lit., "to be made ignorant"]. How can they be made ignorant if they're already smart? Now, you can see that. On the one hand there's education so the people will progress. On the other hand, this government still doesn't truly want the people to understand. They're sent to school, huh? To understand. Once they understand, they don't want them to understand. If they understand, they'll protest. That's what I mean.

In fact we are stamped down if we protest. Stamped down if you protest. If we're honest, is it possible to eat for three or four hundred [rupiahs] for a whole family? What are workers' wages, how can you do it? If they protest, it's said they are being manipulated. Manipulated by whom? Manipulated by not eating. Right? So we're not honest about this. Not honest. The leadership is not honest in this matter. It's as if I felt it, back then. How will it be later? I asked, and the answer is true now. If you're ignorant you'll really always be someone's coolie despite *merdeka*, yeah, that's it. But I think, if that's how it is, there's no need for us to talk about the values of '45, the heritage of the values of '45, because it's meaningless.

. . .

There's a saying that Karo use to describe debtors, rejected lovers, and other social misfits: *bagi belo la ertangké*, "like a betel leaf without a stem." Betel leaves are sold in standard packets of twenty, placed one on top of the other, and counted by stems, so that the stemless leaf is (as the punch line goes) "tied up in the bundle, left out of the count." When Karo men and women began to imagine independence in 1945, they did so in ways that had little, if anything, to do with "Indonesia" as a historically given national entity or even as a conceptually useful political object. The kind of community they imagined in stories of mobilization, aspiration, and even revolutionary violence had to do with more intimate forms of comradeship, equality, and social justice. At the end of the struggle, they found themselves incorporated in the national bundle but have since then been increasingly left out of the count. Over time they mostly had to settle for less than they imagined, a situation that Eben Hezer, for one, acutely recognized in the actions of the New Order regime. "Ignorance" was one way of talking about this situation.

For Eben Hezer, ignorance marked the ground zero of responsible leadership, revealing the duplicity of the current regime, which had fostered compulsory ignorance alongside education. In more personal terms, it also signified the generation gap between the aging Generation of 1945 and the better-educated younger generation of the late New Order period. This was the irony of the so-called transfer of the values of 1945. What was there to transfer? "One time," Eben Hezer said, "the young generation [I., *angkatan muda*] asked me, they said, if we look at '45, the Karo people, with an absolutely minimal education, how could they accomplish all that, they said. What inspired them? Why haven't we inherited it?" All the ambivalence and contradictory implications of ignorance and knowledge played through Eben Hezer's recollected response:

> E.H. SINURAYA: So I said, what is there to inherit? . . . What should I turn over to them? That's the trouble. I didn't understand what they meant that I should hand down. They said that, if that's how it was, that you were all still ignorant, but you were really important [in the struggle]. Why didn't you hand it down to us, because now we're behind all the others. . . . We're going to accuse you, they said to me. Why, what do you have to accuse? I said. Why you didn't hand it down. Why you were capable back then. Those values, why didn't you hand them down to us? It troubled me to think about this.

He imagined himself building a museum dedicated to the Karo freedom fighters, with all their names inscribed on one wall. There would be a recording of Sukarno reading the Proclamation of Independence, to make the point that, "hearing the Proclamation, these were the people who stepped forward." Like the military museums of the 1970s, created explicitly to display and pass on the "values of 1945" to the population as a whole, this imaginary monument was intended to convey the spirit and inspiration of the freedom fighters to its audience. But how could this spirit be transferred from one generation to the next? Eben Hezer pointed to the New Order's "proclamation of development" and the younger generation's indifferent response to it.

> E.H. SINURAYA: If you hear the proclamation of development and don't want to step forward, well, that's how it is now, right? The young genera-tion, in fact they're smarter than us, they should hear the proclamation of development and just step forward. That's how we were, the Proclamation of Independence. So what can I hand down, I'm, I'm—the spirit of '45, right? I thought and thought. What can I hand down, if those who want their inheritance don't want to know [about it]? You know, all I did was hear the proclamation. Joined in right away. Aside from being armed with knowl-edge already, they already know, they've heard the proclamation of develop-ment. That our task now is to fill in development. Why not step forward? For me, it was enough then for the sounding of the proclamation to awaken my spirit. Yeah, as for them, if to this day the sounding of development as a means of filling in independence isn't enough to wake them up, what else can I do?

Despite being saturated with the shifting terms and concepts of mili-tary ideology, Eben Hezer's account charts its own course through the landscape of late New Order Indonesia, playing ignorance as if it were a trump card in the arena of national commitment. This does not mean that his reflections on ignorance and responsibility should be read as a record of resistance. This is not a voice of dissent, engaged agonistically with the nation or even with the state. It is the voice of a patriot, attempting—still, despite nearly fifty years of trying—to find his way *into* the nation, to "fill in independence" from the inside, to become a "part of the count" rather than just another uncounted leaf in the national bundle.

> E.H. SINURAYA: I often say, now, I often say that you are all white-blooded, I say. White blood, because you're not, um—anymore. Why, they said, then your blood must be pure red, they said. Red, but clotted, I said, because I'm already old. So it doesn't flow anymore. But still red, I said. In other words, if I was commanded to defend [the country], maybe to this moment I wouldn't like it. But I'd do it with all my strength. Maybe you with all your knowledge haven't ever thought about this. Maybe you'd just run away. But I'll defend it, I said. It's not in my nature to run anywhere. I'd defend it. Maybe since you're all so smart, if you're afraid of being colonized maybe you can escape abroad, somewhere. That's one way out, right? But not for me, I said. I won't do that.

PEMUDA FEVER

For outsiders like myself, who came to know Indonesia during the peak years of New Order power, the political events of 1998 provided the sense of an ending to a time that, in its carefully cultivated stasis, seemed to be always on the verge of something but never quite got there. John Pemberton has brilliantly depicted this sensibility of arrested anticipation in his account of New Order election campaigns, in which rumors routinely circulated that something was going to happen, but somehow order invariably triumphed and one found that the moment had passed without incident. From a traumatic beginning in bloodshed and repression to an immobilized middle devoted to what Pemberton (1994:7) aptly describes as "that distinctly New Order state of idealized absence in which nothing . . . appears to happen," Indonesia seemed to exist in a state of suspended animation in which, like the Soviet Union before perestroika, "everything was forever" (Yurchak 2005). And so we waited (or I did, anyway) for a future time when we would be able to look back and see the moment when something had already started to happen.

[handwritten margin note: this was the experien of the elec. (2014) in W.P.]

Looking back on the final years of the Suharto regime, it has often seemed to me that the Medan "riot" of 1994 marked such a turning point in Indonesian mass politics. A mood of diffuse anger, frustration, and disappointment was beginning to crystallize in public action, in the double-edged form of demonstration/pogrom that was typical of Indonesian mass mobilizations, especially in the period leading up to and following Suharto's resignation. Between 1994 and 1998, labor unions and social justice NGOs gave way to student organizations as the vanguard groups demanding political reform. Reformasi was, like the *Merdeka!* salute of the 1945 generation, the fetishized password of the new *pemuda* (youth) movement (Siegel 1997a:209). Rather than the strategically limited, practical goals of local NGOs, the aspirations of these student activists were broad and principled.[5] They called for democratic elections, press freedom, social welfare and economic justice, political transparency, and an end to corruption, collusion, and nepotism (KKN, *korupsi, kolusi, dan nepotisme*) in government and business.

A wave of what Doreen Lee (2008) calls "pemuda fever" swept through the activist community. Students nostalgically identified themselves with the various periods of *pemuda* activism marked, in Indonesia, by the years of their specifically politicized generations: the generations of '45, '66, and '78, to which would now be added the generation of 1998, the Reformasi generation. They decked themselves in fashions that, in stylized form, recalled their national predecessors while also referencing the symbols of international struggle—red bandanas, blue jeans, and T-shirts decorated with raised fists and Molotov cocktails or with iconic images of Sukarno, Lenin, and Che Guevara.[6]

Student opposition to the Suharto regime may not have been the determining factor in the dictator's resignation, but it was the Reformasi movement's symbolic center of gravity. Images of student protesters circulated in global news media, underlining the seriousness of the demands for regime change. On May 13, 1998, four university students were shot and killed during a demonstration in Jakarta. In shocked reaction, riots spread through the city and beyond. These once again targeted Chinese businesses as well as properties associated with the Suharto family and cronies. Estimates of the number of people killed in the wave of violence are in the thousands, including many who were trapped in a shopping mall that was set afire by unknown arsonists. It was later revealed that an undetermined number of Chinese women, perhaps in the hundreds, had been raped during the riots, allegedly by military personnel. Within a week, President Suharto stepped down, replaced by his vice president, B. J. Habibie.

At the time we spoke and over the years since, I have often thought of Eben Hezer's anecdote about the "young generation" and their wish to embody the spirit of '45 as a statement of disappointment with the failure of the values and spirit of the founding generation of Indonesian nationhood. Keeping his monologue in its moment and insisting on following the speaker's intention—Eben Hezer's own "sense of an ending" to his story—we can perhaps read it only in that way. If we imagine it in the light of what came after—the Reformasi movement and the fall of the New Order—we might also see it as an aspiration beginning to take shape, a premonitory sign of *pemuda* fever in however inchoate and unrecognized a form. Either way, we establish a configuration in which a present moment (now past, in both cases) becomes a part of the story itself, closing off the open-endedness of "mere succession" with the full stop of conclusion. Yet such anterior "presents" are in turn relentlessly configured by the moving horizon of audiences yet-to-be. The sense of an ending, as Ricoeur says, is particularly acute in stories familiar and honed by repetition, but it is also true that no story is ever the same story twice.

A recent article in the English-language daily the *Jakarta Globe* argued that nothing has really changed in Indonesia since the demise of the New Order (Coates 2010). One could equally well say that everything has changed and continues to do so. In the dozen or so years since Suharto's fall from power, Indonesians have experienced free elections, democratic reforms, regional decentralization and autonomy movements, military and paramilitary violence, a string of horrific natural disasters, moral panics, terrorist attacks, religiously and ethnically inspired fighting, and the emergence of Islam as a powerful political force. A radically expanded media footprint—Internet, cell phone, documentary film and digital video technology, text messaging, blogging, Facebook, Twitter, none of which were very significant and many of which were nonexistent in 1994—has made all of these events accessible in novel and dramatic ways.[7]

History has never been a popular subject in Indonesia, least of all in the pinched and sanitized version promulgated under the New Order, but now it seems to be experiencing a vigorous surge of interest. The long-suppressed massacres of 1965–66 are being—literally— excavated, and a multitude of books inquire into the culpability of various actors in those events, as if the lurid horror of the killings can be neutralized in names and numbers, the madness parsed in explanatory or conspiratorial texts. As part of a resurgence of patriotic sentiment and a new interest in national beginnings, four major films have recently been produced about the independence struggle.[8] In what Karen Strassler (2005:280) describes as a "premature foreclosure," the Reformasi movement itself was almost immediately historicized in public exhibitions where photographs of youth activists served as "memorials to their (already past) moment-in-history." For some, the contemplation of past times offers a refuge from an uncertain, noisy world. Waves of "New Order nostalgia" recall the security, if not the repressions, of authoritarian rule.[9] In a more lighthearted vein, young "history lovers" take part in "Olde Tyme Fun Tours" and group visits to museums and historical sites, sometimes dressed in period costume (Yatun Sastrawidjaja 2010). *Tempo doeloe* ("olde tyme") restaurants serve the urban elite in Jakarta and Bandung with nostalgic fantasies of colonial lifestyles. Each of these configured imaginings of the past imposes its own—perhaps fleeting—sense of an ending and, with it, a trajectory, to the nation's ongoing history. Whether this is a story of change or constancy, of generational decline or the passing of the *pemuda* spirit to a new generation, or of something else altogether depends on the historical pathway mapped by its envisioned end point, as well as its point of departure.

When Sukarno described independence as a golden bridge to the nation's future, he left the end of the journey unspecified, because he felt it was important for Indonesians—that still-imaginary community—to move into the future united by a willing and patriotic spirit rather than divided by their various visions of what might lie on that farther shore. When my Karo informants told their stories of ignorance and eagerness, of stepping forward at the sound of the gong of independence "even if we didn't know what had to be done," of their scattered flight toward safety and danger, of duties completed or "no end of tiredness," of the lurking presence of collaborators or the violent potential of *repolusi*, they were recalling a time like that, when they embarked on a journey into the unknown future with all options open, both good and ill. The outcome of their struggles may not have been what they expected or even what they wanted. That does not make their hopes less vivid, their dreams less poignant, their sacrifices more trivial. Neither does it make the violence they endured, or took part in, less brutal. Possibilities later foreclosed were not so for them. To impose an ending on Eben Hezer's lament for the values of '45, or indeed on any of the stories from the nation's outskirts that I have retold here, would be to pass a judgment on them, in the light of history. That is a judgment they do not need, nor do I wish to make. Because in the end, what they convey, each in its own way, is how it felt to be alive to a moment in which there were no certain endings.

[handwritten marginal note: critiques seem to assume a certain ending]

List of Informants (by date)

Information is listed as follows: Personal name, if known; teknonym, if known (in parentheses); place of interview; birthplace (in parentheses); date of interview(s). Unless otherwise noted, all interviews were audio-recorded and conducted by me. Interviews with an asterisk were conducted in my absence by Jabatin Bangun, Fariana beru Bangun, Julianus Limbeng, Sri Alem Sembiring, and Satria Sembiring Pandia.

Selamat Ginting, Jakarta (Kuta Bangun), November 3, 1993 (not recorded)

Nimai beru Sebayang (Nandé Santoso), Jakarta (Kabanjahé), November 3, 1993 (not recorded), and December 6, 1994

Salamsam beru Ginting (Nandé Juara), Medan (Berastepu), January 4, 1994 (not recorded)

Kumpul beru Muham, Medan (Susuk/Tiga Nderket), April 9 and May 18, 1994

Nandé Madasa beru Ginting, Berastepu, April 15, 1994

Nandé Rikson beru Tarigan, Berastepu (Gamber), April 15 and April 16, 1994

Nandé Lia beru Tarigan, Berastepu, April 15 and April 17, 1994

Namo Bangun (Bapa Kumpul), Berastepu, April 16, 1994

Nandé Murni beru Ginting, Berastepu, April 17, 1994

Nandé Mutiara beru Bukit, Berastagi (Seberaya), April 30, 1994

Ajaren beru Ginting, Tanjung Morawa (Munthé), May 2, 1994

Nandé Berah beru Sebayang, Medan (Perbesi), May 2, 1994

Nandé Sadarman beru Sembiring (Ny. Djaga Depari), Seberaya, May 5, 1994

Anna beru Sitepu (Nandé Wajib), Lau Cih (Gurukinayan), May 7, 1994

Sinek beru Karo, Pancur Batu (Lau Cih), May 9, 1994, and August 28, 1995

Eben Hezer Sinuraya, Medan (Tiga Nderket), May 10, 1994

Nandé Dalam, Mardinding, May 20, 1994

Nandé Jamin, Mardinding, May 20, 1994

Nandé Jaminta, Mardinding, May 20, 1994

Nandé Keris, Mardinding, May 20, 1994

Nandé Kuidah, Mardinding, May 20, 1994

Nandé Rasmin, Mardinding, May 20, 1994

Nandé Sarmin, Mardinding, May 20, 1994

Nandé Semah, Mardinding, May 20, 1994

Nande Tawar, Mardinding, May 20, 1994

Nandé Tega, Mardinding, May 20, 1994

Nandé Ukur Malem, Mardinding, May 20, 1994

Nandé Bahagia beru Tarigan, Mardinding, May 20 and May 23, 1994

Nandé Lina beru Karo, Mardinding (Susuk), May 20 and May 23, 1994

Nandé Marlina beru Ginting, Mardinding (Selandi), May 20 and May 23, 1994

Naksi Singarimbun (Pa Lina), Mardinding, May 20 and May 21, 1994

Nandé Merta beru Ginting, Sukatendel, May 21, 1994

Sabar Singarimbun (Pa Sarmin), Mardinding, May 21, 1994

Anakberu beru Pandia (Nandé Usman), Payung, May 22, 1994

Mbeligai Bangun, Batu Karang, May 22, 1994

Rasi beru Ginting, Batu Karang, May 22, 1994

Meja beru Bangun (Nandé Senantiasa), Payung (Munthé), May 22, 1994

Muhati beru Perangin-angin (Nandé Ndapet), Payung, May 22, 1994

Ngemkem beru Ginting (Nandé Namali), Payung, May 22, 1994

Ngerem beru Singarimbun, Kuta Mbaru, May 22, 1994

Gulamit beru Sembiring (Nandé Abil), Susuk, May 23, 1994

Nandé Bungarem beru Singarimbun, Mardinding, May 23, 1994

Jamu beru Sitepu (Nandé Meré), Kuta Mbaru, May 24, 1994

Pawen beru Sembiring (Nandé Rani), Kuta Mbaru, May 24, 1994

Siti beru Singarimbun (Nandé Sadakata), Kuta Mbaru, May 24, 1994

Mata beru Depari, Seberaya, May 25, 1994

Manis beru Singarimbun (Nandé Kartini), Medan (Kuta Mbaru), May 30, 1994

Urat Tarigan (Pa Kartini), Medan (Kuta Mbaru), May 30, 1994

Setianna beru Tarigan (Nandé Serinaita), Medan (Suka, Kabanjahé), June 1, 1994

Layasi beru Sembiring (Nandé Tobat), Jakarta (Munthé), June 9, 1994

Likas beru Tarigan (Nandé Menda), Jakarta (Sibolangit), June 9, 1994

Piah Malem beru Manik (Nandé Riah), Jakarta (Kuta Pinang), June 11 and July 6, 1994

Roncah beru Barus, Jakarta (Barusjahé), June 12, 1994

Nandé Rosali beru Ginting, Medan (Juhar), June 16, 1994 (not recorded)

Nandé Timur beru Ginting, Medan (Tiga Binanga/Sukanalu), June 16, 1994

A.R. Surbakti (Bapa Waty), Medan (Susuk), June 17, 1994

Bapa Ros Perangin-angin, Medan, June 17, 1994

Jangaku Tarigan (Bapa Prisma), Medan, June 17, 1994

Nandé Dandan beru Perangin-angin, Medan, June 17, 1994

Nandé Ros beru Kaban, Medan, June 17, 1994

Nandé Waty beru Perangin-angin, Medan (Susuk), June 17, 1994

Galang Sitepu (Bapa Arih), Medan (Berastepu), June 20, 1994

Mestik beru Barus (Nandé Lidia), Medan, June 20, 1994

Halimah beru Ginting, Medan (Pancur Batu), June 22, 1994

Tandangen beru Muham (Nandé Nangsi), Medan (Tiga Nderket), June 25, 1994

Basaku beru Bangun (Nandé Sri Arihta), Tanjung Morawa (Payung), June 29, 1994

Yahya Barus (Bapa Sri Arihta), Tanjung Morawa (Kabanjahé), June 29, 1994

Sempa Sitepu (Bapa Jaman), Medan (Ergaji), June 30, 1994

Juda Pinem (Bapa Haroun), Kuta Gamber, July 14, 1994

Beru Sembiring, Medan (Susuk), July 27, 1994

Nandé Berlin beru Sembiring, Medan (Sarinembah), July 27, 1994

Panpan Singarimbun, Medan (Susuk), July 27, 1994

Madasa beru Berahmana, Medan (Perbesi), July 28, 1994

Mulih Kwala Sebayang, Medan (Kwala), July 29, 1994

Sanaria boru Silalahi (Nandé Madison), Medan (Paropo, Kabanjahé), July 29, 1994

D. Sembiring (Bapa Bety), Binjei (Gurukinayan), July 30, 1994

Piahmalem beru Sembiring, Medan (Berastepu), July 31, 1994

Tokih Ginting, Medan (Susuk), July 31, 1994

Terang beru Singarimbun (Nandé Adi), Medan (Tiga Nderket), August 2, 1994

Lenggang Bangun, Medan (Selandi), August 3, 1994

Ingan Bakti beru Karo (Nandé Sekata), Medan (Kuta Buluh, Kabanjahé), August 4, 1994, and Uruk Keci-Keci, August 16, 1994

P. S. Ginting, Medan (Kacaribu), August 6, 1994

Damai beru Tarigan, Uruk Keci-Keci (Buah Raya), August 16, 1994

Kema beru Karo, Uruk Keci-Keci, August 16, 1994

Kolam beru Karo, Uruk Keci-Keci (Beganding), August 16, 1994

Nandé Nomen beru Sembiring, Uruk Keci-Keci (Sukandebi/Naman), August 16, 1994

Pa Selamat Tarigan, Kabanjahé (Bawang/Kabanjahé), August 16, 1994

Pengarapen beru Ginting, Uruk Keci-Keci (Kuta Bangun), August 16, 1994

Raté beru Sembiring, Uruk Keci-Keci (Beganding), August 16, 1994

Nandé Jauhari beru Bangun, Kabanjahé (Kacaribu), August 18, 1994 (not recorded)

Linder Ginting (Bapa Ruth), Medan (Munthé), August 22, 1994

Rasimah beru Ginting (Nandé Petrus), Medan (Kuta Mbaru), August 22, 1994

Nas Sebayang, Medan, August 23, 1994

Nomen Pinem (Bapa Jamal Eka), Medan (Juhar), August 23, 1994

Rugun beru Karo (Nandé Titing), Medan (Medan/Kabanjahé), August 23, 1994

Saman Sembiring (Bapa Mul), Medan (Gurukinayan), August 23, 1994

Biasa beru Surbakti (Nande Thony), Medan (Batu Karang), August 25, 1994

Monika beru Barus, Medan, August 25, 1994

Hasan Basrie Z.T., Medan, August 27, 1994

A.-U. Nasution, Medan, August 27, 1994

"Bahlum Jip," Medan, August 27, 1994

Mena Pinem, Medan (Pernantin), August 27, 1994

Nip Karim, Medan, August 27, 1994

Jem beru Karo, Jinabun, September 15, 1994*

Jenda beru Sembiring, Jinabun (Kuta Buluh Gugung), September 15, 1994*

Nasip Perangin-Angin, Jinabun, September 14, 1994*

Riano Perangin-angin, Jinabun, September 15, 1994*

Sentar beru Sembiring, Jinabun, September 16, 1994*

Nandé Pesta, Batu Karang, April 20, 1995*

Meja beru Tarigan, Batu Karang, April 21, 1995*

Ngidup beru Sembiring, Talun Kenas, July 25, 1995*

Tuhu Limbeng, Talun Kenas, July 25, 1995*

Dekat beru Limbeng, Talun Kenas, August 1, 1995*
Marce beru Perangin-angin, Talun Kenas, August 1, 1995*
Nandé Thomas beru Tarigan, Tanjung Morawa, August 11, 1995*
Bapa Firman Ginting, Kidupen, August 14, 1995*
Nandé Karina beru Ginting, Kidupen, August 14, 1995*
Nandé Terakap beru Sembiring, Kidupen, August 15, 1995*
Reken Ginting, Kidupen, August 15, 1995*
Rajai Ginting, Kidupen, August 16, 1995*
Nandé Tabonal beru Karo, Pernantin, August 23, 1995*
Nangkul Ginting (Bapa Tabonal), Pernantin, August 23, 1995*

Glossary and Abbreviations

D.   Dutch

I.   Indonesian

J.   Japanese

Jv.   Javanese

K.   Karo

M.   Malay

T.   Toba Batak

ADAT (M./I.) custom, customary law

ANAKBERU (K.) ritually subordinate affine, e.g., sister's husband, father's sister's son; also (for men) sister

ANGKATAN (I.) cohort, generation

ARON (K.) agricultural work group, cooperative society; also, name of a Karo squatters organization active in the early months of the Japanese occupation

AZAS KEKELUARGAAN (I.) family foundation (of the state); principle that the family should be the basis of the state and that the state should be organized according to the order of the (patriarchal) family

BADAN OENTOEK MEMBANTU PERTAHANAN ASIA, BOMPA (I.) Agency to Assist in the Defense of Asia, Japanese information and propaganda bureau

BANGSA (I.) nation, people

BANGSA TANEH (K.) people of the land; founding or ruling lineage of a village

BAPA (K.) father, father of _____

BAPAK (I.) father, mister

BARISAN HARIMAU LIAR, BHL (I.) Wild Tiger Brigade; radical militia, spin-off from the Japanese Mokutai

BARISAN PEMUDA INDONESIA, BPI (I.) Indonesian Youth Brigade; in Sumatra, formed in late September 1945, renamed Pemuda Republik Indonesia (PRI) in late October 1945, renamed Pesindo in mid-December 1945

BATALYON DAERAH PERTEMPURAN, BDP (I.) Combat Area Battalion, Karo militia deployed in the Medan Area, May 1946–July 1947

BERU, BR. (K.) woman's natal patriclan (see also *diberu*)

BIBI (K.) aunt (e.g., mother's sister, father's sister, husband's mother), auntie (affectionately)

BORU (T.) Toba Batak equivalent of Karo *beru*

BUPATI (JV./I.) regent, head of *kabupaten* (district)

CAMAT (JV./I.) subdistrict *(kecamatan)* head

DAPUR UMUM (I.) public kitchen, open air cooking area for preparation of meals for soldiers

DAULAT/DOLAT (I./K.) charisma, authority, sovereignty (see also *kedaulatan rakyat, pendaulatan*)

DIAMANKAN (I.) "pacified," euphemism for extrajudicial execution

DIBERU (K.) woman

DUSUN (M.) rural village; in E. Sumatra, the predominantly Karo piedmont area between the coastal lowlands and the interior plateau

ENAK (I.) delicious, tasty, pleasant

ENCIK, 'CIK (M.) term of address for a (secular) female teacher (obs.)

ENTABEH, NTABEH (K.) delicious, tasty, nice

ERKATA BEDIL (K.) the sound of rifle fire (lit., "the rifle speaks," trans. here as "rifle reports"); title of a popular Karo song of the independence struggle

FUJINKAI (J.) women's association; the umbrella organization dealing with women's issues during the Japanese occupation

GENDANG (K.) drum; drum-based musical ensemble, usually of five (the "big" orchestra) or three instruments (the "little" orchestra); also music played by a *gendang* ensemble (e.g., *Gendang lima puluh kurang dua,* "the *gendang* of fifty minus two," a suite of forty-eight tunes)

GERAKAN RAKYAT INDONESIA, GERINDO (I.) Indonesian People's Movement; leftist party in colonial and independence periods

GOTONG ROYONG (JV./I.) cooperative action, mutual assistance

GYUGUN (J.) volunteer soldiers for national defense; Japanese officers training program for Indonesians, equivalent to PETA in Java

HEIHO (J.) auxiliary volunteers; Japanese basic training program for Indonesian support forces

HOLLANDSE-INLANDSCHE SCHOOL, HIS (D.) elite Dutch-language elementary school

IMPAL (K.) cross-cousin (mother's brother's daughter/father's sister's son); also, potential marriage mate

JAGO (I.) fighting cock, thug, petty gangster, boss

JALAN (I.) road, street

JOT-JOT (K.?) spear/bayonet training; onomatopoeic rendering of spear thrust

JUMA (K.) dry (upland) rice field

KAKI TANGAN (I.) collaborator (lit., "feet-and-hands")

KALANGAN RAJA (K.) aristocratic circle/class, social elite. Indicates the affines as well as the members of a ruling lineage.

KALIMBUBU (K.) ritually superior matrilateral patrikin (e.g., mother's brother, mother's father; also wife's father and wife's mother)

KAMI (K./I.) we, exclusive form (we-not-you)

KATONENG-KATONENG (K.) genre of improvised Karo blessing song said to "calm" *(tenang)* the spirit of listeners

KEDAULATAN RAKYAT (I.) authority of the people, popular sovereignty

KEDEP (K.) rice bran

KÉLA (K.) daughter's husband; also (for men), sister's son

KESAIN (K.) village subdivision or ward; also the village common where public ceremonies may be held

KITA (K./I.) we, inclusive form (we all, everyone)

KOMITÉ NASIONAL INDONESIA, KNI (I.) Indonesian National Committee, transitional governing organization in the early independence period

KONINKLIJK NEDERLANDSCH INDISCH LEGER, KNIL (D.) (Dutch) Royal Army of the Netherlands Indies

KORBAN (K./M., FROM ARABIC) victim; sacrifice, esp. animal given as a living sacrifice

KYORING (J./K.) military training

LASKAR (I.) guerrilla, irregular soldier, militia volunteer

LAU (K.) water, body of water, e.g., Lau Renun (river), Lau Kawar (lake)

LINGGARJATI (I.) town in West Java where Dutch and Indonesian representatives negotiated terms for Indonesian independence, November 1946

MAMA (K.) mother's brother or wife's father; also, term of affectionate address by a woman to her sweetheart

MELIAR (K., RELATED TO M., LIAR, "WILD") energetic, enthusiastic, eager; (for women) unruly, promiscuous

MENGUNGSI, PENGUNGSIAN (I.) evacuate, evacuation

MERDEKA, KEMERDEKAAN (I.) independent; independence, freedom

MERGA (K.) (exogamous) patrilineal clan or subclan

MOKUTAI (J.) Wild Tiger Corps; predecessor of BHL

NANDÉ (K.) mother (also father's brother's wife), mother of _____; also, term of address for (female) sweetheart

NASIONAL PELOPOR, NAPINDO (I.) National Vanguard; militia wing of Indonesian Nationalist Party (PNI)

NEGARA (I.) state

NEGARA SUMATERA TIMUR, NST (I.) State of East Sumatra, Malay-dominated "puppet state" set up in December 1947, dissolved August 17, 1950

NEGERI (I./M.) country, land

NETHERLANDS INDIES CIVIL ADMINISTRATION, NICA (E.) military administration created by the British to assist in the transfer of power in postwar Indonesia

ORANG TUA (I.) parent(s)

ORDE BARU, ORBA (I.) New Order, political regime led by General Suharto (1966–98)

ORDE LAMA, ORLA (I.) Old Order, anachronistic label given to the previous Sukarno regime (1950–65) under the New Order

PADI (I.) wet-rice field; also, unhusked rice grain. See also Persatuan Anak Deli Islam

PAGÉ (K.) rice grain or plants (usually dry-field)

PANCASILA (I.) the "five principles" of Indonesian state ideology

PARTAI KOMUNIS INDONESIA, PKI (I.) Indonesian Communist Party

PARTAI NASIONAL INDONESIA, PNI (I.) Nationalist Party formed by Sukarno in 1928; banned by the Dutch and reestablished in 1945 as the sole state party; eliminated soon thereafter but revived in January 1946

PARTAI SOSIALIS, PS (I.) Indonesian Socialist Party

PEMBANGUNAN (I.) development

PEMBINAAN KESEJAHTERAAN KELUARGA, PKK (I.) Family Welfare Guidance, government program for women to improve family life

PEMUDA (I.) youth; a general term for political activists, especially those working outside the structures of government and formal social institutions

PEMUDA REPUBLIK INDONESIA, PRI (I.) Indonesian Republican Youth. See Barisan Pemuda Indonesia; Pemuda Sosialis Indonesia

PEMUDA SOSIALIS INDONESIA, PESINDO (I.) Indonesian Socialist Youth, successor to PRI/BPI as umbrella association of youth militias, December 1945–March 1946; subsequently, militia wing of the Socialist Party (PS)

PENDAULATAN (I.) "sovereignty" (vigilante) operations

PENDIDIKAN NASIONAL INDONESIA, PNI-BARU ("NEW" PNI) (I.) Indonesian National Education, nationalist political party created by Hatta and Sjahrir in 1933 following dissolution of Sukarno's Partai Nasional Indonesia. Designated the "New" PNI to distinguish it from the Sukarnoist PNI. In Karoland the PNI-Baru was associated with Pesindo and the Partai Sosialis.

PENGULU (K.) village head or section chief

PERGERAKAN (I.) political "movement"

PERJUANGAN (I.) struggle, fight

PERSATUAN ANAK DELI ISLAM, PADI (I.) Association of Muslim Sons of Deli, a predominantly Malay militia associated with the sultanate of Deli

PERSATUAN PERJUANGAN, PP (I.) Struggle Union, an umbrella organization of popular militias, January–March 1946 (also known as the Volksfront)

PERTAHANAN RAKYAT SEMESTA, PRS (IN KARO, PÉRÉS) (I.) Total Popular Defense, village-level organization to support armed struggle in Karoland, 1948–49

POESAT EKONOMI RAKYAT, POESERA (I.) Center for the People's Economy, Japanese-era trade association and underground political organization in Karo area

POLITIONELE ACTIE (D.) police action; Dutch term for military campaigns to reassert control over Indonesia, 1947 and 1949

PREMAN (I., FROM D., VRIJ MAN, NONCONTRACT LABORER) casual day laborer, but also urban loiterer, petty criminal, thug. Commonly used today to refer to organized or semiorganized gangsters for (political) hire.

RAJA (M./K.) ruler, chief; "king"

RAJA BEREMPAT (M.) "four kings," administrative capstone of native government in colonial Karoland, consisting of five superior chiefs appointed by the Dutch

RAJA URUNG (K.) colonial native section *(urung)* head, beneath *sibayak/landschap*

RAKYAT (I.) the (common) people, masses

REFORMASI (I.) Reformation, the 1998 movement demanding governmental transparency and an end to corruption; led to Suharto's resignation

RENVILLE ACCORD peace agreement between Indonesian and Dutch negotiators, signed January 1948, on board the U.S.S. *Renville*

REPOLUSI, POLUSI (K.) the "social revolution" of 1946; also, any form of internal violence during the period of the independence struggle

REPUBLIK INDONESIA, RI (I.) Republic of Indonesia

REPUBLIK INDONESIA SERIKAT, RIS (I.) "United States of Indonesia," state created under a Dutch-supported federated plan in December 1949. Superseded in August 1950 by the Unified Republic of Indonesia (RI).

RESIMEN HALILINTAR (I.) Thunderbolt Regiment, Selamat Ginting's Napindo-affiliated militia; later reorganized as Sektor III of TNI Subterritorial VII (Sumatra command)

SARANEN (K.) "instructions," nationalist propaganda and indoctrination campaign of the first year of independence; political rallies

SEI (M.) river

SEKTOR (I.) military operational area created under a territorial command structure, December 1947–December 1949

SEKTOR III operational area of Selamat Ginting's former Halilintar militia Regiment following 1948 territorial reorganization of armed forces; included Dairi and South Karo areas

SENINA (K.) agnatic kin; clan- or subclanmates

SETIA (I.) Serikat Tani Indonesia, Indonesian Farmers' Union (the acronym means "faithful"); Karo squatters' organization in late colonial/Japanese periods

SIBAYAK (K.) lit., "rich person"; title granted to prominent regional leaders according to legend; five "kings" appointed by Dutch to head the Karo native government; also, name of a volcanic mountain on the border of Tanah Karo

SKRINING (I./E.) "screening," pension review for veterans

SRIKANDI (JV.) wife of Arjuna in Mahabarata shadow play; Srikandi Corps, women's military auxiliary training organization

Taman Latihan Petani, TALAPETA (I.) Peasant Training Garden, agricultural, indoctrination, and military training program established by Inoue Tetsuro in association with Gerindo; forerunner of Mokutai and BHL

TANAH (I.) land, territory

TANAH AIR (I.) land-and-water, homeland

TANAH KARO (I.) administrative district *(kabupaten)* of the Karo highlands

TANEH (K.) land, territory

TANEH KARO (K.) Karoland, the Karo plateau of the Sumatran interior

TENTARA KEAMANAN/KESELAMATAN RAKYAT, TKR (I.) People's Security Army, October 5, 1945—January 25, 1946; previously BKR, People's Security Body (September 17–October 4, 1945)

TENTARA NASIONAL INDONESIA, TNI (I.) Indonesian National Army, officially established June 1947

TENTARA RAKYAT INDONESIA, TRI (I.) Army of the Indonesian People, January 1946–June 1947

TURANG (K.) opposite-sex sibling; also poetic term of endearment for sweethearts

VAN MOOK LINE Demarcation line established by Vice-Governor Van Mook at the end of the first Dutch military campaign, marking forward movement of Dutch troops

ZAMAN (I.) time, era; e.g., Zaman Merdeka, "Independence Time"

Time Line

1863	first European tobacco plantation established in "Deli" (east Sumatran lowlands)
1872	"autonomous" native government formed for the residency of Sumatra's East Coast, as part of the Netherlands East Indies
1904	Dutch conquest and annexation of the Karo highlands as part of the East Coast Residency
1942 (March)	Japanese invasion of the Dutch East Indies (Java, March 1, 1942; Sumatra, March 12, 1942)
1945 (August 15)	Japan surrenders to Allied forces
1945 (August 17)	proclamation of Indonesian independence
1945 (September 23)	Indonesian independence announced in Medan
1945 (October 10)	British interim peacekeeping forces arrive in East Sumatra
1946 (March 3–25)	social revolution, transfer of political authority to Komite Nasional Indonesia
1946 (May)	Karo militia battalion sent to the lowland front lines around the city of Medan
1946 (November 15)	preliminary agreement reached between Dutch and Indonesian representatives in negotiations at Linggarjati, West Java
1946 (November 19)	British begin withdrawal of troops from Indonesia

1947 (July 21)	first Dutch military campaign (*politionele actie*, "police action") begins; evacuation of the Karo highlands
1947 (August 4)	first Dutch police action officially ends, fighting continues
1947 (December)	Negara Sumatera Timur (NST, State of East Sumatra) established as political alternative to the Republic of Indonesia in East Sumatra
1948 (January 17–19)	Renville Accord signed by representatives of the Netherlands and the Republic of Indonesia; Karo refugees begin to return home
1948 (November 28)	Indonesian armed forces territorial command structure established, incorporating popular militias into the TNI through the "Sektor" system
1948 (December 19)	second military campaign begins
1949 (May)	peace negotiations begin at the UN-sponsored Round Table Conference in The Hague
1949 (August 14–15)	official cease-fire (in Sumatra)
1949 (December 27)	formal recognition of Indonesian sovereignty, in the form of a "federated" government plan (RIS) that leaves Karoland in the NST, thus outside the Republic of Indonesia
1950 (February–May)	anti-NST demonstrations in the Karo highlands and elsewhere
1950 (August 17)	NST dissolved and East Sumatra incorporated into a province (Sumatera Utara, North Sumatra) of the united Republic of Indonesia

Notes

1. My use of the "ethnographic present" in this description is intended to reflect a kind of temporal neutrality available in the Indonesian language but not in English. To be specific, the descriptive sections of this chapter derive from multiple visits to Karoland between 1983 to 2006.

2. For more on the close but complex relation between the Karo Protestant Church and local custom, see Kipp 1990; and Steedly 1996.

3. Elsewhere in Indonesia the proclamation's date has been officially adjusted to the international standard of Common Era reckoning, but in Kabanjahé the Japanese year 2605 was still being used in the 1990s, as it was in the original Proklamasi text.

4. Some notable exceptions to this general pattern are Reid 1979a; van Langenberg 1976; A. Kahin 1985; Cribb 1991; Frederick 1989; and Lucas 1991. But see also Frederick 2002 on the lack of attention to "rural violence" in studies of the independence struggle.

5. For a more detailed discussion of the social separation between urban, educated *pemuda* (youth) and rural villagers, see Frederick 1989.

6. For another account of this event, see Reid 2009.

7. The National Heroes' Memorial Park in Kabanjahé was begun, with the approval of President Sukaro, in 1951 on the site of the former Juliana Park, on the edge of town (L. Ginting 1995).

8. This number is taken from a 1996 article in the Karo-language newsletter *Sora Mido* (*Sora Mido* 1996). It is the most recent total that I have been able to find, but it is surely much higher now unless the cemetery has reached its capacity.

9. K., *pertangisen kalak lawes erjuang*, lit., "the lament of one who goes to [join the] struggle."

10. The most obvious of these groups are Indonesians of Chinese descent, alleged communists, tribal groups, and inhabitants of those territories forcibly incorporated by the state after 1950, namely, East Timor and Papua. Christians might also be included in this list. I do not suggest that these groups (or members of them) were not active participants in the independence struggle or that they are explicitly persecuted today for perceived nonparticipation in the struggle, but rather that their supposed "infidelity" to the nation during the war has consistently been used as a pseudoproof of contemporary untrustworthiness and an excuse for acts of violence against them.

CHAPTER I

1. Sukarno, "Mentjapai Indonesia Merdeka" (1933), cited in Hering 2002:353; and Sukarno 1945 (my translation). Sukarno's vocabulary of key terms is highly nuanced; I have indicated these in brackets at first use (e.g., people [rakyat], nation [bangsa]) or where necessary for clarity. The speech is widely reprinted. For a summary of the background of this speech and ensuing events leading up to the proclamation of independence, see J.G. Taylor 2004:322–23.

2. The literature on these topics is vast. To mention only a few relevant sources, Gary Hawes (1990), writing of the Philippines, argues that peasant rebellion has to be understood in relation to national and international political economy and in the absence of intermediary mechanisms capable of resolving conflicts. Michael Adas (1981) similarly characterizes a shift in forms of peasant protest from "avoidance" to "confrontation" as a result of the intensification of governmental control under colonial rule, whereby longstanding practices of subtle resistance to state demands were rendered ineffective. See also Kalyvas 2003, 2006; and Ranger 1968a,b, 1985. Hans Pols (2011) provides a critical rereading of colonial and postcolonial analyses of violence in Indonesia.

3. For a sample of recent writings in the anthropology of violence in Southeast Asia and elsewhere, see Hinton 2002; and Whitehead 2004. See Colombijn 2002 and Purdey 2004 for reviews of the study of violence in Indonesia.

4. About twenty additional interviews were conducted in my absence. See appendix 1.

5. Mami, which I have translated as "lady" here, actually denotes a category of equivalence to one's mother's brother's wife. It is also a term of respectful address to an unknown older woman.

6. On the difficulty of writing about rural violence during the independence struggle, given the "absence of any concrete information" from outlying areas, see Frederick 2002, especially 158–60. Frederick argues that in these circumstances academic studies have tended to substitute generalized concepts such as social banditry and criminality for a more particularized examination of events on the ground.

7. For a deeply principled and thoughtful discussion of this problem, see Cribb 2001.

8. I have taken the notions of a "forensic" approach and of "granularity" from Jain 2007.

9. Interview, Nandé Rikson beru Tarigan.

10. Interview, Nandé Namali beru Ginting.

11. Interview, Nandé Timur beru Ginting.

12. These awkward terms only roughly gloss Karo kin categories, which approximate what anthropologists have termed a "Kachin-style" kinship system, based on patrilineal descent, clan exogamy, and preferential matrilateral cross-cousin marriage (MBD-FZS). The best general accounts of Karo kinship are in Singarimbun 1975; and Kipp 1976, 1986.

13. Elsewhere I have argued that wife "giving" and "receiving" is not an accurate gloss for these (untranslatable) terms, which actually describe relationships based on the naming of children. See Steedly 1993:183–85.

14. In a series of articles, Ann Stoler (1985a,b, 1992, 2009) offers a careful and sophisticated archival study of violence in the plantation zone of Deli during the early years of colonial expansion.

15. For more on the founding of the Karo mission, see Kipp 1990:202–20; and Steedly 1996.

16. On land conflicts in Payung Village, see Kipp 1976:45–47; and on land mortgaging, see 40–42.

17. See Steedly 1993:203–23; another account of Pak Tua's life (under the alternative pseudonym "Pa Surdam") is J. R. Ginting 1991.

18. Sinek beru Karo, "Mengungsi ibas revolusi fisik tahun 1947," my translation. The transcribed text and translation of another performance of Sinek's song of the evacuation is in Sembiring 1987. See also chapter 7 of this volume.

19. The concept of provincializing the center is borrowed and adapted from Chakrabarty 1992, where it refers to the project of "provincializing Europe" as a means of recuperating history from the nation.

20. For a view of the fighting in Karoland during the first military campaign from a Dutch journalist "embedded" with the KNIL, see Post 1948.

21. *Turang* is literally the term for a classificatory sibling of the opposite sex, but it is also a "term of endearment" for one's sweetheart, which is how it is meant here. Kipp 1986.

22. At least one popular film, *Turang* (1957), made by Bachtiar Siagian, a director associated with the left-wing LEKRA artists' association, did in fact show women as freedom fighters. The film, which was set and filmed in the Karo highlands, is to the best of my knowledge not preserved anywhere. For a review, see AA 1958. See also Sen 1994:42–43.

23. See Surbakti 1978:180.

24. A particularly thoughtful discussion of ethics and oral history as they relate to human subjects and IRBs, by Linda Shopes, is posted on the website of the Oral History Association. www.oralhistory.org/do-oral-history/oral-history-and-irb-review/. Accessed 7/16/12.

25. Indonesian historian Taufik Abdullah (2009) argues that *independence struggle* and *War of Independence* are the terms preferred by the army and by the New Order regime and used by them to privilege their own role in the conflict. For this reason, he prefers to use the term *revolution*.

26. The female dancers in figure 7 (ch. 2) are wearing a formal version of the *tudung* headdress. In the 1980s these were commonly worn by both urban and

rural women; by the mid-1990s only elderly rural women wore them on an everyday basis, but an elaborate, decorated form of the turbans remained in use on formal or ceremonial occasions.

CHAPTER 2

1. Megawati's appointment as head of the PDI was turbulent and controversial; a government-backed opposition group ousted her from the party leadership in 1996. After massive demonstrations in 1996 she formed a new party, known as PDI-Perjuangan. She was chosen as vice president of Indonesia in 1999; following the forced resignation of Abdurrahman Wahid in 2001 she replaced him as president. She was not reelected in 2004.

2. I discuss this tale in Steedly 1993:175–76. For a Karo text and Dutch translation of the tale, see Neumann 1925.

3. Masty Pencawan, "Untukmu Selamat Gintingku" in Bangun and Chairudin 1994:447–48.

4. See Surbakti 1979:134–37. For more on the importance of uniforms and style among the various fighting groups in East Java, see Frederick 1997.

5. She presumably means "sten guns" here. Sten guns are portable semiautomatic rifles; bren guns are antiaircraft weapons.

6. For an illuminating discussion of the problem of time in oral histories, see Portelli 1991.

7. "The most widely circulated photograph from the expedition depicts Dutch troops standing over a heap of wreckage and bodies in the village of Kuto Réh in the Alas region. . . . In the center background of the picture is what appears to be the lone survivor, an infant, staring out at the photographer. Van Daalen appears as a shadowy figure standing high above everyone else" (Bowen 1991:66). The child was not the sole survivor, but Bowen is not far off: Kempees's casualty list is as follows: killed, 313 men, 189 women, and 59 children; wounded, 20 women and 31 children; uninjured, 2 women and 61 children. Kempees (1905:157–64) gives a detailed account of the Kuto Réh massacre; ironically, the photograph that accompanies this section of his text is of the girl from Kuta Pinang, not that of the massacre itself. See also Siegel 2005.

8. See also Castles 1972:36–37.

9. On Karo sung poetry, see Joustra 1901 and Kozok 1993, 1994; on funeral laments, see also Kipp 1976, 1986.

10. Cf. Andaya 1994; Atkinson 1990; Bowen 1991; Drakard 1990; and Tsing 1990.

11. See Piekaar 1949:183; and Reid 1975:52–53.

12. Brahma Putro and Sinulingga 1977, pt. 2:5; on the PID, see also Reid 1979a:97–98, 103; and Poeze 1994.

13. *Jelutung* (I.) (*Dyera maingayi* or *Dyera costulata* Hook.) is an inferior form of caoutchouc (India rubber). See van Vuuren 1908.

14. Tama Ginting was among the organizers of the Karo district chapter of Pendidikan Nasional Indonesia (Indonesian National Education) in 1937. This was a "noncooperating" anticolonial/antifascist organization associated with

the socialist program of Sutan Sjahrir and Mohammad Hatta. See Mrázek 1994; Reid 1974:8–9; and Surbakti 1978:6–9 and passim.

15. See Kipp 1986 on Karo lovers' discourse. For an illustration of the unexpected meeting and subsequent marriage of *impals*, see, for example, the history of Sibayak Barus Jahé (Joustra 1918).

16. See also Ramadhan 1988:141–42, 148; Surbakti 1979:6, 13–23; Manihuruk 1979:257–69.

17. Tinuk Yampolsky (pers. comm.) suggested the "weightier" meaning of *tugas* in the context of citizenship.

18. Several different versions of this incident have been published. See Bangun and Chairudin 1994:50–52; Manihuruk 1979:105–6; Reid 1979a:154–55; and Surbakti 1978:33.

19. On the formation of the Sumatran TKR, see Biro PRIMA 1976:172–97, 495.

20. See also Manihuruk 1979:112; cf. Reid 1979a:161–65.

21. See Benstock 1988 for a set of essays by feminist scholars (including Marcus) on the "private self" as a trope of women's autobiographical writing.

CHAPTER 3

1. Surbakti's description here seems to be actually of the "oceanic" parade *(pawai samudera)* that took place on October 9, rather than the smaller rally at which the flying of the Indonesian flag was officially enacted. For a detailed description of both events, see Team Asistensi Pangdam II/BB 1977:1:103–7. For an account of the October 9 parade from the viewpoint of an Allied soldier just arrived in the city, see Jacobs 1982:163–64.

2. On the history of the "concept of freedom in Indonesia," see Reid 1998. As Reid notes, the word *merdeka* is richly ambiguous, with a range of connotations that are "positive and expansive" (151). I have tried to convey the flavor of the term's meaning during the period of the struggle by translating it consistently as *independence* in order to capture both its connotations of personal freedom and of national sovereignty.

3. Nandé Madasa beru Ginting, in a group interview in Berastepu, April 15, 1994. See Frederick 1997:220 for a similar story from East Java.

4. For a detailed discussion of the KNI and efforts to create a republican governmental structure in East Sumatra and Tapanuli, see Biro Sejarah PRIMA 1976:148–65.

5. On Lieutenant General Tahir, see Biro Sejarah PRIMA 1976:423–24, 633–71.

6. The word used here was the Indonesian *penerangan* (from *terang*, "bright, clear"). *Penerangan* usually refers to official information and instructions, frequently glossed by Karo as *saranen* (I./K., advice, instructions). *Penerangan* also carries the literal meaning of "lighting," as in *penerangan jalan*, "road lighting." I translate the term as *illumination* here to capture this double meaning.

7. See also Team Asistensi Pangdam II/BB 1977:1:73–74; Manihuruk 1979:103–6; and Biro Sejarah PRIMA 1976:75, 211–12.

8. See Westerling 1952; and Jacobs 1982.

9. On the October 13 violence, see Reid 1979a:159–60; Bangun and Chairudin 1994:55; Edisaputra 1985:68–72; Manihuruk 1979:110–11; Biro Sejarah PRIMA 1976:129–32; and Team Asistensi Pangdam II/BB 1977:1:139–41.

10. Edisaputra 1985:53–56; Biro Sejarah PRIMA 1976:216–28. Cf. Anderson 1972:264–67.

11. On the formation of the PRI in Java, see Anderson 1972:129; on East Sumatra, see van Langenberg 1976:325–28; and Biro Sejarah PRIMA 1976.

12. Cf. Nasution 1958:154, cited in Anderson 1972:235–36.

13. Aneka Minggu, June 19, 1970, quoted in van Langenberg 1976:321. See also Biro Sejarah PRIMA 1976:186–87.

14. On the romanticism of "*pemuda* style," see William Frederick's illuminating essay "The Appearance of Revolution" (1997:231–32).

15. Hobsbawm 1959. For a useful review of Hobsbawm and his critics, with special reference to the Indonesian situation, see Cribb 1991:26–31.

16. As informants pointed out to me, admission into the Gyugun corps, which provided the TKR with most of its officers, usually required a recommendation by a well-connected political figure. While it would have been unusual (though not unheard of) for a member of the inner circle of Karo "royalty" to enroll in the Gyugun program, it was a more likely route to influence for distant kin of local rulers or ambitious youth on the fringes of elite circles, like Djamin Ginting.

17. On the concept of "unfreedom" as the basis of any definition of freedom, see Brown 1995:6.

18 In Malaysia, the term *encik* is a minor honorific for an adult male, the equivalent of the English *mister*. As a term of reference or address for a female teacher, it was specific to West Sumatra, where Encik Muham attended teacher training school. This usage is now obsolete in Indonesia.

19. *Kebangoenan* first appeared in September 1946; *Radikal*, in January 1946. Both continued to be published until the start of the first Dutch campaign in July 1947. There was little difference between the two journals. Many of the same people wrote for and published both.

20. A *tumba* is a measure of dry volume equivalent to about two liters according to a contemporary researcher (Sherman 1990:128–29).

21. For more on Inoue Tetsuro and the Mokutai in Karoland, see Reid 1979a:130–34, 174–75; Reid and Oki 1986:79–110, 191–216; Reid and Shiraishi 1976; and Surbakti 1978:16. Inoue also published a flamboyant memoir of his time in Sumatra (1953), two sections of which are translated in Reid and Oki 1986.

22. The Persatuan Perjuangan, or Volksfront, was formed and led by the communist organizer Tan Malaka, who had a considerable following in East Sumatra as a result of his time spent there as a teacher in a plantation school. On the PP in East Sumatra, see Reid 1979a:225–29 and 230–48; Surbakti 1978:100–102, 144–46; and Biro Sejarah PRIMA 1976:290–91. On Tan Malaka, see Poeze 1976; and Mrázek 1972.

23. The notion of organizations "synonymous" with communism comes from a 1995 speech by Coordinating Minister for Politics and Security Susilo Sudarman, in the aftermath of the July 27 attack on supporters of Democratic

Party head Megawati Sukarnoputri. Blame for the incident was placed by government spokesmen on a small radical student organization, the PRD (People's Democratic Union). As early as 1950 nationalist politicians were linking the violence of the social revolution with the communist-supported Madiun uprising of 1948. See, e.g., Kementerian Penerangan 1953:364–70. T. H. M. Lah Husny (1983), argues that both the Sumatran social revolution and the Madiun uprising were "trial runs" for the so-called September 30 movement of 1965.

24. During the first year of independence, Roegoen Sembiring produced nationalist propaganda posters for the district government. In the postwar period, he became a popular painter of Karo patriotic and village scenes in a style reminiscent of Vincent van Gogh. He was a member of the leftist LEKRA arts organization in the 1960s. Following the 1965 massacres, his work mostly vanished from public view, but I did occasionally see his paintings in the homes of prominent veterans.

25. G. G. Weix, pers. comm.

26. Sarasehan Perang Kemerdekaan di Karo Area, Jakarta, August 5, 1995. The mimic was Santosa Karo-Karo, the son of Nande Santosa beru Sebayang and Koran Karo-Karo, the latter being the Sektor III quartermaster.

27. Cited in Strassler 2010:97–98.

CHAPTER 4

1. For example, on this thinking see Chatterjee 1993:158ff.; and Guha 1983.

2. Dada Meuraxa 1946: front cover.

3. On PRS, see Surbakti 1979:53–60.

4. Partha Chatterjee (1993:116–34) makes a similar point in his discussion of the "woman question" among nineteenth-century Bengali nationalists.

5. See also Kipp 1990, 1998; and Neumann-Bos 1939; cf. van Bemmelen 1992.

6. Muham denotes gender here by indicating a sarong tied in the feminine style (K., *rabit*). A sarong tied in the masculine style is referred to as a *kampuh*.

7. A *pelgan* is a Karo measure of dry volume, equal to about forty liters; a *kaleng* is a petroleum tin holding about twenty liters.

8. Information on the first cohort of Srikandis comes from Zuraida Zainal 1985.

9. Roncah uses the term *pembangunan*, "development," here, presumably a New Order anachronism that has slipped into her narrative.

10. *Amé* is an alternative term for *nandé*, "mother."

11. See, e.g., Brenner 1998:241.

12. See, e.g., Blackburn 2004:97; Newberry 2006; Brenner 1998; and the essays in Sears 1996.

13. As anyone familiar with New Order imaginings of the dangerous masses will recognize, the chaotic threat of politicized popular enthusiasm reaches its representational apex in gendered form, in images of Gerwani, the Communist Party's female auxiliary organization, who were alleged to have performed orgiastic dances during the torturing and killing of six kidnapped Indonesian army generals in 1965. These were depicted in the film *G30S/Pengkhianat*,

shown annually on October 1, and on Hari Kesaktian Pancasila (Pancasila Sanctity Day), inscribed on monuments, and recollected in speeches and newspaper articles, although they seem to be wholly fictional. A great deal has been written about Gerwani in recent years; probably the most thorough account is Wieringa 2002.

CHAPTER 5

1. My account of the evacuation and burning of Bandung draws on Sitaresmi 1997.

2. Sinek beru Karo, "Mengungsi ibas revolusi fisik 1947," in Sembiring 1987 and below, in ch. 7; Djaga Depari, "Sora Mido," in Tarigan 1990:110–11 and in the introduction to this volume.

3. The entire message is "Dutchmen mind your contry [sic] Kaoem Hartawan! Perdjoeangan minta Pengorbanan Harta Bendamoe—Sokonglah!!" (Team Asistensi Pangdam II/BB 1977:93).

4. On the conflict between Chinese and native communities of Medan, and especially the role of the Chinese Poh An Tui militia, see Biro Sejarah PRIMA 1976:224–25; Stoler 1988:232; Team Asistensi PANGDAM II/BB 1977: 122–26.

5. Notes, unrecorded interview, Medan, 1985.

6. Mr. S. M. Amin, who replaced Dr. Amir as lieutenant governor of republican East Sumatra when the latter defected to the British, noted regretfully that "instructions regarding the implementation of the scorched earth program were not followed, or were carried out at will, or in conflict with the intention and words of the instructions" (quoted in Bangun and Chairudin 1994: 158). Roads and bridges were left intact, he reported, while "the destruction was primarily directed at the shops and goods of the Chinese." Van Langenberg (1976:580) extensively lists reports of republican attacks on Chinese communities throughout East Sumatra, including in Berastagi and Kabanjahé. But also see Surbakti 1978:199–200 on militia efforts to control such attacks.

7. Interview with Koran Karo-Karo, in Bangun and Chairudin 1994:154; notes from unrecorded interview with Nandé Santosa beru Sebayang, March 11, 1994.

8. Here is Selamat Ginting's description of their flight from Kabanjahé, from his biography (Bangun and Chairudin 1994:149):

> Kabanjahe itself where I was still located, was continually threatened by gunfire from Dutch planes, so the sabotage squad led by Turah Perangin-angin was ordered to start to burn Kabanjahe. I could not possibly leave by car because of the intensity of the enemy's air assault. I ordered the driver Kongsi Sebayang to take the vehicle to the forest near Kacaribu and wait for me there. And I and Nandé Mburak [Piah Manik] and two Red Cross workers went on foot toward Kacaribu. From Kacaribu we could depart for the new headquarters at Tiga Binanga, whereas the battle headquarters surrounding Kabanjahe was set at Lau Simomo, and Kuta Bangun was chosen as the site for rest and practice for the troops. The East Sumatra Resident was also located in Kuta Bangun. The next day the troops regrouped so that they would be ready to face a new battle.

9. In Toba Batak kinship reckoning, which weighs even more heavily than Karo on the principle of patrilineality, the loss of their only surviving male clan representative would have had a profound effect on the economic and social status, indeed the survival, of the entire family.

10. See also Gintings 1975:40; and Surbakti 1978:221.

11. Both Reid (1979a) and van Langenberg (1976) attribute the mass killings in Karoland to the BHL, yet there seems to be little direct evidence confirming this attribution. Most of my informants insisted that all of the fighting forces in the Karo area, including the TRI, could be implicated in these and other acts of internal violence but that the BHL alone tended to get the blame "because their name was so fierce." That assertion may seem far-fetched, but it is clear that outside observers did tend to misidentify all popular militia units as Wild Tigers and to exaggerate their ferocity. The journalist Hans Post (1948:41), for instance, rather hysterically (and inaccurately) describes the highlands at the time of the first police action as suffering under a "fearful reign of terror" by the Harimau Liar, a group that "counts more criminals in its membership than are locked up in all the prisons in Western Europe put together." This "most extreme group in all of Indonesia," whose members were even said to engage in ritual cannibalism, was, he asserts, the "unrestrained lord and master of this desolate land."

12. Michael van Langenberg (1976:670) notes, "It is almost impossible to even estimate how many persons fled from Dutch occupied regions of Sumatera Timur into Republican-held territory. Dutch sources put the number of refugees from Sumatera Timur to Tapanuli at approximately 50,000. . . . The official Republican history of the Revolution in North Sumatra estimates the number of refugees into both Tapanuli and West Sumatra at approximately 200,000 and into Aceh at about 150,000." This would presumably not include the Karo evacuees in the highlands themselves. Karo speak of virtually the entire population (around 100,000 people) evacuating, though that includes people who simply left their villages temporarily during the fighting, who may or may not have left the district (cf. Kementerian Penerangan 1953:693). For a similar discussion of the difficulty of calculating the number of the dead in other instances of mass violence in Indonesia, see Cribb 2001.

13. The term I translate as "First Lady" is K., *kemberahen*. Sometimes glossed by Karo as "queen," it is an honorific term for a primary (or only) wife.

14. I italicize *our* and *we* here to indicate the Indonesian emphatic particle *pun* (K., *pé*), which is used here to distinguish between the generalized we/*kita* of nationalist agency and the personal but slightly formal we/*kita* that references Setianna beru Tarigan's own household.

15. The memoirs of TRI regimental commander Djamin Ginting were published under the name "Gintings" to indicate his subclan affiliation, Suka, presumably to distinguish him from another TRI officer with the same name, Djamin Ginting Munthé.

16. The letter is reproduced in Surbakti 1978:273–74, among numerous other sources.

17. James Siegel (1998b:2) similarly notes the separation of agents and objects of violence in the Indonesian armed forces museum in Jakarta. This is,

he argues, because "it seems difficult for Indonesians to think that national violence was directed against those clearly not Indonesian."

CHAPTER 6

1. The terms *cult of sacrificial heroism* and *exemplary death* are taken from Aretxaga 2000:43.

2. The term they used, *bodoh*, was a favorite rhetorical trope of Sukarno, who described the Indonesian people as *masih bodoh* (still ignorant) as a result of three hundred years of Dutch colonization. "The people, the Indonesian term is rakyat, were bodoh, which means 'uneducated, inarticulate,' the result of three hundred years of Dutch colonialism. Sukarno claimed the title of Extension of the Tongue of the People for himself. Via massive rallies broadcast over the radio he formulated what the rakyat could not say for themselves. After he spoke, they, presumably, understood what they had previously been thinking and could identify themselves with Indonesia" (Siegel 2006:173). See also Siegel 1997b.

3. In the spirit of full disclosure it is worth noting that Mulih Kwala Sebayang was himself one of the more educated men we spoke to. He had attended the Dutch-language HIS elementary school in Medan and was a classmate of Selamat Ginting at the private INS school in Padang Panjang, though neither of them graduated.

4. H. Amirmachmud, then head of the People's Consultative Council (DPR), in *Kompas*, July 23,1983, quoted in Pemberton 1994:313.

5. Karo refer to *teritis* as a "local delicacy." Because it is made of the contents of the cow's rumen, it is said to aid in digestion. It is usually served on the third day of village harvest festivals, when other meat has run out and hosts and guests alike are often in need of digestive assistance. Many Karo today do not enjoy it. Acting on the ethnographic principle of accepting whatever I was served, I never refused a plate of *teritis*. This quickly became part of the anthropologist's local lore, and when I arrived in villages where I had never been, I was often recognized as "the one who eats *teritis*." People then went out of their way to cook it for me. I was told that, when properly seasoned, it could be delicious, but I can't confirm that claim. Perhaps I never had any that was well seasoned. To me it always tasted (and looked) exactly like what it was. Consider this a warning for future ethnographers.

6. At this time, Djamin Ginting actually commanded TRI Regiment I. After the 1948 reorganization and rationalization of the fighting forces, his command was redesignated as TNI Regiment IV, as P. S. Ginting anachronistically refers to it here.

7. As noted in chapter 2, Kilap Sumagan, "Great Thunderbolt," was the hero of a well-known Karo legendary tale. The name also serves as a Karo translation of the Indonesian "Halilintar," so that its teknonymic form might be rendered as "Father of the Thunderbolt [Regiment]."

8. *Munggil* is a Karo term roughly equivalent to the vulgar Indonesian *mampus*, "dead, croaked." My young Indonesian friends and assistants consistently explained the term as equivalent in obscenity to the English *fuck*.

9. PNI is the Sukarnoist Partai Nasional Indonesia; Murba, the Trotskyite party founded by Tan Malaka; PKI, the Indonesian Communist Party.

10. On the Karo plateau, and especially in the *gunung-gunung* region, there is a strong reluctance to use *engko* in conversation, except, perhaps, to young children. This is in fact one of the most commonly noted regional distinctions in the Karo language. In other areas, especially the lowlands, *engko* is more commonly used, as it is in Indonesian.

11. *Parang mbelin* (K.) can roughly be glossed as "adult male," in the sense of one having full participatory status in village councils and customary debates. The contrastive term is *anak perana*, "bachelor," meaning someone who has not yet achieved that status. Both the implied affection and the explicit marking of status differential seem similar to me to American enlisted men's reference to high-ranking officers in this way.

12. This summary is taken from Bangun and Chairudin 1994:420–22. See also Surbakti 1978:255–56.

13. "Mule in the Yard" was originally published as a short story in *Scribner's Magazine* in 1934; it was subsequently included as chapter 16 of *The Town* (Faulkner 1961:231–56).

14. These included Sempa Sitepu and Eben Hezer Sinuraya (Sitepu, n.d.).

15. This also "lent something of a class tone" to military complaints about the incompetence and corruption of the republic's civilian leadership: "The tendency for officers to be of somewhat lower social status than their civilian counterparts continued into the post-revolutionary period. In the parliamentary years, it lent something of a class tone to military grumblings at the incompetence of civilian politicians. Later, when military officers had assumed many governmental functions (and were taken up by civilian elite families anxious to make an alliance with the powerful parvenus), it exacerbated tensions within the army as a result of resentment by officers who did not experience similar social advancement and who held that those of their colleagues who did had corrupted themselves" (McVey 1971:133–34).

16. What Suharto biographer Richard Elson (2001:192) describes as his "fear and mistrust of the Indonesian people" was an extreme expression of this view of the masses as either passive, quiescent followers of the national (i.e., presidential) will or else dangerous elements of disturbance and subversion.

CHAPTER 7

1. See also Chakrabarty 1992.

2. I obtained a copy of the master recording of Sinek's performance at Toko Serba Sama radio shop in Kabanjahé, as one of a number of unlabeled reels of tape, all of early *katoneng-katoneng* performances. Sinek herself was not certain when this recording was done, since a number of unauthorized recordings of her performances had been made. Sinek played for me a slightly different recording in 1995. A full transcript and English translation of still another recording appears in Sembiring 1987. Variations among these versions consist mostly of different placement of emphatic particles and in alternative formulaic descriptions of locales. Sembiring's more literal translation provides a useful comparison and corrective to my relatively free rendering. Although my translation differs significantly in style, though not in content, from Sembiring's, I have

followed his line and verse breaks. To facilitate comparison of texts and translations, the parenthetical numbers following each passage indicate the verse numbers in Sembiring's published version. For more on the musical accompaniment of *katoneng-katoneng*, see Yampolsky 1992.

3. The term *recognition scene* is from Frye 1957:346, quoted in Fussell 1975:335.

4. Karo usually gloss the term *turi-turin* with the Malay/Indonesian word *sejarah*, "history," rather than *cerita*, "story." The root word *turi* means, roughly, "order" or "sequence." Its best translation might be "narrative" or "chronicle," both of which have the same sequential connotation as the Karo term. See Steedly 1993:204–5; and White 1981.

5. The five-piece gong-drum orchestra is formally referred to as the *gendang lima sedalanen*, "five-together drum [ensemble]." This section is drawn from Yampolsky 1992 and pers. comm.

6. Electronic organs were introduced into Karo popular music in the 1980s; by the mid-'90s they were being used in traditional and quasi-traditional repertoires. The so-called *gendang kibord* (keyboard orchestra) uses a programmed rhythm track instead of actual drums; for pop music this is a modified reggae rhythm that reminds me of skating-rink music. Many older Karo complain about the music's lack of variety and sophistication, but most people seem to enjoy the increased liveliness that *kibord* music generates in dance festivals. Because renting a *kibord* and sound system is less expensive than hiring a full orchestra and because a *kibord* is easier to learn to play than the traditional instruments, it has invigorated the dance scene in highland villages, where it has allowed inexpensive dance classes to be held. Sometimes at weddings and funerals the *gendang kibord* is used for the lengthy formal dancing as well as for the informal entertainment dances featured at weddings. According to my Karo friends, a dance festival or wedding today that doesn't feature a keyboard ensemble for at least part of the program would be considered a poor show. In the period of my first Karo fieldwork, between 1983 and 1985, keyboards and other nontraditional instruments (e.g., guitars) were rarely used in dance festivals but were beginning to appear in some trance rituals.

7. Nandé Waty is referring here to an infamous cable bridge known as "Rambingen" across the deep crevasse cut by the Lau Renun at the border of the Karo and Dairi districts. It was the subject of many stories by evacuees and volunteers, some of whom refused to cross it altogether.

8. For a detailed discussion of Karo terms of address, see Kipp 1986. Sinek and Malem Pagi were actually neither lovers nor siblings; they were simply enacting the performative fiction of seduction conventionally attributed to male-female entertainer teams. I discuss Sinek and Malem Pagi's relationship in more detail in Steedly 1989, which concerns the poetic ambiguity of lovers' discourse in another of their *katoneng-katoneng* performances.

9. Interview, Sinek beru Karo, May 9, 1994.

10. In a speech for Armed Forces Day, 1960, for instance, the former BHL leader Payung Bangun was reported to have advised "Karo artists in particular to compose songs about the revolution and struggle, and not to put forth songs of liberalism, that only pay attention to the individual" (quoted in Ermy

1960:17). For an excellent discussion of the shifting politics of culture in postin-dependence Indonesia, see Yampolsky 1995.

11. This event is described in Ermy 1960.

CONCLUSION

1. On Madiun, see, for example, Swift 2010; Reid 1974; and G. Kahin 2003. For more on events in Sumatra, see Bangun and Chairudin 1994; van Langen-berg 1976:667–739; Manihuruk 1979:354–56; Edisaputra 1985; and Surbakti 1979.

2. See Siegel 1997a:197–207 for a account of the communicative significance of currency exchange in this context, between "red" (Dutch) money and "white" (Indonesian) money.

3. For similar accounts of the "reading" of signs of military involvement in the wave of violence that swept Indonesia following Suharto's resignation, see, for example, Aditjondro 2001; Siegel 1998a, 2006; and Spyer 2002, 2003.

4. *Tempo* 24 (9), April 30, 1994.

5. On the interrelated concepts of "student" and "youth" in New Order Indonesia, see Strassler 2010:219–20.

6. In dressing in the costume of "struggle," the student activists of the Reformasi generation were citing not actual youth attire from the time of independence but rather the imaginings of these that were commonly depicted on the gateways and posters of Independence Day competitions. See, for instance, the portrait of "Laura" in activist costume in Strassler 2010:121; also Lee 2008:72–131.

7. Indonesia now has the second largest number of Facebook users in the world, having had more than a 12,000 percent growth rate in the past two years. www.nickburcher.com/2010/07/facebook-usage-statistics-by-country. html, accessed March 14, 2011. Indonesia has the most prolific users of Twitter as well, with 20.8 percent of Internet users over fifteen who tweet. This figure, cited in August 2010, was only for home or work usage and does not include the potentially much greater number of people who access the Web through Internet cafés or wifi hotspots so is likely to underrepresent current usage. See www.comscore.com/Press_Events/Press_Releases/2010/8/Indonesia_ Brazil_and_Venezuela_Lead_Global_Surge_in_Twitter_Usage, accessed March 14, 2011.

8. Three of these films, *Merah putih* (Red-and-White, 2009), *Darah garuda* (Blood of Eagles, 2010), and *Hati merdeka* (Heart of Freedom, 2011), make up a trilogy following a diverse army unit (one devout Muslim, one pacifist intel-lectual, one Christian from the outer islands) through the fighting in Java. A review in the *Jakarta Globe* (Siahaan 2009) describes *Merah putih* as a "war movie [that] provides an unprecedented level of thrills through its heartpump-ing gun battles, gory knife killings and stunning explosions . . . definitely a fresh alternative in the local motion picture industry." The other film, *Laskar pemimpi* (Troop of Dreamers, 2010), is a comic take on a band of misfit volunteers, featuring players from the musical comedy troupe Project Pop.

9. See, for instance, Winters 2011; and Lundry 2010.

References

AA [Andjar Asmara]. 1958. "Satu epos-gerilya: *Turang*." *Varia* 1, no. 6 (May 28): 11.

Abdullah, Taufik. 2009. *Indonesia: Towards Democracy*. Singapore: Institute of Southeast Asian Studies.

Abu-Lughod, Lila. 1993. *Writing Women's Worlds*. Berkeley: University of California Press.

Adas, Michael. 1981. From Avoidance to Confrontation: Peasant Protest in Precolonial and Colonial Southeast Asia. *Comparative Studies in Society and History* 23 (2):217–47.

Aditjondro, George Junus. 2001. Guns, Pamphlets and Handie-Talkies: How the Military Exploited Local Ethno-Religious Tensions in Maluku to Preserve Their Political and Economic Privileges. In *Violence in Indonesia*, ed. Ingrid Wessel and Georgia Wimhofer, 100–128. Hamburg: Abera Verlag.

Algemeen Rijksarchief, Tweede afdeling (The Hague). 1947. Algemene Secretarie en de daarbij gedeponeerde archieven, 1942–50. Nummer toegang 2.10.14.02. Inv. nr. 2784: "Stukken betreffende het rekest van de Indische gemeenschap van Medan aan Pandit Nehru, waarin hun bezwaren tegen het republikeins regiem op Sumatra, Aug. 1947."

Amin, Shahid. 1995. *Event, Metaphor, Memory*. Berkeley: University of California Press.

Andaya, Barbara. 1994. To Live as Brothers. Honolulu: University of Hawai'i Press.

Anderson, Benedict. 1972. *Java in a Time of Revolution*. Ithaca, NY: Cornell University Press.

———. 1991. *Imagined Communities*. 2nd ed. New York: Verso First published 1983.

Appadurai, Arjun. 1996. *Modernity at Large*. Minneapolis: University of Minnesota Press.

———. 2006. *Fear of Small Numbers: An Essay on the Geography of Anger*. Durham, NC: Duke University Press.

Aretxaga, Begona. 2000. Playing Terrorist: Ghastly Plots and the Ghostly State. *Journal of Spanish Cultural Studies* 1 (1):43–58.

———. 2003. Maddening States. *Annual Review of Anthropology* 32: 393–410.

Arifin Pulungan. 1979. *Kisah dari pedalaman*. Medan, North Sumatra: Diancorporation.

Arry Darma. 1993. *Medan Area: Cuplikan kisah sejarah perjuangan kemerdekaan R.I. di Sumatera Utara/Kota Medan dan sekitarnya*. Comic book. Medan: Inti Juang.

Atkinson, Jane Monnig. 1990. How Gender Makes a Difference in Wana Society. In *Power and Difference*, ed. Jane Atkinson and Shelly Errington, 59–94. Stanford, CA: Stanford University Press.

Bakhtin, Mikhail. 1981. Discourse in the Novel. In *The Dialogic Imagination*, 259–422. Austin: University of Texas Press.

Bangun, Tridah, and Hendri Chairudin. 1994. *Kilap Sumagan: Biografi Selamat Ginting*. Jakarta: C.V. Haji Masagung.

Beekman, E.M. 1988. *Fugitive Dreams: An Anthology of Dutch Colonial Literature*. Amherst: University of Massachusetts Press.

Benjamin, Walter. 1969a. The Image of Proust. In *Illuminations*, 201–16. New York: Schocken Books.

———. 1969b. The Storyteller. In *Illuminations*, 83–110. New York: Schocken Books.

———. 1969c. The Task of the Translator. In *Illuminations*, 69–82. New York: Schocken Books.

Benstock, Shari. 1988. *The Private Self: Theory and Practice of Women's Autobiographical Writings*. Chapel Hill: University of North Carolina Press.

Biro Sejarah PRIMA (Pejuang Republik Indonesia Medan Area). 1976. *Medan area mengisi Proklamasi*. Medan: Badan Musyawarah Pejuang Republik Indonesia Medan Area.

Blackburn, Susan. 2004. *Women and the State in Modern Indonesia*. Cambridge: Cambridge University Press.

Bowen, John. 1991. *Sumatran Politics and Poetics: Gayo History, 1900–1989*. New Haven, CT: Yale University Press.

Brahma Putro and M.N. Sinulingga. 1977. Sejarah perjuangan gerakan Aron Sumatera Timur. 10 parts. *Mimbar Umum* (Medan newspaper), January 27–February 7.

Brenner, Suzanne. 1998. *The Domestication of Desire*. Princeton, NJ: Princeton University Press.

Broek, Jan O. 1942. *Economic Development of the Netherlands Indies*. New York: Institute of Pacific Relations.

Bronson, Bennett. 1977. Exchange at the Upstream and Downstream Ends: Notes toward a Functional Model of the Coastal State in Southeast Asia. In *Economic Exchange and Social Interaction in Southeast Asia*, ed.

K. Hutterer. Michigan Papers on South and Southeast Asia 13. Ann Arbor: Center for South and Southeast Asian Studies, University of Michigan.

Brown, Wendy. 1995. *States of Injury*. Princeton, NJ: Princeton University Press.

Castles, Lance. 1972. The Political Life of a Sumatran Residency: Tapanuli 1915–1940. PhD dissertation, Yale University.

Chakrabarty, Dipesh. 1992. Postcoloniality and the Artifice of History: Who Speaks for "Indian" Pasts? *Representations* 37:1–26.

Chatterjee, Partha. 1993. *The Nation and Its Fragments*. Princeton, NJ: Princeton University Press.

Clifford, James. 1988. On Ethnographic Authority. In *The Predicament of Culture*, ed. J. Clifford, 21–54. Cambridge, MA: Harvard University Press.

———. 1997. *Routes: Travel and Translation in the Late Twentieth Century*. Cambridge, MA: Harvard University Press.

Coady, C. A. J. 1992. *Testimony: A Philosophical Study*. Oxford: Clarendon Press.

Coates, Steven. 2010. 12 Years on, How Sick Is Indonesia's Reformasi? *Jakarta Globe*. May 22. www.thejakartaglobe.com/home/12-years-on-how-sick-is-indonesias-reformasi/376453.

Colombijn, Freek. 2002. Explaining the Violent Solution in Indonesia. *Brown Journal of World Affairs* 9 (1):49–56.

Colombijn, Freek, and J. Thomas Lindblad, eds. 2002. *Roots of Violence in Indonesia*. Leiden, Netherlands: KITLV Press.

Comaroff, John, and Jean Comaroff. 1992. *Ethnography and the Historical Imagination*. Boulder, CO: Westview Press.

Connerton, Paul. 1989. *How Societies Remember*. Cambridge: Cambridge University Press.

Cribb, Robert. 1991. *Gangsters and Revolutionaries: The Jakarta People's Militia and the Indonesian Revolution, 1945–1949*. Honolulu: University of Hawai'i Press.

———. 2001. How Many Deaths? Problems in the Statistics of Massacre in Indonesia (1965–66) and East Timor (1975–80). In *Violence in Indonesia*, ed. Ingrid Wessel and Georgia Wimhofer, 82–98. Hamburg: Abera Verlag.

———. 2002. From Total People's Defence to Massacre: Explaining Indonesian Military Violence in East Timor. In *Roots of Violence in Indonesia*, ed. Freek Columbijn and J. Thomas Lindblad, 227–41. Leiden, Netherlands: KITLV Press.

Cribb, Robert, and Colin Brown. 1995. *Modern Indonesia: A History since 1945*. London: Longman.

Dada Meuraxa. 1946. Kepada Serikandi. *Radikal* 1(7), October: front cover.

Daniel, E. Valentine. 1996. *Charred Lullabies: Chapters in an Anthropography of Violence*. Princeton, NJ: Princeton University Press.

Das, Veena. 1990. Our Work to Cry: Your Work to Listen. In *Mirrors of Violence: Communities, Riots and Survivors in South Asia*, ed. V. Das, 345–98. Delhi: Oxford University Press.

———. 2007. *Life and Words: Violence and the Descent into the Ordinary*. Berkeley: University of California Press.

de Certeau, Michel. 1984. *The Practice of Everyday Life*. Berkeley: University of California Press.

Dirks, Nicholas. 1990. History as a Sign of the Modern. *Public Culture* 2 (2):25–32.

Dobbin, Christine. 1980. The Search for Women in Indonesian History. In *Kartini Centenary: Indonesian Women Then and Now*, vol. 5, ed. A. Zainu'ddin, 56–68. Monash University Annual Indonesia Lecture Series. Melbourne: Monash University.

Drakard, Jane. 1990. *A Malay Frontier: Unity and Duality in a Sumatran Kingdom*. Ithaca, NY: Southeast Asia Program, Cornell University.

Edisaputra. 1985. *Bedjo harimau Sumatera dalam perang kemerdekaan*. Jakarta: Yayasan Bina Satria-45.

Elson, R. E. 2002. In Fear of the People: Suharto and the Justification of State-Sponsored Violence under the New Order. In *Roots of Violence in Indonesia*, ed. Freek Colombijn and J. Thomas Lindblad, 173–96. Leiden: KITLV Press.

Ermy. 1960. Perajaan 5 Oktober '60 di Medan dengan guro2 Aron Apri/ Rakyat. *Terlong* 6:11, 17.

Fanon, Frantz. 1963. Concerning Violence. In *The Wretched of the Earth*, 35–107. New York: Grove Press.

Fassin, Didier, and Richard Rechtman. 2009. *The Empire of Trauma*. Princeton, NJ: Princeton University Press.

Faulkner, William. 1961. *The Town*. New York: Vintage. First published 1957.

Frederick, William H. 1989. *Visions and Heat: The Making of the Indonesian Revolution*. Athens: Ohio University Press.

———. 1997. The Appearance of Revolution: Cloth, Uniform, and the Pemuda Style in East Java, 1945–1949. In *Outward Appearances: Dressing State and Society in Indonesia*, ed. Henk Schulte Nordholt, 199–248. Leiden, Netherlands: KITLV Press.

———. 2002. Shadows of an Unseen Hand: Some Patterns of Violence in the Indonesian Revolution, 1946–1949. In *Roots of Violence in Indonesia*, ed. Freek Colombijn and J. Thomas Lindblad, 143–72. Leiden, Netherlands: KITLV Press.

Frye, Northrop. 1957. *Anatomy of Criticism*. Princeton, NJ: Princeton University Press.

Fussell, Paul. 1975. *The Great War and Modern Memory*. London: Oxford University Press.

Geertz, Clifford. 1973a. After the Revolution: The Fate of Nationalism in the New States. In *The Interpretation of Cultures*, ed. C. Geertz, 234–54. New York: Basic Books.

———. 1973b. The Integrative Revolution: Primordial Sentiments and Civil Politics in the New States. In *The Interpretation of Cultures*, ed. C. Geertz, 255–310. New York: Basic Books.

———. 1973c. Politics Past, Politics Present: Some Notes on the Uses of Anthropology in Understanding the New States. In *The Interpretation of Cultures*, ed. C. Geertz, 327–44. New York: Basic Books.

———. 1973d. Thick Description: Toward an Interpretive Theory of Culture. In *The Interpretation of Cultures*, ed. C. Geertz, 3–30. New York: Basic Books.

Giddens, Anthony. 1991. *Modernity and Self-Identity*. Stanford, CA: Stanford University Press.

Ginting, Juara Rimantha. 1991. Pa Surdam, a Karo Batak Guru. In *The Batak Peoples of the Island of Sumatra*, ed. A. Sibeth, 85–98. New York: Thames and Hudson.

Ginting, L. 1995. Pembangunan Makam Pahlawan di Kabanjahé. *Buletin Tenah* 5:11–13.

Ginting, Malem Pagi. N.d. *Mengungsi*. Cassette recording. Kabanjahé: Toko Remaja.

Gintings, Djamin. 1975. *Titi bambu*. Medan: C.V. Umum.

Gouda, Frances. 1997. Languages of Gender and Neurosis in the Indonesian Struggle for Independence. *Indonesia* 64 (October):45–76.

Guha, Ranajit. 1983. *Elementary Aspects of Peasant Insurgency in Colonial India*. Delhi: Oxford University Press.

———. 1988. The Prose of Counter-Insurgency. In *Selected Subaltern Studies*, ed. R. Guha and G. Spivak, 45–88. New York: Oxford University Press.

Gupta, Akhil, and James Ferguson. 1997. Beyond "Culture": Space, Identity, and the Politics of Difference. In *Culture, Power, Place*, ed. A. Gupta and J. Ferguson, 33–51. Durham, NC: Duke University Press.

Gusdorf, Georges. 1980. Conditions and Limits of Autobiography. In *Autobiography: Essays Theoretical and Critical*, ed. J. Olney, 28–48. Princeton, NJ: Princeton University Press.

Habermas, Jürgen. 1980. Modernity—an Incomplete Project. In *The Anti-Aesthetic: Essays on Postmodern Culture*, ed. H. Foster, 3–15. Port Townsend, WA: Bay Press.

———. 1987. *The Philosophical Discourse of Modernity*. Cambridge, MA: MIT Press.

Halbwachs, Maurice. 1980. *The Collective Memory*. New York: Harper and Row.

———. 1992. *On Collective Memory*. Chicago: University of Chicago Press.

Hawes, Gary. 1990. Theories of Peasant Revolution: A Critique and Contribution from the Philippines. *World Politics* 42 (2):261–98.

Hering, Bob. 2002. *Soekarno: Founding Father of Indonesia, 1901–1945*. Leiden, Netherlands: KITLV Press.

Higonnet, Margaret. 1994. Cassandra's Question: Do Women Write War Novels? In *Borderwork: Feminist Engagements with Comparative Literature*, ed. M. Higonnet, 144–61. Ithaca, NY: Cornell University Press.

Hinton, Alexander Laban, ed. 2002. *Genocide: An Anthropological Reader*. Malden, MA: Wiley-Blackwell.

———. 2005. *Why Did They Kill? Cambodia in the Shadow of Genocide*. Berkeley: University of California Press.

Hobsbawm, Eric. 1959. *Primitive Rebels*. New York: Norton.

Hroch, Miroslav. 1985. *Social Preconditions of National Revival in Europe: A Comparative Analysis of the Social Composition of Patriotic Groups among the Smaller European Nations*. Translated by B. Fowkes. Cambridge: Cambridge University Press.

Husny, T. Haji M. Lah. 1983. *Revolusi Sosial 1946 di Sumatera Timur / Tapanuli disertai pangkal dan akibatnya (proloog dan naloognya)*. Medan: Badan Penerbit Husny.

Indonesia Rapportage. 1945–50. Mailrapport 254/47 (November 26, 1947). Items no. 159/26 and 326/26. Ministerie van Binnenlands Zaken, The Hague.

———. 1946. Verslag van Noord-Sumatra. April 16–30. Ministerie van Binnenlandse Zaken, The Hague.

Inoue, Tetsuro. 1953. *Bapa Jango* [Bapa Djanggut]. Tokyo: Kodan-sha.

Jacobs, G. F. 1982. *Prelude to the Monsoon: Assignment in Sumatra*. Philadelphia: University of Pennsylvania Press.

Jain, Kajri. 2007. *Gods in the Bazaar: The Economies of Indian Calendar Art*. Durham, NC: Duke University Press.

Joustra, Meint. 1901. Naar de landschap Goenoeng2. *Mededelingen van wege het Nederlandsch Zendelinggenootschap* 54:5–90.

———. 1910. *Batakspiegel*. Leiden, Netherlands: S. C. van Doesburgh.

———. 1918. *Toeri-toerîn Karo*. Vol. 2. Leiden, Netherlands: S. C. van Doesburgh.

Kahin, Audrey, ed. 1985. *Regional Dynamics of the Indonesian Revolution*. Honolulu: University of Hawai'i Press.

Kahin, George McT. 2003. *Nationalism and Revolution in Indonesia*. Ithaca, NY: Cornell University Press. First published 1952.

Kalyvas, Stathis N. 2003. The Ontology of "Political Violence": Action and Identity in Civil Wars. *Perspectives on Politics* 1 (3):475–94.

———. 2006. *The Logic of Violence in Civil War*. Cambridge: Cambridge University Press.

Keane, John. 1996. *Reflections on Violence*. London: Verso.

Keane, Webb. 1997. Knowing One's Place: National Language and the Idea of the Local in Eastern Indonesia. *Cultural Anthropology* 12 (1):37–63.

Kementerian Penerangan. 1953. *Republik Indonesia*. Medan: Propinsi Sumatera Utara.

Kempees, J. C. J. 1905. *De tocht van Overste van Daalen door de Gajo-, Alas- en Bataklanden*. Amsterdam: J. C. Dalmeijer.

Kipp, Rita S. 1976. The Ideology of Kinship in Karo Batak Ritual. PhD dissertation, University of Pittsburgh.

———. 1986. Terms of Endearment: Karo Batak Lovers as Siblings. *American Ethnologist* 13 (4) 632–45.

———. 1990. *The Early Years of a Dutch Colonial Mission: The Karo Field*. Ann Arbor: University of Michigan Press.

———. 1998. Emancipating Each Other: Dutch Colonial Missionaries' Encounter with Karo Women in Sumatra, 1900–1942. In *Domesticating the Empire: Race, Gender and Family Life in French and Dutch Colonialism*, ed. Julia Clancy-Smith and Frances Gouda, 211–33. Charlottesville: University of Virginia Press.

Kozok, Uli. 1993. Lamentations of the Karo-Batak, North Sumatra. *Indonesia Circle* 59–60:57–61.

———. 1994. Die Klageliedtradition der Batak Nordsumatras. PhD dissertation, Universität Hamburg.

Lasmidjah Hardi, ed. 1981. *Sumbangsihku bagi Pertiwi.* Vol. 1. Jakarta: Yayasan Wanita Pejoang.

———. 1982–85. *Sumbangsihku bagi Ibu Pertiwi.* Vols. 2–5. Jakarta: Sinar Harapan.

Lee, Doreen. 2008. The Origins of Our Future: Nationalism and Youth in the 1998 Indonesian Student Movement. PhD dissertation, Cornell University, Department of Anthropology.

Lubis, Todung Mulya. 1993. *In Search of Human Rights: Legal-Political Dilemmas of Indonesia's New Order, 1966–1990.* Translated by Sarah Maxim. Jakarta: PT Gramedia Pustaka Utama.

Lucas, Anton. 1991. *One Soul, One Struggle: Region and Revolution in Indonesia.* Sydney: Allen and Unwin.

Lukács, Georg. 1971. *The Theory of the Novel.* Cambridge, MA: MIT Press.

Lundry, Chris. 2010. Sympathy for the Devil. *Inside Indonesia* 100 (April–June). www.insideindonesia.org/edition-100/sympathy-for-the-devil-06061307.

Mamdani, Mahmood. 2002. *When Victims Become Killers.* Princeton, NJ: Princeton University Press.

Manihuruk, A. E. 1979. *Perjuangan rakyat semesta Sumatera Utara.* Jakarta: Forum Komunikasi Ex Sub Teritorium VII Komando Sumatera.

Mansjur. 1976. *The Golden Bridge: "Jembatan Emas" 1945.* Medan(?): n.p.

Marcus, Jane. 1988. "Invincible Mediocrity": The Private Selves of Public Women. In *The Private Self: Theory and Practice of Women's Autobiographical Writings,* ed. S. Benstock, 114–46. Chapel Hill: University of North Carolina Press.

Mason, Mary G. 1980. The Other Voice: Autobiographies of Women Writers. In *Autobiography: Essays Theoretical and Critical,* ed. James Olney, 207–35. Princeton, NJ: Princeton University Press.

McClintock, Anne. 1995. *Imperial Leather.* New York: Routledge.

McGregor, Katharine E. 2005. Nugroho Notosusanto: The Legacy of a Historian in the Service of an Authoritarian Regime. In *Beginning to Remember,* ed. M. S. Zurbuchen, 209–32. Singapore: NUS Press.

———. 2007. *History in Uniform: Military Ideology and the Construction of Indonesia's Past.* Honolulu: University of Hawai'i Press.

McVey, Ruth. 1971. The Post-Revolutionary Transformation of the Indonesian Army: Part I. *Indonesia* 11 (April):131–76.

———. 1972. The Post-Revolutionary Transformation of the Indonesian Army: Part II. *Indonesia* 13 (April):141–81.

Mrázek, Rudolf. 1972. Tan Malaka: A Political Personality's Structure of Experience. *Indonesia* 14:1–48.

———. 1994. *Sjahrir: Politics and Exile in Indonesia.* Ithaca, NY: Southeast Asia Program, Cornell University.

———. 2010. *A Certain Age.* Durham, NC: Duke University Press.

Musjawarah Besar Pedjuang. 1960. *Kenang2an Musjawarah Besar Pedjuang Revolusi 17 Agustus 1945 Se-Sumatera Utara ke-1.* Medan: Panitia Penjelenggara Musjawarah Besar Pedjuang Revolusi.

Nasution, Gen. Abdul Haris. 1982. *Memenuhi panggilan tugas.* 5 vols. Jakarta: Gunung Agung.

Neumann, J.H. 1925. *Si Beroe Rengga Koening ras Poestaka Ginting.* Kabanjahé: n.p.

———. 1927. Bijdrage tot de kennis van de Batakstammen (part 2). *Bijdragen van de taal-land- en volkenkunde.* 83:162–80.

———. 1951. *Karo-Bataks—Nederlands woordenboek.* Jakarta: Lembaga Kebudayaan Indonesia.

Neumann-Bos, G. 1939. C.M.C.M.: Geen puzzle meer. *Nederlandsch Zendingsblad* 22 (October):170–71.

Newberry, Janice. 2006. *Backdoor Java.* Toronto: University of Toronto Press.

Nora, Pierre. 1989. Between Memory and History: *Les lieux de mémoire. Representations* 26:7–25.

———. 1996. Between Memory and History. In *Realms of Memory.* Translated by A. Goldhammer. New York: Columbia University Press.

Onghokham. 2003. The Jago in Colonial Java: Ambivalent Champion of the People. In *The Thugs, the Curtain Thief, and the Sugar Lord,* 113–45. Jakarta: Metafor Publishing. Chapter first published 1984.

Ortner, Sherry. 1995. Resistance and the Problem of Ethnographic Refusal. *Comparative Studies in Society and History* 37 (1):173–93.

Pandey, Gyanendra. 1992. In Defense of the Fragment: Writing about Hindu-Muslim Riots in India Today. *Representations* 37:27–55.

———. 2001. *Remembering Partition.* Cambridge: Cambridge University Press.

———. 2002. The Long Life of Rumor. *Alternatives: Global, Local, Political* 27 (April–June):165–91.

Passerini, Luisa. 1987. *Fascism and Popular Memory: The Cultural Experience of the Turin Working Class.* Cambridge: Cambridge University Press.

Pemberton, John. 1994. *On the Subject of "Java."* Ithaca, NY: Cornell University Press.

Piekaar, A.J. 1949. *Atjeh en de oorlog met Japan.* The Hague: Van Hoeve.

Poeze, Harry A. 1976. *Tan Malaka: Strijder voor Indonesie's vrijheid: Levensloop van 1897 tot 1945.* The Hague: Nijhoff.

———. 1994. *Politiek-politioneele overzichten van Nederlandsch-Indië.* 4 vols. Leiden, Netherlands: KITLV Press.

Pols, Hans. 2011. The Totem Vanishes, the Hordes Revolt: A Psychoanalytic Interpretation of the Indonesian Struggle for Independence. In *Unconscious Dominions: Psychoanalysis Colonial Trauma, and Global Sovereignties,* ed. W. Anderson, D. Jenson, and R. Keller, 141–66. Durham, NC: Duke University Press.

Portelli, Alessandro. 1991. *The Death of Luigi Trastulli and Other Stories.* Albany: State University of New York Press.

Post, Hans. 1948. *Politionele actie.* Vol. 2 of *Bandjir over Noord-Sumatra.* Medan: Deli Courant.

Purba, Tandabelawan. 1946. Sikap angkatan muda (Attitude of the young generation). *Radikal* 1 (February):16–18.

Purdey, Jemma. 2004. Describing Kekerasan: Some Observations on Writing about Violence in Indonesia after the New Order. *Bijdragen tot de Taal-, Land- en Volkenkunde* 160 (2–3):189–225.

Radjab, Muhamad. 1949. *Tjatatan di Sumatera*. Jakarta: Balai Pustaka.

Ramadhan KH. 1988. *A.E. Kawilarang: Untuk Sang Merah Putih*. Jakarta: Sinar Harapan.

Ranger, Terence. 1968a. Connexions between "Primary Resistance" Movements and Modern Mass Nationalism in East and Central Africa, part 1. *Journal of African History* 9 (3):437–53.

———. 1968b. Connexions between "Primary Resistance" Movements and Modern Mass Nationalism in East and Central Africa, part 2. *Journal of African History* 9 (4):631–41.

———. 1985. *Peasant Consciousness and Guerilla War in Zimbabwe*. London: J. Currey.

Reid, Anthony. 1974. *The Indonesian National Revolution 1945–50*. Hawthorn, Australia: Longman.

———. 1975. The Japanese Occupation and Rival Indonesian Elites: Northern Sumatra in 1942. *Journal of Asian Studies* 35(1): 49–61.

———. 1979a. *The Blood of the People: Revolution and the End of Traditional Rule in Northern Sumatra*. Kuala Lumpur: Oxford University Press.

———. 1979b. The Nationalist Quest for an Indonesian Past. In *Perceptions of the Past in Southeast Asia*, ed. A. Reid and D. Marr, 281–98. Singapore: Heinemann.

———. 1998. Merdeka: The Concept of Freedom in Indonesia. In *Asian Freedoms: The Idea of Freedom in East and Southeast Asia*, ed. A. Reid and D. Kelly, 141–60. Cambridge: Cambridge University Press.

———. 2009. *Imperial Alchemy: Nationalism and Political Identity in Southeast Asia*. Cambridge: Cambridge University Press.

Reid, Anthony, and Akira Oki. 1986. *The Japanese Experience in Indonesia: Selected Memoirs of 1942–1945*. Papers in International Studies Southeast Asia Series, vol. 72. Athens: Ohio University Center for International Studies.

Reid, Anthony, and Saya Shiraishi. 1976. Rural Unrest in Sumatra, 1942: A Japanese Report. *Indonesia* 21:115–33.

Ricoeur, Paul. 1980. Narrative Time. *Critical Inquiry* 7 (1):169–90.

Robben, Antonius C.G.M. 1996. Ethnographic Seduction, Transference, and Resistance in Dialogues about Terror and Violence in Argentina. *Ethos* 24 (1):71–106.

Said, H. Mohammed. 1973. What Was the "Social Revolution of 1946" in East Sumatra? *Indonesia* 15:145–86.

Sato, Shigeru. 1994. *War, Nationalism and Peasants: Java under the Japanese Occupation*. St. Leonards, NSW: Allen and Unwin.

Scott, James C. 1976. *The Moral Economy of the Peasant*. New Haven, CT: Yale University Press.

———. 2009. *The Art of Not Being Governed*. New Haven, CT: Yale University Press.

Sears, L., ed. 1996. *Fantasizing the Feminine in Indonesia*. Durham, NC: Duke University Press.

Sembiring, Terbit. 1987. Lagu "Mengungsi": Sada lagu perjuangan kemerdekaan Indonesia. In *Cultures and Societies of North Sumatra*, ed. R. Carle, 394–426. Berlin: Dietrich Reimer Verlag.

Sen, Krishna. 1994. *Indonesian Cinema: Framing the New Order*. London: Zed Books.

Sherman, D. George. 1990. *Rice, Rupees and Ritual*. Stanford: Stanford University Press.

Siahaan, Armando. 2009. "Merah Putih": A War Film with a Western Flavor. *Jakarta Globe*, August 14. www.thejakartaglobe.com/arts/merah-putih -a-war-movie-with-a-western-flavor/324082.

Sidel, John. 2006. *Riots, Pogroms, Jihad: Religious Violence in Indonesia*. Ithaca, NY: Cornell University Press.

Siegel, James. 1997a. *Fetish, Recognition, Revolution*. Princeton, NJ: Princeton University Press.

———. 1997b. Revolutionary Stink and the Extension of the Tongue of the People: The Political Languages of Pramoedya Ananta Toer and Sukarno. *Indonesia* 64 (October):9–20.

———. 1998a. Early Thoughts on the Violence of May 13 and 14, 1998 in Jakarta." *Indonesia* 66:75–108.

———. 1998b. *A New Criminal Type in Jakarta*. Durham, NC: Duke University Press.

———. 2005. The Curse of the Photograph: Atjeh, 1901. *Indonesia* 80:21–37.

———. 2006. *Naming the Witch*. Stanford, CA: Stanford University Press.

Singarimbun, Masri. 1975. *Kinship, Descent and Alliance among the Karo Batak*. Berkeley: University of California Press.

Sitaresmi, Ratnayu. 1997. Social History of the Bandung Lautan Api (Bandung sea of fire), March 24, 1946. Paper presented at NIOD conference Changing Regimes and Shifting Loyalties: Identity and Violence in the Early Revolution of Indonesia, June 25–28, Amsterdam. Accessed September 1, 2008. www.bandungheritage.org/images/stories/dokumen/bandung_sea_of_fire. pdf.

Sitepu, P. 1977. *Buku kesenian kebudayaan tradisional Karo*. Medan: n.p.

Sitepu, Sempa. N.d. Sejarah pertumbuhan suku Karo sebagai landasan GBKP & berkembangnya Gereja Batak Karo Protestan. Typescript.

Sjahnan, H.R., Maj. Gen. (ret.). 1982. *Dari Medan Area ke pedalaman dan kembali ke kota Medan*. Medan: Dinas Sejarah Kodam-II/BB.

Smail, John R.W. 1964. *Bandung in the Early Revolution, 1945–1946*. Ithaca, NY: Southeast Asia Program, Department of Asian Studies, Cornell University.

Sora Mido. 1996. Dirgahayu Kemerdekaan Republic Indonesia ke-51. 2 (1):6.

Spacks, Patricia Meyer. 1980. Selves in Hiding. In *Women's Autobiography: Essays in Criticism*, ed. E.C. Jelinek, 112–32. Bloomington: Indiana University Press.

Spivak, Gayatri Chakravorty. 1993. The Politics of Translation. In *Outside in the Teaching Machine*, 179–200. New York: Routledge.

Spyer, Patricia. 2002. Fire without Smoke and Other Phantoms of Ambon's Violence: Media Effects, Agency, and the Work of Imagination. *Indonesia* 74:21–36.

———. 2003. One Slip of the Pen: Some Notes on Writing Violence in Maluku. In *Indonesia in Transition*, ed. Henk Schulte Nordholt and Gusti Asnan, 181–200. Yogyakarta: Pustaka Pelajar.

Steedly, Mary. 1989. The Play of Pretext (A Love Song for Workers Day, 1963). Unpublished ms.

———. 1993. *Hanging without a Rope: Narrative Experience in Colonial and Postcolonial Karoland*. Princeton, NJ: Princeton University Press.

———. 1996. The Importance of Proper Names: Language and "National" Identity in Colonial Karoland. *American Ethnologist* 23 (3):447–75.

———. 2000. Modernity and the Memory Artist: The Work of Imagination in Highland Sumatra, 1947–1995. *Comparative Studies in Society and History* 42 (4):811–46.

Stewart, Kathleen. 1992. On the Politics of Cultural Theory: A Case for "Contaminated" Cultural Critique. *Social Research* 58 (2):395–412.

———. 1996. *A Space on the Side of the Road*. Princeton, NJ: Princeton University Press.

Stoler, Ann Laura. 1985a. *Capitalism and Confrontation in Sumatra's Plantation Belt, 1870–1979*. New Haven, CT: Yale University Press.

———. 1985b. Perceptions of Protest: Defining the Dangerous in Colonial Sumatra. *American Ethnologist* 12 (4):642–58.

———. 1988. Working the Revolution: Plantation Laborers and the People's Militia in North Sumatra. *Journal of Asian Studies* 47 (2):227–47.

———. 1992. "In Cold Blood": Hierarchies of Credibility and the Politics of Colonial Narratives. *Representations* 37:151–89.

———. 2009. *Along the Archival Grain: Epistemic Anxieties and Colonial Common Sense*. Princeton, NJ: Princeton University Press.

Stoler, Ann Laura, and Karen Strassler. 2000. Castings for the Colonial: Memory Work in "New Order" Java. *Comparative Studies in Society and History* 42 (1):4–48.

Strassler, Karen. 2005. Material Witnesses: Photographs and the Making of Reformasi Memory. In *Beginning to Remember: The Past in Indonesia's Present*, ed. Mary Zurbuchen, 278–311. Seattle: University of Washington Press.

———. 2010. *Refracted Visions: Popular Photography and National Modernity in Java*. Durham, NC: Duke University Press.

Sukarno (Soekarno). 1945. "Lahirnya Panca Sila" (Birth of the Pancasila). Speech to BPUPKI (Badan Penyelidik Usaha Persiapan Kemerdekaan Indonesia). Accessed July 15, 2011. http://presidensoekarno.blogspot.com/2007/03/soekarno-pidato-soekarno-lahirnya-panca.html.

———. [1947] 1984. *Sarinah: Kewajiban wanita dalam perjuangan Republik Indonesia*. Jakarta: Inti Idayu Press (Yayasan Pendidikan Soekarno).

Surbakti, Lt. Col. A.R. 1978. *Perang Kemerdekaan di Karo Area*. Vol. 1 of 2. Medan: Yayasan Pro Patria.

———. 1979. *Perang Kemerdekaan di Tanah Karo, Karo Jahe dan Dairi Area*. Vol. 2 of 2. Medan: Yayasan Pro Patria.

Suryakusuma, Julia. 1996. The State and Sexuality in New Order Indonesia. In *Fantasizing the Feminine in Indonesia*, ed. L. Sears, 92–119. Durham, NC: Duke University Press.

Swift, Ann. 2010. *The Road to Madiun: The Indonesian Communist Uprising of 1948*. Jakarta: Equinox Publishing.

Tarigan, Henry Guntur. 1990. *Piso surit*. Jakarta: Yayasan Merga Silima.

Taussig, Michael. 1989. Terror as Usual: Walter Benjamin's Theory of History as State of Siege. *Social Text* 23 (Autumn–Winter):3–20.

———. 2005. *Law in a Lawless Land*. Chicago: University of Chicago Press.

Taylor, Charles. 1989. *Sources of the Self: The Making of the Modern Identity*. Cambridge, MA: Harvard University Press.

Taylor, Jean Gelman. 2004. *Indonesia: Peoples and Histories*. New Haven, CT: Yale University Press.

Team Asistensi Pangdam II/BB. 1977. *Sejarah perjuangan Komando Daerah Militer II Bukit Barisan*. 2 vols. Medan: Dinas Sejarah Kodam II/Bukit Barisan.

Tempo. 1994. "Medan bergolak." 24 (April 30): front cover.

Tsing, Anna Lowenhaupt. 1990. Gender and Performance in Meratus Dispute Settlement. In *Power and Difference*, ed. J.M. Atkinson and S. Errington, 95–126. Stanford, CA: Stanford University Press.

———. 1993. *In the Realm of the Diamond Queen*. Princeton, NJ: Princeton University Press.

van Bemmelen, Sita. 1992. Educated Toba Batak Daughters as Mediators in the Process of Elite Formation (1920–1942). In *Women and Mediation in Indonesia*, ed. S. van Bemmelen, M. Djajadiningrat-Niewenhuis, E. Locher-Scholten, and E. Touwen-Bouwsma, VKI 152, 135–66. Leiden, Netherlands: KITLV Press.

van der Tuuk, H.N. 1971. *A Grammar of Toba Batak*. The Hague: Martinus Nijhoff.

van Langenberg, Michael. 1976. National Revolution in North Sumatra: Sumatera Timur and Tapanuli, 1942–1950. PhD dissertation, University of Sydney.

———. 1985. East Sumatra: Accommodating an Indonesian Nation within a Sumatran Residency. In *Regional Dynamics of the Indonesian Revolution*, ed. A.R. Kahin, 113–44. Honolulu: University of Hawai'i Press.

van Liere, A.M. 1931. *Vervolgmemorie van overgave van de Onderafdeling Karolanden*. Microfilm. Zug, Switzerland: IDC.

van Rhijn, M. 1936. Memorie van overgave van de afdeling Simeloengoen- en Karolanden. Microfilm. Zug: IDC.

van Vuuren, L. 1908. De handel van Baroes, als oudste haven op Sumatra's Westkust, verklaard: En voor de toekomst beschouwd. *Tijdschrift van het Koninglijk Nederlands Aardrijkskundig Genootschap*, 2nd series, 25: 1389–402.

———. 1910. *Eerste maatregelen in pas geannexeerd gebied*. Zalt-Bommel: H.J. van de Garde and Co.

Volz, Wilhelm. 1909. *Nord-Sumatra*. 2 vols. Berlin: Dietrich Reimer.

Voorhoeve, P. 1955. *Critical Survey of Studies on Languages of Sumatra*. The Hague: Martinus Nijhoff.

Wessel, Ingrid, and Georgia Wimhofer, eds. 2001. *Violence in Indonesia*. Hamburg: Abera Verlag.

Westenberg, C.J. 1904. Nota omtrent de onderwerping der tot nu toe onafhankelijke Karolanden, alsmeed omtrent de beginselen, volgens welke de Bataklanden in 't algemeen en de Karolanden in 't bijzonder 't best bestuurd zullen kennen worden. Appendix to G. Schaap, Gewestelijk Bestuur, Residentie Oostkust van Sumatra No. 4903/4. Mimeograph copy in the Wasson Collection, Cornell University.

Westerling, Raymond "Turk." 1952. *Challenge to Terror*. London: W. Kimber.

White, Hayden. 1981. The Value of Narrativity in the Representation of Reality. In *On Narrative*, ed. W.J.T. Mitchell, 1–24. Chicago: University of Chicago Press.

Whitehead, Neil, ed. 2004. *Violence*. Santa Fe, NM: SAR Press.

Wieringa, Saskia. 2002. *Sexual Politics in Indonesia*. The Hague: Institute of Social Studies.

Wijngaarden, J.K. 1894. Verslag ontrent de zending onder de Karau-Bataks over 1893. *Mededelingen van wege het Nederlandsch Zendelinggenootschap* 38:133–85.

Winters, Jeffrey. 2011. Who Will Tame the Oligarchs? *Inside Indonesia* 104 (April–June). www.insideindonesia.org/feature/who-will-tame-the-oligarchs-22041424.

Wolf, Eric. 1969. *Peasant Wars of the Twentieth Century*. Norman: University of Oklahoma Press.

Yampolsky, Philip. 1992. *Music of Nias and North Sumatra: Hoho, Gendang Karo, Gondang Toba*. Compact disk. Vol. 4 of Music of Indonesia Series. Washington DC: Smithsonian/Folkways Recordings.

———. 1995. Forces for Change in the Regional Performing Arts of Indonesia. *Bijdragen tot de Taal-, Land- en Volkenkunde* 151:700–725.

Yurchak, Alexei. 2005. *Everything Was Forever, until It Was No More*. Princeton, NJ: Princeton University Press.

Yatun Sastrawidjaja. 2010. Playing with the Past. *Inside Indonesia* 101 (July–September). www.insideindonesia.org/stories/playing-with-the-past-01081339.

Zuraida Zainal, ed. 1985. *Serumpun melati di Bumi Pertiwi: Kisah perjuangan Srikandi Sumatera*. Medan: Keluarga Besar Wirawati Catur Panca.

Index of Cited Informants

General Index

Page numbers in italics refer to illustrations.